To Carole & Graham

See you in China;

until then, this

will have to do!

Clay

(AKA: Clay Maidenman)

A Journey
to the East

A Journey to the East

LI GUI'S

A New Account of a Trip Around the Globe

Translated with an Introduction
by Charles Desnoyers

THE UNIVERSITY OF MICHIGAN PRESS
Ann Arbor

2007   2006   2005   2004   4   3   2   1

A CIP catalog record for this book is available from the British Library.

Library of Congress Cataloging-in-Publication Data

Li, Gui, 1842–1903.
    [Huan you di qiu xin lu. English]
    A journey to the East : Li Gui's a new account of a trip around the
globe / translated with an introduction by Charles Desnoyers.
        p.   cm.
    Includes bibliographical references and index.
    ISBN 0-472-11354-2 (Cloth : alk. paper)
    1. Li, Gui, 1842–1903—Journeys.   2. Voyages around the world.
I. Desnoyers, Charles, 1952–   II. Title.
G440.L713   A3   2004
910.4'1—dc21   2003008449

Translator's Preface

Shortly before 11:00 P.M. on Thursday, May 10, 2001, Michele Ridge, the wife of the governor of Pennsylvania, and John Street, the mayor of Philadelphia, stepped down from a horse-drawn carriage and, escorted by local dignitaries, some of whom were turned out in their best nineteenth-century finery for the occasion, ascended the steps of Memorial Hall in the city's vast Fairmount Park to commemorate the 125th anniversary of the opening of the American Centennial Exposition. Memorial Hall had housed the exposition's painting and sculpture collection and had also been the site of the Centennial's inaugural ceremonies in 1876. Specifically designed to be the only major building left standing at the conclusion of the fair, its role as a cultural repository took on a second life when it was transformed into Philadelphia's first art museum at the close of the exposition in November.

Among the most significant objects the new museum inherited from the Centennial were those remaining from the Chinese and Japanese exhibits, which, to this day, constitute a vital core of the institution's East Asian holdings. During the museum's own 125th anniversary celebration—the centerpiece of the city's Centennial festivities—these works were featured prominently in a special exhibit and the accompanying literature emphasized the considerable influence they exercised on late nineteenth-century painting, design, architecture, and decorative arts. But while observers from a host of countries recognized at the time the sensation these objects had created at the Centennial, their significance was captured most appreciatively by a lone Chinese commentator: a young, obscure customs clerk named Li Gui whose participation, though unmentioned in his own country's exhibition brochures, would soon generate considerable notice among the highly placed both at home and abroad.

At the suggestion of a member of the staff of China's multinational Imperial Maritime Customs Service, Li's original charge had been to keep a record of the Centennial in the service of the empire's recent efforts toward industrialization and increased participation in international affairs. Soon, however, from his base in Philadelphia, Li expanded the scope of his fact-finding to include trips to other major cities along the eastern seaboard. As the Centennial drew to a close, he continued on to Liverpool and London, Paris and Marseilles, through the Suez Canal, and on to Aden, Ceylon, Vietnam, and Hong Kong, before returning to Shanghai. What began as a simple record of a historic event had become an epic travelogue; more than this, the direction and character of his journey were seen by Li as nothing less than proof to any doubting readers of the true shape and size of the world. Along the way, the unique position he enjoyed as an unofficial dignitary allowed him access to the notable and powerful while ensuring that he had free rein to comment on them as he saw fit. In so doing he has left us with one of the most significant and, outside China, least-known travel accounts of the nineteenth century.

Just how significant Li's account remains today in China was driven home to me on a dreary October morning in 2002 as I retraced his steps in a now empty Memorial Hall, accompanied by a film crew from China Central Television's program *News Probe*. They were in the United States filming a documentary on the life of another cross-cultural expositor, the educator and diplomat Yung Wing. Li was an admirer of Yung and had visited him at his Education Mission in Hartford, Connecticut. But the symbolic centerpiece of their connection was formed by the visit of the mission's 113 students to the Centennial, where Li accompanied them to various exhibits and interviewed them on their lives in America, after which they were feted by President Grant, the Centennial Commissioners, and assorted foreign dignitaries. In one respect, the incident represented the high-water mark of nineteenth-century Sino-American cooperation: Within a few years, the mission was recalled by its sponsors because of its purported cultural compromises, while the enactment of exclusion legislation soured relations between the United States and China for decades to come. Thus, as I sat on camera in Memorial Hall reading Li's account of the visit of the students to a Chinese audience, I could not help but be struck by the ironic juxtaposition of cultural roles the occasion presented. By turns overwhelmed and exhilarated, with my own lines of mediation between the strange and the familiar increasingly blurred, it later occurred to me that what I experienced that morning must in some small way have paralleled what Li encountered here a century and a quarter before.

This is a historian's translation. By that I mean both that I am a historian by inclination and training, and that the material itself, owing to its depth of description rather than its polish or profundity, will most likely be of interest primarily to other students of history. Though certainly observing the conventions of good literary style, Li's narrative is rather straightforward, and what he chiefly chooses to recount are salient aspects of industry, material culture, social institutions, manners, and mores, rather than fine points of the literature, philosophy, or other intellectual productions of his hosts. Similarly, as a work of translation, I expect its primary audience will not be China specialists, who in most cases are capable of reading Li's account in the original, but rather those looking for uncommon and underutilized primary sources in convenient form: scholars and students of Asian studies, Asian-American studies, American history more generally, and especially those in the rapidly expanding field of world history. Needless to say, I welcome comments and suggestions from all fields.

The title under which I have placed Li's *Huan you diqiu xin lu* (A new account of a trip around the globe) is *A Journey to the East.* Students of Chinese history will of course recognize this as a play on the title of the beloved, fantastical stories of the adventures of the seventh-century Buddhist pilgrim Xuan Zang, *Xiyou ji* (A journey to the west). But it is also the heart of the title of the last section of Li's account and the part that contains his day-to-day journal entries. As such, I believe it to be evocative of the whole on several levels. First, it states clearly the direction in which Li is constantly moving, stressing to his readers in graphic fashion the true configuration of the physical world—as does his choice of the term *diqiu*, or "globe," in his account's full title. Second, it suggests that like Xuan Zang, whose quest for authenticity compelled him to seek the seminal texts of Buddhism among practitioners in the monasteries of India, Li saw his task of evaluating technologies and institutions for use in China as inseparable from observing their operation in their places of origin. Finally, my use of this title is an invitation to readers outside of China to make a provocative shift in perspective: to see themselves as "other" and their own backyards as someone else's back of beyond; to empathetically enter a realm historically inhabited by the greater portion of the world's people, for whom going to the "West" meant crossing the Great Eastern Ocean to remote, exotic lands situated, as Li put it, "on the back of the globe."

While parts of Li's account have appeared in other places in translation, most notably in R. David Arkush and Leo O. Lee's *Land without Ghosts* (Berkeley and Los Angeles: University of California Press, 1989), this volume represents the first full-length treatment of it in English. A great many people have contributed to this project over the years, and space permits me to mention only a few of them. I wish first to thank the Association for Asian Studies and the China and Inner Asia Council for a generous grant in 1995, which enabled me to start this project. Thanks are also due to La Salle University for arranging a research leave for me in the fall of 1996. Special thanks are in order for the reference staff at the Free Library of Philadelphia, the Library Company of Philadelphia, the Historical Society of Pennsylvania, Philadelphia City Archives, Eastern State Penitentiary, the United States Mint in Philadelphia, Independence Seaport Museum, Imperial Maritime Customs Project, the New York Historical Society, Connecticut Historical Society, Antioch College, University of California at Berkeley, University of Pittsburgh, and the Harvard-Yenching Library, all of whom furnished materials for this project. Eithne Bearden, Stephen Breedlove, and Bernetta Robinson-Doane of La Salle's Connolly Library deserve special mention for their skill and determination in ferreting out obscure sources for me. Special mention is also due to Felice Fisher, Lisa Robertson, and Adriana Proser of the East Asian Art Gallery in the Philadelphia Art Museum, for their help with materials on Chinese participation in the Centennial from the museum's archives. Signal help in navigating the difficult terrain of classical Chinese sources was received with great thanks from Michael Nylan of the University of California at Berkeley. Similar thanks for Japanese terms go to Mariko and William La Fleur of the University of Pennsylvania. Help from an unexpected quarter was gratefully received from Jingcao Hu and Qian Gang of China Central Television and An-Min Chung of Drexel University. It goes without saying that my sincerest thanks go as well to the editorial staff of the University of Michigan Press.

Far more than my own efforts, this book is the product of the support and advice of my friend and mentor for more than twenty years, Professor S. M. Chiu, formerly of Temple University, and his wife, Helen. I can never fully repay them for their kindness and expertise through all of those afternoons spent poring over this text at their house, fortified by tea and cake. I can only offer again to them my profoundest thanks. Needless to say, any errors that remain are mine alone.

Finally, this book is dedicated to a person of unsurpassed courage, admirable insight, piercing intelligence, exquisite patience, and most especially an all-encompassing sense of humor, my wife and partner through all, Jacki. "Many have done excellently, but you exceed them all." *Wo ai ni.*

Contents

BOOK III: NOTES ON SIGHTSEEING

BOOK IV: DIARY OF A JOURNEY TO THE EAST

Contents

xii

Introduction: A Journey to the East

PASSAGES

Travel, in the younger sort, is a part of education; in the elder, a part of experience. He that traveleth into a country before he hath some entrance into the language, goeth to school, and not to travel.

— Francis Bacon

The seventh and eighth [December 22 and 23]. Continuing southeast. Approaching Ceylon on a southerly course.

— Li Gui, "Diary of a Journey to the East"

It was an encounter that went unrecorded and, most likely, undetected by the participants. On the evening of December 23, 1876, a few hundred miles off the Malabar Coast of India, the Peninsular and Oriental steamer *Peshawur,* bound for Aden and points west out of Galle on Ceylon, slipped silently past the *Ava,* a French *paquebot* on a southeasterly course for that port. The passing was one of hundreds regularly taking place along well-traveled routes marking the sinews of empire as Europeans pressed ever more deeply into South and East Asia. It would not be worthy of comment — save perhaps as testament to the growing ordinariness of long-distance travel — were it not for some unusual passengers aboard the two vessels. In the relatively short, complex, and troubled history of China's relations with the industrializing West[1] their passing on board these ships, though unknown to either group, signaled the opening of a new phase in an era already marked by profound transformation.

Aboard the *Peshawur* were the first resident Chinese diplomatic representatives of modern times, Guo Songtao and Liu Xihong, on their way to take up their posts in a circuit that would ultimately include Great Britain, France, and Germany.[2] They were, of course, by no means the first Chinese to travel so far outside the empire. In addition to the tens of thousands long involved in the vast commerce of the Nanyang, the Southern Ocean, their predecessors over the last few centuries had included crewmen aboard Portuguese caravels and Spanish galleons, Christian converts bound for Paris and Rome, and, most recently, hundreds of thousands of gold-seekers, merchants, and laborers—free and indentured—headed to the Americas and Australia. Indeed, by 1876, Chinese communities of various sizes could be found in a majority of the world's great cities. From Singapore to San Francisco, New York to New South Wales, their expanding and often insecure enclaves occupied a position in many ways analogous to that of the foreign treaty port communities in China. An important difference, however, was that the Westerners in China had wrested their ports by means of the two Opium Wars (1839–42 and 1856–60) and were now protected by their diplomats and gunboats. With the coming of Guo and Liu, along with Chen Lanbin and Rong Hong (Yung Wing) to the United States, Spain, and Peru, and He Ruzhang to Japan, the overseas Chinese communities would now at least have the former, if not the latter. Thus the progress of the *Peshawur*'s passengers marked a vitally important transition in China's presence abroad, which was to mature with remarkable swiftness during the following half-decade.[3]

The passengers on board the Messageries Maritimes mail packet *Ava* numbered among them the last of an earlier sort of Chinese traveler and his interpreter. Until 1866, when the elderly Manchu official Bin Jun had reluctantly agreed to accompany the Inspector General of the Chinese Imperial Maritime Customs Service, Robert Hart, on leave to England, no Chinese official had traveled to the West in any capacity in modern times. In the decade following, no fewer than five major delegations were dispatched to Europe and the United States. Of these, perhaps the most significant were the 1868 Burlingame Mission, in which the former U.S. minister to China volunteered his services as a Chinese ambassador-at-large, and the Chinese Education Mission (1872–81).[4] Headquartered in Hartford, Connecticut, the Education

Mission was the inspiration of Rong Hong (1828–1912), better known by the Cantonese pronunciation of his name, Yung Wing. Yung and his senior colleague Chen Lanbin constructed a total immersion program of Western studies for 120 selected Chinese boys, supplemented by tutoring in the Confucian classics. The object of their efforts had been to create a nucleus of expertise with which to nurture China's nascent *ziqiang,* or "self-strengthening" movement, aimed at bolstering the Confucian state through the help of new foreign technologies. Perhaps equally important, the mission provided China's first sustained "window on the West" and made Chen and Yung natural choices to be China's first permanent diplomats in the United States.[5]

With the exception of Yung Wing, the men involved in all of these missions were members of China's scholar-official class. An important part of their duties during their travels had been to keep diaries of their experiences as a way of augmenting the scant information available in China about the outside world. Young at thirty-four, and unknown outside of a small group of *yangwu* (foreign affairs) specialists and members of China's Imperial Maritime Customs Service, the diarist aboard the *Ava,* Li Gui (1842–1903), styled Xiaochi, was now on the final leg of a historic journey around the world as he passed Guo and Liu on their way to England. Strangely, given the importance of the event, his diary does not indicate that he was told the envoys were en route, though, as he toured many of the same sights as Guo and Liu in Galle only two days later, his guides would surely have mentioned the pair's visit. To compound the irony further, the *Peshawur* was actually running ahead of schedule; had it left port on its appointed date, Christmas Day, Li would certainly have availed himself of such an opportunity and sought an audience with the ministers.[6]

Lost chances and puzzling omissions aside, however, Li's diary of his travels, *Huan you diqiu xin lu* (A new account of a trip around the globe) ultimately exercised considerable influence among the small coterie of Chinese self-strengtheners, as well as on subsequent generations of reformers and revolutionaries. Li Hongzhang (1823–1901), China's most powerful official and a vocal champion of *ziqiang* programs, wrote its foreword; Guo himself, whose favorable observations on England in his official journal, *Shixi jicheng* (Record of an envoy's journey to the West), later inspired antiforeign riots in his hometown of Changsha, was said to have kept a copy of *A New Account* ready to hand later during his service in London; Kang Youwei, the force behind the "Hundred Days" of reform in the summer of 1898, was also an avid reader, as was Mao Zedong in his early years.[7]

With the coming of permanent diplomatic observers abroad, accompanied by staffs of attachés, interpreters, clerks, and other trained information gatherers, Li Gui in many respects represents the last of the roving "amateur" diarists of the previous decade. Unencumbered by diplomatic protocol or official responsibilities, intensely interested in everything around him, by turns frankly impressed and impressively frank about what he sees, his journal in its scope and subject matter is, on balance, perhaps the most insightful and entertaining nineteenth-century Chinese account of the world. On this score, the silent encounter of the *Ava* and the *Peshawur* might be said to mark another sort of passing as well.

GHOSTS OF THE HEAVENLY KINGDOM

Considering the influence of Li's journal, relatively little is known of his life.[8] He was born in 1842 to a fairly wealthy family in Xia Village in Jiangning *fu,* or prefecture, not far from the great walled city of Nanjing; at the time, perhaps seventeen miles distant.[9] His early years appear to have been pampered ones. He was tutored at home, a practice that, owing to the considerable costs involved, was generally undertaken only by the well-to-do. Here he developed an early zest for the classics as he prepared for the local, provincial, and metropolitan examinations that marked the surest route to wealth and power in imperial China.

Education in Confucian[10] China was a rigorous process, heavily dependent on memorization. A child's formal schooling usually began at age eight and consisted of reading and recitation of ever-larger blocks of text from primers, followed by the classics and their multiple commentaries. By at least one estimate, a student who by his early teens had memorized the core group of classical texts (*Analects, Mencius, Book of Changes, Book of Documents, Book of Poetry, Book of Rites,* and *Commentary of Mr. Zuo*) would have at his command 431,286 characters.[11] With so much at stake in terms of potential wealth and prestige for student, tutor, and family the process was conducted under considerable pressure and often accompanied by periodic doses of corporal punishment for the lazy or inept. By Li's time, too, a number of study guides to aid in cramming for the different levels of exams were in wide circulation, despite repeated attempts by local officials to ban them.[12] Though apparently thriving within this system, he was later pointedly critical of its potential for corruption and its emphasis on rote and recitation in comparing it with American and English pedagogy and curricula.[13]

As he neared his teens, a time when the better students were already preparing for their first exams, his progress along the standard path to an official career suffered what ultimately became a permanent interruption. On March 19, 1853, the Taiping army, having fought its way north from a mountain stronghold in Jintian, Guangxi province, entered Nanjing. On securing the city they changed its name to Tianjing, the Heavenly Capital, and proclaimed it the seat of their new state, *Taiping tianguo* (the Heavenly Kingdom of Great Peace). In Xia Village the transition at first brought few drastic changes, as the immediate vicinity remained in the hands of the Qing dynasty's forces. Li later recalled it as a time in which "we met with no calamities at the hands of the rebels."[14] In nearby areas, however, the insurgents pursued a policy of ruthless extermination of officials and gentry, a practice with which Li was soon to become agonizingly familiar.

The Taipings, through the revelations of their leader Hong Xiuquan (1813–64), had knit together a belief system that combined an explosive mixture of Protestant Christian revivalism and Chinese millenarian traditions with a rough and ready social policy of communitarianism. Given their animus toward the Confucian order, the unsettled conditions and loyalties in the area, and the constant threat of attack, Li's education was probably conducted intermittently during this time, if at all. In any case, with the local examination centers under Taiping control, any chance of passing the initial round of tests and achieving *shengyuan*, or licentiate, status was now out of reach for the foreseeable future.[15]

In 1860, uncertainty gave way to disaster. On May 6, a second attempt to besiege the Heavenly Capital by the Qing Army of the Jiangnan Command was broken and routed. Its leader, Zhang Guoliang, committed suicide, and the defeated soldiers fled through Jiangning prefecture in reckless confusion, while the pursuing Taipings attacked anyone unlucky enough to have remained in the newly occupied areas. Blocked by dangerous currents as they attempted to ford a swollen river to safety, Li and forty members of his family doubled back through a gap in the lines in a desperate effort to find shelter in their now abandoned village. A rebel foraging party happened across them, however, and cut down twenty of the women, children, and elderly hiding in a nearby field – among them Li's wife, mother, and infant daughter. Helpless to flee, and certain to be discovered, the remaining family members barricaded themselves inside a vacant compound where "we could do nothing but fold our hands and await our own destruction,"[16] Li later wrote. Within a few days, it came. The survivors were flushed from their stronghold and seized, their remaining possessions scavenged as they looked on. Under a driving rain, they were placed under guard in a tent along with their captors' pack animals to await their disposition.

Two decades after his capture, Li wrote a remarkable, searing memoir of his ordeal, *Sitong ji* (Bitter memories). Like countless other survivors whose emotional lives had been irrevocably scarred, he appears to have found both solace and frustration during the intervening years in repressing and compartmentalizing his experience; in seeing his ordeal as something that, while perhaps endurable, would forever remain inexpressible. A chance meeting toward the end of his global journey with "a certain gentleman," however, "made me discontented when I examined myself" on this score and convinced him to record his story.[17] While Li refrains from naming this individual, the details of the meeting strongly suggest that he was prompted by the scholar and journalist Wang Tao, whom he had met in Hong Kong in January 1877. The result of Wang's urging was one of the most riveting captivity narratives in any language.

Even by twentieth-century standards of programmatic brutality, *Sitong ji* still shocks. Tied by their queues to a long lead rope, the captives were marched roughly 250 miles during the following months from Jiangning to the region around Suzhou and, ultimately, to the rear areas near the Taiping siege of Hangzhou. Early on, Li bore horrified witness to Taiping interrogation methods: Each captive was asked in turn if he wanted to go home; if the answer was yes, he was immediately beheaded. The rebels, with heads in hand, then gleefully informed the stunned onlookers that they had simply honored the victims' requests and "sent them home." On being condemned, Li's father and four uncles bribed a guard to spare Gui and his two cousins, which, for a time, gave the boys a measure of protection. Appalling sights were routine throughout the march: charred corpses of dismembered men and women tied to trees; infants and mothers sliced in half together; and everywhere a sere landscape peopled by the hollow-eyed, half-starved, and ragged stumbling along the roads and squatting by the waysides. Though at several points the rebels forced his assistance in writing and record keeping, the educated remained fair game and Li lived in constant fear of his manners and appearance giving him away. Finally, in the confusion following a failed Taiping bid to recapture Hangzhou, Li was asked by some refugees behind the lines to write letters for them and smuggle them to relatives in Shanghai. Taking advantage of the opportunity he was able to make his way by boat to the city in the fall of 1862.[18]

Like many educated men of his generation, Li's experiences during the Taiping years appear to have exercised a profound influence on his conceptions of government, society, and the motivations behind human behavior. The ideological and social threat posed by the insurgents had called into question the most basic premises of the Confucian order: filial piety, reciprocal responsibilities within an interlocking social hierarchy, and particularly the guiding role of the scholar-gentry. Hence, the inauguration of the reign of the infant Tongzhi emperor in late 1861, officially designated as a "restoration" *(zhongxing)*, signaled that substantial reform would accompany the "return to order" *(tongzhi)* and rebuilding of the country once the war had been concluded.[19] Within this broader context, Li emerged from his ordeal with his Confucian fundamentals intact—in some respects, strengthened from their collision with the "foreign" ideology of the Taipings—but like many of his contemporaries, he carried with him an enhanced sense of the need for flexibility in practicing them. For example, the Confucian emphasis on agriculture was underscored in *A New Account* when Li lamented that huge tracts of land still remained unreclaimed a dozen years after the end of the conflict. But he strongly advocated the use of Western labor-saving tech-

nologies to bring them back into cultivation and registered his
impatience with those who dismissed their use in China as unsuitable. In addition, the appalling loss of life during the war—with
estimates running as high as thirty million—as well as his own
tragedies, engendered a considerable degree of empathy for the
sufferings of those on both sides.[20]

While we can only speculate about the degree of psychological
trauma to which the teenage Li was subjected during his captivity,
it appears that he continued to find revisiting the war in later years
therapeutic. In addition to *Sitong ji*, he also produced a four-vol-
ume military history of the Nanjing area during the rebellion, *Jinling bing shi huilue*, in 1888. Moreover, his keen sense of the collective suffering of the region extended even to the ordinary Taiping
soldiers—several of whom showed him surprising kindness and, on
at least one occasion, actually saved his life—and tended to human-
ize them somewhat in his eyes. One might speculate, too, that the
wrenching experience of being forced to accommodate his captors
in an alien and hostile environment might have prepared him in
some ways to overcome any later apprehensions he might have had
about dealing with foreigners, whether at home or abroad.[21]

Ironically, the defeat that had such disastrous personal consequences for Li set in motion events that ultimately created an
entirely new direction for his career. The rout of the Jiangnan
Command and the continuing Taiping threat to the treaty port of
Shanghai encouraged an unprecedented degree of cooperation
between the Qing and the foreign powers. In early June 1860, less
than a month after the Jiangnan defeat, the American adventurer
Frederick Townsend Ward recruited the first company of what
would ultimately grow into the famed Ever Victorious Army. Composed of Chinese troops officered and drilled by foreigners, it soon
became the most effective strike force of the Huai Army of Li
Hongzhang, who was already building a reputation as one of the
preeminent Qing commanders. Li's troops, together with Zeng
Guofan's Hunan forces, besieged the Heavenly Capital yet again
and this time beat back a Taiping relief army of one hundred thousand in the fall of 1862. By this time, Li Gui had made his way to
Shanghai and, through the intercession of a friend, found employment as a secretary at the headquarters of the Ever Victorious
Army.[22]

Long before Li settled into his new duties, the dislocations of the rebellion had spawned a more ambitious and, ultimately, longer-lived Sino-foreign venture. In the winter of 1853–54 the rebels had come dangerously close to cutting off and besieging the capital at Beijing. Only the cold and the exploits of the Mongol cavalry of Prince Senggelinqin had turned them back. That same year, a secret society called the Small Swords had taken advantage of the situation and seized control of the Chinese city (as distinct from the treaty port) of Shanghai. The foreign powers, faced with their treaty obligation to remit customs duties to the Qing in the absence of local control, deputed their consuls to temporarily collect them. When order had been somewhat restored the following year, Qing officials agreed to an arrangement in which special customs inspectors were to be drawn from the foreign community for the duration of the rebellion as a hedge against future interruptions in collection. The newly enhanced revenues, the result of eliminating a large portion of the kickbacks and payoffs endemic to the old system, encouraged an expansion of the new customs service to all the treaty ports by 1858. From this informal arrangement grew the famous and controversial Imperial Maritime Customs Service, guided during its first five years by Horatio Nelson Lay.[23]

Lay was forced to step down in 1863 in the wake of a scandal involving the purchase of a fleet of British ironclad gunboats for his Chinese sponsors. His successor was the colorful Robert Hart. For forty-seven years until his death in 1911 the famed Inspector General, fastidious, tart-tongued, incorruptible, and autocratic, knit together a service in his own image that wielded perhaps more power than any other organization in the empire. As it grew and gained the grudging confidence of Chinese officials in the ports, the IMC drew liberally from the growing numbers of ambitious, educated Chinese like Li Gui who lacked official positions, as well as from lower-level staff members of the *mufu*, or private bureaucracies of powerful officials, and those with linguistic or other *yangwu* skills. The IMC also recruited young, adventurous, non-Chinese candidates according to strict national quotas devised by Hart. They were then tutored in the written language and the Beijing regional dialect called *guanhua*, or Mandarin, that functioned as the lingua franca of officials, as well as the appropriate regulations and protocol, thus creating a truly international civil service.

Officially, the Maritime Customs Service was an arm of the Chinese government and generally about 80 percent of its members were Chinese; in practice, Hart wielded sufficient power within its highly centralized structure to frequently influence the policy directions of the government. Considering himself staunchly loyal to China, he nevertheless arrogated to himself a unique understanding of where the empire's best interests lay.[24] No one, however, could gainsay the effectiveness of the new system. Through the latter part of the nineteenth century, the efficiency of the customs service accounted for an ever-larger portion of the government's revenues, despite the artificially low tariff limits imposed on China by foreign treaties.

In 1865, the Englishman Herbert Elgar Hobson, recently arrived in Ningbo to take charge of the customs office there, invited Li Gui to join his staff as a secretary in charge of correspondence and archival work. Hobson had joined the IMC in 1862 and apparently met Li during his initial appointment as liaison to the Ever Victorious Army headquarters in Shanghai, where he served as an interpreter for its new commander, Charles George ("Chinese") Gordon.[25] As part of Hobson's staff, Li's work in the IMC gradually accustomed him not just to the routines of bookkeeping, inspections, and the many dodges of smugglers, but to the larger workings of the new world system of trade and economics steadily pulling China into its orbit.[26]

The various traditions within Confucianism, particularly that of Mencius (385?–312? B.C.E.), tended to see commerce and its agents as necessary but ultimately corrupting. As members of a new class whose wealth and power had been acquired outside the older agrarian social structures of Zhou (1122–221 B.C.E.) China, merchants were early on regarded as parvenus and social parasites. On the one hand, they were needed to circulate scarce commodities throughout the state; on the other, they produced nothing and merely trafficked in the goods of others for profit *(li)*. Such a single-minded quest for *li*, if allowed to run unchecked, was considered the first step toward the ruin of good government. As Mencius said to King Hui of Liang in the opening lines of the *Mengzi* (Mencius), "I bring only humanity *(ren)* and righteousness *(yi)*; why must Your Majesty speak of profit *(li)*?"[27] Instead the sages, again especially Mencius, put a high premium on safeguarding *min sheng*, the "people's livelihood." In practical terms, this concept was used to justify state monopolies on or heavy regulation of strategic industries like iron and salt, along with support of agriculture and periodic attempts at land reform and redistribution. In the seventeenth and eighteenth centuries, Jesuit missionaries were sufficiently impressed with this aspect of Chinese economic thinking that it found its way through them into the theories of the French Physiocrats, whose spokesman, François Quesnay, was dubbed the "Confucius of Europe."[28]

For Chinese grappling with the new economics of the foreign treaty ports, however, it was especially unsettling to confront powerful nations now supported with apparent success by theories directly contrary to Confucian doctrine. Though his travels in America and Europe would later give him a somewhat more balanced view of Western economics, Li set out with the perception that nations like England, the United States, and France had been built almost entirely upon trade and commerce. As his journey progressed he repeatedly, and ruefully, considered that they often surpassed China in their attention to supporting "the people's livelihood" as well. Unlike most of his fellow diarists, Li's ten years in the Maritime Customs Service had already given him a more nuanced appreciation of the complexity of the relationships among commerce, industry, government, and society that had so rapidly evolved in the nineteenth-century Euro-American world. But in many ways, *A New Account*, filled as it is with observations on how wrong his perceptions had once been, suggests just how narrow the possibilities were for a more than superficial understanding of the workings of the outside world within the distorted littoral space of the treaty ports. Li's transforming encounter would come instead at a site that, for a brief six months, proved irresistibly attractive to millions throughout the world as the highest expression of Thomas Carlyle's "Age of Machinery, in every outward and inward sense of that word": the American Centennial Exposition.[29]

"CHINA AT THE CENTENNIAL"

In 1864, while both the Taiping Rebellion and the American Civil War slowly ground toward their endgames, the first of several proposals was put before Congress for an exposition to mark the centenary of the founding of the United States. The model for such an event had been 1851's Great Exhibition in London. In addition to attracting more than six million visitors, the exhibition's architectural triumph, Joseph Paxton's spectacular Crystal Palace, had become a world landmark overnight. Within it was offered the most extensive collection of curiosities and advanced technology yet assembled, cementing Great Britain's self-advertised reputation at midcentury as "workshop of the world." National prestige aside, the gathering's chief function had been commercial, and this first world's fair, as well as its successors in Paris (1855) and London again (1862), were seen by participants as ideal venues for the large-scale international marketing of their goods. Proponents of such exhibitions, most prominently Great Britain's Prince Albert, also hoped that these exchanges would promote peaceful competition and greater amity among nations.[30]

After several more proposals in the late 1860s, Congress approved a bill in March 1871, authorizing an "international exhibition of arts, manufactures, and products of soil and mine" to be held in Philadelphia, the site of the nation's founding, in 1876.[31] It had not, however, authorized any funds for the exhibition, and the men in charge, General Joseph Hawley of Hartford, John Welsh of Philadelphia, and Alfred Goshorn of Cincinnati, faced a considerable challenge in drumming up financial support for the effort. In addition to objections that the project amounted to an unseemly exercise in national vanity, there was considerable skepticism as to whether the United States in its geographical isolation would draw enough participants and visitors for the sponsors to pay back their investors. Further compounding the fiscal woes of the newly formed Centennial Commission was the onset of a long-term financial slump in the wake of the Panic of 1873.[32]

Nevertheless, the preparations continued, if fitfully. In late 1873, having rejected the plans of better-known architects, the commissioners in desperation hired twenty-seven-year-old Hermann J. Schwarzmann, recently arrived from Germany, who had previously worked for the city's Fairmount Park Commission. Schwarzmann designed and supervised the construction and placement of nearly all the major buildings at the exposition. His surviving masterpiece, the Art Gallery—today known as Memorial Hall—is believed to have been a prototype for Paul Wallot's design of the

German Reichstag building.[33] Under Schwarzmann's drive, a 284-acre section of Philadelphia's Fairmount Park was transformed into an otherworldly city of 249 buildings ranging from the Main Exhibition Hall—at 1,880 feet in length and twenty-one acres in area the largest building in the world—to assorted annexes, carriage houses, and comfort stations.

Unlike earlier exhibitions, particularly the most recent in Vienna in 1873, meticulous provisions were made for the housing and transportation of visitors. The Pennsylvania Railroad erected an enormous depot adjacent to the exhibition and, along with the Reading Railroad, built numerous sidelines and spurs to the fairgrounds; the Philadelphia streetcar companies ran fleets of oversized omnibuses; and river craft of all sizes and capacities ferried people to and from special landings on the Schuylkill River. Inside the grounds, visitors had their choice of transport by narrow gauge railway, by the world's first steam-powered monorail, or by rolling chairs within the larger exhibition buildings. By opening day, May 10, 1876, helped at the last minute by an appropriation of $1.5 million from Congress, all preparations were essentially complete.

Meanwhile, in 1873, the commissioners had sent invitations to dozens of foreign governments to participate in the exposition. In the end, thirty-seven countries, including both China and Japan, and twenty colonial dependencies and territories sent delegations and exhibits. China had earlier participated in the Vienna exhibition and, quite minimally through intermediaries, in Paris in 1867. The Qing court, therefore, through Prince Gong, the head of the Zongli Yamen (Foreign Affairs Office), pledged its cooperation with the effort.[34] Nonetheless, the dubiousness with which the imperial court and the majority of Chinese officials regarded foreign ventures of any kind, and the prospect of career problems attending any official sent overseas, effectively left China's participation in the hands of the Imperial Maritime Customs officials. For their part, Hart and his staff, seeing themselves as agents of China's progress, maneuvered to keep the exhibit free from any outside interference by other Chinese officials. Directives went out to IMC commissioners in the ports to gather "treasures of man and nature from China's eighteen provinces," as the sign on the *pailou*, or ceremonial gate, marking the entrance to the Chinese exhibit later put it.

Given their limitations, the commissioners did their work remarkably well. Chinese goods had sold credibly in Vienna, and the commissioners planned to expand proven categories of luxury merchandise—porcelain, cloisonné, furniture, carvings, tea, and silk—to include a wide array of inexpensive everyday items such as foodstuffs, medicines, fans, parasols, cotton clothing, shoes, and the like. The Chinese exhibit thus became one of the Centennial's few self-consciously ethnographic displays in its attempt to show the full range of the empire's material culture.[35]

On February 17, 1876, the *North China Herald and Supreme Court and Consular Gazette,* the organ of Shanghai's foreign merchant community, took notice of the preparations. In this case, however, it temporarily abandoned its customary stance of bemused skepticism toward China's self-strengthening efforts. Under the headline "China at the Centennial," it noted, "There can be little doubt that China will equal if not excel Japan in the exhibition of products, both natural and artificial, at the forthcoming Centennial at Philadelphia." It went on to list a number of categories of items, and cited the Chinese collectors Hu Guangyong—the famous Hangzhou banker who had displayed his invaluable collection of cloisonné and porcelain at Vienna—and Song Sing-king, with his large array of furniture from Ningbo, "the heaven of carvers." Moreover,

> The entire collection is estimated to be worth upwards of Tls. 100,000, and not the least worthy feature of it is, that the whole of the workmanship is Chinese—not so much as a foreign nail having been used in the construction even of the packing cases, which it might be mentioned, are made so as to enable them to be converted into counters without interfering with their use as cases.[36]

As the commissioners set about canvassing collectors, merchants, and officials for objects to display, Gustav Detring (1842–1913), the Chefoo customs commissioner and confidant of Li Hongzhang, suggested to Li Gui that he could provide a valuable service by going along with the delegation to Philadelphia and writing an account of it. Detring had been one of the IMC commissioners in Vienna and was all too aware of the limitations posed by the lack of knowledgeable Chinese staff there. Perhaps more importantly, he had become a friend and mentor to Li Gui when he was commissioner at Ningbo and seems to have acquired a sound understanding of his skills and character. Li, enthusiastically it appears, agreed to go, and as testament to his relationship with Detring dedicated *A New Account* to him. Interestingly, his diary also reveals that Li did the calligraphy for the main *pailou* as well as the eastern and western gateways marking the Chinese exhibit, though the characters, he notes without comment, "were suggested by Mr. Detring."[37]

Although the Chinese exhibit included a number of workmen to set up and dismantle it and more than a dozen Chinese staff with some understanding of foreign tastes, no Chinese officials were scheduled to go. The Chinese Centennial commissioners included Robert Hart's brother "Jem" (James); Customs Commissioner Alfred Huber—who had recently gone to America to assist Chen Lanbin in investigating the atrocious condition of Chinese laborers in Cuba; Edward B. Drew, who had been with Detring in Vienna; and J. L. Hammond, both from the customs service. Edward Cunningham, W. W. Parkin, and Francis P. Knight, all prominent merchants, rounded out the delegation. Knight, who had also been the American consul in the northern port of Niuzhuang since 1867, would strike up a close friendship with Li Gui during their travels together and emerges in the account as his Virgil during their five months in the United States. Knight would later unsuccessfully suggest that Li be named as the first Chinese instructor at Harvard, a post ultimately occupied by another Ningbo resident, the scholar Ke Kunhua.[38]

Li's position was thus an unofficial one, and he went unmentioned in the Chinese exhibit's catalog. Nonetheless, his account of the Centennial was to come at a critically important time. By the 1870s, a number of the projects of *ziqiang* proponents were beginning to mature. To cite just a few, the Tongwen Guan (Institute of Foreign Languages), founded in 1862 to assist the new Zongli Yamen, the Chinese Foreign Affairs Office established the year before in the wake of the Second Opium War (1856–1860), had now blossomed into a full-scale technical institute; the Kiangnan (*Jiangnan*) Arsenal, built upon machinery brought back by Yung

Wing from America in 1865, had spawned other munitions plants as well as a modern shipyard in Fuzhou; the China Merchants' Steam Navigation Company, chartered in early 1873, now vied with foreign firms for control of China's river trade; and the success of the Education Mission in Hartford (1872–81) had already inspired plans to send students to Britain, France, and Germany. As Hart noted shortly thereafter, "Thus, gas, mines, Rail, wire, Audiences, Representatives Abroad, Extension of Customs, Merchant Steamers, Ships of war, etc., etc., etc., are all 'under weigh' [*sic*]. I really think China begins to move!"[39]

In many ways, however, the sponsors of these initiatives were still operating in the dark. Starting from the premise that China required nothing more than "strong ships and effective cannon" to bolster its defenses in the face of the Western threat, they had somewhat unsystematically moved toward trying to understand the foundational institutions from which the Western countries drew their strength. As noted above, by the middle of the decade, the view among self-strengtheners had become that trade and commerce formed the base on which rested the West's military power. But exactly how the one produced the other remained open to speculation. What, for example, was the role and nature of invention and entrepreneurship; how had Western mechanical expertise so outstripped that of China, and so recently at that; by what mechanisms did government, commerce, and industry reinforce each other; and perhaps most important, what were the social and moral implications of these developments in toto? Did they represent a genuine systemic alternative to Confucianism, or something else?

This last question was crucial not just for the self-strengtheners but for their opponents as well. The resistance of officials who feared for the holism of the Confucian polity increased considerably as *ziqiang* programs began to trend from technological improvements toward institutional reform. Though based on the time-honored Neo-Confucian concepts of "root and branch" *(ben-mo)* and "essence and function" *(ti-yong)*, the self-strengtheners' formula, *zhongxue wei ti, xixue wei yong* (Chinese studies for the essence, Western studies for practical application) was, according to its critics, an unworkable attempt at syncretism: "Chinese studies" and "Western studies," founded on incompatible premises, could not be used to support one another, they argued. To the insistence of the self-strengtheners that only appropriate Western studies would be utilized, and then only to bolster the Chinese "essence," opponents countered that *any* introduction of foreign technology or institutions brought with it its own cultural baggage, with unanticipated and corrosive repercussions.[40]

As with the new economics, then, despite the efforts of earnest cultural emissaries in the treaty ports, any claim to a genuine understanding of these systems abstracted from the context of their places of origin was to mistake a greatly truncated glimpse for the whole. Thus, even as he was readying to depart for Philadelphia, Li had become at least as interested in examining the entire mosaic of social, political, philanthropic, and service institutions of his hosts as he was to view their economics and technology.

THE BACK OF THE GLOBE

Three days after the official opening of the Centennial on May 10, 1876, Li Gui and his Cantonese interpreter, Chen Chiyuan, boarded the Mitsubishi Company's American steamer *Nevada* in Shanghai and proceeded slowly down the Huangpu toward the open sea. By chance, Knight was also aboard and bound for Philadelphia, beginning the close friendship that would provide a number of important opportunities for Li in the United States. An international group of passengers including Chinese, Japanese, Europeans of various nationalities, and, of course, Americans rounded out the first-class passenger list. In order to encourage exhibitors to come to the Centennial, the American government had shortly before signed shipping agreements with participating countries reducing the passage fees of official travelers by half.[41]

From the moment he walked up the *Nevada*'s gangway, Li was confronted by his own "otherness" amid his new surroundings. Almost immediately he realized that all the prepared foods he had taken with him were unneeded in the face of the dining service available to first-class passengers. Moreover, as he explained parenthetically to his readers, fresh bedding was routinely provided all passengers, unlike the service aboard traditional Chinese vessels.[42] This proved especially beneficial since for much of his Pacific crossing he was confined to his bunk, wracked by seasickness. In fulfillment of his duties, he carefully noted the routine of the crews and the navigational techniques of the ship's officers. Despite his sometimes desperate discomfort, however, like travelers in any age he also rhapsodized about moments of wonder and transcendent beauty, as here on Japan's Inland Sea: "Leaning on the rail and gazing into the distance, the shining mist descended onto the very foreheads of the people onshore, as if in a painting come to life."[43]

The *Nevada* made Nagasaki in thirty-nine hours, the first of several stops in Japan. Here, Li was able to see firsthand the dramatic changes so recently wrought by the Meiji government. In Japan, as in San Francisco, Singapore, Saigon, and Hong Kong, his principal guides were prominent members of the local Chinese communities. In all cases, these were dominated by the system of *huiguan*—mutual aid associations organized along regional and clan affiliations—that functioned as intermediaries for the communities with local authorities. Nearly everywhere, Li's conversations with area Chinese convinced him of the desperate need for the protection provided by consulates, which, he noted, were soon to come with the imminent dispatch of resident Chinese ministers. The presence of so many Chinese communities on nearly every continent no doubt also drove home to him the vast potential of China's recent expansion into the international arena.[44]

Nowhere were the promise and problems of China's own self-strengtheners' goals more dramatically on view than in Japan. Li took his first ride on a passenger train during a side trip from Kobe to Osaka; he visited the customs house in Nagasaki, done in Western style with officers dressed in Western uniforms; he commented on Japan's new use of international standards of coinage; and he visited a science museum with Western and Japanese machinery on display. At the same time, it appeared to him that the Japanese had in most respects successfully preserved the cultural foundations of their civilization. For example, the Buddhist shrines he visited were well attended and, except in the ports, the written language had not given way to foreign script. Yet he also felt the need to strike a cautionary note: During the Tokugawa period (1603–1867), he wrote, Japan's government had allowed its minister, the shogun, too much power; now the country was strong and expansive, and busily engaged in reform, but the trend toward wearing Western fashions, changing the calendar, and even eliminating the traditional communal bathhouses might have been done, he felt, "somewhat unthinkingly."[45]

At Yokohama, passengers bound for America boarded the Pacific Mail Steamship Company's *City of Peking*. Iron-hulled and 420 feet in length, it was the largest ship in the Pacific Mail fleet, and Li was suitably impressed with its first-class accommodations. Like the company's other steamers, it also contained a cavernous steerage or "common berth" area for the emigrant trade to San Francisco. Though it was capable of carrying a thousand passengers, on this trip Li found only "109 Chinese and 18 foreigners" in the common berth. Two weeks into the voyage, when he had recovered somewhat from his seasickness, he went below to interview some of them.

For Li, it was his first real brush with the problem that loomed largest in nineteenth-century Sino-American relations. Guo Songtao's mission to England notwithstanding, it was the treatment of Chinese emigrants in the Americas that had been the principal catalyst for sending Chinese diplomats abroad in the 1870s.[46] It was also the reason behind the first Chinese ministers to the United States receiving additional assignments to Spain—because of Spain's possession of Cuba—and Peru, both of which had large concentrations of Chinese laborers. But while Chinese had come to these places by means of the infamous "coolie" or "pig" trade—kidnapped, gulled, or bullied into signing fictitious labor contracts and working under conditions scarcely distinguishable from slavery—those in the United States had come as so-called free emigrants. Attracted initially by the news of gold in California, for which boomtown San Francisco was ever after known as *Jin Shan*—Gold Mountain—and later by the chronic labor shortage in the American West, Chinese were soon to be found in nearly every trade and craft practiced on the Pacific Coast. The enormously difficult and dangerous construction of the Central Pacific Railroad was almost entirely the product of Chinese labor, and by 1876, Chinese communities could be found scattered along nearly every rail line west of Omaha.

Their hard work, thrift, and success had also bred enmity among competing groups. By the early 1870s, it had resulted in a variety of local and state anti-Chinese ordinances as well as riots, assaults, and lynchings, most notably in Los Angeles in 1871. Now, even as Li was en route in May and June 1876, Chinese were being attacked in California at Antioch, Tehachapi Pass, Carson, and Truckee. Several years before, in 1873, a statewide "People's Protective Alliance" had been formed of anti-Chinese and labor groups. Abetted by the depressed economic conditions of mid-decade, and with recent Irish immigrants in prominent roles, they preached a volatile mix of race, class, and ethnic warfare against the Chinese and their employers under the slogan "the Chinese must go!" Their tactics ran the gamut from simple intimidation to beatings and mob violence. As the men in the *City of Peking*'s steerage explained to Li, the latest reports of "Irish" activities arriving in Hong Kong had reduced the numbers on this voyage by nearly 90 percent. When he asked why they came anyway in the face of such hostility, they replied simply that they were "driven by famine." Hearing this, "I felt enormous pity for them," he wrote.[47]

The voyage was not especially rough, and, once recovered, Li settled into a routine of reading, writing, walking on deck, and socializing in the ship's main saloon. On the whole, he seems to have found his fellow first-class passengers agreeable. One afternoon, however, he lunched with a group of missionaries, several of whom had spent decades in China. When one of them complained to him about the constant, and apparently orchestrated, tensions between his converts and their neighbors, Li politely opined that perhaps the best way to solve the problem was for his tablemates to be a bit less skillful at their work.[48]

The technical aspects of running the ship also occupied his attention. Li spent time with Captain Maury, as he would with the officers on his other voyages, and he was especially taken with conceptions of time and distance used in navigation, which run like a leitmotif throughout his account. The specific terminology used in the title of his work, *A New Account of a Trip Around the Globe,* is aimed at demonstrating conclusively to his readers that the earth is in fact a sphere on which China and America stand on opposite sides, representing, literally, the "front and back of the globe." While most educated Chinese were aware of this in theory, he says, perhaps eight of ten could not bring themselves to accept it as fact; he himself had once been among them. Having traveled "over eighty thousand li" to the east, however, from Shanghai to Shanghai, he believes the point to now be sufficiently proved. Hence, the travel portion of *A New Account* is titled "Diary of a Journey to the East." Significantly, on the last line of the journal, the captain of the *Ava* points to the ship's chronometer and says to Li, "Look! In Shanghai it is 5:00 P.M.; in London, it is just 10:00 A.M.!"[49]

On June 11, after eighteen days at sea, the ship passed through the Golden Gate and anchored off the Pacific Mail Company's wharf in San Francisco. After clearing customs, Li, interpreter Chen, and Knight settled into rooms at the plush Palace Hotel. Billed as the best in the world at the time, and featuring hot and cold running water, electric signals to alert the bellhops, spiral stairs, and elevators, its appointments drew admiring entries—as they would other Chinese travelers.[50] Li would expand on the role of such travel amenities and their larger implications in separate essays in *A New Account* on running water, hotels, the noise of traffic in the cities, and the niceties of social relations with Westerners. During his stay in San Francisco, he visited with the leaders of the region's *huiguan*—the famous Six Companies—as well as the Japanese vice-consul, Takagi Saburo, and the former American minister to China, Frederick F. Low. They provided him with the background to write an essay on the "actual condition" of the Chinese in America and a brief history of the Six Companies.[51]

On June 16, Li, Chen, and Knight took a ferry to Oakland, where they boarded a Central Pacific train for the long journey east. Li found the layout and workings of the train fascinating, though the rigors of the heat, noise, and marginally palatable food took their toll on him during the weeklong trip. As before, he took careful note of the Chinese communities along the way. In Evanston, Wyoming, where one-quarter of the population was composed of Chinese railroad workers, he felt pangs of homesickness while eying a display of Cantonese clothes on sale in the local restaurant. The emptiness of the American West impressed him, as did the ethnic and religious diversity of the United States. But while the diary explains to his Chinese readers how the terms *white, black,* and *red* are used as racial designations, there is little evidence that his guides imparted to him an authentic sense of their respective conflicts or relative status in the social hierarchy. For example, the only African-Americans he had encountered at this point were Pullman porters and attendants. His introduction to Native Amer-

icans, a brief incident in Sidney, Nebraska, during which a group
of Lakota entered the train and teased the passengers, occasioned
an account of the reservation and agent system, but one implying
that the major Indian nations had all been pacified. Ironically, the
pivotal battle at the Little Bighorn was fought only a few days later
on June 25. If Li was later aware of it—and since it pushed the coverage of the Centennial from the front pages of the Philadelphia
papers for two weeks in early July, it is hard to imagine he was
not—he did not record it. One might assume in any case that as
heir to a tradition that had seen itself for millennia as controlling
and civilizing the nomadic peoples along its own borders, Li would
likely have been inclined to view the situation from the perspective
of his hosts.

The phenomenon of Mormonism also piqued his interest. Li
provides a capsule history of the ostracism of the Church of the
Latter Day Saints from the east and of their great migration to
Utah. His conclusion is that although the Mormons had placed
themselves outside the accepted canons of Christianity due to their
practice of polygamy, the policies of the American government
toward them are actually quite generous. Though subjected to a
form of internal exile, he says, they are neither actively persecuted
nor forced to convert, and will be welcomed back if they change
their practices to more accepted norms.[52]

On June 23, the train pulled into Philadelphia, where Li stayed,
with interruptions for side trips to Washington, D.C., Hartford,
and New York City, until the end of October. He arrived, as did the
other passengers, "exhausted":

> In all, the meals and snacks were not terribly satisfying, the
> drinks were of ice water or tea with milk, I was dirty and
> greasy, and it had all become simply unbearable. Beyond
> this, the thunderous racket of the train's machinery has
> affected my hearing. What an arduous trip! Yet . . . if not for
> the train, how could it have been accomplished?[53]

THE COSMOS OF THE MACHINE

Li's home for the next several months was in many respects a city
in transition, and most of the changes had been neither easy nor

welcome. A century before, Philadelphia had been the largest city in British North America and the second largest in the English-speaking world. As the site of the Declaration of Independence and the framing of the Constitution, it was in terms of its historical significance arguably the world's most important city in the late eighteenth century. In the 1790s, it had served as the new nation's capital, and within the living memory of its older residents had been the country's most populous and cosmopolitan city, as well as its financial center, until overtaken by New York in the 1830s. From midcentury, following the city's incorporation of several neighboring municipalities and fueled by the railroad boom, the development of nearby coal and steel concerns, and successive waves of immigration, it had been transformed into the nation's premier industrial center.[54]

By 1876, although Philadelphia's population had multiplied twelvefold since the turn of the century, it had slipped to the status of second city and was on its way to being eclipsed by Chicago within a few years. Yet its overall wealth and tradition of civic amenities had kept pace with the century. The site of the Centennial, Fairmount Park, remains even today the largest urban green space in the country. The city's Waterworks, the machinery for which was concealed inside a complex of small Greek temples, was the first such urban water system in the United States and a popular tourist destination. The Almshouse and Municipal Hospital complex was the largest in the world, while its mental hospital, College of Physicians, and prisons were celebrated at home and abroad for their efficacy and innovation. Even as the new sprawl of factories and redbrick row houses pushed its borders ever outward, and class and ethnic tensions, which had reduced the city to near anarchy a few decades before, simmered just beneath the surface, Philadelphia still projected an air of deeply rooted gentility and unpretentious good taste. Li summed it up this way:

America's richest and most populous areas are concentrated in its northeastern states. Within these, accordingly, are the three largest cities. The first is called "New York," the second, "Philadelphia," and the third, "Boston," and the prosperity of their trade and commerce follows in this order as well. As for the extent of their respective areas, number of

multistory houses, and spaciousness of streets and boulevards, however, Philadelphia must take precedence.[55]

This impression of spaciousness was now taxed to the utmost by
the influx of people for the exhibition. On an average day during
the Centennial the city's population of 817,000 expanded by more
than 10 percent; on Pennsylvania Day, September 28, the nearly
275,000 visitors set a one-day attendance record. By the close of the
Centennial on November 10, an estimated 10 million people had
passed through its turnstiles, nearly doubling the figures for London's Great Exhibition.[56] Even with the unprecedented attention
given to accommodating the visitors, rooming houses and hotels
were overbooked for the duration. Though they moved twice during their stay, Li and Chen had been lucky enough to secure rooms
through the aegis of the Maritime Customs officials already on site.
In *A New Account*, he reported that it was common for visitors to
take lodgings as far away as New York City, coming and going each
day by train. In addition, he said, the constant traffic provided an
ideal sellers' market for all manner of necessities, the prices of
which, in some cases, climbed to seven times those of comparable
items in Shanghai.[57]

Nearly one-third of *A New Account* is taken up by the first book,
"Mei hui jilue" (A brief account of the American exposition). By
way of explaining the rationale for the celebration, Li supplies an
overview of the founding of the United States, complete with what
had by now become an obligatory apotheosis of George Washington as the embodiment of virtues characteristic of famous Chinese
leaders of antiquity.[58] This is followed by boilerplate descriptions
of the layout of the fairgrounds, mode of financing, and the names
and purposes of the principal exhibition halls, each of which are
then explored in detail: the Main Building, Machinery Hall, Art
Gallery (Memorial Hall), Agricultural Hall, Horticultural Hall, the
Women's Pavilion, the American Government Building, and
Judges Hall.

Anxious as Li was to omit no piece of information no matter how
trivial, some stretches of the first book are, in effect, laundry lists
of exotica. In addition, since an important reason for Li's coming
in the first place had been to survey the exhibition's vast holdings
of advanced technology, he dutifully describes the workings of

machines and industrial processes in mind-numbing detail. Interspersed among these somewhat barren stretches, however, are lively, astute, and wonderfully human observations on a wide range of subjects, some peculiar to his position as a Chinese traveler, some recognizable to anyone who has ever wandered too far from the familiar.

This last reaction was one often cited by those recounting their first experience of standing in the Main Building, gazing about dumbfounded and disoriented. For Li, the feeling was intensified by his being made an unwilling participant in the show:

> The handful of Chinese seen by the foreigners here had all been in work clothes, so one dressed more elegantly had the crowds continually closing in on him to catch a glimpse of yet another novel sight. I met with no one who did not exchange a kind word or, effusive in his admiration, offer me additional good wishes. Nonetheless, everyone pressing in on me at every turn was like being surrounded with no means of escape.[59]

As he explored the various halls, the overriding purpose of the exhibition, as related to him by officials at the different displays, formed a steady refrain. Initially, he admitted, he was rather dubious about the utility of such gatherings. "Now, however, I have come to realize that their purpose in fostering friendly relations [among nations], rewarding human talent, aiding in the diffusion of products, and connecting those who have with those who lack is beneficial to the country, and thus not at all pointless." This concept of international commerce, he admits ruefully, has been slow to catch on in China: "We Chinese alone seem capable of thinking that the intent of the Westerners in undertaking these exhibitions rests on principles against which we should guard at any cost." And yet, other countries spend vast amounts of money showcasing their goods at these venues; could they all be misguided?[60]

Though modest by the standards of the larger exhibitors, China's showing was certainly considered a success, though not an unqualified one. The Centennial judges awarded the exhibit thirty-five medals overall, and Hu Guangyong's porcelains and cloisonnés, and the distinctive oval-arched Ningbo bedstead and meticulously detailed wooden screens moved one observer to comment that "John Chinaman has an eye to solid comfort in the midst of all his love of gaudy color and gingerbread ornaments."[61] As Li wrote with justifiable pride, "All of this prompted visitors and dignitaries of other countries . . . to gasp in admiration at their beauty on seeing them for the first time, and to even exclaim, 'Now we know the ingenuity of the Chinese surpasses even that of the Westerners!'"[62] It was nonetheless also the opinion of some foreign observers that the enormous investment in man-hours required to produce such masterpieces might have been better spent on more practical projects, while their strict adherence to traditional forms was not sufficiently "progressive" for modern tastes. Still, the completeness and exoticism of the exhibit made it extremely popular with the public, and the sales figures show that comparatively little was shipped home unsold.[63]

While pleased at China's showing, Li was also clear about areas requiring improvement. The porcelains were extremely popular and had sold out early; ". . . antiques and satins, however, with their high asking prices, found comparatively few buyers since Westerners generally rely on Chinese purchasing agents for them."[64] Genuine Chinese green tea also moved well, but retailing it would have been far easier if it had been prepackaged in one-pound boxes instead of the large tea chests used in the wholesale and export trades. Perhaps more important, he said, was that its quality and purity must be more tightly controlled and the use of various fillers abandoned. Similarly, selling silk by weight was not advisable either since "its thickness and quality become thoroughly jumbled." In sum, "If we speak of developing effective practices, then purity without deception in such areas of commerce is something we must work toward improving every day." In his later comments on the quality and marketing of French and Italian silks, British porcelain, and Indian tea, he revisited this point, observing that in all of these cases China had already lost, or was in the process of losing, market share.[65]

Insight into just such effective practices could be found directly across the aisle at the Japanese exhibit. The *North China Herald*'s predictions notwithstanding, it was Japan's display that caused the biggest stir at the exposition. Japan's exhibition space was more than twice that of China's; moreover, like several of the other major exhibitors, the Japanese had constructed a separate outdoor pavilion along traditional lines, which drew admiring comments for its tasteful simplicity and skillful construction. Collectively, it can be said that both China and Japan at the Centennial sparked a powerful interest in East Asian arts in the Victorian world; of the two, however, it was Japan that self-consciously sought and received the most attention.

Ironically, a large measure of what made Japan's exhibit so attractive to the Western public, in contrast to the purposeful tra-ditionalism of the Chinese displays, was its balanced tension between time-honored arts and the products of Japan's developing industrial plant. The Chinese exhibit's organizers had assumed that the Centennial audiences would view items made along West-ern lines as simply inferior copies and, perhaps worse, as not authentically Chinese. For the Meiji government, which had com-mitted itself to a national policy of *bunmei kaika*, or "civilization and enlightenment," as a step toward revision of its own unequal treaties, it was vital to play up the angle of progress as defined by their adherence to the new Western norms.[66] As he had been in Japan, Li was quick to notice the movement toward goals in so many ways congruent with his own. But there were also aspects of Japanese aims about which he was less enthusiastic. His opening description captures nicely the exhibit's desired effect:

> The display cases and tables were fashioned along Western lines, and the furnishings were also manufactured using Western techniques. In the middle of an open area deco-rated all around with bonsai, water pipes rose up to a bronze fountain with pearls of water flowing down; a sight very much worth seeing.[67]

On the other hand, all the personnel and their families had aban-doned the national dress for Western clothes and uniforms. As Li dryly noted, "If not for their black hair and sallow *[mianhuang]* faces, one could scarcely distinguish 'east' from 'west.'"[68]

As did the other visitors, Li found Japan's porcelains, bronzes, lacquerware, and other arts commendable, though in some cases inferior to Chinese types. He was especially taken with the landscape painting and bold calligraphy of the Tokyo artist Ryūho (Fukushima Nei, 1820–89). There were also numerous machines on display, though it appears Li found these a bit disappointing compared to the overwhelming array in the American, British, and German exhibits. Still, he said, "I find this country to be carefully studying Western institutions, technology, and manufacturing, determined to unlock their deepest secrets." Moreover, he believed the interrelatedness of such initiatives, though much feared by certain cultural guardians in China, to be vital to their success: "For example, opening mines . . . helps the country, while strengthening the military through administrative reform, and building machine shops, mints, offices for telegraphs, posts, steamships, and railroads benefits the nation and people even more."[69] Even now, he said, the Japanese are scouring the country for skilled people to use in these new endeavors and laying plans to have an exposition of their own in the near future. The candidates for such positions, he noted—perhaps with a touch of envy— must be "excellent with the brush, bold and generous, discerning and skilled, and unwilling to drift complacently along in old ways of thinking."[70]

The cultural offerings of nearly all of the exhibitors exercised considerable fascination for Li, and he lavished a good deal of prose on the nature and prices of innumerable items. A Russian silver tea service, a life-sized French nativity scene, German pianos and music boxes, British optics, Turkish carpets, Australian gold, and American convertible furniture all captured his attention. Exhibits dealing with current issues in Sino-Western relations quite naturally also came in for discussion. At the display for British India, he detailed for his Chinese readers the strategy of the British in creating a tea industry in Assam in order to reduce the flow of specie out of their empire—and into China. He found the taste of the Indian product, however, decidedly inferior.[71]

More troubling by far was the ever-expanding opium trade. For Li, as for nearly all Confucian commentators, opium was the object lesson in how the drive for profit undermined both private morality and the public good. As his entries on London, Aden, Ceylon, Singapore, and Hong Kong show, he was for the most part impressed by English governance, even in the colonies. He writes that in India, however, the huge revenues from opium production and sales in China had propped up the economy of the Raj for so long that it was now impossible for either side to curb it. As for those colleagues who argued for legalization and taxation, he demanded plaintively: "Isn't it far too easy to argue that we have no alternative?"[72]

Perhaps most impressive for Li, as they were for the majority of the spectators, were the weapons and machines on display. The revolution in arms beginning roughly at midcentury that produced breech-loading, rifled cannon and explosive shells, repeating small arms, and various forerunners of machine guns now placed countries like China, whose industrial bases were barely in their formative stages, at an enormous disadvantage. In addition, the Qing court, unlike Meiji Japan, had no systematic strategy for weapons procurement and development. Powerful regional officials like Li Hongzhang acted essentially as independent purchasers on the international arms market and were always on the lookout for new weapons. And now, for the world's arms makers and their customers, the Centennial had become the biggest showcase of all.

As they had in so many other industrial categories, American arms manufacturers like Hotchkiss, Colt, Remington, and Winchester emerged at the Centennial as major forces in creating high-quality, innovative weapons. Li provided detailed descriptions of the workings of the Gardner battery gun, the Gatling rotary machine gun, and the new Winchester '73 lever action rifle, and was suitably impressed by the ease of operation and effectiveness of all of them. The most awesome weapons on display, however, were the new, all-steel Krupp breech-loading cannons located in Machinery Hall. Able to penetrate two feet, five inches of iron plate with its thirteen-hundred-pound shells, the larger of the two pieces looming over the German exhibit was sufficiently menacing to give spectators pause as the press trumpeted it as "Germany's Killing Machine!"[73] Li Hongzhang was impressed enough with Krupp's arms over the coming years that he would become one of the company's best customers — as befitting the title of "China's Bismarck" given him by the foreign community. Alfred Krupp, it was said, kept a picture of him over his bed.[74] Li Gui's reaction was more succinct: "*Yi!*" he exclaimed.[75]

The potential of machines to multiply human power and supply human wants had conferred upon them a kind of reverence more commonly associated with religious objects, and nowhere was this commingling of the sacred and profane more in evidence than in the fourteen-acre Machinery Hall. Surrounded by devices for every conceivable purpose, the onlookers could be forgiven if they expressed themselves along the lines of Lancelot Smith, Charles Kingsley's protagonist in his novel *Yeast,* when he said that such technology was surely a sign that "we are, in some ways at least, in harmony with the universe."[76] Thus, although the exposition's inaugural ceremonies were carried out on the steps of Memorial Hall, the real opening took place immediately following when President Grant and Emperor Dom Pedro of Brazil climbed the central stairway of the colossal Corliss steam engine in the center of Machinery Hall. Standing together on the operator's platform high above the awed spectators, they pulled their respective levers under the direction of designer George Corliss and set the mechanism's thirty-foot, fifty-six-ton flywheel into motion. Rated at a sustained fourteen hundred horsepower, the world's largest engine ran noiselessly on steam piped in from twenty remote boilers. What made it most impressive as a display, however, was that nearly all of the hundreds of machines in the hall—with the conspicuous exception of those in the British exhibit—were connected to it by means of geared shafts and overhead belted pulleys. As Frederic A. Bartholdi, the arm of whose Statue of Liberty was on prominent display near the Agricultural Hall, put it, the Corliss in motion had "the beauty, and almost the grace of human form."[77]

Li, too, confessed to having been transfixed by the almost supernatural quality of so many machines springing to life each day and performing their respective tasks by means of unseen forces: "The display of machinery was immense . . . so many that it was impossible to count. . . . one must now proclaim the state of the cosmos to be that of one vast machine!"[78] Though he tried, he said, to single out and write about the ones with "real utility," he was overwhelmed by the immensity of the display, the difficulties of understanding the movements of the devices, and their often-deafening clatter. Those he did describe included power looms, silk reelers, assorted papermaking machines, brick makers, nail cutters, tin platers, rope twisters, and rotary printing presses, to name just a few. More important than detailing their operational features, however, was to once again stress to his readers the importance of employing machines in general. He notes the fierce competition among manufacturers for innovation, a feature he revisits in the American Government Building by way of discussing U.S. patent law. However, he says, it is often objected that:

> We Chinese have a saying: "Where there are secret dealings, there are sure to be ingenious minds; the ancients, there- fore, did not encourage them." However, this is certainly not a maxim for us to follow today![79]

We can no longer afford to mouth such paeans to Daoist primi- tivism, he said, but should instead "buy all those [machines] with- out exception that might benefit the people."[80]

The Agricultural Hall—appropriately, perhaps, resembling a Gothic cathedral—and the flamboyantly Moorish Horticultural Hall held a number of attractions for Li, though his self-confessed lack of expertise in farm machinery placed him at something of a disadvantage. As he observed, "America's land is extensive and its population sparse. Thus, the business of agriculture could never succeed without utilizing the power of machines." Unfortunately, "the foreigners I questioned did not understand a great deal about them either. . . . As a result of this, I quite frankly have no way to describe their particulars." Nevertheless, he felt that since condi- tions in Western countries are not terribly different from those in China, such machines would be useful as a substitute for man- power in the areas still depressed from the Taiping Rebellion and for the thinly settled regions of China's northwest. Once again, he noted, the Japanese are busily doing just this on their northern island of Hokkaido, and importing Chinese farm laborers to boot.[81]

His powers of aesthetic appreciation faced an agreeable chal- lenge in the Art Gallery. The cultivation of skills in the "three excellences"—poetry, painting, and calligraphy—was an integral part of a traditional Chinese education, though their guiding prin- ciples departed from Western concepts in several important respects. For example, within the stylized confines of themes such as lone pines, craggy mountains, and tiny human figures, the Chi- nese artist's skill lay in his ability to suggest the subject matter's inner essence; to create a transcendent exchange with the viewer in which outside appearances are stripped away and the *dao* immanent in the creative effort of the artist emerges. The media in which the artist works lend themselves to this as well. A painting or piece of calligraphy brushed on paper in ink cannot be painted over. Thus the moment of spontaneous creation is seen as supremely important in revealing the character and inner state of the painter. The ultimate goal of the process is, as one writer put it, "to liberate the visual beauty of an abstract structure of lines"; or perhaps more succinctly, "to act like nature does."[82]

The realism and attention to detail so characteristic of Western painting was, of course, also aimed at revealing the inner essence of the subject. The development of techniques using oils on canvas, however, meant that a more studied, gradual approach could be taken in constructing the work itself. For Li, this took a bit of getting used to, though he was certainly impressed with the result:

> According to those well versed in Western art, *yin* and *yang* [i.e., darkness and light, or light and shadow], details of perspective and depth, position and placement must each be considered in their turn and clearly defined in painting. . . . Viewed up close, the brushstrokes seem crude and disorderly, like chicken scratches, and the colors appear to jut out abruptly and unevenly. As the viewing distance is gradually increased, however, they become wonderfully lively and vibrant, and remarkably true to life.[83]

Like other Chinese diarists, Li seems to have been under the impression that the relative social freedom of Western women, as well as attire that exposed their shoulders and décolletage, meant that it was quite common for them to be painted in the nude. Thus, he includes comments on the difficulties of technique in depicting "noble women" in various states of undress. Nevertheless, as in China, he says, painting is the province of the literati, though in the West, artists tend to specialize as professionals because of the demands of the discipline, since "idle craftsmen" are incapable of producing such sophisticated work.[84]

The borders of Chinese and American concepts of the role of gender were drawn in bold relief during Li's visit to the Women's Pavilion. Yet it is also here that he most startlingly defies expectations, both in his reaction to the place of women in America and, more significantly, in his own vision of what it ought to be in China. This contrariety made Li's entry on the Women's Pavilion the first piece of *A New Account* to be published in translation, appearing almost in its entirety in the August 17, 1878, issue of the *North China Herald*, which billed it as "of more than passing interest."[85]

The circumstances under which a separate women's exhibit had come to be were equally interesting. Though they seldom pronounced themselves so enthusiastically, the sentiments of both European and Chinese observers tended to echo Sarah Bernhardt's famous encomium of America as a "country . . . where women reign." Earlier, too, Alexis de Tocqueville had attributed the "singular prosperity and growing strength" of the United States chiefly "to the superiority of their women." In nearly all his visits to factories and institutions in the United States and Europe, Li, too, noted the high percentage of women engaged in a wide variety of occupations.[86]

The Centennial Commission had originally planned to include exhibits of women's activities and crafts in the Main Building. When space and politics precluded this arrangement, a Philadelphia-based coalition called the Women's Centennial Committee campaigned nationwide to raise funds to build a separate hall in which to showcase the accomplishments of women. Though criticized as accommodationist by Susan B. Anthony and Lucretia Mott, who advocated a women's boycott of the exposition, the committee's president, Elizabeth Gillespie, a great-granddaughter of Benjamin Franklin, proved a highly effective organizer. As Li carefully noted, "The building's design was conceived by women, as was the superintending of its construction, its decoration, and the placement of the exhibits. . . . Even the personnel selected to staff the pavilion's exhibits were all women."[87]

On entering, one saw a woman stationary engineer operating a steam engine, which ran various small devices throughout the hall. Though he doesn't mention it, Li would have been intrigued to discover that one of the most widely sold items there, the Suplee sewing needle, had originally been fabricated by a Chinese craftsmen to the designer's specifications and was being marketed as "the joint result of Yankee training and Chinese skill."[88] What impressed him most, however, was the open, forthright manner of the women. Here his views echo almost word for word the pronouncement of Tocqueville regarding their "masculine strength of understanding and manly energy"[89]:

> All of the staff were happy to answer my questions and did so tirelessly, with a poise and dignity completely unlike the demeanor of girls kept secluded in the home [as were Chinese girls]. On the contrary, they possessed a manly vitality, and I came to regard them with great respect and affection.[90]

Intriguing as well was the contemporary political agitation in the United States and England for women's suffrage. For Li, "Their arguments, though unprecedented, do seem justified." After all, he notes, education for women in many countries is now widespread, in some cases even compulsory, and no country can afford to waste the talents of half its population. Moreover, women are certainly no less intelligent than men, and their "inner calm" allows them to concentrate more effectively. Yet in China, he says, women and their talents are presently disparaged and female infanticide widespread; how are we to account for this?

His answer is one recently revisited by scholars. The nature of education for women has changed radically over the past two millennia, he writes, and for the worse. As late as the Eastern Zhou period (770–221 B.C.E.), even though their position was already eroding, women still held positions of power and influence; now, however, "there is even a saying, 'Only a woman without ability is virtuous.' *Yi!* This one sentence is harmful to all women." His solution, which builds toward its climax with a step-by-step assuredness reminiscent of classical models of argumentation, moves from educational reform for women through development of reason and right conduct, to utilization of their abilities, which would then stop the discounting of their intelligence and, finally, end the drowning of infant girls, "of its own accord."[91]

Having come this far, however, he stops just short of what we might think of as the final step. While earlier admitting the justice of Western women's demands for political rights, he qualifies his approval of their ultimate aims: "As far as the views of the English and American women are concerned, however, they surely go too far." Given his overwhelmingly male company, it was therefore not surprising that "on this, my Western friends wholeheartedly agree."[92]

MEANDERINGS

The material on the Centennial ends with some brief notes on the Judges Pavilion, where Li adds almost as an aside that it was there that he met President Grant. The context for that meeting, as well as all of his essays on American and European cities, and short pieces on Western practices and mores, are contained in the second and third books of *A New Account*, "Youlan suibi." A literal rendering of *suibi* would be the somewhat romantic-sounding "following the brush"; a more idiomatic and functional translation, however, might be "notes," "brief essays," or "jottings." In any case, Li's two books of "notes on sightseeing" cover a wealth of material on everything from the state of the Chinese in San Francisco to the delights of French cuisine, interspersed with visits to such prominent figures as American secretary of state Hamilton Fish; New York governor and presidential candidate Samuel J. Tilden; diplomat and educator Yung Wing; and the Oxford scholar, missionary, and translator James Legge. In nearly all cases, his visits to factories, schools, prisons, hospitals, military installations, and cultural institutions spark deft observations on their functions in their respective societies and, perhaps more important to his Chinese readers, comparisons with conditions in China.

As previously noted, with the exception of his brief stay in San Francisco, his visits to American cities were all done from his base in Philadelphia. This section therefore begins with a fairly extensive overview of the city and its notable sights. Of these, one of the most interesting for Li, as it was for a great many visitors before and since, was the great experiment in prison reform undertaken within the brooding, fortresslike Eastern State Penitentiary.

The squalid, overcrowded conditions that had marked Philadelphia's late colonial era Walnut Street Jail pushed early-nineteenth-century reformers toward a shift in emphasis from punishment of the incarcerated to their transformation. The city's deep-running Quaker sensibility also inclined toward the view that individual reflection on one's wrongs away from the corrupting influence of other prisoners would lead to penitence and reform. In terms of prison architecture, this insistence on solitary confinement was linked to the hub-and-spoke designs emerging in Europe as variations of the Utilitarian philosopher Jeremy Bentham's Panopticon. At Eastern State, or Cherry Hill as it was more widely known, a three-story rotunda was constructed as an administrative center from which radiated seven spokes of cellblocks, the doors of which were all visible from the hub, thus providing maximum efficiency in guarding the inmates. The whole of the complex was then surrounded by massive stone walls with crenellations and battlements to inspire awe and reflection among the citizenry. On completion in 1829, each prisoner had his own generously proportioned cell with such innovative features as a primitive flush toilet, sink, central heat and ventilation, and a private exercise yard. Its whitewashed interior and arched windows at the end of each cellblock were intended to add a vaguely religious aura to the building, an effect completed by the lone circular window atop the wall of each cell called the "God's Eye." Inmates were not only forbidden to communicate with one another, but also prevented from even seeing each other's faces. When transferred from cell to cell, all were required to wear hoods to disguise their identities and were referred to only by their prison numbers. At Eastern State, it was claimed, the prison had become a *penitentiary*.[93]

Almost from the day of its completion, the complex on Cherry Hill had become one of the nation's most popular tourist attractions, though the so-called Pennsylvania System remained the subject of bitter debate. The design itself was widely imitated, and modified versions were even built in China during the last years of the Qing.[94] The most contentious issues, however, revolved around the efficacy and unintended effects of solitary confinement. During the celebrated 1842 visit that yielded his unflattering *American Notes*, for example, Charles Dickens excoriated the system as a psychologically barbaric recipe for madness, "immeasurably worse than any torture of the body."[95] Li's impression, on the other hand, was far more favorable.

While it is unclear from his own writings how familiar he may have been with Chinese prisons, Li did not shrink from comparing them to the Philadelphia model:

I consider foreign prisons to be completely unlike those in China. In the first place, there is a desire for cleanliness; in the second, the food and drink are well balanced; third, work and rest are appropriately regulated; fourth, there are opportunities for learning a craft; finally, the warden and staff show consideration in every way for the condition of the men, like a father and elder brothers to sons and younger brothers . . . This is the utmost in admirable laws and generous intentions. If such practices resemble anything, it is in regarding a prison as something akin to a Buddhist monastery.[96]

Li was equally impressed with his visit to the Pennsylvania Hospital for the Insane and the nearby Municipal Hospital and Almshouse. By 1876, the hospital and the Almshouse, sometimes called "Blockley" and administered by the city's Guardians of the Poor, had become perhaps the largest charity medical institution in the world, with about four thousand patients at any given time. The medical staff donated their services, and, Li noted, the chief surgeon, Francis F. Maury, even contributed his own money to the institution. Li watched avidly as Maury performed an operation to remove bladder stones. In a statement bound to resonate with Confucian readers, he wrote, "The chief physician, Dr. Maury, possesses extraordinary medical abilities. His skills are imbued with a humanity [ren] that proceeds from a profound generosity of spirit."[97]

Li's visits to Washington, D.C., Hartford, and New York City tended in many ways to reinforce this impression of wealth and power used in the service of the people's livelihood. His stay in Washington was brief but busy. He had hoped to visit the president at the White House, but was disappointed to find him out of town on vacation. He still managed to discuss theories of civil service administration with Secretary Hamilton Fish in the State Department, wrote in favor of an American-style postal system to replace China's complex arrangement of civil and military couriers, and visited the U.S. Naval Observatory.[98]

In terms of China's existing self-strengthening programs, the visit to Hartford was perhaps more significant. The city was the site

of the Chinese Education Mission and the longtime home of Yung
Wing, who, by mid-decade, had achieved considerable prominence as the nation's most recognizable Chinese-American. Born
in Guangdong in 1828, he attended several missionary schools
before being invited to come back to the United States with one of
his teachers, Samuel R. Brown (1810–80). There he attended Mon-
son Academy in Massachusetts and became the first Chinese to
graduate from an American university, Yale, in 1854. He had long
since converted to Christianity and in 1852, while a student at Yale,
became a U.S. citizen. His lifelong goal had been to help China
modernize more or less along American lines, and he had proposed schemes of various sorts to both the Taiping leadership and
the Qing. In early 1864, he was sent back to the United States by
Zeng Guofan (1811–72) to purchase the machine tools for a factory
that when opened in September 1865, became the famous Kiangnan *(Jiangnan)* Arsenal. In 1872, after years of lobbying Zeng, Li
Hongzhang, and other prominent officials, the first group of students, with Yung and Chen Lanbin in charge, sailed for America
to set up the Chinese Education Mission.[99]

From the time of its arrival, the local and national press followed
the progress of the Education Mission avidly. By the time of Li's
visit, Yung Wing had become a national celebrity, numbering
among his circle President Grant, Mark Twain, Yale president
Noah Porter, and Connecticut education commissioner B. G.
Northrup. By all accounts his closest friend was his pastor at the
Asylum Hill Congregational Church, the Reverend Joseph
Twichell. Twichell, also a Twain intimate, had just the year before
officiated at Yung's wedding to Mary Louise Kellogg, whose father
had long been associated with the Education Mission. In 1874 and
1875, Chen and Yung were sent on missions of investigation to
Cuba and Peru, respectively, to gather evidence of the frightful
abuse of Chinese laborers there. As a result of their success in
these inquiries and their growing expertise in foreign affairs, they
were appointed joint ministers to the United States, Spain, and
Peru in September 1875. On the eve of Li's arrival in Hartford,
Yung had just been awarded an honorary L.L.D. by his alma
mater.

Though the mission was considered an unalloyed success in
America, it remained quite controversial in China. Yung's fervid

Christianity had been suspect from the beginning and was the principal reason the mission's sponsors made Chen his senior colleague. Moreover, certain cultural compromises had been permitted in order to ease the boys' relations with their hosts. They often wore Western clothes, like Yung himself; they concealed their queues under their hats; they had even formed a baseball team, "The Orientals," and played local clubs. In short, there was great fear that as living experiments in self-strengthening, they had already become irredeemably Westernized.[100]

Li carefully weighed these perceptions as he visited with the boys. Their initial meeting had taken place in August, when all 113 students had come down to the Centennial. He had already seen examples of their work on display at the Connecticut state exhibit in the Main Building, and immediately found himself taken with their skill and self-assurance. Asking pointed questions about their daily lives, dress, and curriculum, he professed himself fully convinced that the mission's goals were well on their way to being achieved. When they are finished, he said, they will be fully able to serve the imperial court in any capacity. As a parting gesture for both the Chinese students and a group of Japanese also studying in America, a luncheon was held with President Grant, the Centennial commissioners, the Japanese delegates, and assorted other dignitaries in the Judges Hall. The event received extensive coverage in the Philadelphia and Hartford papers, which called the boys "exceedingly bright looking and well behaved." Amid the general bonhomie of the welcoming addresses, the *Philadelphia Inquirer* reported that the Pennsylvania education superintendent, J. P. Wickersham, had even suggested a mission of "two to three hundred" American boys be sent to China, "to learn what good they could do there in exchange." His parting suggestion that side by side with the next contingent of boys, China "should send their sisters along also," was met with thunderous applause.[101]

Arriving in Hartford three weeks later, Li, accompanied by interpreter Chen and Knight, went to meet Yung Wing at the mission headquarters. The *Hartford Courant,* always alert for Education Mission news, summarized their itinerary over the next several days, noting that "Mr. Li is a highly educated Chinese gentleman, who is taking careful notes of what he sees in this country for use after he returns to his own country. He will probably publish a work in Chinese giving the results of his investigations here."[102] Yung showed him the plans for the new building, which Li felt would more properly express the national dignity *(tigong)* than their present lodgings. Moreover, in their deportment with each other and with their host families, and especially in their Chinese and Western studies, it was evident to him that the boys were acquiring both *ti* (essentials) and *yong* (practical application) in proper proportions. Yung Wing himself, said Li, is living proof that China can certainly trust Chinese who have lived abroad to be loyal servants of the throne.[103]

Yung arranged for the group to tour the Pratt and Whitney factory, the Colt works, and the Cheney Brothers textile mill in nearby South Manchester. Li was particularly impressed by the interrelationship between Pratt and Whitney and Colt, whereby the one would custom design machinery for the other, and each manufactured items on contract from other companies. Gatling, for example, had licensed Colt to produce its famous revolving barrel machine gun; Li also found Colt manufacturing the Gardner gun he had seen demonstrated in Philadelphia. Yung himself had a long-standing relationship with the Colt factory, having brokered a purchase of Gatling guns for China in 1873. As a parting gift, the plant manager presented Li with a brand-new "Peacemaker" revolver.[104]

Li's final excursion in America came in October with a trip to New York City. Here his host for much of the time was the wealthy "Sugar King," Henry O. Havemeyer. Havemeyer, along with General Hector Tyndale, had been among the most active buyers of Chinese and Japanese art at the Centennial.[105] Li had met Havemeyer's family in Philadelphia, and the invitation to visit him in New York perhaps originated during one of their exchanges. The Sugar King proved an active and engaging host. The group visited a public school—whose methods, Li noted approvingly, favored silent reading over the rote learning of his own education—a firehouse, police station and court, the offices of the *New York Sun,* a customs house, his host's sugar-refining mill, and the theater. He found the efficiency and openness of the court particularly admirable. Yet as well intentioned and lenient as the laws and punishments were in America, he mused, why do there seem to be so many arrests? And as for swearing an oath on the Bible, he opined, this is so much superstitious nonsense. The climax of the trip came with a visit to Governor Tilden, who, Li carefully recorded, was currently in a race for president. The two talked for quite some time and, on parting, exchanged autographed pictures.[106]

On October 26, Li and Chen headed for the American Line's Christian St. wharf in Philadelphia, where they boarded the steamer *Lord Clive* for Liverpool. The care with which the Maritime Customs' Centennial staff looked after them was evident throughout their parting. Hart, Hammond, and Huber came on board to see them off, the men shaking hands with considerable emotion. Before they left, Li noted gratefully, they implored the captain to take special care of them during the voyage.

In the event, they needed it. The passage was much rougher than the Pacific crossing five months earlier. At one point, a well-meaning shipmate dropped by Li's cabin to reassure him that these conditions were normal for an Atlantic crossing. Li, lying miserably in his bunk replied, "'How can I be worried about dying when, to be honest, I can scarcely stand this tossing around?' My friend then had a steward bring me some milk, and after drinking it I felt a bit better. Not a moment later I threw up again."[107]

After two weeks at sea, they made Liverpool. Jem Hart in Philadelphia had cabled James Duncan Campbell, the head of the IMC's London office, to arrange for Li to be met in Liverpool by some of his staff. They then took the train to London. Li was immediately taken by the charms of the English countryside in autumn, though he was bowled over by the immensity and bustle of the capital. Unlike the United States, which is a new country, he said, one is immediately struck by the traces of antiquity here, and the place has the air of "a still vigorous aristocratic family." He noted the famous fog, rendered toxic at times by enormous volumes of coal smoke, and how it had blackened the city's buildings.[108]

At the London office he was delighted to find several Maritime Customs men he had known in China home on leave. It is indeed a happy occasion, he said, to meet old friends in such a remote corner of the world.[109] His colleagues had arranged an appropriate itinerary of visits for him to London's palaces, Windsor Castle, St.

Paul's Cathedral, Westminster Abbey, and the Houses of Parliament. The visit to Parliament occasioned an overview of representative government as a whole. The English system, he observed, is the basic model for such systems in the West. Its debates are carried out in the open and are reported in all the newspapers so that the entire country may be informed about the great issues of the day. Thus all classes of society are involved at some level, and policy is carried out by consensus.[110] For the self-strengtheners concerned with institutional reform aimed at facilitating "officials, merchants, and people" working together, firsthand reports of these systems in operation in the United States, Great Britain, and most recently, Japan, held considerable appeal. In the hands of the next generation of reformers like Kang Youwei and Liang Qiqiao, the goal of constitutional monarchy would become central, though their efforts were to bear fruit only during the last days of the empire.

As he had been in the United States, Li was fascinated by the accelerating pace of technology in transportation, communications, and warfare. "In America, many of the streets have iron rails laid in them for running streetcars. . . . This city, however, has underground tunnels through which trains are run."[111] The Underground's stations themselves, with ticket offices, newsstands, and vendors of all sorts, seemed like a kind of fantasy world to him. The efficiency of the General Telegraph Office, with its links by cable to nearly every continent, he found miraculous. No less impressive was the pneumatic message delivery system within the building, tying together the telegraph and postal systems. The pressing need for ever-increasing speed in information gathering and dissemination was driven home again during his visit to the *Times* of London. Emphasizing the role of the press in the West, Li questions by implication those in China who see world affairs as secondary, if at all:

> I note that Westerners have established newspapers from a desire to thoroughly understand the world's affairs. People must comprehend world affairs in order to be capable of participating in them. Thus, the founding of these newspapers can indeed be said to be quite advantageous and their benefits considerable.[112]

Li's interest in military technology, whetted as it had been in America, was honed further during visits to the Woolwich Arsenal and Portsmouth Navy Yard. He witnessed the construction of built-up heavy artillery and was fascinated by the improved, wire-guided Whitehead "fish" torpedo. Equally impressive was gun cotton, the explosive power of which was five times that of black powder. At Portsmouth he visited an Arctic exploration vessel and a new ironclad with fore and aft turrets.[113]

His cultural exposure was taken care of by excursions to the South Kensington Museum, the Crystal Palace, the British Museum, and Oxford. At Oxford, Li paid a call on James Legge (1815–97), at the time perhaps the premier Western scholar of China, who had just been awarded a professorship at the university. Legge took the group on a tour of the colleges, and Li found its system of specialization and independent study a fascinating contrast to the rigidly structured curriculum and examination system of China. He did, however, find it unfortunate that the tuition and expenses of the university often prevented poorer students from entering, in contrast to the widespread philanthropic endeavors that seemed to mark the West more generally.[114]

Of all the places he visited, Li found Paris, "the West's most scenic city," best suited to his own tastes. Unfortunately, he spent only a few days there, and those were made somewhat difficult by the language barrier. Chen Chiyuan did not understand French, and only after considerable searching was someone hired from the hotel staff with enough knowledge of English to enable Li and Chen to communicate with him after a fashion. Nevertheless, the boulevards were broad and scenic and planted with trees for shade along the sidewalks; the shops "arranged like the cells of a honeycomb, orderly and pleasing to the eye. The buildings are six or seven stories, with the doorways on each level protected by ornamental iron grilles painted a golden color, extraordinarily pretty in a way that neither England nor America comes close to approaching."[115]

Li's activities in France were exclusively cultural: He visited the Louvre, Les Invalides, the Arc de Triomphe, Tuileries, Notre Dame, the Paris Opera, and took in a performance of the circus. The monumental architecture of Paris he found most impressive, and the spirit of Napoleon seemed to hover over much of what he saw. He noted that the city was still rebuilding after the disastrous war with Prussia and the rising of the communards, though "it is already the very picture of peace and tranquility, and the country's wealth and prosperity are everywhere evident."[116]

Most impressive of all, however, was the food. As the playwright and sometime government minister Jean Giraudoux would later say to a Chinese colleague, "Our countries were made to get along. They are the only ones which have both a *cuisine* and a *politesse.*" Li would likely have agreed. "The food from the hotel kitchen is absolutely wonderful and everything is delicious. In England, they still have not achieved this level of refined preparation, and in America, even less so." As it happened, Li received an invitation to lunch from his colleague Alfred Huber, recently returned home from the Centennial, who no doubt confirmed this sentiment.[117]

After dinner that evening, Li and Chen boarded a train for Marseilles, where they would take ship for the final leg of their journey back to Shanghai. On December 3, they made their way to their staterooms aboard the *Ava,* a thirty-five-hundred-ton screw steamer operated by the Messageries Maritimes as a mail and passenger carrier along a regular circuit of French, British, and Dutch Asian colonial possessions. The crew and passengers reflected the expanding imperial interests of the French: Of the 172 officers and sailors on board, there were "50 black men, 23 Chinese, and the rest are French." For their part, those in first-class "were educated people, with half of the group composed of French military officers and missionaries. The passengers are for the most part English, French, and Dutch. . . . In fact, officials and merchants are constantly coming and going among the possessions of these three countries. The rest of the passengers are Germans, Americans, Japanese, and Indians."[118]

After passing through the Suez Canal, the subject of a separate short essay, and stopping for coal at Aden, the ship made Galle, the primary port of call on Ceylon in the 1870s, on the evening of December 24. On Christmas Day, Li and Chen took a catamaran ashore, where they engaged a carriage and, following in the footsteps of Guo Songtao two days before, went to visit the Valukarama (Sand Hermitage) Buddhist temple. Like Guo, Li made a small donation and was given a look at some ancient Pali scriptures written on palm leaves.[119]

On New Year's Day, the *Ava* made Singapore. As in Aden and Galle, Li was once again able to glimpse the workings of the British colonial administration at close quarters. Given his qualms about Britain's designs on China, he was much impressed with the efficiency and relative fairness of Singapore's government. Perhaps more significantly, his docents were members of the local Chinese community. Li had two days to spend on the island, his departure being delayed pending the arrival of the packet boat from Java, so he took the time to visit the exquisite garden of expatriate Cantonese merchant Ho Ah-Kay, known to the Europeans as Whampoa. As had Guo in his diary, Li observed that Ho was highly regarded by both the British and the Chinese, and was currently serving as both an advocate on the Singapore bench and acting Russian consul. Guo was so impressed that he selected him to be the first Chinese consul in the Straits Settlements the following year.[120]

One thing that had commended itself to Li's attention in Singapore was the evenhandedness of the tax structure. The same could not be said of Saigon, his next stop and the showplace of French colonialism in Asia. One cannot escape the feeling that Li was particularly struck by the disparity between the quality of the good life in Paris and the abuses to which the French subjected the Vietnamese and Chinese in Saigon. Here, he said, the French hoped to put themselves into a position comparable to that of England in India. By way of funding their designs, "the French view the increasing numbers of Chinese coming here day by day as an avenue to financial benefit, and have developed new regulations specifically aimed at taking advantage of them."[121] Touring the Chinese city of Cholon, he learned that his countrymen were assessed no fewer than six separate taxes, in addition to which they were required to carry landing permits subject to yearly renewal. Export taxes were levied as well as tariffs, and all those engaged in trade had to carry their licenses on their persons. "Alas!" he exclaimed. "There is no place in the entire world so annoyed by this kind of tyrannical treatment. Compared to the English regulations in Singapore, they are truly as far apart as heaven and earth."[122]

A few days later they landed in Hong Kong, and for the first time in eight months, Li and Chen set eyes on Chinese soil, if only from a distance. Then as now, "When evening arrives, lamps illuminate everything brilliantly from the shore up to the many-storied buildings with countless thousands of lights—a magnificent spectacle." The following day, he spent an enjoyable afternoon with the redoubtable writer Wang Tao (1828–97). Having fled to Hong Kong because of his alleged support of the Taipings, Wang had been James Legge's associate for many years while the latter labored to translate the Chinese classical canon into English. In the late 1860s Wang lived with Legge in Scotland for two years and had acquired considerable insight into the pressing issues of Sino-foreign relations. He had also been instrumental in cofounding and editing one of the most successful Chinese-language newspapers, *Tsun wan yat pao,* in 1873. As he had with Yung Wing in Hartford, Li felt himself in the presence of someone extraordinary, though here he felt Wang's talents to be unjustly obscured by his exile so close to home: "Although we sat and talked, he constantly wanted to get up and move about. How sad to meet by chance someone living in this strange and distant land whose talents remain unknown to the world!"[123]

ATOP TAI SHAN

Arrived . . . Per M.M. str. *Ava,* from Marseilles—Mr. And Mrs. Viguier, Messers. Cracken, Li Hsiao Chi and Chin Cho Henen.
—*North China Herald,* January 18, 1877

Five days later, on January 17, 1877, Li arrived back in Shanghai. Having journeyed more than eighty thousand li over the course of 260 days, during which, he wrote, he was ill more than half the time and unable to keep up with his writing, he was now ready to edit and collate his material for printing and distribution. His preface bears an early date of March 1877; Li Hongzhang's foreword, done in his own distinctive calligraphy, is dated April of the following year. An initial run of three thousand copies underwritten by the Zongli Yamen, with maps by the firm of Ernest Grelier, "Corner of Nanking and Szechuan Roads, Shanghai," were printed. Most of these were sent to like-minded *yangwu* officials and their subordinates. Demand swiftly justified a second printing, and an early copy may have been among the photographs and other materials pertaining to the Centennial presented by Gustav Detring to Chen Lanbin on the eve of the minister's departure for the United States in late April 1878. Some sections may also have been leaked or given out to foreign sources, as evidenced by the excerpt on the Women's Pavilion in the *North China Herald*. In any case, Li's diary was quickly anthologized and appeared in successive versions of Wang Xiji's famous compendium of travel accounts, *Xiaofanghu zhai yudi congchao* (Geographical collectanea from the "Little Square Teapot Studio") in 1878, 1892, and 1894.[124]

The prestige imparted the work by Li Hongzhang's backing ultimately helped Li Gui secure an official position. In 1880 he memorialized both Li Hongzhang, at the time superintendent of trade for the northern ports, and his counterpart in the south, Liu Kunyi, offering seven proposals for self-strengthening and diplomacy based on the observations made in *A New Account*. A few years later, one of Li Hongzhang's protégés, Xue Fucheng, was named *taotai* of the circuit centered at Ningbo and employed Li Gui as a *yangwu* expert. That such expertise was desperately needed was brought out shortly after in August 1884, when the French escalated their campaign for control of Vietnam by launching a surprise attack on the Chinese naval base at Fuzhou. In one hour, the Chinese lost the core of their steam fleet and the harbor facilities that had been built up so painfully and expensively during the preceding decades.[125]

Having been sensitive to the French threat in Vietnam nearly a decade before, Li now urged Xue to move aggressively with his remaining forces. The opportunity came on March 1, 1885, when the French fleet attempted an assault on Zhenhai in Zhejiang province. The Chinese batteries opened fire on the French as soon as they were in range and, after three days of punishing exchanges, drove them off. Li later reported that he had watched the battle through his telescope from nearby Baoshan, perhaps reminded of the devastation during his days of captivity with the Taipings. For Xue, the victory and his account of it, *Zhedong zhou fang lu* (The defense of the eastern coast of Zhejiang) helped secure additional promotion. By decade's end—and no doubt with briefings from Li—he was dispatched as Chinese minister to Great Britain, France, Italy, and Belgium. Shortly after the battle, in 1885, he recommended Li for a position as expectant subprefect in Jiangnan, though it was not until 1893 that a vacancy materialized for him to occupy. In the meantime, Xue, as Li Gui's patron, wrote a preface for his protégé's 1888 *Jinling bing shi huilue* (A brief military history of Nanjing).[126]

During this period Li also played a pivotal role in the development of China's modernized postal system. By the mid-1880s, the empire had no fewer than six different government and private modes of mail delivery: the *yizhan* and *pu* systems of government mounted and foot couriers for official correspondence and travelers; *wenbao*, for the correspondence of the Zongli Yamen and Chinese diplomats; *xingju*, or private carriers, in most larger cities; the postal systems of the assorted foreign governments and municipal councils in the treaty ports; and, after 1878, the Maritime Customs postal service. While Robert Hart had continually lobbied for a Western-style system since the 1860s, the arrangements already in place had in fact done a reasonably good job in terms of convenience and reliability and had only recently been surpassed by Western systems in terms of speed and uniformity.

Li's visits to the Post Office Department in Washington, D.C., and the General Post Office and General Telegraph Office complex in London had convinced him not only of the increased efficiency of the Western systems, with their uniform rules, fee schedules, and combining of official and civilian mail, but of their profitability as well. China's system cost on average about 5 to 7 percent of the government's annual expenditures. The postal systems of the United States and Britain, with their low fees and high volume, created substantial surpluses for their respective governments.

Hence, in 1885, Li submitted a proposal through Xue Fucheng, along with another IMC man, Henry Kopsch, detailing a Western-style system to be adopted in China and appending the new Hong Kong postal regulations as a possible model. While attracting general approval from Zeng Guoquan, the Superintendent of Trade for the Southern Ports, the Yamen sidelined it until after the Sino-Japanese War. Finally, the Qing Imperial Post was created after considerable review in 1896, with Kopsch as its first Postal Secretary.[127]

Established at long last as an advisor and foreign expert, and now with a modest official post, Li was sent to Shanghai at the outbreak of the Sino-Japanese War in 1894 to attempt to negotiate aid from the British. In 1895 he published a short report, *Tongshang biao* (Statement on trade),[128] and after the end of the war, he was invited by Li Hongzhang's powerful rival, Zhang Zhidong, to advise on the plans for police and municipal administration during the opening of a foreign concession in Suzhou in 1897. The following year, at the height of his career, he suffered an apparent stroke. Increasingly incapacitated, he lingered for nearly five years before finally passing away in 1903.[129]

How are we to assess Li's role as cultural intermediary and interpreter? In some respects the effect of his account suggests that of a camera obscura: It projects an occluded image of the outside world into a confined space through the pinhole aperture of a single person's experiences. As in the device itself, the image is correct in most particulars, yet inaccessible, distorted at the edges, and appears in some important respects to be inverted—at least according to the expectations of many of Li's readers. Moreover, the aperture itself is clouded by multiple layers of preconceptions; by an admittedly insufficient understanding of geography, science, and mechanics; and above all, by an utter dependence on well-meaning, if occasionally self-serving, guides, the quality of whose information is largely governed by the limitations of Chen Chiyuan's five short years of English language training in Hong Kong. Yet, despite all these barriers, Li's account not only displays a striking degree of fundamental accuracy but, as this introduction suggests, a marked gift for unexpected insight. His meditations on the difficulties of compassing and reconciling different perspectives, and his attempts at self-analysis in his attitudes toward crime and punishment, lodging, entertaining, and noise by means of discussions with his hosts create a revealing, though limited, layer of metanarrative within the conventions of travel literature to which he felt himself bound. His asides to his Chinese readers alone provide a rich cultural vein to mine on subjects as varied as weights and measures, the naming of cities, wedding and funerary customs, clothing, agriculture, and the role of machines, to name just a few. When one adds to the list his short essays on Western manners and mores, hotels, and running water, it also becomes possible to discern an approach that diverges markedly in places from a mode of late Qing thinking that might be termed "occidentalist."

Appropriating elements of postmodern theory as employed by Edward Said in dissecting European literary constructions of the

Islamic world in his pioneering *Orientalism*, some scholars have suggested parallel attitudes identifiable within nineteenth-century Chinese perceptions of the West: easy, essentialist assumptions of cultural "otherness"; the inability to disentangle what Joseph Levenson once termed "the incompatible questions" of "truth" and "mine" regarding history and value; the belief that Western science and technology sprang from earlier Chinese discoveries; and perceptions of "perverse" practices stemming from the West's antipodal geographical position, among others.[130]

As *A New Account* demonstrates, Li was not completely immune from any of these assumptions, and one frequently sees him struggling to place some startling piece of new information into a familiar frame of reference. But by his own frequent admission, what was familiar within that frame grew considerably over the course of his journey. In this, along with his immediate predecessors in writing on the West, Bin Jun, Zhang Deyi, Zhi Gang, and Sun Jiagu, he is part of a long continuum in Chinese travel writing, the historical function of which had been in part to correct gross misconceptions while fitting the territory in question into compatible constructs so as to more effectively order the world.[131]

His sure-handed positing of the world as a globe orbiting the sun, for example, based as it was on his own unbroken "journey to the east," put to rest not only his own doubts but signaled to his readers that they may now safely do the same. Whether they hewed to the ancient cosmology of a square earth and round heaven or the more elaborate critiques of Western heliocentrism leveled by Ruan Yuan (1764–1849), the new outlook, by means of interaction with an approved observer, could now be viewed as comfortably within the ken of shared cultural experience. In making the globe his territory, he is at once free to set a distinct tone of critical inquiry while broadening to an unprecedented degree the possibilities of its ordering. He is thus on a grand scale what Richard Strassberg characterizes as a kind of literary explorer:

> By applying the patterns of the classical language, writers symbolically claimed unknown or marginal places, transforming their "otherness" and bringing these within the Chinese world order.[132]

In addition to symbolically bringing vast new territories under the transforming sway of the *ru* discursive tradition, *A New Account* is also noteworthy in its concrete expectations of Chinese agency in world affairs. As such it represents a distinct, though by no means isolated, strain of countervailing thought during a time often depicted by historians as one of political retreat and retrenchment.[133] Some have even argued in this connection for Li's "modernity," citing his seeming ability to step outside the limitations of his own cultural subjectivity in his admiration for things foreign and recommendations for reform in China. Yet it might also be argued that such an approach suggests a Confucian worldview—shared to a considerable degree by his fellow travel writers—that is far more elastic and optimistic than is generally appreciated. Against a backdrop of relative peace, the dispatch of officials abroad, millions of Chinese living around the world, and a wide array of apparently well-begun self-strengthening efforts, perhaps it is not surprising that Li, like Robert Hart, would see China's participation in international expositions as evidence of a trend toward expansion and perhaps even convergence with the West—a kind of ultimate *ti* and *yong* relationship. Given how conceptually freighted Confucian discourse is in this regard, with its key assumptions of a universal, China-centered polity and carefully arranged hierarchical relationships, it is perhaps suggestive that Li Hongzhang describes the present situation of Sino-foreign relations in his foreword to *A New Account* as being "in some respects like those of a family"—terminology employed as well in the imperial credentials carried by Qing envoys.[134]

As the Chinese diplomat Wu Tingfang wrote a little more than a generation later, "Of all the nations in the world, America is the most interesting to the Chinese."[135] One could argue that this was already true in Li's time, and it was an interest shared in at least one area with European observers. Both to some degree sensed in the newness of the United States the tension between its boundless possibilities for reinvention and its unsettling rootlessness, the result, according to Henry James, of having "no sovereign, no court, no personal loyalty, no aristocracy, no church, no clergy." Or as the title of a recent collection of Chinese accounts of America puts it, it was a "land without ghosts."[136]

On the other hand, nearly all nineteenth-century Chinese

accounts of America differ fundamentally in purpose from those of European travelers. As a number of commentators have noted, writers like Tocqueville, Dickens, and Trollope saw the young United States as the place where the promises and perils of Enlightenment and revolution were in the process of being played out. In cultural terms, however, they tended to see Americans as coarse and bumptious, naive and derivative, often humorously so. One recalls Oscar Wilde's line from *A Woman of No Importance* that when good Americans die, they go to Paris, but when bad ones die they go to America.[137]

For Li and other early Chinese travelers, the exact structure of the American political system and its experimental nature were seldom of more than passing interest. More significant were the general condition of apparent cooperation among all classes in decision making and the effectiveness of individual institutions — the post office, mint, army and navy, and assorted philanthropic establishments — that bore comparison with similar systems in China. By the time of Li's visit, the phenomenon of political parties and their role in the mounting difficulties experienced by Chinese communities in California and the American West was also beginning to come under scrutiny. Far more interesting to all observers, however, was the figure of George Washington. As Kevin Scott Wong and others have observed, beginning with Wei Yuan, Lin Zexu, and Xu Jiyu in the 1840s, Washington's role in resisting British oppression, his sage leadership as a founder of the country, and his refusal to create a hereditary dynasty elevated him to comparisons with the ancient "model rulers" Yao and Shun.[138]

Unrestrained by the complex legacy of European-American cultural relations, Chinese writers felt free to make other correlations with their own ancient past. The very newness of the United States and its place on the opposite side of the globe made it a convincing test case for Confucius's dictums that virtue, too, may be found among the barbarians and that human nature everywhere is essentially the same. For Li, the breathtaking extent to which the new technologies had been employed in the service of the "people's livelihood" only tended to reinforce this impression of the Americans' intuitive adherence to universal norms of proper behavior. Indeed, Chang Fan-chen, drawing in part on Li's account, terms the emerging Chinese view of America at this time as that of a "barbarian paradise."[139]

Careful readers of *A New Account* will note many apparent similarities in form and content with Western travel literature. This is equally true of other works within the long and varied history of Chinese official accounts of far-flung territories, with their opening geographical and historical notes and careful descriptions of items of ethnographic interest to literati and scholar-officials. From the very first travel accounts of the *Shan hai jing*—rendered as the *Classic of* [or *Guide through*] *Mountains and Seas* (ca. 320 B.C.E. to 200 C.E.)—through Han accounts of peripheral territories such as Japan, "The literary forms of Chinese travel writing evolved out of a matrix where narrative was dominated by the impersonal style of official, historical biography, and subjective autobiographical impulses were largely subsumed within lyric poetry."[140]

On the other hand, such subjectivity frequently surfaced within an orientation toward community with the past by means of visits to famous sites such as mountains, shrines, scenic landmarks, and so forth.[141] Between the eighth and twelfth centuries, the first-person, belletristic conventions for relating such experiences had been defined within the genre of the *youzhi* (travel account), while the more straightforward narratives of day-to-day events were to be found in the related *riji* (travel diary). On the whole, third-person accounts, viewed as being more akin to histories, were generally listed under the category of "records" *(ji)*, as with Fa Xian's classic fourth-century journal *Foguo ji* (A record of the Buddhist kingdoms).[142]

The overwhelming number of Chinese travel accounts deal with sites in China, and by the nineteenth century there had emerged a kind of fusion of the *youzhi* and *riji* forms, occasionally interspersed with lyric poetry in reaction to famous sights as a way of connecting with the past and establishing a temporal link with future readers.[143] But these conventions resonated best with readers for whom the places visited were likely to be recognizable; once beyond the pale of the Sinitic and Buddhist spheres, the language itself might appear familiar, but the sites described—aside from stock themes such as mountains, waterfalls, sunrises, and so forth—would necessarily become increasingly alien. Thus, although Li's account is organized according to the *youzhi* tradition of placing individual essays on the sites visited in the foreground while relegating the travel diary itself to the end, his material more closely resembles the "journalistic" sort found later on in the century in the work of Huang Zunxian, Liang Qiqiao, Wang Tao, and others.[144] Interestingly, Wang Xiji, in anthologizing *A New Account*'s final book, perhaps unknowingly completed the process, taking the editorial liberty of weaving the various essays appearing in the earlier "Youlan suibi" sections into the travel record "Dong xing riji" (Diary of a journey to the east) matching them to their appropriate chronological entries along the way. In many respects, therefore, Li represents a bridge figure between these two trends, employing long stretches of straightforward eyewitness description followed by a summary coda of reflection and opinion on the matter at hand. One might say, too, that his account represents the middle ground on a continuum extending from the extreme imaginative experientialism of post-Enlightenment European travel writers—as in Coleridge's comment that "part of my 'Travels' will consist of excursions in my own mind"—to the heroic restraint of the earliest modern Japanese observers of the West.[145]

In one important area, that of world geographies and atlases (*tuzhi* and *zhi*, or gazetteers), Li and his fellow travelers represent a more decided break with the recent past. In the eighteenth century, Jesuit adherence to Tychonian constructs of the solar system had caused Western astronomy to suffer in Chinese eyes when these were later dropped in favor of heliocentric models; Jesuit cartographic techniques as a result were similarly tainted by association, though less dramatically.[146] Such politically influenced neglect contributed to geographical information about the non-Chinese world being in short supply by the time of the First Opium War. A primary resource, for example, was the collection of *Hai lu* (ca. 1820), or "maritime records," based on the reminiscences of a blind, aged Cantonese interpreter and sailor. Drawing on available foreign materials in translation, Lin Zexu, the imperial commissioner in charge of suppressing the opium trade in Canton, and Wei Yuan, a local scholar, compiled two far more useful works, *Sizhou zhi* (Gazetteer of the four continents, 1841) and Wei's *Haiguo tuzhi* (A geography of the maritime countries, 1844, 1849, and 1852). A shorter, but more serviceable compilation with sections borrowed directly from European atlases was Xu Jiyu's 1850 *Yinghuan zhilue* (A brief description of the maritime circuit). Xu's work remained a standard reference through much of the nineteenth century and was a preferred source for travel writers in guiding their own observations abroad. Li, for example, refers to it more than once and appears to have lifted his account of the American Revolution from it almost word for word.[147]

All of these new works, however, were the result of homebound research. During the decade ending with Li's journey, the first wave of Chinese traveler-diarists accumulated a vast amount of new information by personal observation, which was now available to Chinese officials as they began their postings abroad in the late 1870s. If the world was to be symbolically ordered in the literary sense, and seemingly on the verge of being so in the diplomatic sense, the necessary knowledge for "practical application" was now at least being acquired in a far more extensive and systematic fashion, thanks to their efforts.

As a figure who steadfastly resists easy categorization, perhaps the most meaningful thing we can say of Li Gui is that his account represents an important primary source in recent efforts to develop what Paul Cohen has called a more "China-centered" perspective on modern Chinese history. For students of the American past, Li's observations on nineteenth-century life, like those of Tocqueville or Dickens, will perhaps expand the body of much-needed outsider views of the republic. For world historians calling into question long-standing assumptions about the effects of imperialism, such a first-person account by an individual traversing the cultural borderlands of the East Asian encounter must necessarily enrich the literature. Perhaps a fitting perspective on his efforts was one offered more than two thousand years before by Mencius, and utilized by Chinese writers ever since:

> Confucius ascended the eastern hill, and the state of Lu
> appeared to him small. He ascended Tai Shan and all the
> world appeared to him small.[148]

For a brief eight months, Li Gui had peered out at the world from atop Tai Shan. If anything, though, he found it far larger than he could have ever imagined.

TRANSLATOR'S NOTES

As Herrlee Glessner Creel famously observed, literary Chinese, or *wenyan,* with its classical structure and modern vocabulary, is "terse to the last degree." Li Gui's prose is often particularly so, which makes rendering it into English in a way that does justice to its laconic richness especially difficult. Additionally, some rhetorical devices of literary and official style — the intensification of points through parallelism and repetition, or the iteration of hierarchies of causation, for example — do not necessarily present themselves as elegant or sophisticated modes of argument in English. Similarly, the persuasive power of correlation and part/whole argument, so central to older Chinese systems of thought, has long been superseded in the West by discursive systems privileging analytic or evolutionary approaches. Finally, the vast body of Chinese classical allusions, some with close English counterparts, some impossibly obscure, all at some level necessary for an understanding of the literary language, presents a fresh set of challenges for the foreign reader.

Thus, the translator is necessarily faced with fundamental tasks of interpretation, and in the case of historical documents, doubly so. In this, one is continually confronted with choices in rendering such a work into modern idiomatic English ranging from literal to free translation, and this account undoubtedly contains abundant examples of both extremes. Nonetheless, the aim throughout has been to present it in such a way as to be recognizable as the work of one who is young and well educated, yet whose temperament is decidedly pragmatic and unpedantic. An additional consideration, in terms of his descriptions of foreign technology and institutions, has been to adopt a tone suitable for one who has some passing acquaintance with many of these, but no deep understanding of any of them.

Though Li's record as presented here is fundamentally complete, some brief sections have been glossed for editorial reasons. By far the largest segment of *A New Account* deals with the Centennial and sites around Philadelphia. As previously noted, these contain some arid stretches, especially those involving the minute workings of machines, or long lists of certain categories of items.

In several cases, these have been glossed in favor of clearer or briefer descriptions of similar things covered elsewhere in the record. In addition, Li's accounts of the Philadelphia House of Correction and the Educational Home orphans' school have been glossed in favor of full accounts of the more famous Eastern State Penitentiary and New York City's Foundling Asylum.

Chinese methods of reckoning dates are many and varied. For the most part Li refers to years by where they fall in the reign of a particular emperor, as in "the second year in the reign of the Guangxu emperor" for 1876. This is frequently augmented by an appropriate combination of one of the ten "heavenly stems" and twelve "earthly branches" of which the sixty possible combinations constitute a cycle. Thus, in addition to giving the imperial reign year for 1876, both Li Gui in his preface and Li Hongzhang in his foreword also designate it as the *bingzi* year. In cases where the year in question is significant to Westerners, Li also generally gives it in the Western style. Though lunar months and solar terms carry their own literary designations, for the most part, Li follows the common method of listing them by their order in the lunar calendar, that is, *first month*, *second month*, and so on. The Chinese lunar calendar generally overlaps the Western solar year by a month to six weeks, with the new year coming at the end of January or early February. It also requires a short intercalary month every three years, and in 1876 this fell in late June and early July. As with the years, seasons, months, and days, the twelve two-hour divisions of the day have their own designations, in this case appropriating the names of the twelve "earthly stems." On the whole, these have been given as their English equivalents in the text. Similarly, the Chinese "hour" or *shi*, the equivalent of two English hours, is noted in brackets where appropriate.

Though Li's instructions to his readers include Chinese equivalents for foreign weights and measures, these are, he freely admits, only approximations. He is in addition sometimes vague as to which kind of measure is being employed at a given time. Therefore, the designations *English* and *Chinese* are also given in brackets within the text for these where known. Other information required for clarity is also supplied in intertextual brackets or in the notes; all asides contained in parentheses are Li's. Though the

Chinese terms for weights and measures are given in pinyin romanization with English equivalents where they first occur, for the sake of convenience they are given below as well:

1 *cun* = 1.41 inches, 3.581 centimeters
1 *chi* = 12.1 inches as a walking measure, 30.734 centimeters;
    14.1 inches as a linear measure, 35.814 centimeters
1 *zhang* = 141 inches, 3.581 meters
1 *li* =1821.15 feet, a third of a mile; 0.555 kilometers
1 *mou* or *mu* = .16 acres, .064 hectare
1 *liang/tael* = 1.327 ounces, 37.62 grams
1 *jin/catty* = 1.33 pounds, 603.277 grams
1 *dan/picul* = 133 pounds, 60.477 kilograms
1 *shi* = 160 pounds, 72.574 kilograms
1 *dou* = 2.34 gallons, 10.31 liters
1 *shi* = 23.4 gallons, 103.1 liters[149]

Transliterations of personal and place names in Chinese accounts of foreign lands almost always prove problematic, and those in *A New Account* are no exception. Where these are known for certain, they have been put into their direct English equivalents; those in doubt are given in pinyin transliteration with the possibilities rendered in brackets or, in cases where more detail is required, in the notes.

While often approximating the familiar divisions of chapter, book, and volume in Western literature, the Chinese terms *juan* and *ce* that appear in the text and notes do not have exact English equivalents. *Juan*, for example, is etymologically descended from the character for "scroll" and can mean, variously, "book," "volume," or "chapter." Similarly, *ce* originally depicted the joining together of bamboo slips—one of China's earliest writing media—and is also therefore usually rendered as "book" or "volume." In this translation, the four *juan* into which Li's work has been divided have been rendered as "books," both because they were separately bound in the original edition and because each is divided into chapter-length sections. Since the divisions in other works cited may vary considerably in length and character, however, they are given as *juan* and *ce* throughout.

Finally, as mentioned earlier, Li's account is organized according to a hierarchy of his mission's priorities. That is, his first book is dedicated to coverage of the Centennial, his second and third are taken up with cities visited and brief topical essays, and the last is occupied by the actual travel diary. Readers wishing to follow the account in chronological fashion should therefore begin with the front matter and skip directly to book IV. They may then follow Li's directions at the end of the chapters "From San Francisco to Philadelphia," "From Philadelphia to London," and "From London to Marseilles," referring them to the appropriate essays, and conclude with "From Marseilles Back to Shanghai."

NOTES

1. It should be noted that the terms *West* and *Western* used here refer primarily to the nations of Europe and North America guided by ideologies springing from the Enlightenment and its aftermath and powered by the Industrial Revolution during the nineteenth century. Mindful that such terms are misleadingly reductive, I employ them here principally because of their use by Li and his colleagues as referents for these areas and their inhabitants. For a full discussion of the "fictive" elements of such constructs, see Michael Nylan, *The Five "Confucian" Classics* (New Haven: Yale University Press, 2001), 367–68.

2. The standard work on the careers of Guo Songtao and Liu Xihong, including translations of diary excerpts, is J. D. Frodsham, *The First Chinese Embassy to the West* (Oxford: Clarendon Press, 1974). See also the ministers' journals, *Yangzhi shuwu yiji* (Guo) 12 *juan* (1892); and *Yingyao riji* (Liu), in *Xiao-fang hu zhai youdi congqiao,* comp. Wang Xiji (Shanghai: n.p., 1892), 8871–8970.

3. The literature on the overseas Chinese, the coolie trade, and the sending of the first diplomatic missions abroad is far too vast to list more than a few representative works here. Some standard English language treatments include Robert W. Irick, *Ch'ing Policy toward the Coolie Trade, 1847–1878* (Taipei: Chinese Materials Center, 1982); Shih-shan Henry Tsai, *China and the Overseas Chinese in the United States, 1868–1911* (Fayetteville: University of Arkansas Press, 1985); Yen Ching-hwang, *Coolies and Mandarins* (Singapore: Singapore University Press, 1985); and Immanuel C. Y. Hsu, *China's Entrance into the Family of Nations: The Diplomatic Phase, 1858–1880* (Cambridge: Harvard University Press, 1960). For detailed sources on the roles of Chen Lanbin and Yung Wing in the diplomatic process, see Charles Desnoyers, "Self-Strengthening in the New World: A Chinese Envoy's Travels in America," *Pacific Historical Review* 60 (1991): 195–219; and "The Thin Edge of the Wedge: The Chinese Educational Mission and Diplomatic Representation in the Americas, 1872–1875," *Pacific Historical Review* 61 (1992): 241–63.

4. In addition to Bin Jun's trip with Hart, these included the 1868 Burlingame Mission, which resulted in an immigration treaty with the United States; the official Chong Hou's mission of apology to France in 1870 to settle claims resulting from the Tianjin Massacre; the Chinese Education Mission,

1872–81; and the sending of Imperial Maritime Customs personnel to represent China at the Vienna Exposition in 1873. The official account of the Burlingame Mission may be found in *Chouban yiwu shimo. Tongzhi* (n.p., 1880), 51:27b; Burlingame was accompanied by two officials, Zhi Gang and Sun Jiagu. Zhi kept a travel diary, *Chu shi taixi ji* (The first mission to the far West), as did a young interpreter, Zhang Deyi. Zhang (1847–1919) had earlier accompanied Bin Jun and later served with Guo Songtao; from 1902 to 1906, he was ambassador to Great Britain in his own right. An English translation of his diary during the Burlingame Mission, *Ou mei huanyou ji* (An account of travels in Europe and America), may be found in Simon Johnstone, *Diary of a Chinese Diplomat* (Beijing: Chinese Literature Press, 1992).

5. In addition to the materials on Chinese emigration and diplomacy mentioned above, see Yung Wing's autobiography, *My Life in China and America* (New York: Henry Holt, 1909); Thomas LaFargue, *China's First Hundred* (Pullman: University Press of Washington State, 1942); William Hung, "The Closure of the Educational Mission in America," *Harvard Journal of Asiatic Studies* 18 (1955): 51–73; Edmund Worthy, "Yung Wing in America," *Pacific Historical Review* 34 (1965): 265–87; and Kevin Scott Wong, "The Transformation of Culture: Three Chinese Views of America," *American Quarterly* 48, no. 2 (1996): 217–25.

6. The ironies continue. According to earlier rumors circulating among Imperial Maritime Customs officers, Guo's party was originally supposed to have taken up their posts by way of the American Centennial Exposition in Philadelphia—Li Gui's principal destination. He therefore might have had the opportunity to travel with them. See Chen Xiafei and Han Rongfang, eds., *Archives of China's Imperial Maritime Customs Confidential Correspondence between Robert Hart and James Duncan Campbell, 1874–1907*, vol. 1 (Beijing: Foreign Languages Press, 1990), no. 233, p. 180.

7. Zhong Shuhe, ed., *Zouwen shijie congshu* (English title given as *From East to West*) (Changsha: Hunan People's Press, 1980, 1985), 186. The edition cited here is 1985.

8. Principal references include ibid., 169–87; the introduction to an earlier (1980) Hunan People's Press edition of *Huan you diqiu xin lu*, 1–8; R. David Arkush and Leo O. Lee, *Land without Ghosts* (Berkeley and Los Angeles: University of California Press, 1989), 41; Chang-fang Chen, "Barbarian Paradise: Chinese Views of the United States, 1784–1911," Ph.D. diss., Indiana University, 1985, 125–39, passim; and Daniel William Garcia-Lahiguera, "The Diaries of Li Gui," M.A. thesis, University of California, Berkeley, 1993. See also Li Gui, *Sitong ji* (Bitter memories), 2 *juan* (n.p., 1880).

9. Zhong, *Zouwen shijie congshu*, 170. This sketch of Li's early years is drawn largely from Zhong, 170–74, which remains the only relatively complete account of his life.

10. Like the term *Western*, *Confucian* is used here as a convenient shorthand, in this case to compass the intellectual tradition of the *ru*, or classical scholars, as understood by the educated in the nineteenth century. Hence it includes both the canon approved for the various grades of official examinations as well as a wide variety of texts and commentaries outside of the official Confucian corpus. See Nylan, *The Five "Confucian" Classics*, especially 8–22 passim and 366–67.

11. Ichisada Miyazaki, *China's Examination Hell* (New Haven: Yale University Press, 1981), 16.

12. Ibid., 17.

13. See, for example, Li Gui, *Huan you diqiu xin lu* (A new account of a trip around the globe) (Shanghai, 1878), book II, 29a–b; 39a–b. The different versions of *A New Account* are cited hereafter as "S" (the original Shanghai, 1878, edition); "XFH" (that contained in the *Xiaofanghu zhai yudi congchao* [Geographical collectanea from the "Little Square Teapot Studio"], 1878–94); and "HPP" (Hunan People's Press, 1980, 1985). Hence, in addition to the citation above from the Shanghai edition, the material referenced may also be found in XFH *juan* XII, 102 a–b, pp. 10135–36; and 104b, 105a; 10141–42; and HPP, 264, 270.

14. Li Gui, *Sitong ji* (Bitter memories), 2 *juan* (n.p., 1880), *juan* I, 1a.

15. For the above dates see Colin Mackerras and Robert Chan, *Modern China: A Chronology from 1842 to the Present* (San Francisco: W. H. Freeman, 1982), 52. The Taiping Rebellion represents perhaps the single largest field in nineteenth-century Chinese historiography, and space allows little more than a hint at its richness here. Among the more important works in English are John King Fairbank, *Trade and Diplomacy on the China Coast* (Stanford: Stanford University Press, 1969); Philip Kuhn, *Rebellion and Its Enemies in Late Imperial China* (Cambridge: Harvard University Press, 1970); Franz Michael and Chung-li Chang, *The Taiping Rebellion: History and Documents,* 3 vols. (Seattle: University of Washington Press, 1966, 1971); Elizabeth J. Perry, *Rebels and Revolutionaries in North China* (Stanford: Stanford University Press, 1980); Vincent C. Y. Shih, *The Taiping Ideology: Its Sources, Interpretations, and Influences* (Seattle: University of Washington Press, 1967); Jonathan D. Spence, *God's Chinese Son* (New York: Norton, 1996); Teng Su-yu, *Historiography of the Taiping Rebellion* (Cambridge: Harvard University Press, 1962); Rudolf Wagner, *Reenacting the Heavenly Vision: The Role of Religion in the Taiping Rebellion* (Berkeley and Los Angeles: University of California Press, 1982); Frederic Wakeman Jr., *Strangers at the Gate: Social Disorder in South China, 1839–1861* (Berkeley and Los Angeles: University of California Press, 1966); and Mary C. Wright, *The Last Stand of Chinese Conservatism: The T'ung-Chih Restoration, 1862–1874* (New York: Atheneum, 1966). For contemporary accounts, see Prosper Giquel, *A Journal of the Chinese Civil War, 1864,* ed. Steven Leibo (Honolulu: University of Hawaii Press, 1985; Theodore Hamberg, *The Visions of Hung-siu-tschuen, and Origin of the Kwang-si Insurrection* (Hong Kong, 1854); and Thomas Taylor Meadows, *The Chinese and their Rebellions* (London: Smith, Elder, 1856).

16. Li, *Sitong ji, juan* I, 3a–4b.

17. *Ibid.*, introduction, 2b.

18. *Ibid., juan* I, 4b, 5a–b, 6a, 14b, 20b; *juan* II, 3b, 21b. Zhong, *Zouwen,* 170, 171. Mackerras, *Modern China,* 78.

19. Wright, *Last Stand,* 18, note "f."

20. See, for example, the preface and introduction to *Sitong ji,* and the afterword, excerpted in Zhong Shuhe, *Zouwen,* 170–71.

21. Zhong Shuhe inclines toward this judgment as well. See *Zouwen shijie congshu,* 171, 174.

22. Ibid., 171. The scholarship on both Li Hongzhang and Zeng Guofan is

extensive. In addition to their collected correspondence, *Li Wenzhong gong quanji*, ed. Wu Rulun, 165 *juan* (Nanjing, 1905–8), and *Zeng Wenzhong gong quanji*, 10 *ce* (Shanghai, 1888), see their biographies in Arthur Hummel, ed., *Eminent Chinese of the Ch'ing Period*, 2 vols. (Washington, D.C.: GPO, 1943–44), 1:464–71; 2:751–56; Stanley Spector, *Li Hung-chang and the Huai Army: A Study in Nineteenth Century Regionalism* (Seattle: University of Washington Press, 1964); and Jonathan Porter, *Tseng Kuo-fan's Private Bureaucracy* (Berkeley and Los Angeles: University of California Press, 1972). For the Ever Victorious Army, see Caleb Carr, *The Devil Soldier* (New York: Random House, 1992); and Richard J. Smith, *Mercenaries and Mandarins: The Ever Victorious Army in Nineteenth Century China* (Millwood, N.Y.: KTO Press, 1978).

23. Wright, *Last Stand*, 181; John K. Fairbank, Katherine Frost Bruner, and Elizabeth MacLeod Matheson, eds., *The I.G. in Peking: Letters of Robert Hart, Chinese Maritime Customs, 1868–1907*, vol. 1 (Cambridge: Harvard University Press, 1975), introduction, passim; Robert Ronald Campbell, *James Duncan Campbell: A Memoir by His Son*, Harvard East Asia Monograph Series no. 38 (Cambridge: Harvard University Press, 1970).

24. Fairbank, Bruner, and Matheson, *The I.G. in Peking*, 12. In 1875, fourteen hundred of the eighteen hundred persons (or 78 percent) on the IMC staff were Chinese; the percentage continued to increase throughout the century. For comments on Hart's position, see Campbell, *James Duncan Campbell*, 46. Marxist scholars as well as some nineteenth-century Chinese officials had from the beginning contested Hart's contention that his overriding goal had been to "make China strong" through close ties to England. See Chen and Han, *Archives*, viii, xi, xiv.

25. Fairbank, Bruner, and Matheson, *The I.G. in Peking*, 50. See also Richard J. Smith, "Li Hung-chang's Use of Foreign Military Talent: The Formative Period, 1862–1874," in *Li Hung-chang and China's Early Modernization*, ed. Samuel C. Chu and Kwang-Ching Liu (Armonk, N.Y.: M. E. Sharpe, 1994), 125. Zhong Shuhe mistakenly identifies H. E. Hobson as the missionary Benjamin Hobson. See *Zouwen shijie congshu*, 172.

26. Zhong Shuhe, citing entries from Li's papers, notes that he was already in the process of studying the complex economics of imperialism. *Zouwen shijie congshu*, 172.

27. *The Works of Mencius*, trans. James Legge (Oxford: Clarendon Press, 1895; reprint, New York: Dover, 1970), bk. I, pt. 1, chap. 1, lines 2–3 (pp. 125–26).

28. D. E. Mungello, *The Great Encounter: China and the West, 1500–1800* (Lanham, Md.: Rowman and Littlefield, 1999), 89. See Quesnay's *Le Despotisme de la Chine* (1767).

29. Thomas Carlyle, "Signs of the Times," in *Critical and Miscellaneous Essays* (New York: 1896), 60.

30. As the prince put it, "The progress of the human race, resulting from the common labour of all men, ought to be the final object of the exertion of each individual. In promoting this end, we are accomplishing the will of the great and blessed God." From the official catalog, quoted in C. H. Gibbs-Smith, *The Great Exhibition of 1851* (London: Her Majesty's Stationery Office, 1950), 26. For a recent critical evaluation see Jeffrey Auerbach, *The Great Exhibition of 1851: A Nation on Display* (New Haven: Yale University Press, 1999).

31. James D. McCabe, *An Illustrated History of the Centennial Exhibition*

(Philadelphia: National Publishing, 1876), 170; see also John Maass, "The Centennial Success Story," in *1876: A Centennial Exhibition,* ed. Robert C. Post (Washington, D.C.: Smithsonian Institution, 1976), 11.

32. McCabe, *Illustrated History,* 659–66; Maass, "The Centennial Success Story," 11.

33. Maass, *The Glorious Enterprise* (Watkins Glen, N.Y.: American Life Foundation, 1973), 53–56.

34. Correspondence on the Centennial may be found in Zongli Yamen from Avery, May 8, 1875; Zongli Yamen to Liu Kunyi, May 11, 1875; Zongli Yamen to Hart, May 11, 1875; Zongli Yamen from Hart, October 9, 1875; Zongli Yamen from Avery, October 28, 1875; Zongli Yamen to U.S. State Dept., December 31, 1875; Institute of Modern History, Academia Sinica files, Zongli Yamen, *Ge guo saihui gong hui* (International Exhibitions). Reprinted in *Zhongmei guanxi shiliao* (Historical materials on Sino-American relations) (Taipei: Institute of Modern History, Academia Sinica, 1968), nos. 36–38, 91, 124.

35. The most extensive study of Chinese participation at the Centennial is Jennifer Pitman, "China's Presence at the Centennial," M.A. thesis, Bard College, 1999.

36. *North China Herald,* February 17, 1876. It is worth noting that Li Gui's description follows that of the *Herald* almost word for word. See *A New Account,* S: bk. I, 9b; XFH: *juan* 12, 79b, 1009o; and HPP: 206. The final worth of the articles in the Chinese exhibition was valued at about sixty thousand taels, or a bit over ninety thousand 1876 U.S. dollars. For material on Hu Guangyong, see C. John Stanley, *Late Ch'ing Finance: Hu Kuang-yung as an Innovator,* Harvard East Asia Monograph Series no. 12 (Cambridge: Harvard University Press, 1966).

37. For the comment on the calligraphy, S: bk. 1, 9b; XFH: *juan* 12, 79b, 1009o; HPP: 206; for the dedication, see author's preface, *A New Account,* S: bk. I, 2a; HPP: 194.

38. For Huber's work with Chen Lanbin in Cuba, see Chen Lanbin, A. Huber, and A. MacPherson, *The Cuba Commission Report* (Shanghai: Imperial Maritime Customs, 1876; reprint, Baltimore: Johns Hopkins University Press, 1993); for a list of China's Centennial commissioners, see Imperial Maritime Customs, *Catalog of the Chinese Exhibition* (Shanghai: Imperial Maritime Customs Press, 1876), i. For Knight's efforts to find Li Gui a post at Harvard, see the *North China Herald,* May 13, 1879; for Ke Kunhua, see Ruthann Lum McCunn, *Chinese American Portraits* (San Francisco: Chronicle Press, 1988), 20; also "The History of Harvard-Yenching Library" http://www-hcl .harvard.edu/harvard-yenching/history.html.

39. Fairbank, Bruner, and Matheson, *The I.G. in Peking,* 233. For early self-strengthening initiatives, see Wright, *Last Stand,* 148–250; Chu and Liu, *Li Hung-chang;* and Albert Feuerwerker, *China's Early Industrialization* (Cambridge: Harvard University Press, 1958). For more recent materials in Chinese and English, see Institute of Modern History, Academia Sinica, *Proceedings of the Conference on the Self-Strengthening Movement in Late Ch'ing China, 1861–1894,* 2 vols. (Taipei: Academia Sinica, 1988).

40. In addition to the above, representative discussions of the philosophical difficulties related to self-strengthening may be found in Thomas Metz-

ger, *Escape from Predicament* (New York: Columbia University Press, 1977), 167–88; Paul A. Cohen, *Discovering History in China* (New York: Columbia University Press, 1984), 22–47; Joseph R. Levenson, *Confucian China and Its Modern Fate*, 3 vols. (Berkeley and Los Angeles: University of California Press, 1958, 1964, 1965); and Tu Wei-ming, *Way, Learning, and Politics: Essays on the Confucian Intellectual* (Albany: State University of New York Press, 1993), 161–69.

41. *A New Account*, S: bk. IV, 1a–b; XFH: *juan* XII, 91a, 10113; HPP: 317.

42. Ibid.

43. Ibid., S: 5a; XFH: 92a, 10115; HPP: 320. Cf. Douglas Howland, *Borders of Chinese Civilization* (Durham, N.C.: Duke University Press, 1996), 82. Howland here cites the correspondence between the notion of *dong you*, "a journey to the east," and its broader connotations of travel to Japan. He further notes that "it is not merely coincidental . . . that Li Gui, Wang Zhichun, and He Ruzhang, en route to the East, all rapturously describe a sunrise at sea."

44. This is implied, for example, throughout Li Hongzhang's foreword to *A New Account*. See also Charles Desnoyers, "Toward 'One Enlightened and Progressive Civilization': Discourses of Expansion and Nineteenth-Century Chinese Missions Abroad," *Journal of World History* 8, no. 1 (1997): 135–56.

45. *A New Account*, S: 8a–b; XFH: 93a, 10117; HPP: 323.

46. The most direct expression of this view may be found in Irick, *Ch'ing Policy*.

47. *A New Account*, S: 10b, 11a; XFH: 93b, 94a, 10118–19; HPP: 325. In addition to the works mentioned above in note 2, standard references in English on labor and immigration history remain Alexander Saxton, *The Indispensable Enemy: Labor and the Anti-Chinese Movement in California* (Berkeley and Los Angeles: University of California Press, 1971); and Stewart C. Miller, *The Unwelcome Immigrant: The American Image of the Chinese, 1785–1882* (Berkeley and Los Angeles: University of California Press, 1969).

48. *A New Account*, S: 10a–b; XFH: 93b, 10118; HPP: 325.

49. *A New Account*, S: 1a–2b, 43a.; XFH: 125a, 10181; HPP: 312–13, 353.

50. Chen Lanbin and his retinue stayed at the Palace Hotel two years later, in July 1878. See Chen's diary, *Shi mei jilue* (A brief account of my trip to America) in Wang Xiji, *Xiaofang hu*, vol. 12, p. 10049.

51. *A New Account*, S: bk. III, 28a–31b; in XFH, this essay is untitled and folded into the daily entries on Li's stay in San Francisco. See 94b–95b, 10120–22; HPP: 300–304.

52. Ibid., bk. IV, S: 13b–22a; XFH: 95b–98a, 10122–27; HPP: 328–36, passim.

53. Ibid., S: 22b–23a; XFH: 98a–b, 10127–28; HPP: 336.

54. An important work on Philadelphia history remains Russell F. Weigley, ed., *Philadelphia: A Three-Hundred-Year History* (New York: W. W. Norton, 1982). See also Kenneth Finkel, "Philadelphia in the 1820s: A New Civic Consciousness," in Norman Johnston, with Kenneth Finkel and Jeffrey A. Cohen, *Eastern State Penitentiary: Crucible of Good Intentions* (Philadelphia: Philadelphia Museum of Art, 1994), 9–20, passim.

55. *A New Account*, S: bk. II, 1a–b; XFH: 107a, 10145; HPP: 240. The city's population as of April 1876 was 817,448, up 21.2 percent from the 1870 federal census. Li's remarks reflect the contemporary conception of Philadelphia as

"a city of homes" with more housing stock than Baltimore, Boston, St. Louis, and Louisville combined in 1870. McCabe, *Illustrated History*, 28–29.

56. Average daily attendance varied from 36,050 in May to 115,315 by November. Total attendance from May 10 to November 10 was 9,910,966, versus approximately 6 million for the Great Exhibition of 1851. See Maass, "The Centennial Success Story," 21–22. Attendance figures may also be found in Richard R. Nicolai, *Centennial Philadelphia* (Bryn Mawr, Pa.: Bryn Mawr Press, 1976), 84.

57. *A New Account*, bk. II, S: 3b; XFH: 107b; 10146; HPP: 242.

58. For an overview of the evolving Chinese view of George Washington, see Scott Wong, "The Transformation of Culture," 208–11.

59. *A New Account*, bk. I, S: 8a–b; XFH: 79a–b, 10089–90; HPP: 205.

60. Ibid., S: 6a–b, 10a; XFH: 78b–79a, 80a, 10091; HPP: 203, 207.

61. McCabe, *Illustrated History*, 418.

62. *A New Account*, S: 9b; XFH: 79b, 10090; HPP: 206–7.

63. The Chinese exhibit sold approximately $53,000 worth of goods. Pitman, "China's Presence," 44.

64. *A New Account*, S: 9b–10b; XFH: 78b–79a, 10090–91; HPP: 207.

65. Ibid. Indeed, Li appears to have been a witness to this trade watershed. According to A. W. Kirkaldy, "During the days of the tea clippers, the great bulk of the tea consumed in the United Kingdom came from China, but of recent years India and Ceylon have very successfully competed in this market, with the result that but very little Chinese tea is consumed in this country. . . . [The trade] reached its maximum in the year 1876 with a total of nearly £23,750,000." *British Shipping: Its History, Organisation, and Importance* (London: Kegan Paul, 1914), 344.

66. A recent treatment of Japanese self-perception during this time may be found in Robert Eskildsen, "Of Civilization and Savages: The Mimetic Imperialism of Japan's 1874 Expedition to Taiwan," *American Historical Review* 107, no. 2 (April 2002): 388–418. For a discussion of *bunmei kaika*, see pp. 391–93.

67. *A New Account*, S: 11a; XFH: 80a, 10091; HPP: 208.

68. Ibid.

69. Ibid., S: 12a–b; XFH: 80b, 10092; HPP: 209.

70. Ibid.

71. Ibid., S: 18a–b; XFH: 82a, 10095; HPP: 214.

72. Ibid. Li remained vitally interested in the opium problem and later wrote *Yapian shi lue* (A brief account of the opium trade), 2 vols. (Beiping: Beiping tuxuguan, 1931). The work contains a wealth of statistics drawn largely from English sources and concludes with Guo Songtao's famous address to the British Society for the Suppression of the Opium Trade.

73. Post, *1876*, 82; Franz Realeaux, the German commissioner general, pronounced himself discomfited by his country's display of militarism at the exhibition: "It seems that seven eighths of the space are occupied by Krupp's giant guns, the 'killing machines' which stand like a menace among the peaceful works of the other nations. Is this the real expression of Germany's 'mission?'" *Brief aus Philadelphia* (Braunschweig: Friedrich Vieweg und Sohn, 1877, 6); cited in Maass, *The Glorious Enterprise*, 107.

74. Joanna Waley-Cohen, *The Sextants of Beijing* (New York: Norton, 1999), 185.

75. For Li's comments on the American weapons, see *A New Account*, bk. I, S: 15a–b; XFH: 81a–b, 10093–94; HPP: 211–12. For his observations on the Krupp guns, see S: 36b–37b; XFH: 87b, 10106; HPP: 229–30.

76. Quoted in Michael Adas, *Machines as the Measure of Men* (Ithaca: Cornell University Press, 1989), 139.

77. Post, *1876*, 13, 31. Curiously, Li mentions nothing of the Statue of Liberty's arm, though its proximity to the Agricultural Hall and the American Restaurant would have taken him by it on several occasions.

78. *A New Account*, bk. I, S: 28a–b; XFH: 85a, 10101; HPP: 222–23.

79. Ibid. The saying quoted is from the Daoist work, the *Zhuangzi*, chap. 12.

80. *A New Account*, bk. I, S: 28a–b; XFH: 85a, 10101; HPP: 222–23.

81. Ibid., S: 41a–42a; XFH: 88b, 10108; HPP: 233–34.

82. Chiang Yee, *Chinese Calligraphy* (Cambridge: Harvard University Press, 1938, 1954, 1973), 207; Simon Leys, "Poetry and Painting: Aspects of Chinese Classical Esthetics," in *The Burning Forest* (New York: Holt, Rinehart and Winston, 1985), 23. Leys is quoting a sentiment expressed by Flaubert. Significantly, he notes that "artistic creation and cosmic creation are parallel; they differ only in scale, not in nature." Twelfth-century calligraphy theorist Jiang Kui expressed himself in similar terms: "Perfection of art is surely linked to spirit. . . . The distinction between discord and harmony is the difference between good and bad calligraphy." In *Xu Shu Pu (Sequel to the "Treatise on Calligraphy")*, in Sun Qianli and Jiang Kui, *Two Chinese Treatises on Calligraphy*, trans. Chang Ch'ung-ho and Hans H. Frankel (New Haven: Yale University Press, 1995), 28.

83. *A New Account*, bk. I, S: 39b; XFH: 88a; HPP: 232.

84. Ibid. The occasion for Li's musing was a large painting lent by the British Crown titled *The Marriage of His Royal Highness the Prince of Wales*, by W. P. Frith. For Chinese attitudes toward Western female nudity, see, for example, Frodsham, *First Chinese Embassy*, lvii and 128. Here, Liu Xihong matter-of-factly and, of course, erroneously, informs his readers that, "in the front court [of Buckingham Palace] is a painting of Victoria herself lying down quite naked."

85. "Mr. Li Kwei on the Education of Women," *North China Herald*, August 17, 1878.

86. Sarah Bernhardt quoted in Joseph Hariss, "The Divine Sarah," *Smithsonian* 32, no. 5 (2001): 75; Alexis de Tocqueville, *Democracy in America* (New York: Penguin, 1956, 1984), 247.

87. *A New Account*, bk. I, S: 45a–b; XFH: 89b, 10110; HPP: 237 Li was mistaken, however, in insisting that the pavilion itself was designed by women; it was in fact designed by Schwarzmann. As Elizabeth Gillespie later noted, "I heard the praises sung of a woman architect in Boston [Emma Kimball of Lowell, Massachusetts] and I wished I could annul the contract with Mr. Schwarzmann. To this hour I feel pained, because I fear we hindered this legitimate branch of women's work instead of helping it." E. D. Gillespie, *A Book of Remembrance* (Philadelphia, 1901), quoted in Maass, *The Glorious Enterprise*, 121; Post, *1876*, 173. The Philadelphia papers also reported the activities of various women's groups on a regular basis. See, for example, the *Philadelphia Inquirer* for June 16, p. 3, and July 6, p. 5. The later article covers an

attempt to read a "Declaration of the Rights of Women of the United States" on July 4 at Independence Square.

88. Post, *1876*, 165, 167.

89. Tocqueville, *Democracy in America*, 244.

90. *A New Account*, bk. I, S: 45a–b; XFH: 89b, 10110; HPP: 237.

91. Ibid. The most explicit work in this regard is Lisa Raphals, *Sharing the Light: Representations of Women and Virtue in Early China* (Albany: State University of New York Press, 1998). Like Li Gui, Raphals traces a shift in perceptions of women and, consequently, their education to the more hierarchical philosophical synthesis of the Han period (202 B.C.E. to 220 C.E.). Later developments in this regard are explored in Patricia Ebrey, *The Inner Quarters: Marriage and the Lives of Chinese Women in the Sung Period* (Berkeley and Los Angeles: University of California Press, 1993). It is striking to lay Li's comments on education alongside those of Mary Wollstonecraft:

> The education of women has, of late, been more attended to than formerly; yet they are still reckoned a frivolous sex and ridiculed or pitied by the writers who endeavor by satire or instruction to improve them. . . . All the writers who have written on the subject of female education and manners . . . have contributed to render women more artificial, weak characters, than they would otherwise have been; and consequently, more useless members of society. . . . Strengthen the female mind by enlarging it, and there will be an end to blind obedience . . . the grand end of their exertions should be to unfold their own faculties and acquire the dignity of conscious virtue.

A Vindication of the Rights of Woman (reprint, Mineola, N.Y.: Dover, 1996), 9, 21, 24.

92. Ibid., S: 46a; XFH: 90a, 10111; HPP: 238.

93. Johnston, *Eastern State Penitentiary*, 31–45, passim.

94. Ibid., 79. The first prison of this type opened in Hubei in 1906. See also Michael R. Dutton, *Policing and Punishment in China: From Patriarchy to "the People"* (Cambridge: Cambridge University Press, 1992), 158.

95. Charles Dickens, *American Notes for General Circulation* (reprint, Avon, Conn.: Limited Editions, 1975), 98.

96. *A New Account*, bk. II, S: 8a–b; XFH: 109a, 10149; HPP: 246–47. The reference to fathers and sons, and elder brothers and younger brothers, is a pointed correlation to two of the "five relationships" of Confucianism.

97. Ibid., S: 13a; XFH: 110b, 10152; HPP: 250.

98. Ibid., S: 19a–27a; XFH: 99b–101b, 10130–34; HPP: 255–62, passim.

99. For Yung Wing's early years, see his autobiography, *My Life*, 1–66; and LaFargue, *China's First Hundred*, 17–35. Yung's Yale days are covered in Worthy, "Yung Wing in America," 269–72. For his proposals to Hong Rengan (1822–64) of the Taipings, see *My Life*, 123–25; for his journey to the United States to purchase machinery, *My Life*, 155–60. Yung also claimed to have attempted to volunteer for the Union army as a courier but was dissuaded because of his official mission for China.

100. Ibid., 205–14. LaFargue, *China's First Hundred*, 50–51. The fullest documentary record in English is found in Hung, "Closure of Educational Mis-

sion." Ultimately, unfavorable reports sent back to the Zongli Yamen by the mission's last director, Wu Zidong (Wu Jiashan), coupled with the refusal of the American military academies to admit the students, ended the mission in 1881—despite a determined last-minute lobbying effort by Grant, Twain, and others.

101. *A New Account*, bk. III, S: 25a–27b; HPP: 298–300. *Philadelphia Inquirer*, August 25, 1876, 8. See also *Hartford Courant*, August 22, 24, 25, and 29 for accounts of the boys' activities.

102. *Hartford Courant*, September 13, 1876.

103. *A New Account*, bk. II, S: 28a–b; XFH: 102a, 10135; HPP: 262–63.

104. Ibid., S: 29b–33b; XFH: 102b–103b, 10136–38; HPP: 264–67. Gatling Gun Company, Minutes of the Board of Directors, August 12, 1873, cited in Worthy, "Yung Wing in America," 277.

105. Pitman, "China's Presence," 74. See also Allen Johnson and Dumas Malone, *Dictionary of American Biography*, vol. 4 (New York: Scribner's Sons, 1931), 404–5.

106. *A New Account*, bk. II, S: 34a–46a; XFH: 104a–106b, 10139–44; HPP: 268–77. Translated excerpts of Li's visits to the police court, firehouse, theater, and the Women's Pavilion at the Centennial can also be found in Arkush and Lee, *Land without Ghosts*, 41–48.

107. Ibid., bk. IV, S: 24a–26a, XFH: 120b–121a, 10155–56; HPP: 337–38.

108. Ibid., bk. III, 1a–2b; XFH: 113b, 10158; HPP: 278–79.

109. Ibid., S: 4a; XFH: 114a, 10159; HPP: 281.

110. Ibid., S: 4a–5b; XFH: 114b, 10160; HPP: 281–82.

111. Ibid., S: 3b–4a; XFH: 114a; HPP: 280.

112. Ibid. For the telegraph office, S: 5b–6a; XFH: 114b, 10160; HPP: 282. For the *Times* of London, S: 7b–8b; XFH: 115b, 10162; HPP: 284–85.

113. Ibid., S: 17b–20a; XFH: 118a–119a, 10167–69; HPP: 292–95.

114. Ibid., S: 8b–17a; XFH: 115b–118a, 10162–67; HPP: 285–92.

115. Ibid., S: 21a–22a; XFH: 119b–120a, 10170–71. Note: this version includes the travel account from London to Paris placed separately in book IV in the Shanghai and Hunan Peoples' Press versions (HPP: 295).

116. Ibid., S: 22a–24b; XFH: 120a–122a, 10171–73; HPP: 296–98.

117. Ibid., bk. IV, "Dong xing riji," S: 30a–30b; XFH: 121b–122a, 10172–73; HPP: 342–43. Jean Giraudoux, quoted in Sanche de Gramont, *The French* (New York: Putnam, 1969), 304.

118. Ibid., S: 32a–b; XFH: 122a–b, 10173–74; HPP: 344.

119. Ibid., S: 37a; XFH: 123a, 10177; HPP: 348. For Guo's visit, see *Yangzhi shuwu yiji*, translated in Frodsham, *First Chinese Embassy*, 26.

120. Ibid., S: 39a–b; XFH: 124a, 10179; HPP: 350. Frodsham, *First Chinese Embassy*, lii, liii, 81, 89.

121. Ibid., S: 40b–41a; XFH: 124b, 10180; HPP: 351. Literally, "treating them as fish and meat."

122. Ibid., S: 41a–b; XFH: 124b, 10180; HPP: 352.

123. Ibid., S: 42a–b; XFH: 124b–125a, 10180, 10181; HPP: 352–53. For a short, detailed biography of Wang, see Hummel, *Eminent Chinese*, 2:836–39. The best extended study remains Paul A. Cohen, *Between Tradition and Modernity: Wang T'ao and Reform in Late Imperial China* (Cambridge: Harvard University Press, 1974).

124. Zhong, *Zouwen shijie congshu,* 172; the name and address of the Grelier firm appears on the illustrations of original copies of *A New Account;* for Detring's gifts to Chen Lanbin see *Shi mei jilue,* 10045 (1a); *North China Herald,* August 17, 1878.

125. Hummel, *Eminent Chinese,* 1:332. Zhong, *Zouwen shijie congshu,* 172–73. Hummel places the date of Xue's intendancy as 1884; Zhong has it as 1883.

126. Hummel, *Eminent Chinese,* 1:332; Zhong, *Zouwen shijie congshu,* 172–73.

127. The most complete study on late imperial China's modern postal system remains Ying-wan Cheng, *Postal Communication in China and Its Modernization, 1860–1896* (Cambridge: Harvard University Press, 1970). For the different systems, see p. 6; for Chinese postal costs as a percentage of government expenditures, see p. 32; for the role of Li Gui, see pp. 84–85. Li's proposal is no longer extant, though parts of it are referred to in Zongli Yamen to the Throne, March 20, 1896, in *Huangchao Dao Xian Tong Guang zouyi* (Memorials of the Dao Guang, Xian Feng, Tong Zhi, and Guang Xu periods), by Wang Yenxi and Wang Shumin (Shanghai, 1902), 14: 7b. For additional citations, see Cheng, p. 124. I am indebted to Mr. Qian Gang, Chief Researcher of China Central Television's *New Probe* for calling Li's role in this regard to my attention.

128. Li Gui, *Tongshang biao* (A statement on trade), 4 *juan* (n.p.: Haichang guan, 1895).

129. Zhong, *Zouwen shijie congshu,* 173–74.

130. Edward Said, *Orientalism* (New York: Pantheon, 1979). Representative works exploring the applicability of critiques of Orientalism to China and East Asia—along with non-Western Orientalist avenues of categorization—include Leys, "Orientalism and Sinology," in *The Burning Forest,* 95–99; Cohen, *Discovering History in China,* 149–50; Louisa Schein, "Gender and Internal Orientalism in China," *Modern China* 23, no. 1(1997): 69–98; James Hevia, *Cherishing Men from Afar* (Durham: Duke University Press, 1995); Haun Saussy, *Great Walls of Discourse* (Cambridge: Harvard University Press, 2001), especially 118–45; Laura Hostetler, *Qing Colonial Enterprise* (Chicago: University of Chicago Press, 2001), 81–100; review symposium on Orientalism, *Journal of Asian Studies* 39, no. 3 (1980): 481–517; a recent general survey may be found in "Review Essays: Orientalism Twenty Years On," *American Historical Review* 105, no. 4 (2000): 1204–49. For a recent treatment of Occidentalism in late-twentieth-century China, see Xiaomei Chen, *Occidentalism* (Lanham, Md.: Rowman and Littlefield, 2002). The Levenson quote may be found in "'History' and 'Value': The Tensions of Intellectual Choice in Modern China," in *Studies in Chinese Thought,* ed. Arthur Wright (Chicago: University of Chicago Press, 1967), 150. It should be noted that the term *Occidentalism* has come to be employed in at least two ways that differ from my usage of it here. One definition, stemming from the work of Roland Barthes, sees it as a self-conscious privileging of "Western" values in the "West"; the other usage posits it as a "counterdiscourse" to that of Orientalism in modern non-Western societies, as in the work of Xiaomei Chen on post-Maoist China. My approach here, however, is closer to what John K. Fairbank referred to as "culture-centrism." It is not a "counterdiscourse" in this sense because it was not brought into being by the imposition of Orientalism from the outside. It is instead a constellation of long-held assumptions by China's elites that had as yet suf-

fered little in the way of fundamental contradiction or critique. For more extended discussion of the points raised here, see Stein Tonnesson, "Orientalism, Occidentalism, and Knowing about Others," *Nordic Newsletter of Asian Studies*, April 1994: 1–9 (online version, http://nias.ku.dk/nytt/thematic/orientalism/orientalism.html); Fernando Coronil, "Beyond Occidentalism: Toward Nonimperial Geohistorical Categories," *Cultural Anthropology* 11, no. 1 (1996): 51–87; James G. Carrier, "Occidentalism: The World Turned Upside Down," *American Ethnologist* 19, no. 2 (1992): 195–212; and James G. Carrier, ed., *Occidentalism: Images of the West* (Oxford: Clarendon Press, 1995).

131. Richard Strassberg, *Inscribed Landscapes: Writings from Imperial China* (Berkeley and Los Angeles: University of California Press, 1994), 3–6.

132. Ibid., 6.

133. Many of the works on self-strengthening listed here include some degree of Chinese agency as an implicit assumption. More directly, Cohen, in *Discovering History in China,* calls for a "China-centered" approach to the period as a partial antidote to the "ethnocentric bias" of most Western works on modern China. Recent accounts featuring Chinese agency more generally are Waley-Cohen, *The Sextants of Beijing;* Kenneth Pomeranz, *The Great Divergence: Europe, China, and the Making of the Modern World Economy* (Princeton: Princeton University Press, 2000); and Andre Gunder Frank, *ReOrient: Global Economy in the Asian Age* (Berkeley and Los Angeles: University of California Press, 1998); for a critique of Gunder Frank's "unabashed Sinocentrism," see Victor Lieberman, ed., *Beyond Binary Histories* (Ann Arbor: University of Michigan Press, 1999), 4.

134. For Li's modernity, see Chen, "Barbarian Paradise," 139. A wider survey of the literature on perceptions of Chinese expansion may be found in Desnoyers, "Enlightened and Progressive Civilization." For Li Hongzhang's comments, see *A New Account*, preface, S: *vb–via* (my numbering), and HPP: 192. XFH does not contain Li's preface.

135. Wu T'ing-fang, *America through the Spectacles of an Oriental Diplomat* (New York: Stokes, 1914), v.

136. Henry James, *Hawthorne* (1879), chap. 2; Fei Xiaotong, "A World without Ghosts," in Arkush and Lee, *Land without Ghosts,* 181. Fei noted, "In a world without ghosts, life is free and easy. American eyes can gaze straight ahead. But still I think they lack something and I do not envy their lives."

137. Oscar Wilde, *A Woman of No Importance* (1893), act I, scene II.

138. Scott Wong, "The Transformation of Culture," 208–11. See also Xiong Yuezhi, "Difficulties in Comprehension and Differences in Expression: Interpreting American Democracy in the Late Qing," trans. William Rowe, *Late Imperial China* 23, no. 1 (June 2002): 1–27.

139. Chen, "Barbarian Paradise."

140. Strassberg, *Inscribed Landscapes,* 4.

141. Howland, *Borders of Chinese Civilization,* 80.

142. Strassberg, *Inscribed Landscapes,* 32–42, passim.

143. Ibid.; Howland, *Borders of Chinese Civilization,* 80.

144. Ibid., 3, 4.

145. Samuel Taylor Coleridge, *Satyrane's Letters,* ii (*The Friend,* December 7, 1809, no. 16, *Biographia Literaria*); for the earliest Japanese accounts of the United States and the West more generally, see Masao Miyoshi, *As We Saw*

Them: The First Japanese Embassy to the United States (Tokyo: Kodansha, 1994). One might speculate that, like Miyoshi's Japanese envoys, whose accounts tended to emphasize those things they could enumerate or control in an alien environment (*As We Saw Them*, 100–114), Li's obsessive detailing of the prices and categories of objects, along with his struggle to describe the workings of complex machinery, might represent something of a similar impulse. Given the nature of how he understood his mission, he did in any case see it as an important part of his duties.

146. Waley-Cohen, *The Sextants of Beijing*, 111–14.

147. For Li Gui's history of the American Revolution, see *A New Account*, bk. I, S: 1b–2a; HPP: 200. For Wei Yuan and Xu Jiyu, see Jane Kate Leonard, *Wei Yuan and China's Rediscovery of the Maritime World* (Cambridge: Harvard University Press, 1984); Fred Drake, *China Charts the World* (Cambridge: Harvard University Press, 1975). For translations of Xu's account of the role of Washington in the founding of the United States, see Scott Wong, "The Transformation of Culture," 209; Arkush and Lee, *Land without Ghosts*, 20–23; and John K. Fairbank and Su-yu Teng, *China's Response to the West* (Cambridge: Harvard University Press, 1954), 44–46.

148. *Mencius*, bk. VII, pt. 1, chap. 24, line 1 (p. 463). Significantly, the passage ends, "Thus, he who has contemplated the sea, finds it difficult to think anything of other waters, and he who has wandered in the gate of the sage, finds it difficult to think anything of the words of others." For other travel writers employing this passage, see Strassberg, *Inscribed Landscapes*, 20–21.

149. Adapted from Frederick Wakeman Jr., *The Great Enterprise*, vol. 1 (Berkeley and Los Angeles: University of California Press, 1985), xiii; reprinted in Strassberg, *Inscribed Landscapes*, xxii.

A NEW ACCOUNT OF A TRIP AROUND THE GLOBE

By Li Gui, Xiaochi, of Jiangning

Xiaochi is Li Gui's *zi*, or "courtesy name."

Foreword

The opening of the second year in the reign of the Guangxu emperor of the Great Qing, the *bingzi sui* [1876], marked the centenary of America. The Americans held an exposition in the city of Philadelphia, gathering there an extensive collection of the antiquities, daily necessities, flora and fauna, and categories of the arts of various countries. In addition to China, thirty-six countries participated in this exhibition, which was called the "Centennial Exposition," and also "the Great Exposition." It was undertaken from a desire to study the products of different countries and foster cordial relations among them, and in so doing followed the lead of the European exhibitions in staging the affair.

At the suggestion of Mr. [Gustav] Detring, the Imperial Maritime Customs commissioner for Chefoo,[1] Li Gui of Jiangning journeyed to attend the exposition. Traveling east from Shanghai, he passed through Japan and crossed the Great Eastern Ocean [the Pacific], arriving in the city of San Francisco. He then traveled more than 10,000 additional li over land before arriving in this city [Philadelphia], where he entered the exhibition grounds and explored them freely for over four months. During this time he also visited the capital city of Washington, D.C., as well as Hartford and New York. His mission at the exhibition completed, he left Philadelphia and sailed eastward on the Great Western Ocean [the Atlantic] to the capital cities of London, England, and Paris, France, following

---

1. Literally *Dong*, for Shandong; the office itself was in Chefoo, also called Yantai. Centennial records list Detring as still at his former post in Ningbo. See McCabe, *Illustrated History*, 234.

which he crossed from the Mediterranean to the Red Sea through the Suez Canal, and by turns passed through Ceylon [Sri Lanka], Singapore, Saigon, and Hong Kong. All incidents en route have been faithfully recorded. In the course of this service[2] he covered more than 82,300 li in all over land and sea for more than eight months. Thus, to his one book titled "A Brief Account of the American Exposition," two comprising "Notes on Sightseeing," and one called "Diary of a Journey to the East"—to which are appended a map of the globe and a full plan of the exposition grounds—the entire work bearing the title *A New Account of a Trip Around the Globe,* I beg to add this foreword.

Since the inauguration of commercial relations, the various countries of the West have daily exerted their intelligence, talents, and efforts in mutual competition. In pursuing their plans for wealth and power, they have followed each other in vying for the newest railroads, telegraphs, warships, and weapons. Moreover, they have paid particular attention to commercial matters as something without which their nations could not sustain themselves. This is not a practice limited to a single place but one, in fact, dictated by general circumstances. Hence, item by item, this record of the abundance and scarcity of goods, the ease and difficulty of the topography, the successes and failures of government admonitions, the ingenuity with which machines are constructed, and the similarities and differences of people and customs has been kept. That which has not been heard or seen has not been included. This journey of Gui's, therefore, has not been made in vain.

At present, friendly Sino-foreign relations are in some respects like those of a family. For example, the imperial court has already sent special envoys to serve in the capitals of England, Germany, France, and America and has also sent students abroad to study. The many nations of the world[3] are thus in a sense like the thresholds of homes between which light carriages come and go unceasingly on the road. Ambitious gentlemen, if they exert themselves to

2. The character used here is *yi*, meaning "servant" or "subordinate." Used as an official term, it carries with it the implication of conscription or service in far-flung border regions.

3. *Wu zhou zhong yi;* literally, "interpreting the five continents." *Zhong yi* is a term generally used for the translations of the multiple languages of remote border peoples; hence it conveys the sense of "many nations"; "five continents" is a euphemism for "the world."

the utmost in their investigations, can derive much from their strong points while avoiding their shortcomings. The benefits of this to the entire nation will thus be extensive. But beyond this, how can just one description of things serve as an adequate mirror for mutual evaluation?

The fourth year of the reign of the Guangxu emperor, *mouyin*, third month [April 1878]. By Imperial Order, Superintendent of Trade for the Northern Ports, Grand Guardian of the Heir Apparent, Grand Secretary, Governor-General of Zhili, Earl of the Guards of the First Rank, Commandant of Cavalry (Hereditary) Posted to Hefei,

Li Hongzhang

Author's Preface

In the second year of the reign of the Guangxu emperor, *bingzi* [1876], America held its Centennial Exposition. Previously, that country's minister in Beijing had requested the Zongli Yamen[1] to direct the Superintendents of Trade for the Southern and Northern Ports to distribute a proclamation through the local officials giving explicit instructions to craftsmen and merchants to send items to the exposition. They also decided on the amount of funds to allocate and, citing the precedent of the Austrian Exposition [1873], instructed the Inspector General of the Imperial Maritime Customs, [Robert] Hart, to send customs officers to superintend the exhibit. They thereupon designated those who were to supervise matters relating to the exposition in this country, namely, Chefoo Customs Commissioner [Gustav] Detring and Fujian Commissioner [Edward Bangs] Drew; as well as those to manage things on site at the exposition, Canton Commissioner [James] Hart, former Tianjin Commissioner [Alfred] Huber, the Hu [Swatow] Commissioner [James Lennard] Hammond, and also an American gentleman and merchant residing in China, [Francis P.] Knight.[2]

1. Officially known as the Zongli ge guo shiwu yamen (Office in General Charge of Foreign Affairs), the Zongli Yamen was created in January 1861 by Prince Gong (Yixin) in the wake of the Anglo-French occupation of Beijing and the imposition of the revised Tianjin treaties of 1858. The Yamen was meant to handle all Chinese foreign affairs, though in practice, powerful officials like Li Hongzhang sometimes tended to work around it. In 1901, in the aftermath of the Boxer Rebellion, it was replaced by the Waiwu bu, or Foreign Office.

2. In addition to the previous posting of Detring mentioned in the Centennial materials, McCabe lists Drew as Chefoo commissioner, with Hammond at Swatow, as above. *Illustrated History*, 234.

Aside from these, there were numerous other gentlemen and minor officers who assisted in this enterprise. I [Gui] am not clever[3] and had formerly worked as an unworthy clerk in the Zhejiang [Ningbo] customs office archives for a decade or so where I formed a close friendship with Mr. Detring, which is something rather rare. Consequently, when the suggestion came from Mr. [Robert] Hart for someone to be sent to attend the exposition, he [Detring] urged me to go and observe the scene there, keep a detailed record of what I experienced throughout the trip, and bring it back to China in order to have reliable documentation of the event. He was therefore being nothing more than circumspect and thorough, as well as desirous of friendly diplomatic relations and the extension of human talent, in the hope that our country and people would benefit from their effects. I have carefully recorded the regulations and circumstances of the exposition, its beneficial plans and excellent implements, and singled out those for selection and adoption in an entire book titled "A Brief Account of the American Exposition." Those travels through the major American cities in their turn as well as in England and France, together with what was seen and heard on the trip out from Shanghai, around the globe, and back to Shanghai; all political and social conditions, and accompanying opinions on them by Westerners, are recorded entirely in the sections separately titled "Notes on Sightseeing" and "Diary of a Journey to the East." The name of the complete work is *A New Account of a Trip Around the Globe.* Though painfully aware of the mediocrity of the insights that follow, I cannot fail to help commend them to your attention, though they surely do not do justice to reality.[4]

The completion of this book is undoubtedly due principally to the efforts of Mr. Knight and all the Imperial Maritime Customs officers who accompanied, advised, and guided me in various places. Nevertheless, hammering out the wheels is, in truth, the

3. *Gui bu min.* Li here echoes a line from the opening of the *Xiaojing* (Classic of filial piety) in which Confucius has just explained to his disciple Zengzi that the ancients "had the highest virtue and the essential *dao.*" When asked if he understood, Zengzi replied, "Can bu min," "*Can* [Zengzi's personal name, i.e., 'I'] am not clever. How can I be sufficient to understand it?"

4. Literally, they are "surely in the same category as the cranes of Duke Yang"; a reference from Prince Liu Yiqing (403–44), *Shishuo xinyu* (A new account of tales of the world), indicating that the name does not match the reality.

beginning of a great chariot, and without Mr. Detring how would this trip around the globe have been initiated or this record completed? As the ultimate source of this account, it is therefore dedicated to him.

—The third year of the reign of the Guangxu emperor, year of *dingzhou*, spring, second month, final ten days [the last week of March 1877], Li Gui, recorded in Yong [Ningbo], at River Bridge Customs House.

Instructions to the Reader

- The opening map of the exposition grounds in this book is copied from an American original. The legend has been translated into Chinese to make its main points understood so that it may be properly viewed.
- In the Main Building, it is only fitting to discuss China first. As for addressing the different countries in sequence and fully surveying the contents of the hall, however, it is not my intention to cover each and every one. Those not included in this account are of lesser importance and may therefore be counted as insignificant.[1]
- In Machinery Hall, details are provided only for America, England, and Germany. Generally speaking, the other countries are similar to these three and have therefore been omitted.
- The Art Gallery, and the Agricultural and Horticultural Halls are each discussed only in general terms and are not differentiated by country since they have so many more objects than the Main Building and Machinery Hall.
- The narratives describing the various buildings within the exposition are not uniform in their depth of discussion. Due to the size of the halls, the abundance of objects, and the density of the crowds, no one person could have actually visited all of them, as he would have been too fatigued to see and hear everything. Hence, some inaccuracies are in fact unavoidable.

1. Literally, "From the *Odes of Gui* onwards, no remark was made"; i.e., of no importance.

- "Notes on Sightseeing" includes the different things seen and heard en route from Philadelphia to the French capital of Paris. The places I did not reach, I did not presume to include. The level of detail is uneven because the days of sightseeing were many and because the interpreter accompanying me was, on occasion, not completely conversant in the languages of England, France, and America.
- The places through which we passed were not limited primarily to England, France, or America; the others, however, were mostly dependencies through which trains or ships traveled and, being unable to stay briefly and explore, we never got to [visit] them.
- In "The Visit of the Chinese Education Mission Students to the Centennial" [chap. 17], which follows the different essays, the words have been hastily composed and so it is arranged separately after other "Notes."
- All of the terms used for official titles, places, names and descriptions of objects, degrees of measurement, etc., were taken from the translations of knowledgeable interpreters. Although documentation was gathered from a variety of inquiries, in the end, I fear it is not without errors.
- Things in Chinese and foreign languages differ considerably. Therefore, small translation notes have been added,[2] occasionally along with other types of references, all in the hope that readers will consult the original sources and familiarize themselves with what they have not yet studied.
- In Western countries, mileage [li] is calculated differently on land and sea. In measuring the distance on land, every mile is equivalent to 3.3 Chinese li; on the water, it is calculated by measuring the sun at precise times and every mile is equivalent to 3.8 Chinese li [i.e., nautical miles]. Also, in Western countries, one mou [acre] is approximately six Chinese mou. However, these measurements have been taken entirely from inquiries of Westerners and in the final analysis I am not completely sure of their accuracy. For the time being, however, these methods of calcu-

2. In the original Shanghai (S) and *Xiaofanghu zhai yudi congchao* (XFH) versions, parenthetical notes are made intertextually in small print; in the Hunan People's Press edition, they are placed in parentheses.

lating distance and acreage will serve in this book to illustrate the ways in which they depart from Chinese techniques.

- Those things using *zhang* [a linear measure of 141 inches] and *chi* [12.1 inches] in this book, such as the height and width of the walls of houses, depth and surface dimensions, and [other] various objects, have been ascertained as such and are therefore given in *zhang* and *chi*. Those for which we depended entirely on the descriptions of Westerners are given in the yards and feet of Western countries. In the case of those things I have personally seen, they are all, in brief, expressed in China's *zhang* and *chi*.
- As for *tons, pounds, yards, gallons, cubic, gold pounds, shillings, francs, pence,* and so on, these are made clear in the accompanying notes, and are thus not reiterated here.
- This entire journey lasted not quite 260 days, though I missed [by being confined to his cabin or railroad car] half of the land and sea travel due to illness. Following my return, I compiled and proofread the manuscript, and completed this account in only three months. Omissions due to haste are consequently unavoidable.

BOOK I
A Brief Account of the American Exposition

CHAPTER 1. THE ORIGINS OF THE AMERICAN EXPOSITION

The continent of North America is the site of the country of America, called in the foreign language [English] "United States," which may be rendered as *Hezong guo*. It is also called *Milijian* ["American"] and, commonly, "the Flowery Flag [Country]," and is one of the large and powerful nations of the West. Located in the earth's Western Hemisphere, its position with reference to the globe is directly opposite to that of China. From ancient times it had remained unknown and was inhabited solely by red-skinned aboriginal peoples (whom Westerners call "Indians"). Three hundred eighty-four years ago, the Spanish (now *Xibanya Guo*)[1] official Columbus discovered it while exploring lands across the seas. Later, English missionaries arrived as well. Seeing that the climate was suitably mild and the land vast, they felled trees to fashion rude dwellings, cultivated the soil, preached their religion, and founded settlements. Gradually they began to kill some of the aboriginal raiders as a warning to those who repeatedly proved impossible to civilize.[2] As time went on, the number of English emi-

---

1. Li's preceding transliteration in this sentence, which he updated parenthetically here, uses the characters *Risipaniya Guo*.

2. Li's meaning here is somewhat murky. The character *hua* can mean simply "change," or it can imply religious conversion or, more broadly, to become "civilized." Given the long history of the term as used in connection with China's border peoples, the third choice seems the likely one in this instance.

grants increased by the day. The rootless and dispossessed of other European countries crossed the seas to join them, expelling the aborigines and, turning their energies completely to agriculture, gradually opened up and developed the surrounding lands.

For the English, whose principal aim in sending high officials, stationing troops, founding coastal cities and villages, facilitating trade, and establishing customs duties and taxes there was the benefit of the state, it was very much an overseas paradise. Enacting such laws, however, proved to be quite unpopular, for while the various officials stationed in America had all been sent by the English Crown, they were dependent upon the Americans for their positions and salaries. The American territories repeatedly petitioned to send a representative to the English Parliament to open negotiations on the matter, but the English steadfastly refused. Thus, even as the Americans patiently endured this state of affairs, behind the scenes the idea of rebellion was already beginning to develop.

As the fortieth year of the reign of our dynasty's Qianlong emperor [1776] drew near, the English, who had been at war with the French territories on this continent for some time, urgently required funds to pay their soldiers and so repeatedly and arbitrarily levied extortionate taxes. The tax on tea (which was brought from China) sent from England to America had customarily been paid by the seller; now, not only were the rates doubled but the buyers were also ordered to pay a tax. The Americans could no longer stand such harassment, and so in Boston (the name of a place in the northeast corner of America) they dumped the tea into the ocean and, raising their arms and crying out in one voice, the people of the entire country rose in revolt and chose [George] Washington to be their commander.

Washington,[3] a native of a different region in America [i.e., Virginia, not Boston], had once distinguished himself in battle serving the English but, seeing no reward, had since retired here and

3. Like many Chinese writers before and since, Li transliterates "Washington" as *Huashengdun.* Perhaps in the belief that the final syllable, *dun,* represents Washington's family name, he uses it to refer to Washington in this sentence. In this he follows Xu Jiyu, whose account of the American Revolution, as noted in the introduction, is recounted here almost word for word. Cf. Fairbank and Teng, *China's Response,* 44, for an English rendition of Xu.

enjoyed the complete confidence of the Americans. On receiving the acclamation of the entire country's multitudes, Washington realized that under the circumstances he could not refuse [the command] and thereupon marshaled his forces to fight. The English brought in troops and fought a bloody war of seven or eight years without victory until finally acquiescing to the formation of a state by Washington's coalition. They retained control of their northern territory of Canada while the fertile lands to the south were all ceded to Washington. It was on this basis that America was founded.

In the second year of the reign of the Guangxu emperor [1876], one hundred years of nationhood was celebrated. (In Western countries, one hundred years is similar in significance to China's cycle of sixty *jiazi* and *ji* of twelve years.) Previously, their officials and people had met in discussion and proclaimed:

> When Washington founded the nation, its people were few and its states numbered a mere thirteen. Now our country's developed territory grows vaster by the day, there are a total of thirty-nine states, and our population surpasses 40 million. Although these multitudes may be attributed to immigration, such rapid growth must surely be due to the effectiveness of our government as well. Those things for which all the great powers of Europe are counted as grand, vastness of territory, a powerful military, a people at peace and in plenty, has not our country now surpassed them in some ways and lagged behind in others? Even as we view the general trend of events, how do we know that in the future we will not be able to forge ahead of them? On this auspicious occasion, therefore, it is appropriate to recommend mounting a most splendid affair in order that it may be forever remembered.[4]

For this reason, they chose the city of Philadelphia in the state of Pennsylvania to construct buildings and set up an exposition in

---

4. Though this speech appears similar to the sentiments expressed in President Grant's opening address at the Centennial, the phraseology is closer to the Centennial Commission's 1873 request for a presidential proclamation underscoring the enterprise as a truly national effort. See McCabe, *Illustrated History*, 181–82 and 290–92.

which the competition was extended to the products of the entire world, giving it the appropriately grand title of "Centennial Exposition," or "Great Exhibition."

CHAPTER 2. SOME GENERAL COMMENTS ON THE FAIRGROUNDS

In the second year of the reign of the Guangxu emperor, the year 1876 according to the Western calendar, the American city of Philadelphia, following the precedent of the European expositions, opened its Great Exhibition.[1] [The organizers] notified other countries in advance of their plans to celebrate the nation's centennial with an exhibition of the world's great treasures, artifacts, unique skills, and diverse talents, and peoples far and wide were invited to participate in a spirit of friendship in order to reward and encourage their abilities.

The site of the exposition was in Fairmount Park, in the northwest corner of the city. It occupied an area of over thirty-five hundred *mou* and was enclosed by a wooden barricade with seventeen gates.[2] Inside the grounds, five halls were erected to house different kinds of objects: a Main Exhibition Building for a wide variety of goods; a Machinery Hall; an Art Gallery;[3] an Agricultural Hall; and a Horticultural Hall. The immensity of the area, the towering architecture, the impressive abilities, and the beauty of the objects on display were absolutely unprecedented on the five continents. The five halls are estimated to have cost $4.5 million in foreign money. In addition to these, more than 150 buildings of various sizes were also constructed,[4] including a hall for the objects of the American government, a pavilion for the works of women, assorted stables and carriage houses, an administration building for exhibition officials, and an office for assistance with official business. The

1. The official title was the United States International Exhibition.
2. Approximately 584 acres by Li's rough reckoning of six *mou* per acre; a more exact calculation using the standard of 0.16 acres per *mou* puts the site at 468 acres. The actual size of the site turned over to the Centennial Commission was in fact 450 acres, with the exhibition grounds taking up a total of 287.
3. Now called Memorial Hall; it was intended to be the only building to remain after the close of the exhibition.
4. The actual number of buildings, including the five main halls, was 249.

other countries also set up offices for their exhibition personnel within their designated areas.

A customs house, banks, telegraph and post offices, a license bureau (for the issue of special permits), and police stations were also located on the fairgrounds, as well as a photography studio, taverns, restaurants, and shops for a wide array of other items. All of these [concessions] were leased to the people and arranged for the convenience of the visitors. Two railroad lines of thirty-three li [roughly eleven miles] were specially constructed to move the crowds about the area, with each passenger paying five cents per trip, while the exhibition halls had small man-powered vehicles[5] for those who found it inconvenient to walk. In the evening, gas lamps lit up everything like a multitude of stars, and a system of underground pipes provided all of the sites with a continuous supply of running water. The total cost of these items was more than $4 million, with the final construction expenses for the buildings totaling an estimated $8.5 million in foreign money. In addition to a $1.5 million award from the national treasury and the contributions of wealthy businessmen, shares were issued like those of a commercial enterprise, and from the purchase of these by the merchant community a sufficient pool of capital was acquired. After tending to business, the gate receipts (everyone entering the exposition paid fifty cents, in addition to the rents from all the shops on the fairgrounds, etc.) were collected and used to pay back the investors when enough had been accumulated. The people were quite enthusiastic about buying the shares, as they believed them necessary to ensure the exposition's success; whether they ultimately recouped their investments was of secondary importance.[6]

On July 4, 1874, according to the Western calendar (this is said to be the day on which Washington founded the nation), work began, and on January 1, 1876, declared complete. An official to preside over exhibition business was publicly chosen along with thirty-two assistants. In addition, there was a group of two hundred promi-

---

5. Literally *renli xiaoche;* a reference to what were called "push chairs" at the exhibition.

6. In the event, the investors ultimately lost money on their shares, making back only twenty-three cents on the dollar. Worse still, the U.S. government sued to reclaim its $1.5 million contribution, arguing the case up to the Supreme Court before winning its claim. Maass, *The Glorious Enterprise,* 126.

nent men who assessed the quality of the objects, and those displaying exceptional talent or beauty were awarded medals at the conclusion of the exhibition (along with a plaque of merit). There were eight hundred police on special duty, and as for the gatekeepers, managers, and workers everywhere, they were nearly impossible to count. The daily outlay for salaries, workers' food, and miscellaneous expenses came to about $8,000 in foreign money.

Thirty-seven countries brought goods to the exposition. All in all there were forty-six officials in charge of managing exhibition business (these were not differentiated as "great or minor officials"; all were called in English "Chief Commissioner"). Aside from these, there were two to three hundred officials and gentlemen (called in English "commissioner"), about two thousand delegations of business representatives sent to the exhibition (in English "commissions"), and roughly sixty thousand people bringing industrial and commercial products (in English "exhibitors").[7] As for the levels of funding among the participants, suffice it to say that the amount provided by our China proved ample, so I need not elaborate.[8] Countries like England, France, and others were inclined to spend from $100,000–$200,000 to many hundreds of thousands of dollars in foreign money. The number of objects at the exhibition was practically unlimited, and all of them were beautiful and practical. Each display was required to be prepared before the end of June and to have everything appropriately arranged for viewing. Visitors who wished to see all of the items, walking a circuit of the different exhibits every day, would have covered a distance of fifty-six li [about nineteen miles] and required two days to finish. It was truly an incredible display of the very best of the ten thousand treasures; the height of human talent and ingenuity!

America had the greatest amount of exhibition space, about 50–60 percent, with England next, followed by France, Germany, Russia, and Austria[-Hungary] down to the smallest, Chile and Peru. The rules of the exposition stipulated that all objects had to be sent before the opening of the fair, and each exhibitor was

7. The official figures give the number of exhibitors as 31,000. Perhaps Li's numbers reflect estimates for staff and assistants as well. Post, *1876*, 22.

8. China's funds totaled about sixty thousand taels, or approximately ninety thousand dollars in 1876.

required to supply an inventory of the names, count, and valuation of their goods, as well as a declaration from the customs house at the exhibition, before the items could be displayed in the halls. Those desiring to sell merchandise could do so at any time. First, a voucher would be issued while the goods remained on site. When the exhibition closed [for the day], those holding vouchers paid the price agreed upon earlier in silver, while the customs duties were handled either by the seller or the buyer. Unsold goods were to be returned to their place of origin duty-free.

On the seventeenth day of the fourth month of this year, May 10 on the Western calendar, the exposition opened; the twenty-fifth day of the ninth month, November 10, marked its close. The gates opened every day at 9:00 A.M. and closed at 6:00 P.M. Every visitor had to present a fifty-cent ticket to the gatekeeper each time to enter, as it was not permissible for two people to pay a dollar together or for one to pay two twenty-five-cent pieces (there was a booth next to the gate where money could be exchanged for tickets). Every official involved in managing the exposition held a special permit to enter that had to be examined by the gatekeeper. Those running the industrial, commercial, and other affairs of the exposition had to first obtain a special pass from the license office. Following this, they had their pictures taken in the photography studio for a half-dollar in foreign money and pasted onto the passes, which then allowed the holder to enter the grounds without having to pay each time. Occasionally, someone came without his or her pass, in which case the ticket price of half a foreign dollar had to be paid.

It is estimated that more than 130,000 people were on hand for the opening day of the exposition, with the American "president" (the nation's head in America, the translation of which means "great leader") and the emperor of Brazil presiding over it together. On the eleventh day of the eighth month [September 28] the visitors to the exhibition from the various cities in Pennsylvania surpassed 250,000[9] and the count for the six months during which the

9. The actual figure for the opening day was 186,000; the largest single turnout was on the "Pennsylvania Day" cited by Li, when nearly 275,000 people passed through the turnstiles. Post, *1876*, 13. Among the notable events of the opening ceremonies was a *Centennial Inauguration March* composed by Richard Wagner. Wagner later remarked that the best thing about the piece was the five thousand dollars he received for it. Maass, *The Glorious Enterprise*, 41.

exhibition was open averaged about 60,000 visitors per day. Of the various halls and pavilions, only the Art Gallery [Memorial Hall] is to remain in use as a landmark after the closing of the exhibition. Arrangements have already been made by the state of Pennsylvania to purchase the other four great halls for different purposes. The rest of the buildings will be dismantled and rebuilt as offices. To say more about this, a widely published map has been appended here. In order to convey the sense of the map more completely, I have included a brief translation of its headings into Chinese.

I had once characterized the staging of this exhibition by the Americans as seemingly pointless. Now, however, I have come to realize that their purpose in fostering friendly relations [among nations], rewarding human talent, aiding in the diffusion of products, and connecting those who have with those who lack is beneficial to the country, and thus not at all pointless. Moreover, the thirty-seven nations gathered at the exhibition all receive substantial benefits, so their expenses are certainly not wasted either.

Obviously, even a single family cannot satisfy its needs through local resources alone; what then of a nation? Therefore, the selection of the world's unique skills and abilities at this exhibition allows a host of items beneficial to a state's plans for its people's livelihood to be collected in one place so that from among them the most useful ones may be drawn. The value placed on improving relations among the thirty-seven countries, the quality and extent of their human talent, and the attractiveness and relative abundance or scarcity of their goods are there for all to see. In the future, increasing attention is certain to be focused on strengthening these relations, utilizing human talent more effectively, and improving the collection and display of products. At the same time, the rigorous testing cannot but enhance the abilities of a nation's people, and its products will benefit accordingly as a means of enriching them . . .

Li continues in this vein, noting that exhibits for international expositions must be carefully planned, and that the participants not only tend to show a profit for their efforts, but that the investment in the exchange of information "is essential and appropriate in carrying out a nation's long-term plans."

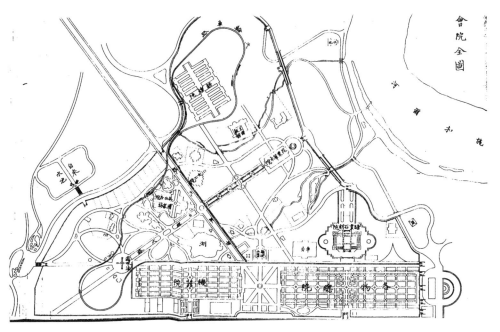

A Complete Plan of the Exhibition Grounds. The long rectangular structures at the edge of the map contain the Main Building and Machinery Hall. Immediately above the Main Building is Memorial Hall (the Art Gallery) with the small Judges Hall just above the cross-walks separating the two largest buildings. The cruciform structure further above Machinery Hall is the American Government Building, while directly across one of the two main boulevards from it is the Women's Pavilion. The Agricultural Hall is the large building enclosed in the loop of rail line toward the top of the map, below which is the American Restaurant and, at the end of the other main boulevard, the Horticultural Hall. The body of water depicted below the map legend is the Schuylkill River. (From *Huan you diqiu xin lu*, Shanghai, 1877–78; courtesy of University of Pittsburgh.)

CHAPTER 3. THE MAIN BUILDING

This hall was on the south side of the fairgrounds with its main entrance facing east, and large entrances on the west, south, and north all reaching to a height of 80 feet. There were about thirty auxiliary doors, very much smaller, with the flags of all the [partic-ipating] countries mounted alongside, their colors dazzling to the eye. The building was 1,880 [English] feet long, 464 feet wide, and completely supported by iron beams and pillars, with walls fash-ioned of great glass panels, lofty, open, and translucent inside and out. Twelve great towers rose above it, with the four central ones reaching a height of 135 feet. Climbing one of these to view the objects of the various nations, one could see them even from a distance as clearly as the lines on one's hand.

Inside the building were seven aisles running east and west, while fifteen ran north and south. The flooring consisted of wooden boards into which ponds and pools had been cut in numerous places, some round, some square, some octagonal, each of them wonderful it its own way. In the middle of these were bronze pillars supporting raised platforms through which pipes were run. Water flowing from the ends of the pillars cascaded back into the pools like sprays of pearls on the snow, gladdening the heart and refreshing the mind. Numerous benches placed in the aisles allowed visitors to rest, and four concession stands were set up inside the north and south entrances so that food and drink were always convenient. The Main Building was the largest in size; outside its south entrance was a series of identical annexes, and the grounds of the building spread over six *mou.* The cost of the entire complex came to 1.6 million foreign dollars . . .[1]

> *Li here details the classification scheme of the objects, the location of the exhibits of the different participants, and the way in which visitors could follow a guideline placed at the intersection of the two main aisles to see the displays in sequence.*

Every day the visitors from the different countries numbered in the tens of thousands and were evenly divided between men and women. Jammed shoulder to shoulder, following hard on each other's heels, they crowded together bustling with life. Apart from the Chinese, only the Turks appeared to dress in a distinctive fashion, the attire of the rest being generally uniform in style. Wandering among them was like entering the bazaars of five great capitals, with tens of thousands of treasures on display, and I found myself in a state of utter amazement—and not a little apprehension. In addition, the handful of Chinese seen by the foreigners here had all been in work clothes, so one dressed more elegantly had the crowds continually closing in on him to catch a glimpse of

---

1. The overflow of goods from the Chinese exhibit—mostly food products and medicinal herbs—was displayed in the Mineral Annex. The area of the Main Building itself was just short of twenty-one acres.

yet another novel sight. I met with no one who did not exchange a kind word or, effusive in his admiration, offer me additional good wishes. Nonetheless, everyone pressing in on me at every turn was like being surrounded with no means of escape. I had hoped to capture the particulars of this time and place with special care, but they simply defied description.

The rationale of the Westerners in gathering together the world's ancient and modern objects in a single place is the product of noble aims and painstaking efforts. That is, they accept no limits in seeking to extend their studies to include knowledge gathered from all parts of the world. Such secrets are not, as a matter of course, for the sole benefit of those who can uncover them, but rather for the good of the public, who are as yet largely without them. Thus they have spared no effort in tirelessly and continually overcoming the obstacles to searching them out, and the annoyances of asking leave and making inquiries, in the hope that a thorough knowledge of the world might be obtained through their efforts. As for what I have seen and heard, in all honesty I cannot give a comprehensive survey of it. Nevertheless, without fear of burdening the reader with trivial details, or of venturing to be vulgar or shallow, those things I have experienced are recorded below:[2]

The objects sent by China to the exhibition filled 720 crates, and were valued at approximately two hundred thousand silver *liang* [taels; a bit less than $300,000]. The display area was smaller than that of Japan and somewhat insufficient for its purpose. This, however, was not due to our having been assigned inadequate exhibition space. Rather, it was because our country had originally arranged for an area of only eight thousand square feet, so [the organizers] were at first unprepared for our additional goods. Our location was inside the western door of the hall; to the left were the areas of Chile and Peru; to the right, Japan, Egypt, and Turkey; with Italy, Norway, and Sweden opposite. To the north, a *pailou* [a wooden ceremonial gateway] had been set up on which were written the three large characters *Da Qing Guo* [The country of the great Qing]. A horizontal sign read "Items from China's Celestial Treasures," with complementary couplets also proclaiming: "A

---

2. Literally, "to the left"; the original text was written vertically, right to left.

spectacular gathering of the works of man and nature from China's eighteen provinces" and "Celebrating the Centennial with sincere friendship." These were the words Mr. [Gustav] Detring [see author's preface] suggested I compose. On the east and west sides were the outer gates, which flew the [Qing] standard of the green dragon on a yellow field in the manner of an official's *yamen* [office], and were most dignified in appearance.

Entering the ceremonial gate, several display cases were set up in the center, eight or nine feet in height and styled along the lines of a temple. There were also a number of gilt wooden cases faced with large plates of glass displaying the silks and satins, carved ivory, antiques, silverware, and precious objects of various provinces. To the left were arranged assorted cloisonné pieces from *daotai* [Intendent of Circuit] Hu of Wulin[3] [Hangzhou]; to the right, one found Cantonese lacquerware, embroidery, mirrors, and screens. Behind these were different styles of rosewood chairs and couches; further back were carved wooden items from Ningbo and the porcelain selected by the Imperial Maritime Customs officials, as well as an assortment of antiques from He Ganchen of Guangzhou[4] [Canton]; in back of these was an office near a window. Though the area appeared somewhat cluttered, it was laid out according to a scheme designed to enhance the beauty of the displays. The articles were all finished in Chinese styles and, furthermore, made entirely by hand without the aid of machines. All of the wooden frames for the objects and display cases, as well as the tables, chairs, beds, cushions, and the paintings and calligraphy decorating the business office were also without a trace of foreign style. All of this prompted visitors and dignitaries from other countries, without exception, to gasp in admiration at their beauty on seeing them for the first time, and to even exclaim: "Now we know the ingenuity of the Chinese surpasses even that of the Westerners!"[5]

3. The famous Shanghai financier and banker, Hu Guangyong, often referred to by Westerners as "Taotai Hu." See introduction.

4. This is probably an error; He Ganchen is identified in the IMC *Catalogue of the Chinese Imperial Maritime Customs Collection at the United States International Exhibition, Philadelphia, 1876* (Shanghai: Statistical Department of the Inspectorate General of Customs, 1876) as being from Shanghai. There is, however, a contributor identified as He Ajing who is from Guangdong.

5. Western commentators remarked about the quality and style of the exhibit as well. McCabe, for example, notes: "Every part of the enclosure is of the gaudiest character,

Outside of the south door was an annex [the Mineral Annex] where the silks, teas, cereal grains, and medicines of the various provinces were displayed separately from the Main Building, all of which had also been arranged by Imperial Maritime Customs. There were not less than seven hundred types of medicinal products exhibited, along with assorted varieties of silks and teas. The foreigners stress that the desire to exchange goods more easily with others is the underlying purpose behind the staging of these expositions. They therefore consider all goods to be useful, because of their potential to increase knowledge and experience, and thus beneficial, rather than curiosities simply pleasing to the eye. China's silks, teas, porcelain, satins, carved utensils, and cloisonné were acclaimed as the best among the various countries, while the bronzes, lacquerware, silver work, rattan, and bamboo articles took second place; items like jade garnered little interest. It may be recalled that although our country sent goods to the competitions at previous expositions in France and Austria [1867 and 1873], we nonetheless reaped no commercial advantage from them owing to the lack of Chinese staff there. This time, therefore, we brought along more than a dozen industry and trade people who well understood the tastes of the Westerners in their day-to-day dealings with them. I have heard that in a year or two, France will again have a large exposition.[6] Those of us attending such exhibitions in the future will need a keen grasp of the most effective ways of displaying our goods, as opposed to those employed on previous occasions when our expectations proved groundless.

The porcelain at the exhibition sold out early. The antiques and satins, however, with their high asking prices, found comparatively few buyers since Westerners generally rely on Chinese purchasing agents for them. Tea as a commodity proved quite popular among the people, though they disliked the mixing of filler [e.g., refuse from cheaper teas, sometimes even including chopped willow leaves] with the thick green variety. Also, the tea chests originally

and here and there rise tall pagodas and towers ornamented with the most brilliant colors. The display gathered within the enclosure is rich, valuable, and exceedingly interesting. . . . Close by these begins the display of inlaid tables and stands . . . as handsome and as well executed as anything of the kind in the Japanese section, which is saying a great deal. . . . The display of porcelain and pottery . . . fully sustains the reputation of the celestials for skill in this branch of industry." *Illustrated History*, 418.

6. The next French Exposition Universalle was held in Paris in 1878.

A New
Account
of a Trip
Around
the Globe

100

sent abroad were a bit large and thus unwieldy to bring out for individual purchases. It would have been better to instead have every pound (equivalent to twelve *liang* [Chinese ounces]) in a small box, so that together the amount in the boxes would have been equivalent to a chest. Selling silk by the catty [*jin;* 1.33 pounds] is not a sound practice either, as its thickness and quality become thoroughly jumbled, and it is easy to see why Westerners have recently taken a considerable dislike to it. If we speak of developing effective practices, then purity without deception in such areas of commerce is something we must work toward improving every day.

Considering that the intent of countries in holding expositions is primarily to display friendship and extend human talent, particular emphasis is placed on the four words *expand and strengthen commerce.* For the most part, though, we Chinese have not seen this as advantageous, nor, since so few of us have gone abroad, have we fully grasped its implications. Still, can it be the case that others do their utmost to understand the precise thoughts of foreigners and eagerly spend hundreds, thousands, tens, or even hundreds of thousands of dollars of their capital competing in enterprises that are not advantageous? We Chinese alone seem capable of thinking that the intent of the Westerners in undertaking these exhibitions rests on principles against which we should guard at any cost. Yet as a means of enriching the country on the one hand, and benefiting the people on the other, how could this second [after Vienna in 1873] exposition attendance be considered wasteful?

Japan's exhibition area was perhaps twice the size of China's and wonderfully organized. The display cases and tables were fashioned along Western lines, and the furnishings were also manufactured using Western techniques. In the middle of an open area decorated all around with bonsai, water pipes rose up to a bronze fountain with pearls of water flowing down; a sight very much worth seeing. A gold-lacquered horizontal sign hanging between the roof trusses bore the four large characters *Di Guo Riben* [The empire of Japan] surrounded by flags with white areas and red centers. The business office was on the extreme western end, and the officials in charge all dressed in Western clothes, sometimes bringing their wives and children along (their families also wearing Western clothes). If not for their black hair and sallow [*mianhuang*] faces, one could scarcely distinguish "east" from "west." One of the officials, a man named Saigo, is a general and has visited China.[7]

The bronzes and lacquerware were the most beautiful pieces. Vases fired entirely of blue-black colors with gold and silver inlays, landscape paintings, people, plants, and trees were of matchless skill. One of these depicting a sea god and more than two feet high was priced at $3,500. A Western buyer had already arranged for the purchase of a vase only two feet in height for $1,000. A wooden, black-lacquered plaque about three feet in height and width with gold and ivory inlays on an antique stand, exquisite and unusual, was priced at $5,000. Small boxes eight or nine inches long and two inches wide, said to be types of pieces from two centuries ago, without the slightest damage and stored in a glass display case like antiques, were priced at $250. There was also a pair of large porcelain vases about six feet high, similar to the *dan* style [slender neck and bulging middle], which, though their exterior decoration was beautiful, did not appear to be as sturdy in quality as Chinese types; these were also priced at $2,000. The ivory carvings were not so good, though their gold inlays were exquisite. Samples of cloisonné were of lesser quality, inferior to Chinese types. Other things, like calligraphy and paintings, satin, and rattan were also on display. I saw one landscape painting with extremely vigorous colors and details, the inscription of which read:

A New
Account
of a Trip
Around
the Globe

101

Scattered peaks, shadows fall, the afternoon sunlight slants,
A tiny bridge leans on the pebble shore.
Like a duck's foot, now an oriole, the tallow tree glows red
Autumn's flush turns home to its craggy tor.

The sender inscribed on the painting was Ryūho [Fukushima] Nei [1820–89] of Tokyo.[8]

7. Saigo Yorimichi or Tsugumichi, the younger brother of Saigo Takamori and commander of the Japanese expeditionary force to Taiwan in 1874. Saigo reviewed U.S. troops with General of the Army William Tecumseh Sherman, Prince Oscar of Sweden, and Centennial Commission president Hawley among others during the July 4 festivities at the exposition.

8. For a more detailed look at a number of the pieces in the Japanese exhibit, see Joe Earle, *Splendors of Meiji: Treasures of Imperial Japan* (St. Petersburg, Fla.: Broughton International, 1999), 36–41.

A New
Account
of a Trip
Around
the Globe

102

As for practical items, with the exception of some very fine blocks for printing with movable type, all the items were manufactured by the Japanese according to Western methods. There were also a number of small, skillfully made machines on display. The techniques employed in producing them are already in widespread use, and it is likely that these are even now superior to the originals. Below the south window were metals, ores, types of coal, no less than several dozen kinds and over a hundred samples all set out for examination. The porcelain manufacturing techniques of the people in the Hizen [Arita porcelain from Saga/Nagasaki] region were the most excellent. The bronzes, lacquerware, and ivory were mostly made in Tokyo. It was said that this abundance of goods sent to the exhibition cost the Japanese government $270,000 in gold, but I have never been able to confirm this.[9]

I find this country to be carefully studying Western institutions, technology, and manufacturing, determined to unlock their deepest secrets. For example, opening mines for the five metals and coal helps the country, while strengthening the military through administrative reform, and building machine shops, mints, offices for telegraphs, posts, steamships, and railroads benefits the nation and people even more. Hence, among the four classes of the people [officials, peasants, artisans, and merchants], all those who closely follow foreign affairs or can speak or write foreign languages are gathered together, overlooking no one, so that their services may be obtained and encouraged in the future. They are also now selecting people to send to future exhibitions, along with special officials to observe and record their impressions. Rumor also has it that in one or two years, after the French have held an exposition, they [the Japanese] will host one of their own—closely following the formula of this one—to enhance their country's reputation. In selecting candidates for these positions, their official responsibilities will, in all cases, require them to be excellent with the brush, bold and generous, discerning and skilled, and unwilling to drift complacently along in old ways of thinking.

Nearby Japan were the exhibits of Egypt, Turkey, Portugal, Spain, and Denmark, whose areas were smaller and whose articles

9. McCabe reported that Japan's appropriations to defray the expenses of their exhibit and outside building complex came to an astonishing $600,000 in gold, more than Great Britain, France, and Germany combined. *Illustrated History,* 221.

were not terribly outstanding; I therefore will not describe them in detail. Nevertheless, Spain's silks and satins were not inferior to those of France; the use of strips from the rice paper plant[10] in Portugal for fashioning flowers and trees, birds and animals, ships and carts, and other toys was very clever; the carpets of Turkey were thick and soft, and much prized among the countries of the West; and Egypt's ancient stone artifacts, as well as gold, silver, and copper coins—no less than eleven hundred items—drew vast crowds day after day. Turkey and Egypt also exhibited weapons, saddles, and jewelry in styles similar to those of China, which was quite strange.

The American articles in the Main Building occupied approximately 30–40 percent of the total area. There were no less than two to three hundred assorted wooden cabinets, iron racks, and glass booths constructed in various styles for the objects on display, and all were of the utmost excellence. The placement of the products, which were all arranged according to separate categories, was done without the slightest bit of disorder. For example, there were medicines, soap, paint and lacquer, pigments and dyes, inks, books, pens and paper, perfumes, bricks, tiles, porcelain, glassware, assorted types of lamp stands, articles for the library, kitchenware, horse carriage equipment, metal ware, weapons . . . [Li goes on to list two dozen more categories of articles here]; there was nothing that they lacked. There were calculated to be 1,588 categories in all, so it can certainly be said to have been a rich display.

Among the iron objects was a type of large vault of the newest design and most unusual. It was about ten [Chinese] feet high and similarly deep and wide. Above and below and on all four sides it had iron plating approximately two [Chinese] feet thick, and the inside was layered with sandstone. The double doors and their locking pins were built to operate entirely by a mechanism like a clock. It is locked for a predetermined time and the doors can only be opened at that moment. If the appropriate time has not yet come, one cannot open the doors even if one has the key. Valuables stored inside it cannot be damaged by fire, and it is impervious to water as well. This indeed is an invaluable item for government repositories, the homes of the wealthy, and some of the

A New
Account
of a Trip
Around
the Globe

103

---

10. Actually, fig tree fiber.

larger business firms. Its weight was estimated to be 75,000 pounds, and it was priced at $10,000 (with the door lock at $3,000). There are much smaller models, and there are those that are round like a sphere, priced from thirty or forty dollars to several thousand.

There was one object about seven [Chinese] feet high and wide, and one foot deep, like a large, fairly ordinary looking cabinet. But with one pull of a lever mechanism it turns into a small room space. Both sides have louvers, and the front becomes a door and the middle a bed with a soft, thick mattress. Next to the bed is a cupboard under which is a cabinet with assorted toiletries arranged within. Then with another pull of a lever it returns to its original form; the price for this is only $200. There was also what appears to be a wooden cupboard, in front of which is a half-table. When the tabletop is opened, there is a sparkling crystal mirror, washing articles are prepared, and next to them is a drawer holding stationery. Here again, there is a lever on the cupboard door that with one pull reveals a bed to relax on underneath, and the price for both items comes to $175. These are all set up by Westerners in spare rooms or carried along when traveling so that they can make arrangements for themselves anywhere . . .

> *There follow several pages on gold, precious gems, and jewelry, the quantity and quality of which "makes the eyes dizzy." Among the noteworthy articles are two miniature gold and silver-plated ships fashioned by a blind craftsman, a diamond necklace priced at $80,000, and assorted emeralds and pearls. There were also fossil leaves and pieces of wood. Of the minerals, the most impressive were the giant pieces of coal weighing over a hundred tons from New York. After a few incongruous sentences on carpets from San Francisco, Li turns his attention to weapons.*

There were Gardner guns, which had just been manufactured during the last few months. These were sent especially for the competition at the exposition, and their method of operation is the latest and most ingenious. Underneath there is an iron tripod mount and on top sit two gun barrels placed side by side. The ends of the barrels have openings into which are inserted brass magazines seven or eight [Chinese] inches high, two inches wide, and sixth tenths of an inch thick, holding the ammunition. There is a small hand crank on the side of the frame. The bullets from the brass magazines enter the gun chambers, firing as they are introduced, and the gun can fire four hundred rounds per minute. Each weapon costs $650 in foreign money. There is one with four side-by-side barrels also employing this method, every one of which carries three thousand rounds of ammunition and costs $1,200.

A New
Account
of a Trip
Around
the Globe

105

There were also Gatling rotary guns, the system of which uses ten barrels bundled together like a sheaf. These are mounted on a carriage and capable of firing eight hundred to a thousand rounds per minute. Its ammunition is arranged like that of the "Gardner" gun [i.e., in a brass magazine]. The biggest has a caliber of eight-tenths of an inch, and the ammunition [magazine] weighs eight pounds; it has a range of seven li [two and a third miles], and can fire three hundred rounds per minute; its cost is $2,800. One after another, all of the European countries have purchased them.

In New York State there is a famous factory called "Winchester," which has a newly designed double-barreled rifle. It is particularly handy and convenient—weighing no more than ten pounds—and its bullets can penetrate four inches of wood at twenty-two hundred yards.[11] Because the gun barrel has an identical one mounted beneath it, it is called the "double-barreled gun." The lower barrel stores sixteen cartridges with powder and bullets, and as each shot is fired another is brought into the upper barrel, firing the sixteen in succession. Every rifle costs forty dollars. One suddenly confronted with an enemy need not worry about having a shot loaded. All of these are completely effective weapons for defense.

Under the south window rose six pavilions, each of which consisted of three levels. Displayed here were the instructional methods and materials of the entire country's schools and academies, as well as student texts and essays. Revised copybooks for all the dif-

11. This appears to be an overstatement. Ballistics tables for the 44–40 cartridge with black powder load used in the gun indicate that performance drops off severely after 500 yards. With sufficient elevation, the 2,200-yard distance may be theoretically possible, but with no appreciable penetration. One possible explanation is that Li may have meant 2,200 feet, in which case a penetration of four inches of wood would be within the weapon's capabilities. See Ray Bearse, *Centerfire American Rifle Cartridges 1892–1963* (London: Thomas Yoseloff, 1966), 153–55 and tables 1 and 2; and Berkeley R. Lewis, *Small Arms Ammunition at the International Exposition Philadelphia, 1876* (Washington, D.C.: Smithsonian Institution Press, 1972).

A New
Account
of a Trip
Around
the Globe

106

ferent school levels and grades were on hand for purposes of comparison. The students can critically examine themselves and by means of exhortation for the diligent and warnings for the lazy, exert themselves every day in their studies. In encouraging people's talents, these are indeed fine methods and good intentions. The curricular materials and compositions of our Chinese students at the Hartford school in the state of Connecticut [see chapters 13 and 17] are also on display here. I have seen samples of their painting, maps, mathematics, biographies, and horticulture, all of which are quite up to standard. Their Chinese-language essays, such as "An American Travel Diary," "Hartford School Diary," "In Celebration of the Centennial," "American Geography," and "Social Customs," are all clear and readable as well. Every composition had several pages of foreign-language translation appended to it, and the Westerners examining these found them most commendable. My interpreter[12] told us that in his own foreign-language writing he can approximate the meaning of Chinese ideas, but in the use of Latin (ancient Rome is held to be the historical seat of European culture, and European gentlemen have traditionally been expected to memorize Roman literature the way Chinese read the Classics; this language is called "Latin") there are a number of points he does not understand. Considering this, he felt that a student educated for two years at Hartford has attained the equivalent of his own studies of five years in Hong Kong. Indeed, one can see the diligence, expert teaching methods, and preparation involved.

North of New York State is the territory called Canada (an English possession), which produces many kinds of furs. Every pelt of very fine, soft, wildcat fur such as lynx was priced at fifty dollars. The sea otter, seal, marten, fox, muskrat, otter, and lynx were all as good as those from Russia, though the price was quite high.

England's exhibition area is large and its products abundant, resplendent, and magnificent enough to dazzle the eyes of the visitors. About thirty large cases have been set up, each more than ten [Chinese] feet tall and wide. In the center of the exhibit there was something resembling a platform with a pavilion of several stories on it, and no fewer than fifty or sixty small cabinets. All of the objects were classified according to category, with the goods of

12. Li's interpreter, Chen Chiyuan, is introduced in chapter 27 at the beginning of the travel portion of his account.

England's dependencies also arranged mostly in cases, and displayed separately to the west of this area. A horizontal signboard hung from the roof supports draped with many flags, and there were two fountains, which were also excellent.

Their porcelains are considered to be of the highest quality—finely crafted and spotlessly pure and white—though relatively inexpensive. At one time, none of the Western countries possessed porcelain and so sought it from China. Returning home, they focused their efforts on analyzing it, and only then were they successful in unlocking the secrets of its manufacture. Now they no longer rely on Chinese techniques and, in fact, have surpassed the Chinese-made products. Their teacups, trays, vases, *yu* vessels [like an urn or spittoon], moreover, were painted with scenes of Chinese figures, landscapes, trees, and flowers and accompanied by signs with descriptions of Chinese clays and techniques written in large script. The earthenware was mostly yellow, and baked without straw. In depicting people, the artwork was exceptionally fine, and we Chinese cannot match it.

The woolens and cotton cloth are also highly prized. All of it is manufactured on spinning and weaving machines and is of good quality and cheap. Chinese people like to use it and a great deal is sold: In terms of the flow of China's gold and silver to other countries in trade, this is the most extensive commodity aside from opium.

In the midst of the glassware there was a chandelier that was ten [Chinese] feet tall, weighed twelve hundred pounds, and held 166 candles. The entire lamp was made up of 30,000 tiny interlocking pieces and priced at $5,000. A wine cup with figures in relief, superbly wrought, carried a price of $150. A water vase only seven to eight inches high cost $200. It was said that the man who fashioned these had formerly been awarded a certificate of merit at the London (the name of England's capital city) Exhibition [of 1862]. As for the rest, such as clocks, watches, telescopes, and microscopes, there was nothing they lacked and nothing that was not excellent.

There were two gold watches completely inlaid with diamonds and made by hand that were capable of running for eight days. One was priced at $3,000 and one at $1,800. The microscopes ranged from two to three inches up to two to three feet in length,

A New
Account
of a Trip
Around
the Globe

108

some for use with one eye, some for both eyes, and can magnify objects from ten to two thousand times. One of the staff members at the exhibit took a drop of water and placed it on a glass slide for viewing, and one could see insects [*sic*] like fish, soft-shelled turtles, crabs, and scorpions swimming about in it. He also pricked his finger with an acupuncture needle and placed a drop of his blood [on the slide], and, within the yellowish smear, one could see similar fishlike creatures, along with ones that looked like rice tassels. There was a telescope, six feet, four inches long, with the diameter of a large bowl. The mount, five feet high, had a mechanism in the center to raise and lower it, next to which was a brass dial engraved with degree calibrations and employing the latest techniques for checking the precise measurement of distances . . .

*Li then moves into a description of a gold- and silver-inlaid vase,
an emerald pendant, gold bracelets, and diamonds.*

As for the products of dependencies like India, Australia (known colloquially as "The New Golden Hills"),[13] and the African territories, these too were all displayed separately. Accordingly, the five metals, mining, fine woods, wool, coffee (similar to a bean; Westerners use it as a substitute for tea), tea leaves, wheat, and millet were the most numerous items. Half of the commodities of India are reminiscent of those of China, and the tea harvest grows larger each year—though its flavor is not especially pleasing. Nevertheless, it is widely marketed and I heard that perhaps more than eighteen thousand *dan*[14] worth was shipped to England during the Western calendar's year of 1875. How much is shipped to all the neighboring countries or used within the country of origin is unknown. This has come about in recent years because they have been paying careful attention to methods of [tea] cultivation, and consequently do not have to rely so much on tea from other countries. Thus it stems from concerns about the flow of gold and silver to foreign countries.

13. San Francisco had originally acquired the name "Golden Hills" or "Gold Mountain" during the gold rush of the late 1840s. When gold was discovered in Australia in succeeding decades, the continent acquired the name of New Golden Hills, and San Francisco became "Old Golden Hills."
14. A unit of weight, sometimes called a *picul*, equivalent to 133-1/3 pounds.

I also heard that the value of the Indian opium sold every year in China totals £10 million (every "pound" is a piece of gold money, equivalent to about five foreign [U.S.] dollars). Their laws allow the populace to cultivate it in various places, and the harvest is then sold to the [British] imperial government, after which it is divided up and sold to merchants, the common people being prohibited from dealing in it themselves. The Crown then shares the yearly profits with the people and the individual merchants. The entire country of India and the imperial government have thus come to rely on these revenues in their budget estimates, while the merchants and people have likewise become steeped [lit.] in their dependence on them. Furthermore, all of this opium goes to China, where the damage has spread like wildfire and is, of course, well known to all. That it seems as if nothing can stop it is likewise well understood, and as such the cultivation of poppies[15] in China even now grows more widespread every year. This invasion from within and without is so disastrous, how can anyone stand to keep silent about it? Or say: "Shouldn't our China adopt laws like those of India in the hope of profiting from this calamity?" I say: Isn't it far too easy to argue that we have no alternative?

A New
Account
of a Trip
Around
the Globe

109

Australia's gold production is extremely prosperous. There are a number of sites along its coast and also along the adjacent southeast corner of New Zealand, and over the past twenty-five years gold worth a total of $130,823,025 has been extracted from them.[16] In their display areas were several gilded wooden pavilions [actually obelisks] with a sign proclaiming in black letters: "Diagrams of Certain Years of Gold Exports in Foreign Money." The borders of each pavilion were painted like so many paths for certain years, with several years grouped together on each one. One could follow how much gold was obtained during those several years and where it was refined by means of [the displays on] the different-sized pavilions set up to inform the people of these particular points. It seems to me that our country, too, once pursued mining and valued the five metals. But the costs have increased nine- or tenfold over those of ancient times, and because of this we no longer mine.

15. *Yingsu*; Li, however, appears to have mistakenly used the homophonous character *ying* (orioles) instead of the correct one meaning "jar" or "pitcher."

16. Li seems to have had access only to partial statistics. The full value for New South Wales alone was given as $167,949,355. McCabe, *Illustrated History*, 374.

A New
Account
of a Trip
Around
the Globe

110

This lack of mining is precisely the cause of the mining disasters of later dynasties. Moreover, it causes us to choke on wasted resources, and as a policy must therefore be considered ill conceived. If we are prepared to explore suitable methods and not remain stuck in the ruts of former dynasties, then how can disaster proceed from disaster?

Australia also produces exceedingly long, fine, soft wool used in high-quality woolens. Every year they export tens of millions of dollars worth. Additionally, they produce coal, iron, and stone in great quantities.

I saw the skeleton of a giant bird. Its legs were more than two feet long and, combined with its neck, its height came to a full six feet. Under it lay an egg as large as a melon, while next to it were two smaller birds, like chicken hens of three or four *jin* in weight. I asked about this and learned that it was an ostrich raised in the African desert. Its short wings prevent it from flying, but it can run with the speed of a galloping horse, and is even capable of delivering mail. These skeletons and eggs were found in the desert and the eggs were hatched there by means of an incubator. The chicks, I heard, had been hatched for only two or three days. The eggs are fashioned into very hard and durable cups and bowls, while the feathers—fluffy, and yellow, white, and black in color—are used to decorate the hats of Western women. I also saw a huge skeleton, seventeen or eighteen feet long, four legged, with short front legs and large rear ones; it is very long and slender from head to tail, like a crocodile. It is called a "lizard" [*leishade*], which may be translated as a type of reptile. It comes from Australia, and China has no creature like it.

Coming to a place at the end of the exhibit, I saw several items arranged in display cases. They were made of fine blue-and-white cotton, soft and thick, more than a [Chinese] foot high, with a large upper opening and a smaller one below, like a garment for the upper part of a person's body. I did not understand what these were used for, and a member of the staff told me that they were articles for controlling and shaping a woman's body [i.e., corsets]. They are used, he said, to lift and emphasize the breasts while narrowing the waist, in order to enhance the beauty of the figure. He then asked me, "Don't the Chinese also use these?" I replied: "In ancient times, we Chinese considered narrow waists to be attractive as well, and the so-called '*Chugong [Chu Palace]* waists' were similar to these. The notion of emphasizing the breasts, though, is actually opposed to Chinese custom. In any case, a small bosom cannot really be enhanced [very much], so what then?" "That's not a problem," he said. "There is another set of articles, like two cups, which can be fastened directly to the breasts." *Yi!* This is as dangerous an idea as the Chinese custom of foot binding and, worse still, the parts of the body affected are more important!

Facing east in France's exhibit area, there is a pavilion with an archway fashioned in the style of a Catholic cathedral. This is due to the zealous advocacy of Catholicism on the part of the French . . .

The different styles of French horse carriages are detailed, and Li is favorably impressed with French textiles—especially silk, the machine-made variety of which, he notes, surpasses Chinese makes in smoothness and firmness. Again, he comments on the tendency among the commercial nations of the West to create domestic industries in order to avoid the flight of revenue overseas to pay for essential imports. Following this is a page on "gold and silver objects, bronze and stone statues, ivory utensils, tortoise shell articles, time pieces, and assorted other kinds of goods." Li then returns to the subject of religion.

Further to the north, it was like an entirely different world. Amid three very old wooden huts, piles of rice straw and wheat straw were strewn about as if on a farmstead. Inside, one encountered nothing but painted wooden figures with the most extraordinary clothes and ornaments, some sitting, some kneeling, some crying or laughing.

A woman of surpassing beauty was performing the *koutou* [kowtow]. In the middle of the area a straw basket was placed in which an infant lay, while a species of ox sniffed at him from behind. I did not quite understand all of this and when I asked, it was explained to me that this was a scene depicting the birth of Jesus, and that the infant was actually Jesus. The beautiful woman was Mary, the mother of Jesus. In a space to the left, statues of contemporary Catholics and clergy approached the mother of Jesus kneeling in worship. In an area to the right were men and women, all resplendent in a variety of clothes. In the middle was a statue draped in

A New
Account
of a Trip
Around
the Globe

III

A New
Account
of a Trip
Around
the Globe

112

red depicting Jesus, his feet and face bearing wounds, in a scene of his ascent into heaven. The sculpture was so vivid it seemed on the verge of life, and as an eyewitness, it appeared absolutely real to me. I had to reflect for a moment before I realized it was all an illusion. *Yi!* Such skills are absolutely uncanny![17]

Germany, or *Deyizhiguo* [Deutschland], which the Chinese call "German," and which was formerly known as "Prussia," occupies an area of Europe that from ancient times has produced objects of culture and refinement. At this exhibition, therefore, books, pictures, musical instruments, paper, and pens constituted the greater part of their offerings. Other items, like woolens of all colors, clocks and watches, ivory, glass, metalwork, and weapons were excellent as well. The porcelain is particularly noteworthy, and there were no less than dozens – perhaps hundreds – of types of perfumes and toilet water among their many finer goods. Two screens, more than three [Chinese] feet square, each painted with a scene of several ladies and gentlemen relaxing in the woods, were on display there. They are both the work of contemporary artists, but their relative quality is so difficult to judge that it is as if they were painted by the same hand. The price of one, however, was twenty-four hundred dollars, while the other is only forty dollars. This business of painting, it would appear, is the same whether in China or abroad.

There was a huge piano, tall and perhaps twenty [Chinese] feet on a side, resembling a small room. The inside was taken up entirely by a mechanism of strings and cords, while the outside was furnished with a kind of narrow table and stool. When the table is opened, there are keys arranged in a row inside, with strings and cords running from the space under the table into the little "room." As the pianist sits and plays, great ringing sounds, or those like the clash of battle, or gentle ones like the whispering of children, enable the listeners to relax and forget their weariness. Every day [the pianist] necessarily played several collections of pieces, and the people from the dozens of countries in the hall were unstinting in their praise of him. Next to this there was also

17. This was the exhibit of the Parisian firm of Raffl & Co., makers of church statuary. McCabe reports, "A crowd is always gathered about the space, and the group receives as much notice, perhaps, as anything in the French collection." *Illustrated History,* 382–83.

one [a piano] more like a long, narrow half-table. The pianist was quite refined and elegant, and in front of the assembled onlookers he played a composition especially for me. As one with no real understanding of music, however, I am afraid I must have disappointed him despite his generous intention. I have heard that in Western countries the literati are quite skilled at the piano, and the Germans are said to be the best. Their techniques in manufacturing musical instruments are also the most refined. At the eastern end of the exhibit there was a music box about ten [Chinese] feet tall, four feet wide, and a bit more than a foot deep. All four sides were covered in glass inside of which was a wheel and axle, both ends having square iron strips extending toward the outside. Winding a large key produced the eight musical tones in harmony, and the singers know these as well as the words and rhythm. Such large instruments and music boxes are proclaimed as the height of perfection.

A New
Account
of a Trip
Around
the Globe

113

Of the Russian goods, silver utensils, furs, and emeralds are said to be the best. There was a tea tray fashioned from a single piece of silver, weighing about eighty ounces, with vines engraved in it and plated with gold. On it were arranged some white towels piled perhaps five [Chinese] inches high, and when the tray was tilted, it showed their decorative folds of crepe and water stains, as if [the towels] had been used for wiping up tea water. Uncertain as to whether it had been left in this condition by the artisans or by those who were cleaning it, I paid no attention to it. Later, through the explanations of the staff, I began to realize that the hand towels on the tray were actually crafted in silver as a part of it, and that it was, in fact, a piece unique in all the world. The next day, I returned with my Western friends to see it again. My friends gazed at it for quite some time and also had difficulty distinguishing the real from the illusory in it. On asking the price, they said it was five hundred dollars . . .

Other aspects of the Russian exhibit that caught Li's eye were the large display of furs, emeralds mined in Siberia, and the ornate vestments of an Orthodox bishop.

Afterward, we returned to the business office and had an agreeable chat with the exhibit official in charge of selecting the prod-

A New
Account
of a Trip
Around
the Globe

114

ucts for the public. According to what he said, the worth of the goods sent to the exhibition that they intended to sell was about $1.5 million; that of the articles brought specially to the exposition but not for sale he did not know. He went on to say that competition is now considered to be the most important thing, since it can strengthen friendly relations among nations, broaden their horizons, and join together the commerce of the world. Because of this, he noted, his country was not worried about the costs of the exhibition, though they were as much as one to two hundred thousand dollars.

Austria's products were also numerous, though I did not record many of them. The staff led us to a place where we saw three objects inside a glass cover. In the center was a piece of white gemstone like a goose egg, only flat, and brilliant with a luster of the five colors like mother-of-pearl reflecting the sun. They said it comes from the Austrian mountains, and that this white gemstone is the largest, costing twenty-five thousand dollars. To the right of it was a bracelet on which was carved a likeness of the nation's monarch, inlaid all around with gems, and worth ten thousand dollars. To the left was a pendant like the bracelet but slightly smaller, priced at six thousand dollars. These objects are regarded as national treasures and were specially selected for the exhibition to broaden people's understanding and experience. Although they carried prices, they were not offered for sale.[18] Below were arranged some twenty-four stone objects of different sizes, green, but of unusual brilliance; the white gemstone is extracted from this stone. There was also a case containing an amber chandelier, octagonal in form and about three [Chinese] feet high, with forty candles, costing eight thousand dollars. We were told that it took many craftsmen to build and took a year to complete, and one can certainly see this in the fine detail. The furs, bronze ware, and musical instruments were all excellent, their *hu* and *qin* [*erhu* and *luqin*] more or less similar to those of China.[19]

Italy was in the northwest corner of the Main Building and its display area was not very large. Among their articles, sculptures of

18. Li appears to be describing the collection of meerschaum carvings at the Austrian exhibit.

19. The *erhu* and *luqin* are stringed instruments that Li is equating to a violin and a zither.

stone and bronze, and terracotta figures were the most numerous, and among the Western countries that excel at carving statuary, Italy is considered the most prominent . . .

Li here describes the manufacture of fine straw hats and marvels at the cleverness of some of the faux antique marbles and bronzes.

A New
Account
of a Trip
Around
the Globe

115

There was a great deal of natural silk, and all sizes of cocoons were also fully prepared and displayed. On inspection, however, the white variety of silk does not have the brilliance of Chinese types because of the region [where it is produced]. I was told that this country's production of silk is like that of Indian tea, and other countries compete to buy each year's harvest. Their methods of production are uniform, unlike those of Chinese silk, which suffers from uneven quality. Should we not worry that their silkworm techniques, also obtained from China and successfully imitated, are used to seize profits from China?

More of their bronze and stone antiquities, ivory, and ironware excavated from the ground were displayed in the Art Gallery, all of them over two thousand years old. There were stoves, desks, five types of kitchen implements, a serrated steelyard balance, incense burners, bronze pitchers and mirrors, bronze and stone seals, all of them identical to Chinese types. It also appeared that they contained writing similar to the kind of script found on [ancient] *ding* vessels,[20] but so corroded that I could not make it out. I note that it was Italy that unified all of ancient Europe under Rome, and that the *Han Shu* [*History of the Former Han*] records that the country of *Da Qin* [Rome] had contact in that era with China. Seeing these things now, I wondered if they were obtained from China at that time or if they copied the [Chinese] styles and made them for themselves? It is a shame that the writing on these scripts could not be deciphered and that I was unable to investigate their origins.

The products of Switzerland were all average, except for the manufacture of clocks, which may indeed be called "without rival in the entire world," and cost from $4 to $2,500. Among them was a type as small as a foreign button that can run for six days and

20. Three-legged bronze ritual vessels; among China's earliest, some dating from the fifteenth century B.C.E.

A New
Account
of a Trip
Around
the Globe

116

costs $2,000. One kind of pen, about four [Chinese] inches long, made of gold, square on top and round on the bottom, was inlaid with three clock faces, all as small as goose eyes. On the upper face are the hours and minutes; on the middle one are the Westerner's weeks; on the lower face are the days of the month, and the whole article costs $2,200. There was also a gold finger ring inlaid with clock dials as small as beans. The script is barely distinguishable, and it, too, is able to run for six days and costs $2,500. Although it has been running for several years, it has not lost a second. There is also an ordinary type of clock whose face has five hands: hour, minute, day, month, and week, all running simultaneously; moreover, it can ring out the quarter hours. Its cost is $1,050. These are all handmade without the use of machines, every one so exquisitely ingenious that I cannot quite fathom it. If I had not seen them with my own eyes it would surely have been difficult to believe. Their chiming clocks and music boxes were excellent as well.

As for Norway and Sweden, more than half of their products were made entirely of iron and steel. Various kinds of furs were also in great supply. Norway produces a fish oil that is able to control tuberculosis. They said that this kind of oil is produced from the liver of fish taken from the Arctic Ocean and refined into medicine [i.e., cod-liver oil]. There are men in China who sell this oil and use it to treat coughs and choking, and every bottle costs a half-dollar. I once tried it.

As for the two countries of Peru and Chile, their areas were the smallest, with little to record. Peru had one large case, its interior of wooden boards, its outside covered with glass, in which were displayed several human remains, all of whom appear to be sitting. Their bones have not come apart, and the skin and flesh have dried up and withered to a black color, the hair also remaining intact. The clothes were all cotton prints, and the bodies completely tied up with fine string hung with small brass bells and knives, clamshells, and various items, and one could not distinguish between the men and women. There was a child wrapped in cotton as well, also apparently sitting, with the wadding very black and stiff like iron. In the top of the case were arranged a dozen or so bones, some of which were long like a horse's head, some very round and twice as large as those of an ordinary man, also with long black hair still attached to the skin. Their form was enough to shock one. I asked them that since it was known that these mummies are a thousand years old and that their skin and flesh have not withered away, and since they had been dug up twenty-seven years ago, whether or not they understood the method used at the time to coffin them? They also had a clay jar, flute, vase, jars, dozens of items, the quality of which was rather crude, on which were painted the faces of devils and tigers, all of it permeated with an air of antiquity. There were also many kinds of bows and arrows, a bronze begging bowl, straw baskets, clamshells, and sea snails. The bow was made of a tree branch, the arrow shafts were like reeds, and the arrowheads made of black wood. The straw baskets were all skillfully made. Nearly all of these were funerary objects, and though they were generally inferior to the other goods at the exposition, they [the Peruvians] wanted to have experts examine them. The remainder of their objects, which included many kinds of birds and animals, fur, and bones, were quite pretty and very unusual.

Chile's medicinal herbs were many. Each kind of plant and tree closely resembled types found in China. In the middle an octagonal pavilion had been set up, fully stocked with nuggets from gold and silver mines. There was a black silver ore from the bottom of a mine, unrefined, yet shiny enough to see one's reflection. It was similar in appearance to a jumbled pile of stones and quite heavy— about fifty ounces—and valued at four thousand dollars. On asking why it was worth so much, they replied that it was most rare and thus very precious. Perhaps this is the so-called black gold of the Chinese.

Beyond these, there are more than ten remaining countries, but their articles were not really unusual and, in addition, I did not have the free time to record them.

CHAPTER 4. MACHINERY HALL

This hall was adjacent to the Main Building and its [principal] entrance faced toward the south. Exiting the Main Building's western portal and crossing over slightly more than a hundred paces, one then entered this hall's eastern gate. The building was 1,402 [English] feet long and 320 feet wide. Its roof trusses were made entirely of iron, and the walls were of brick and stone, topped by

A New
Account
of a Trip
Around
the Globe

118

glass, with a floor of wooden planks. Five aisles ran east and west, and eleven north and south, all of them very broad, and the visitors shuttled back and forth in dense profusion. The total cost came to eight hundred thousand dollars in foreign money. In the allocation of space, the largest area belonged to the Americans, whose machines occupied about 80 percent of the room from east to west; then to the east were England's machines, taking up perhaps 10 percent; the rest, such as Germany, France, Russia, Austria, Belgium, and Brazil, were in the remaining space in the section to the east. The areas of the various countries displayed their national flags together with woolen banners or feather plumes and signs indicating the countries in large script, so that visitors could identify them at a glance. Two railroads were built inside and outside the entrance and there were locomotives to move the assorted machines into the hall. Outside the hall's north entrance there was a lake with an area of twenty *mou* [a little over three acres] complete with a fountain spraying water into the air, and pieces of lifesaving equipment used on oceangoing vessels floating about in it.

The display of machinery was immense, with machines for digging coal, pumping water, forging and smelting, land cultivation, dredging [another fifteen kinds of machines are listed] . . . every kind of machine—so many that it was impossible to count. There is now probably nothing done without the aid of machines. That which creates the machines is a machine; that which drives the machines is also a machine. To this one must now proclaim the state of the cosmos to be that of one vast machine.[1] Moreover, improvements are constantly springing from the minds of the ingenious, and these advances stimulate still more innovation. No sooner is a machine developed than it is copied, and the competition continues without letup. From sun up to sun down, and again from sun down to the new day, how wondrous is this business of mechanical innovation! We Chinese have a saying: "Where there are secret dealings, there are sure to be ingenious minds; the

---

1. This passage is somewhat ambiguous. The original Shanghai edition, lacking modern punctuation, allows the reader to infer the parallel construction of the phrases, *zao ji zhe jiqi ye, yun ji zhe you jiqi ye.* The editors of the HPP version, however, decided to make the *zao* the last word of the previous sentence. Chang-fang Chen, in electing to leave the parallel structure intact, renders it as "only a machine can create more machines and only a machine can operate a machine." "Barbarian Paradise," 129. I have, with minor differences, followed suit.

ancients, therefore, did not encourage them."[2] However, this is certainly not a maxim for us to follow today! If we were to employ those with such "ingenuity" solely as tools for the benefit of the country and people, then they would not scheme to profit themselves and their relatives. In that case, why not try to use them? As for the proper use of machines, we must not speak of citing the ancients' well sweeps[3] and generalize about the use of such devices as inappropriate, but instead, buy all those without exception that might benefit the people.

As I wandered about gazing at these machines, I wanted very much to single out and write about those with real utility. In this, however, I was hindered by the complexity of their workings, which proved impossible to completely recount. In addition, the group of visitors was very large and the movements of the machines were deafening, so when meeting with others, I quite often could not hear them speak. The interpreter, too, could not help but distort some things in conveying the finer points of the different devices to me. For all of these reasons, I am able to report only on those things that I could see and inquire about with comparative ease. In light of this, these three brief accounts of the American, English, and German machines have been selected and prepared. As for the other countries, like France, Austria, and so forth, their items were not numerous and consisted entirely of those which these three countries had. Hence, they have not been recorded.

America's territory is vast but its population is sparse, so the people tend to depend on machines in all their activities as a substitute for human labor. Consequently, they pay particular attention to their power and precision, and are unrivaled in this regard among other nations. In the center of this hall stood a giant machine, with a wheel more than thirty [English] feet in diameter and the power of fifteen hundred horses. It was so constructed that the power for the wheel was provided by steam from a remote location (outside the hall there was a separate building in which two boilers[4] were set up) through iron pipes, which were run to the various machines. The motion of the great wheel, as well as that of

A New
Account
of a Trip
Around
the Globe

119

2. The passage is from the *Zhuangzi*, chapter 12, and reads, "Where there are clever devices, there are sure to be secret dealings; where there are secret dealings, there are sure to be ingenious minds."
3. The contrivance criticized in the above passage from the *Zhuangzi*.
4. This appears to be an error; there were in fact twenty boilers.

A New
Account
of a Trip
Around
the Globe

120

every steam-driven device in the hall, drew its steam from this source. The devices that did not require steam were driven solely by leather belts, the various machines having been equipped with pulleys of various sizes around which the belts were wound. These in turn were attached to pulleys and shafts in the iron ceiling trusses, where their movement could be engaged as needed. All of the machines for tasks like pumping water, printing, spinning, sawing, and milling utilized them. The engine was called "Corliss," after the name of the American who constructed it. Every day at the *weichu* hour [1:00–3:00 P.M.] the engine was started. Such an enormous machine, running without a sound and requiring only one man to operate it, was most extraordinary.

Inside the western entrance was a pool 140 [English] feet long, 60 feet wide, and 8 feet deep, surrounded on all sides by railings [the Cataract]. Mounted on the railings were iron pipes of all sizes from which water cascaded back down into the pool. Inside the railing was a veranda where many benches were set up for people to sit and watch. Farther behind this were all manner of water-pumping machines used to circulate water through the pipes into the pool and to draw the water in from the bottom of it. The water from the various devices made a turbulent sound as it was drawn and recovered, circulating continuously. In Western countries all of the mines having water inside use these devices to pump it out. These were presently installed in the hall because they wanted to acquaint people as much as possible with their excellence and utility and, furthermore, from a desire to pursue the latest innovations. This caused me to consider that the waters of China's rivers and streams rise and fall frequently, with drought and flood proving equally disastrous. In the highlands of the northeast, agricultural land is everywhere difficult to irrigate. When it comes to water conservancy, therefore, urgent crises could be more ably managed through the use of such machines. If the results proved beneficial and convenient, they could be duplicated and thus be of assistance everywhere.

There were also small types of water pumps and very many fire engines, all of which were first rate. I saw a steamship only five [Chinese] feet long, equipped with all manner of fittings. A member of the staff applied some steam to the ship and used various devices to run it like those on a full-size vessel, its excellence beyond understanding. The American [John] Roach [of John Roach and Son Works] built this distinctly new type of model warship. The stern has two screw propellers running together and moves forward and backward, right and left, as per the operator's wishes. There was a gun turret with two guns. The turret has a wheel mechanism for rotating in any direction. It was said that the bore of the guns is twenty inches in diameter, and the ship is 300 [English] feet long and 16 feet wide,[5] drawing only 18 feet of water. Seeing its shallow draft and its ingenuity and maneuverability, it is most suitable for speeding into inland waters . . .

A New
Account
of a Trip
Around
the Globe

121

Li next details the mechanics of a bucket dredger and then moves on to outline the workings of a papermaking machine, following which he surveys the printing trade.

A little to the east were the printing presses, no fewer than dozens of varieties of all sizes, just then in the process of printing books, newspapers, and pictures with unmatched speed. There was one type that is extremely small and ingenious. It was set up on a small square table and was only about a [Chinese] foot high and eight inches wide and made of iron. In the middle of it was a clever device embedded with ink, and an iron plate was set up under which were arranged all the letters of the foreign alphabet, twenty-six, like chess pieces, operated by a woman on the staff [i.e., a typewriter]. Paper is placed on the iron plate then, using a technique similar to that of playing the piano in foreign countries, it prints certain letters by means of her hands pressing certain alphabetical keys, while inside the machine an impression of each letter is struck. These are connected together to form words very nimbly and quickly. Offices all buy one, since its uses are many and its cost is only in the range of a little over one hundred dollars. Unfortunately, however, it does not print Chinese characters . . .

There follow descriptions of new models of sewing machines, a power loom from New York State, nail cutters, and tin platers. Li seemed particularly taken with a machine used to etch glass.

---

5. This is undoubtedly a mistake, perhaps a transposition for 61 feet. The vessel was a monitor-type gunboat called the *Puritan.*

A New
Account
of a Trip
Around
the Globe

122

Nearby there was a crowd of spectators around a machine for carving patterns or the names of gift-givers on glassware. The strokes of the characters it produced were neat and uniform. The method involved using a delicate brass tube to trace the form to be carved, and on the tube was embedded a tiny piece of steel as small as a coin, like a polished jade wheel plate, whose edge was extremely sharp. Steam shoots out from inside the tube, which surges against the wheel and makes it turn, by means of which it then carves. Accordingly, I tried to write some Chinese characters for it to carve but the operator was too busy to do it. This, however, was only because the many strokes in Chinese characters are not as easy to work with as the twenty-six alphabetical characters strung together into words.

There was an envelope machine, very unusual, that combined the stationery and glue and folded it entirely within a rotating mechanism with incomparable speed. Every hour it can make several thousand envelopes and requires only one female worker nearby to count, wrap, and box them.

There was also a cotton-weaving machine about which I felt particularly confused concerning its principal features, seeing it but not understanding what I was seeing. By means of different colored threads, it can weave extremely lifelike pictures of the virtuous leaders and famous officials of different countries. Flowers, trees, landscapes, whatever, all of it was indistinguishable from paintings and without revealing a trace of being woven [i.e., a Jacquard loom]. Each of these machines, too, requires only one operator.

At the English exhibit they had installed their own engine to power their country's machines, as they did not rely on the main American engine. Their wool-spinning and weaving machines were the newest and most excellent, and the cost was also not so high. I counted four machines, two for weaving cloth, one for wool, and one for camlets. Every one can make about 120 yards per day (every *yard* is about two Chinese feet, five inches). There is one operator and also perhaps a person to superintend the four machines together. Every machine costs only one hundred dollars, but they cannot be run without steam power. There are, however, also small steam engines available, of only two horsepower, for four hundred dollars. Purchasing one of these can power about twenty machines, so this problem is certainly easy to solve . . .

The next section deals in painstaking detail with the workings of a British silk-reeling machine, hemp spinners, a cotton spinner, cotton gin, printing press, and coal breaker before moving on to the German exhibit.

A New
Account
of a Trip
Around
the Globe

123

The Krupp steel cannon of Germany is considered to be the very best. Gleaming and dazzling to the eye, its excellence is unsurpassed. Its length is twenty-seven feet with a breach circumference of eight feet, a circumference of eighteen feet in the midsection, a bore of sixteen inches, and it weighs sixty-two tons.[6] The breach has an opening to receive the powder and shell and closes quickly and easily. The projectile is three feet, five inches long, and its rear diameter is nine inches. Of the pointed explosive types, the iron one weighs 1,030 pounds, while the one of steel, 1,150 pounds. The solid iron type weighs 1,369 pounds. The chamber receives a powder charge of 280 pounds and every firing of the gun costs three hundred dollars. The shells are capable of covering a distance of fifty-three li [nearly eighteen miles] and can penetrate two feet, five inches of iron plate within 540 yards. *Yi!* With the construction of such immense guns firing such enormous shells, it is no surprise that even ironclad warships cannot be completely relied upon. I have heard that England is also casting huge guns, though whether they are the equals of this one is unknown.[7] The mount is also made of iron, thirty-two feet long, ten feet wide, and five feet high. The distance from the muzzle to the floor is twelve feet, and both sides of the mount have wheels with gearwork, the turning of which can elevate or lower the gun. It also has an iron hook for lifting the projectile into the gun. The movements of the mechanism are simple and convenient, with three wheels on the bottom of the mount on both sides. It can be traversed quite well but cannot

6. The character I have rendered as "circumference," *cu*, is usually given as "diameter." It seems obvious, however, that given the actual dimensions of the gun, such a definition would be incorrect. The bore of this gun was 13.85 inches, and it did indeed weigh sixty-two tons.

7. Stopping at Woolwich Arsenal in England later in his journey, Li was told of the current construction there of guns weighing a hundred tons and of the planned construction of guns of up to two hundred tons. See chapter 15.

A New
Account
of a Trip
Around
the Globe

124

move straight ahead because it is made strictly for use in forts and
batteries. It is manned by a crew of eight, and the gun and mount
together weigh 104 tons and carry a price of about one hundred
thousand silver *liang*. There was also a gun of identical style,
though a bit smaller, mounted on a large carriage. Two men ride
on the sides of the carriage, and this is used during a charge to
break the enemy. Powder and ammunition are transported in a
separate caisson, also with two men riding on it. There is, in addition, a model that is even smaller, only around three feet long
and carried on horseback. Another horse carries the gun carriage
and another the limber chest, and this one is used for mountains
and rugged terrain.

Note: This man Krupp is a German who built a factory in the
region of Essen that bears his name. The complex covers an area of
ten thousand *mou* [about sixteen hundred acres], and its workers
and craftsmen number 16,200. The highest-quality military ordnance made there is reserved for the use of the German army,
though most of what the factory produces is purchased abroad. All
types of things like railroad carriages, rails, and assorted iron
goods are also manufactured there. At this exhibition, dozens of
items related to iron mining are displayed, along with those of all
the enterprises associated with extracting materials from the
mountains. My understanding is that the construction of factories
in other countries is undertaken either by the government or by
the issuing of shares, and that Krupp is the only man to have set up
a factory using his capital alone. He owns the coal and iron as well,
so there is no need to purchase them from others. Not only are his
steel guns hailed as the best weapons for defense, but his family is
also immensely wealthy to an extent rarely seen.

CHAPTER 5. THE ART GALLERY
[MEMORIAL HALL]

Among the five great halls, this one is considered outstanding. The
beautiful stone, fine ironwork, and glass in its construction are
incomparably solid, and the cost for labor and materials has been
calculated at $1.5 million. The reason for this is that all of the other
halls and buildings were scheduled to be dismantled at the conclusion of the exposition, with only this one remaining to serve as

a memorial of the event. The building is 365 [English] feet long and 210 feet wide, with a dome rising to 150 feet in the center, round like an inverted bell, and topped by a statue of a goddess. The entrance faces south, directly opposite the Main Building's north entrance, and separated by only a few dozen paces. A statue, perhaps twenty feet high, of a soldier holding a rifle stands in front of the doors, and both sides are flanked by great bronze equestrian statues of military commanders. One ascends more than ten steps to go in, very wide and grand. Above them is a covered corridor lined with stone statues.[1] Entering a door there is a large room, forty feet deep and sixty wide, filled with stone and bronze statuary. In the place of honor among the statues of stone were renderings of the American founding father, Washington; among the bronzes in the south and east corners were those of the current German chancellor, Bismarck—several more than ten [Chinese] feet high. The rest, such as numerous gods, generals, goddesses, and *luohan* [in Buddhism, *arhats,* or those who have attained enlightenment through their own efforts] of all sizes are in some cases depictions of actual people and in others products of the imagination. There were also statues of black men from Africa, Indians, Muslims, and red-skinned aborigines [from America], as well as those of men and women who were completely nude (their lower bodies sometimes hidden from view by leaves or strips of silk), no less than thirty or forty in all. Then, entering another great room, one again found nothing but statues of ancient and modern notables, with marbles depicting the crucifixion of Jesus in the majority.

Entering yet another door there was a transverse aisle winding around with doors on all sides, and one could not tell in which direction one was heading. One could only follow in the footsteps of the other people and assume their position in turn. On the doors were large signs in the foreign languages of certain countries denoting the areas of those countries' exhibits of paintings. The rooms themselves were irregular in terms of style and area. Paint-

A New
Account
of a Trip
Around
the Globe

125

1. The Hall, which subsequently became the first home of the Philadelphia Art Museum, remains in use for a variety of functions today. The statue capping the dome is a figure of "Columbia." The soldier holding the rifle was called, variously, "The American Volunteer" or "The American Soldier" and carved by the New England Granite Company. The bronze equestrian pair was not, as Li believed, a depiction of military figures but rather views of the winged horse Pegasus and his mythical handlers.

A New
Account
of a Trip
Around
the Globe

126

ings filled the four walls, with no unused space: large ones up to twenty or thirty [Chinese] feet wide, and ten or twenty feet high; small ones, no more than a foot or so square, all of ancient and modern people and landscapes. A certain number of the paintings in the hall were to be reproduced and printed in a special book, so that visitors could view them later on. The number of rooms occupied by the different countries varied according to the number of paintings they brought, which ranged in cost from several tens of dollars to thousands and tens of thousands of dollars. There were [also] some priceless works from family collections that had been sent to the exposition for special viewing and study.

England had a large painting of the marriage of its crown prince to a Russian princess, depicting the ceremony in the church [*The Marriage of the Prince of Wales*, by William Powell Frith]. The prince's formal dress, as well as the princess' regalia and gown, was completely white (Western custom regards white as an auspicious color for clothing on joyous occasions; black is reserved for mourning clothes), and the gown left her back and shoulders bare to the bosom. The royal family followed in their court robes. The clothes of the royal family were of many colors—the dress of the women also leaving the shoulders and back bare to the bosom— and the party included perhaps a hundred people. On the left stood a tall pavilion in which the queen of England was seated; three or four noblemen and women were seated with her, all of them members of the royal family. To speak of this scene of the event, the brushwork without pretense or ostentation, the facial features so lifelike, how could one know its price? A small German painting of a bust of a woman, only about two [Chinese] feet in area, carried an asking price of eight thousand dollars. There were far more than a hundred paintings of Washington among the pieces, though it was a French rendering of him on horseback that was the most riveting. I had heard that the Americans have an even better one though, unfortunately, I did not get to see it.[2] The various other countries all have a great many rare works, and it was nearly impossible to record them all.

According to those well versed in Western art, *yin* and *yang* [i.e., darkness and light, or light and shadow], details of perspective and

2. This may be a reference to the famous Gilbert Stuart portrait of Washington, which was on display in Memorial Hall.

depth, position and placement must each be considered in their turn and clearly defined in painting. Most of the works here are oil paintings done on canvas, though there are also some painted on paper. Viewed up close, the brushstrokes seem crude and disorderly, like chicken scratches, and the colors appear to jut out abruptly and unevenly. As the viewing distance is gradually increased, however, they become wonderfully lively and vibrant, and remarkably true to life. In painting noble women, depicting them as clothed is relatively easy, while nudes are especially difficult. This is because the flesh of the body, with its skin, muscles, bones, hidden girth, etc. must all be done with great care, and one's inadequacies [in terms of skill] cannot be concealed in the slightest. Carving stone and casting bronze statues demand similar levels of technique. Those entering these crafts of painting and sculpture certainly have no intention of making the nude display its inelegant aspects, and the works collected in this hall were fashioned entirely by the literati of various countries, idle craftsmen being incapable of producing them. The stone statues of Italy are particularly excellent, while the French and English are said to number among them the best painters.

A New
Account
of a Trip
Around
the Globe

127

CHAPTER 6. AGRICULTURAL HALL

Agricultural Hall is on the exposition's northern corner; its length given as 826 [English] feet and its width as 540. It is about 50 feet high with its four walls constructed of brick, above which is also glass, and cost three hundred thousand dollars. Its southeast [corner] is perhaps one li distant from the Main Building,[1] and it is one of the five halls. Every kind of tool for reclaiming wasteland, weeding fields, mowing crops, killing weeds, catching fish and seafood . . . [another thirty categories of tools and produce are listed here] has been prepared for inspection by experts in the field. Categories of items relating to food and drink are the most numerous, and, aside from coffee, all of them are things found in our country. As to the agricultural implements, no more than 10–20 percent are recent American inventions.

1. Li is apparently referring to one of the boulevards on the exposition grounds, Agricultural Avenue, which linked the corner of the Agricultural Hall to an entrance in the Main Building.

America's land is extensive and its population sparse. Thus, the business of agriculture could never succeed without utilizing the power of machines. I have examined these one by one, the majority of them being quite large and heavy. Nonetheless, how they are employed according to the requirements of the land, the businesses for which they are used, and the details of their operation have all been difficult to comprehend. The foreigners I questioned did not understand a great deal about them either, as they were not actually farmers and so had a limited knowledge of agriculture. As a result of this, I quite frankly have no way to describe their particulars. At present, there is a great deal of land remaining unreclaimed since the war [the Taiping Rebellion, 1851–64], a situation ideally suited to the use of such machines. Later, if we propose to reclaim the vast lands of the northwest, we should make a point of purchasing some for use in lieu of manpower. Conditions in Chinese and Western territories are not terribly different, and agriculture has always been China's most pressing need. To double the power and simplify the work, therefore, would be something the entire country would be sure to welcome. Here, although I have not been able to completely understand them, I have tried to ask the foreigners not just about the convenience and ingenuity of the machines, but especially, too, about their methods of cultivation and crop selection: How do they grow so abundantly? How can they be made to really thrive? How can we reduce the waste of chaff and bran husks? By comparing these things point by point, we could be certain of applying them in a productive manner. The people would then voluntarily seize the opportunity to compete with each other in following such an example, all as a consequence of this agricultural machinery. Thus, with agricultural machinery, we could indeed create a country without wasteland and a people without vagrants. The granaries would be full, and customs and teachings would grow more honest and sincere.[2] Japan has now

2. Cf. *Lunyu* (Analects), 13:9: Ranyu said: "The people having grown so numerous, what next should be done for them?" "Enrich them," was the reply. "And when one has enriched them, what next should be done?" Confucius said, "Educate them." Also, see *Mencius*, bk. I, pt. 1, chap. 7, line 24 (p. 149): "Let there not be taken away the time that is proper for the cultivation of the farm . . . and the family of eight mouths supported by it shall not suffer from hunger. Let careful attention be paid to education in the schools—the inculcation in it especially of the filial and fraternal duties, and grey-haired men will not be seen upon the roads, carrying burdens on their backs and heads."

purchased eighteen models of various machines, at a total cost of fifteen hundred dollars. I understand that in the northernmost territory of their four islands [Hokkaido], the climate is bitter cold in the winter. They want to increase the level of cultivation in the region, but the Japanese themselves are reluctant to settle there. They therefore have purchased these machines and plan to recruit Chinese laborers to come and reclaim the land. Obviously, these are issues to which they have devoted considerable attention.

A New
Account
of a Trip
Around
the Globe

129

The majority of items of food and drink that constitute the daily necessities of all Westerners are different in character from those consumed by Chinese. Nonetheless, the liquor is especially good and the finest grapes are fermented into wine. The white wines of Germany's Rhine River, France's champagnes and red wines, and Portugal's sherry, for example, have long been known in China. Their asking prices, however, are excessive, so they are not for drinking under everyday circumstances. The salt and sugar are pure, white, and fine, surpassing that produced in China, while things like butter, cheese, and coffee Chinese do not bother to ask about purchasing. Of the articles displayed in the Japanese exhibit, aside from fishing nets, wood blocks, tea, salted fish, rice, and salt, even the most trivial items without exception carried the five characters *quan ye liao chupin* ["an Industrial Promotion Board (*Kangyo Ryo*) product"].[3]

CHAPTER 7. HORTICULTURAL HALL

This hall was on the northwest corner of the exhibition grounds, and was 383 [English] feet long, 193 feet wide and cost three hundred thousand dollars. The construction methods employed made it bright and appropriate for flowers and plants, and its beauty was enhanced by carvings and ornamentation. There was a vacant area outside the entrance that followed the contours of the building. Dozens of plantings of different flowers just coming into bloom were set off by an abundance of green stalks, as if brocaded or

3. The Kangyo Ryo, or Industrial Promotion Board, was the initiative of then interior minister Okubo Toshimichi (1830–78). Its aim was to foster by governmental activism the coordinated development of the empire's domestic and export economy within the board's three divisions of Agriculture, Commerce, and Industry. Li's implicit comparison of this approach with China's halting efforts at increasing exports would likely not be lost on his readers.

painted, only even more gorgeous. The varieties, however, were not numerous, as only those most pleasing to the eye were selected.

A New
Account
of a Trip
Around
the Globe

130

Entering the center door, there was a large room called the Conservatory, translated as *Nuan ge* [Hothouse], its window arches all of glass. There was a pool below, in the center of which stood a bronze statue fifteen [Chinese] feet high. An apparatus of pipes was so arranged that water was drawn up from underneath the statue to its head, flowing continuously back down all around like pearl droplets.[1] Surrounding all were the flowers and plants and fruit trees of different countries, not less than several thousand varieties . . . [over a dozen are then listed] most of which I cannot name. Some had bright red stamens and pistils; some were beginning to flower; some beginning to bear fruit; some were overripe; and there also were some that were not terribly uncommon. Yet one did not see lotus or bamboo, which was a considerable omission. The four corners of the room all had small pools cut into them next to which were long benches set up for visitors to rest. On the south and north there were side rooms holding assorted delicate potted plants. A platform was built along the upper story running east and west for viewing from afar. Leaning on the balustrade and looking down from the center of the veranda was like entering a valley of ten thousand flowers. The flowers and plants of the entire room were presented to the eye below, and made for a wonderfully satisfying and pleasing sight. The rest of the rooms were mostly arranged with books on horticulture and implements for shading, protection, and irrigation. Outside the north end of the hall, there was a separately built room also holding many unusual varieties of flowers and plants.

There was also a special entrance for Western methods of cultivating flowers and grafting plants. The flowers that were not colorful were made so; blooms of one color were made to have many colors, all transformed by the use of chemicals and water. Sour fruits were made fragrant and sweet by means of grafting them to other trees. Those forming hard fruit also became spongy and crisp by being grafted to other trees. These secrets are assuredly difficult to fathom, but the wondrous transformation was certainly

1. This was the famous fountain designed by the American sculptor Margaret Foley.

real! Now, as with all the products displayed at the exhibit, these are continually being improved and refined.

CHAPTER 8. THE AMERICAN GOVERNMENT BUILDING

A New
Account
of a Trip
Around
the Globe

131

The Government Building was specially constructed to store and display the products of the various American states and territories, and also to act as a museum. It was to the north of Machinery Hall, perhaps five hundred feet in length and three hundred feet wide, and cost sixty thousand dollars to build. A large entrance faces the east. In front of the door are some pieces of dried [petrified] wood, enclosing an area of about thirty [Chinese] feet, and it is said that these were found along the shore and were many thousands of years old. Entering the door, on the left one encountered different models of historic weapons, guns, and ammunition through the years. All of them were individually marked for inspection, so that the strong points of the modern ones might be compared with those of older models. In back of these were miniature versions of naval vessels, sails, and lines, with their anchors and helms on display, also labeled for comparison through successive years. There were medical instruments, scalpels, and needles—perhaps several hundred kinds—as well as a number of medicines. Still further back were various foodstuffs.

Also on display were small models of assorted kinds of machines, all wonderfully nimble and ingenious. An American law [states]: Anyone among the people who has an original idea for building a machine must first construct a model and send it to officials for examination. If it proves truly useful, then [the inventor] is rewarded with much gold or a ceremonial plaque. He is also given a certificate granting him a monopoly on the profits from it for a certain time [i.e., a patent; this is the Patent Office exhibit] and prohibiting others from copying or counterfeiting it. These models are then stored in a government repository. I heard that recently, nearly five to six thousand people seek these patents in America every year, and year after year the number increases with no sign of letting up. No wonder such skillful machines emerge in an endless stream! And this is true not only of machines; writing a new book or discovering an effective medicine is handled in the same fashion. This law originated in England, with other countries closely following suit, and it has now been in effect for more than two hundred years . . .

A New
Account
of a Trip
Around
the Globe

132

A section follows detailing an exhibit of American food fishes preserved in a large ice cabinet.

Further back were the weapons of the red-skinned aborigines, their vessels and vehicles, headdresses and clothes, utensils, and images of their gods. These images were made of large logs, cut in half and carved into representations of demons [i.e., totem poles]. Each log had five or six images on successive levels, painted in many colors, and strange and ugly beyond description. Their clothes were made entirely of animal skins, with some also using fur and feathers in completing their dress. Their boats were made from hollowed-out tree trunks, while their knives, spears, bows and arrows resembled those of ancient China.

Further back was mining, with large pieces of iron as heavy as ten thousand catties. Connected to this was also a room for carvings, stone chips [i.e., quartz] used as material for glass, and a great lighthouse lens. The remaining space was filled with statues of famous generals, their attire and arms all appropriate to the period, and each one lifelike. There were also statues of the red-skinned aborigines, and their features are much like those of Chinese people. Their hair is also black, and worn draped over their backs or tied up in a bun on top of their heads like [a bunch of] drooping flowers.

In the northeast corner there was a square room used as a telegraph and post office for obtaining the news of different states. Nearby, an anemometer, rain gauge, thermometer, and barometer were set up, and the visitors pressed in close to see them. The head official and staff were affable and cordial. The one accompanying me was a member of the staff of the Judges Office, Mr. Fay[?].

CHAPTER 9. THE WOMEN'S PAVILION

The plans for the exposition had originally called for women's crafts to be displayed in the Main Building, rather than having a special hall constructed for them. The women of the entire country were dissatisfied with this, however, maintaining that it showed a light regard for the work of women, and thus for women themselves. As a result, they made plans to raise the funds required to build a separate hall that would showcase the works of women.

This building was to the east of Agricultural Hall, 192 [English] feet square in length and breadth, and surrounded by more than five *mou* [a bit less than an acre] of grounds. It was octagonal, resembling a tent, and had eight doors with a central pavilion rising to a height of eighty feet. The building's design was conceived by women, as was the superintending of its construction, its decoration, and the placement of the exhibits. [In conception and execution] it was entirely new, ingenious, and unusual, and cost a total of one hundred thousand dollars. Various kinds of books, paintings, maps, and needlework done by women, as well as the techniques of each craft and skill, were all collected and displayed here. In a separate room was an exhibit of school supplies and curricular materials for women. Even the personnel selected to staff the pavilion's exhibits were all women. I toured the entire building and saw works on astronomy, geography, science, and mathematics—as well as sewing and cooking—all displayed, and there were also a number of ingenious tools and implements. All of the staff were happy to answer my questions and did so tirelessly, with a poise and dignity completely unlike the demeanor of girls kept secluded in the home. On the contrary, they possessed a manly vitality, and I came to regard them with great respect and affection.

According to our Western friends accompanying us, the practice in the West is to consider men and women as equals, and to give women the same education as men. Hence, women are quite able to comment on important affairs and accomplish considerable feats. In the fifth month of this year [May 22–June 21, in 1876] a newspaper came out in which a woman noted, "All of the official positions in our country are occupied by men, and the president elected shortly will doubtless be a man as well. How is it that we women cannot also run for office? This is a grave injustice."[1] I have heard that in England there are also women who desire to enter

1. This is possibly a reference to local coverage of an upcoming conference to be held in the first week of July by the Women's Suffrage Association, with Julia Ward Howe, Lucy Stone, Susan B. Anthony, and Elizabeth Cady Stanton in prominent attendance. See *Philadelphia Inquirer* for June 16, 1876, 3. In the event, the convention met in Horticultural Hall and at the First Unitarian Church at Tenth and Locust Streets and produced a strongly worded "Women's Declaration of Rights" read at noon on July 4. *Philadelphia Public Ledger*, July 4, 1876.

A New
Account
of a Trip
Around
the Globe

133

A New
Account
of a Trip
Around
the Globe

134

Parliament and join in taking part in national affairs. Their arguments, though unprecedented, do seem justified. In recent years
schools for girls are to be found in all countries, without exception.
In English universities, men and women take examinations for
admission as equals, while in Germany education is compulsory
for girls as young as eight and their parents are held legally
accountable for compliance. In America there are perhaps three or
four million women teachers and students. These trends are developing day by day because of the desire to fully utilize the abilities
of women: Men and women are to be found in roughly the same
numbers throughout the world, so if only men are educated and
not women, then only half of the people will be useful. Women are
not inferior to men in intelligence. In fact, in some respects their
capabilities are superior to those of men, and their inner calm
allows them to concentrate without distraction. If their talents are
ultimately stifled from a lack of education and encouragement, is
this not a serious betrayal of Heaven's purpose in creating people?
In other countries, therefore, the births of both boys and girls are
treated as equally joyous occasions. In China, the situation is just
the opposite: The low regard in which women are held and the
drowning of infant girls can be stopped by neither law nor reason.
Why, in fact, is this so?

The answer, in my view, is that it is caused solely by the decline
of women's education. I note that officials in the Zhou dynasty
[1122–221 B.C.E.] included priestesses and women clerks, and Han
[202 B.C.E.–220 C.E.] regulations mandated that records be kept of
the imperial concubines. As for women's education, then, it was
made use of in the past. The names of learned women appear
among the *Tian Guan*'s [the Zhou dynasty's Ministry of State] inner
offices, and their virtue, words, magnanimity, and skills were
deservedly extensive. But these ancient positions do not accord
with the usages of later dynasties, which emphasized only the
teaching of elegant speech in women's education. Hence the *Yijing*
[*The Classic of Changes*] counsels high positions for them in the
inner precincts [of the court], the offices listed in the *Li Ji* [*The
Book of Rites*] include posts for women skilled in working with silk
and hemp, the verses of the *Chunqiu* [*Spring and Autumn Commentaries*] commend their services, and the *Xiaoya*'s [*Lesser Odes*]
words approve their opinions on food and drink. During the house

A New
Account
of a Trip
Around
the Globe

135

of Zhou's eastern sojourn [770–221 B.C.E.], the virtue of women was surely in decline.[2] Nevertheless, as with Jing Jiang ["Her Serenity," the title of Lady Ji] of Lu in her discussions on work and rest with her son, Earl Wen [Wen Bo], our former sages expressed an especially high regard for them. In the early Three Dynasties period [Xia, Shang, and Zhou, 2205–221 B.C.E.], then, women's learning flourished, but over the succeeding generations it gradually deteriorated. Now there is even a saying, "Only a woman without ability is virtuous." *Yi!* This one sentence is harmful to all women. Are their so-called abilities to consist of nothing more than composing and chanting frivolous poetry? If this is what is called "ability," they might just as well be without virtue. If we could reconstitute women's education so that all might study and develop their reason, the true path of women would be strengthened and their abilities would also be put to use. The tendency to discount their intelligence would then be remedied, and the custom of drowning infant girls would stop of its own accord.

As far as the views of the English and American women are concerned, however, they surely go too far. On this, my Western friends wholeheartedly agree.

CHAPTER 10. THE OFFICE OF THE EXHIBITION OFFICIALS [JUDGES HALL]

This office was well situated in the middle of the exhibition grounds and was 150 [English] feet deep, 115 feet broad, 34 feet high, and three stories tall. The building's prospects on all sides had flying turrets around which were flags, very grand in appearance, at a cost figured to be thirty thousand dollars. This is where the exposition's officials maintained their offices. A specially selected committee of two hundred natural scientists and learned men examined all the objects for their merits and defects and were grouped in twos and threes in each office. The top men selected from Philadelphia received a salary of six hundred dollars per month; those chosen from Pennsylvania and elsewhere received

2. The "surely" in this sentence is probably to emphasize that women must also have shared in the general ethical decline said to characterize the Eastern Zhou period within the *ru* tradition. Numerous examples of this perception may be found in the narratives of the *Chunqiu* and *Zuo Zhuan* (Commentary of Mr. Zuo).

one thousand dollars per month [i.e., salary plus living expenses]. The central gallery was 60 [English] feet deep by 80 wide. Above, there was a veranda, and below were arranged a number of long benches. All who wished to discuss exhibition matters, change the rules and regulations, explain or publicize affairs—even by means of using musical instruments and songs—could do so. There were long corridors on both sides leading to the back of the hall. These had police on duty at the doors, quite solemn and grave. I have listened to several piano performances here, and on the sixth day of the seventh month [August 24], I also met the president.[1]

A New
Account
of a Trip
Around
the Globe

136

1. The occasion for Li's meeting President Grant was a banquet thrown by the Centennial officials for the Chinese Education Mission students and a number of Japanese dignitaries and visitors. See chapter 17 for a full account.

BOOK II
Notes on Sightseeing

CHAPTER 11. THE AMERICAN CITY
OF PHILADELPHIA

America's richest and most populous areas are concentrated in its northeastern states. Within these, accordingly, are the three largest cities. The first is called "New York," the second, "Philadelphia," and the third, "Boston," and the prosperity of their trade and commerce follows in this order as well. As for the extent of their respective areas, number of multistory houses, and spaciousness of streets and boulevards, however, Philadelphia must take precedence. Furthermore, we can say that of the great cities of the globe, it ranks twelfth in size. In the second year of the reign of the Guangxu emperor [1876], which was the centenary of the founding of the American state, a great exposition was held in celebration of the event. The exposition was held in Philadelphia because when the decision was made to found the national state, this was the place where Washington formed his coalition [of the colonies] against England.

The city stands on the west bank of the Delaware River in the state of Pennsylvania, and its area is calculated at 426 square li.[1] Its harbor is accessible to the outside, enabling merchant ships to sail directly to the city. The roads and streets run north and south, and east and west, as straight as an arrow and from sixty or seventy to one hundred [Chinese] feet wide. In the center of the city is a

1. In 1876 the city's area was reckoned at 120 square miles, slightly smaller than Li's figure.

A New
Account
of a Trip
Around
the Globe

138

major avenue named *Boluo siteli,* which may be translated as
"Broad Street." It runs more than thirty li [ten miles] north to
south, and at a prominent place along it the office of Philadelphia's
mayor is under construction (a "mayor" is similar to the Chinese
position of *zhifu* [prefect]), grand and imposing in appearance, and
said to cost $1.5 million in gold.[2]

The streets are paved with cobblestones and incorporate within
them a system like that used for railroad cars, with level rails especially designed for use by horse trams. The edges of the streets are
slightly lower and lined with trees planted to block the wind and
provide shade, while pedestrians come and go entirely on generous brick sidewalks running along both sides. (The streets and
thoroughfares of Western countries are generally like this.) Multi-
level houses are built of red brick or stone, and are from two or
three to five or six stories tall. The bridges are mostly of fine ironwork, very solid and ingenious, some having a length of more than
a thousand [Chinese] feet, and a width of seventy to eighty. A particular bridge along *Zhierranger* [Girard Avenue] in the western
part of the city is considered to be exceptional in this regard. There
are perhaps a dozen railroad lines, some of which pass directly
through the city. Gazing upward, one sees electric wires on
wooden poles at every turn, almost too many to count, as each pole
has up to fifty or sixty wires hanging from it.

The climate of the area might best be summarized as *shanzuo,*
"east of the mountains" [i.e., the Taizhong Mountains; the climate
is similar to Shandong]: not too damp, with sandy soil and many
trees; a delightful place to live. The population is over 817,000, and
there are more than 151,000 homes. For the most part, the factories
and stores are located within the city, and Chestnut and Walnut
Streets enjoy a particularly brisk trade. More than three hundred
Chinese have also come here, engaging in laundry and cigar-mak-
ing businesses. Recently, a Cantonese man from San Francisco
named Zheng rented a room on Chestnut Street and opened a
shop selling Chinese goods. A Japanese man has also opened a
store.

Gas lighting and running water are supplied entirely by means

2. Still the nation's largest municipal building and, with its 510-foot tower, the tallest
masonry structure of its kind, Philadelphia City Hall faced endless delays over financing and obsolescent internal systems before its final completion in 1902.

of pipes winding all about beneath the city before emerging. The length of all the pipes is roughly calculated at more than two thousand li [about 670 miles].[3] Horse-drawn vehicles of all types are reckoned in the tens of thousands, and there are also what are called "streetcars" (the Western language pronounces this [*che*] as "car"), fashioned like rooms of perhaps twenty [Chinese] feet in length, five feet in width, and six feet in height. Both sides of the cars have long benches mounted underneath glass windows, and they can seat thirty people. Those used for the crowds at the exposition, with the cars filled to capacity inside and out [i.e., on running boards], can hold more than eighty people sitting and standing. Under each car are four wheels, and it is pulled along a track by a team of two horses, traveling a bit faster than an ordinary carriage. There is also a model that does not use horses but is instead propelled mechanically. Both inside and outside of the city these cars may be found at successive intervals on all the streets, so that regardless of the place or time, they are convenient to the people (Western countries all have them, but America's are the best and most numerous). Every ride costs only five to nine cents.

A New
Account
of a Trip
Around
the Globe

139

In the northwestern part of the city there is a huge park, called *Feima pake* [Fairmount Park] (*Pake* is translated as "park"), which, including both land and water, covers more than sixteen thousand *mou* [about 2,730 acres]. The exposition grounds are in its southern part. No other country has a park as large as this, and its luxurious copses of trees, winding river course, ponds, and pavilions are all laid out according to a design. It is intended as a place of relaxation for both officials and people, and the park grounds are patrolled by more than a hundred police. Taverns, restaurants, guesthouses, carriage houses, and stables have all been set up, and in the afternoon, the traffic flows in an endless stream. The majority of the visitors are women, mostly from rich and prominent families. Whether sitting on the ground chatting, or leaning on a railing gazing into the distance, or riding horses, playing ball, sailing small paddleboats, or rowing, everyone relaxes in his or her own fashion, all of it subsidized by the government. There is a zoo (called in the Western language a "zoological garden") nearby, with birds, sea

3. These estimates are essentially correct. An 1875 set of figures gives the mileage of the gas pipes laid beneath the streets as 600 with that of water mains as 546. See McCabe, *Illustrated History*, 29.

A New
Account
of a Trip
Around
the Globe

140

life, animals, insects—every kind of creature. For example, I saw
tigers, leopards, lions, elephants, bears . . . [a dozen other animals
are listed]. There was also a creature resembling an ass, essentially
white in color with black stripes, like those of a tiger [i.e., a zebra];
and one like a short spotted deer with its head as tall as twice the
length of its body (the Western language calls it a "giraffe," while
the *Yinghuan zhilue*[4] calls it *chang jing lu* [long-necked deer]); its
strength is astonishing. There are dozens of kinds of large and
small monkeys, and well over a hundred varieties of rare birds of
all gorgeous colors, as well as some that appear powerful and
extremely savage and hideous. There was also a large ostrich
weighing two hundred pounds. The price of admission is twenty-
five cents.

The thirteenth day of the intercalary fifth month of this year,
July 4 according to the Western calendar, is the day on which
Washington founded the nation. The evening before, at 7:30 P.M.,
the vice president and the mayor of Philadelphia attended a banquet with the exhibition officials of various countries, after which
they took carriages to sightsee. The lamps of all the streets and
thoroughfares lit up the heavens, and the sound of guns shook the
earth. There were hundreds of amusements on hand, and the
exploding fireworks and flags draped everywhere all contributed to
the festivities. Many hundreds of police were on hand to keep the
peace, marching in orderly ranks. The next three days saw similar
scenes of celebration, and it was undeniably a very grand affair.

For the occasion of this exhibition, the visitors from various
countries numbered tens of thousands per day. Though there were
a great many newly opened hotels, and many residents also rented
out rooms, there were still not enough accommodations for everyone. Consequently, there were some people who went to New York
City to find lodging, coming here in the morning and returning in
the evening. The distance to New York from Philadelphia is over
three hundred li [about one hundred miles], barely two hours by
train, so there was a constant stream of traffic to and from this center throughout the night. Simply because so many people stopped
here, the price of goods could not help becoming inflated, in some
cases to twice that of comparable items in Shanghai; in others, to
three, four, or even six or seven times as high. Since the residents

4. *A Brief Description of the Maritime Circuit,* by Xu Jiyu (1848, 1850).

could largely monopolize this traffic, they held their ground, not yielding an inch, and so were able to reap substantial profits along the way.

In the middle of the intercalary fifth month [early July] the weather was oppressively hot, with the thermometer going as high as 105 degrees [Fahrenheit]. Within a span of six days, 198 people came down with heatstroke, and the horses felled could not even be counted. Every afternoon there was certain to be a large thunderstorm, and buildings were damaged by lightning. It cooled down somewhat during the rain, but within an hour or two of when the showers stopped the heat returned.[5] By the first month of autumn, it becomes cool enough to live indoors; before midautumn, people wear heavy cotton clothes and some even gather around the stove; by about the ninth [Chinese] month, the trees have all lost their leaves and one already sees huge snowflakes . . .

A New
Account
of a Trip
Around
the Globe

141

In the section following, Li accepts an invitation from Philadelphia mayor William Strumberg Stokely to visit the House of Correction, an institution for youth and light offenders opened in 1874 near the Pennypack Creek in what is now Northeast Philadelphia. His impressions of the facility in terms of its cleanliness, order, and intent to reform the inmates closely parallel the ones below of the famous Eastern State Penitentiary.

Pennsylvania has two prisons for serious offenses, one in Philadelphia and the other in Pittsburgh. Upon conviction, those whose sentences range from more than a year to several years, decades, or even life, are all sent to these two prisons. On the twenty-first day of the sixth month [August 10, 1876], accompanied by a Western friend named [John] Welsh [?],[6] I went to visit the

---

5. Along with events at the Centennial and the battle at the Little Bighorn, the record heat dominated Philadelphia news coverage. See for example the *Philadelphia Inquirer* for July 10 and 11. Among other things it was reported that there were 176 infant deaths in the city due to temperatures of 102 and 103 degrees for July 9 and 10, respectively.

6. Li's transliteration of this name is *Weiersi,* for which a good possibility would be John Welsh, a Philadelphian and head of the Centennial Board of Finance. Unfortunately, the guest registers of the prison only go up to 1854, and the "Warden's Daily Journal" and "Minutes of the Board of Inspectors and Board of Trustees" in the Pennsylvania State Archives do not contain any entries for Li's visit. See Record Group 15, Series 15.50 and 15.44.

A New
Account
of a Trip
Around
the Globe

142

prison in Philadelphia [Eastern State Penitentiary] and record
some of the things I saw and heard there.

The area of the prison grounds is more than fifty *mou* [7.6 acres]
and bounded by a thirty-foot stone wall, very strong and solid.
Entering the main gate, there is a set of iron rails laid for the horse
trams used in transporting prisoners under guard. There are doors
on both sides for the warden's office and living quarters, and a
small garden outside with an abundance of flowers and plants. The
warden, Mr. [Edward] Townsend,[7] greeted us, and we entered and
sat for a bit. He then led us back the way we came, and we passed
through two doors. First on the left is a room where the prisoners'
registers are kept, listing assorted information on the number of
offenses, names, places of birth, year, appearance, addresses, and
so forth. Looking over the books for several years, the [inmates']
occupational preferences, family circumstances, and reasons for
conviction and sentencing can be traced over time. There is also a
book in which all visitors, men or women, regardless of their status
as officials or private persons, must first record their names at the
start of the tour (in Western countries, regardless of whether it is a
palace, official building, factory, or famous place of any sort, all visitors must give their names on entering). After recording all of our
names, Mr. Townsend accompanied us as we entered a courtyard
lush with flowers and plants and followed a path shaded by trees.
In the middle of the grounds, a large building rises up like a tower.
It is three stories tall, and appears to have seven sides, each of
which has a door, with a single door on the outside for entrance
and exit. The six remaining inside doors all open onto long corridors lined with cells as far as the eye can see.

Every corridor is connected to thirty or forty cells, each of which
has a door with a wooden sign indicating the prisoner's number.
Mr. Townsend led us on a special visit to one of the cells, as the
prisoners were just then at work. Every one is eleven feet deep and
six feet wide, with a floor of wooden boards. They are furnished
with a bed, table, toilet, work tools, a register for warm air (in
Western countries, when circumstances prevent the use of stoves
throughout large buildings, many have a main furnace in the basement, with iron registers mounted in the wall spaces of the rooms,

7. Edward Townsend was the warden of Eastern State Penitentiary from 1870 until
1881.

and warm air is blown in by means of a rotary fan. In the summer the furnace is shut off and there is another large rotary fan that draws warm air out from all the registers; because of this they are also called "ventilators"),[8] a water tap and a gas lamp. The lamp's jet and chimney are inside the cell, but the thumbscrew used to adjust the gas is on the outside wall. The reason for this is that in the evening there is a fixed time at which the lights must be put out, and the prisoners are not permitted to do this themselves. At the top of the cell there is a window, which admits a good deal of light [the "God's Eye"], and in the rear, a door. Passing through the door, one finds a bit of ground, five or six feet wide, with flowers and plants. Every day the inmates must go into this area and march at the half-step for forty-five minutes for their exercise. The four walls of stone and the windows of iron certainly guard against escape, and it is calculated that the six corridors have a total of 580 identical cells, each holding one prisoner. The women inmates are on an upper level.

Of the articles they make, like wooden furniture, leather goods, clothing, sewing, and so forth, there is a fixed amount to be completed every day, and the current price varies according to official costs. If production exceeds the quota, the workers whose additional labor resulted in the increase have half the value of the overage returned to the public funds of the places where their offenses were committed, and the other half earns interest from the prison administration against the day when their sentences are completed and they become eligible to receive the accumulated amount. In the case of those incarcerated for life, the money goes to their dependents. As for items requiring the work of two men, since each cell has only one inmate, a prisoner is brought under guard from another cell in the morning and returned in the evening. During these transfers, a cloth covers his face and he is not allowed to see anyone in order to preserve his anonymity. In all of this their [the prison authorities] purpose is quite generous. On first entering

A New
Account
of a Trip
Around
the Globe

143

8. While Li is correct in his overall description of the use of forced hot air systems in Western buildings, the registers at Eastern State were strictly ventilators by the time of his visit. The original heating system had employed stoves installed below the corridors with convection ducts mounted in the cells. These had not only proved inefficient but also subjected some of the prisoners to carbon monoxide poisoning. Within a decade of the prison's opening, a pressurized hot water system with radiator pipe loops in the cells was installed. Johnston, *Eastern State Penitentiary*, 43.

A New
Account
of a Trip
Around
the Globe

144

the institution, those unable to work are required to learn, while those who are frail are enabled to master light skills that they would otherwise find too strenuous. Every day there are three meals: breakfast, consisting of a cup of coffee and a piece of bread; a lunch of meat soup, a piece of beef (or mutton or pork; each in turn at regular intervals), more bread, and vegetables; and a cup of tea and a piece of bread for dinner. Everything is spotlessly clean, and no stale or spoiled food is reused in their meals for fear of illness.

On the second floor of the central building there is a library of more than nine thousand books. The librarians are all prisoners, as are those who do the binding and repairs. A catalog of the library's books has been compiled, and each of the prison cells is provided with a copy. A certain number prisoner desiring a particular book writes its title down on a strip of wood and, having first obtained the library's permission to take it out, receives it in the course of several days. The book must then be returned on the due date. The third floor serves as a spacious chapel where the clergy preach and read [Scripture] to reform the inmates. As for the various kinds of rooms for the staff, guards, and workers, and the huge kitchen, bathhouses, and toilets, all are spotlessly clean. In the rear of the kitchen, a kind of machine is installed that provides all the milled grain, cooked vegetables, and hot tea, in addition to supplying warm air [sic] to all the heating registers.

A person standing in the middle of the tower building has a complete view of all seven sides [from which the corridors of cell-blocks radiate]. In the evening the bright lights on the buildings illuminate everything like the day. Because of this, among the several hundred rooms in the complex, this building is considered the control center.

I consider foreign prisons to be completely unlike those in China. In the first place, there is a desire for cleanliness; in the second, the food and drink are well balanced; third, work and rest are appropriately regulated; fourth, there are opportunities for learning a craft; finally, the warden and staff show consideration in every way for the condition of the men, like a father and elder brothers to sons and younger brothers [i.e., as within the Five Relationships of Confucianism]. As a result, not only do all the visitors among them not feel as if they are in a prison, but even those incarcerated for a long time tend to forget the fact of their confinement.

By his appointed release date, the inmate has acquired a craft or has some money saved and is completely able to arrange for the support of himself and his family, perhaps even passing it [the money] on to his sons and grandsons. This is the utmost in admirable laws and generous intentions. If such practices resemble anything, it is in regarding a prison as something akin to a Buddhist monastery.[9] Still, we must also observe how they adapt such methods to circumstances. The essential point is the goal of not demeaning human life, which necessarily facilitates harmony and cooperation and eliminates petty squabbles and disagreements. As the hearts of others display repentance and reform, one's own spontaneously does so as well. A Westerner asked me: "How do you find the criminal law of foreign countries?" I replied: "Actually, the laws are most admirable and quite generous in intent, but are they not perhaps a bit too lenient?" He answered: "This is true. However, we Westerners seek comfort and fear the anxiety and depression of confinement. For example, the men we see here in prison have already shown extreme cruelty to others. Even those condemned for capital offenses, however, are merely imprisoned, which depresses their will and ambition. By allowing them to have some happiness grow in their hearts though still depressed at their confinement, one may then hope that they will repent and reform. We Westerners also have a very fierce nature, and in cases where inmates are shackled for fighting, they must then spend the rest of their sentences in chains." Thus, the punishment of criminals in foreign countries is indeed bound, to some extent, to be lenient . . .

Following this visit, Li made an excursion to the Educational Home for "orphan and destitute children of all creeds,"[10] which occasioned another meditation on Western institutions devoted to the

9. Interestingly, Norman Johnston's history of Eastern State makes exactly the same point:

A British prison administrator [Alexander Paterson] once likened a prison to "a monastery inhabited by men who do not choose to be monks." Eastern State Penitentiary was intended by its creators to operate in many ways like a monastery, and most certainly the prisoners were there unwillingly. (*Eastern State Penitentiary,* 47)

See also Wang Tao's notes on foreign prisons, which bear a close resemblance to Li's comments. Cohen, *Between Tradition and Modernity,* 128–29.

10. James Laughery Paul, *Pennsylvania Soldiers' Orphans Schools* (Harrisburg: Lane S. Hart, 1877), "Educational Home."

A New
Account
of a Trip
Around
the Globe

146

"people's livelihood." This was followed by visits to area medical facilities.

There is an institution for the mentally ill [the Pennsylvania Hospital for the Insane, founded in 1841] about ten li to the west of Philadelphia. Mr. Welsh, a Western friend accompanying our party, explained: "Thirty-five years ago, the mentally ill were all sent to a hospital in the city [Pennsylvania Hospital] to recuperate alongside the [physically] sick. Their hands and feet were shackled and they were not permitted even the slightest movement. The medications were also not as yet effective. Those who recovered, therefore, were comparatively few. From discussions among the gentry and people, it was felt that the well-being of the mentally ill had long since been compromised by shackling them and housing them with patients suffering physical ailments. Moreover, because they continued to be infected by others day after day, with illness compounding illness, it was not surprising that the medicines had little effect. A suitable place would have rooms to provide security for their persons. With their hands and feet free, their vigor would return. By seeing famous doctors, the origins of their illnesses could be explored. With many kinds of flowers, plants, and trees, their hearts and minds would be gladdened and refreshed. Finally, by carefully selecting intelligent people to attend them, they would be protected from their own unpredictable behavior. In cases of extreme illness, only the patients' hands would be manacled and they would be confined to their rooms, after which they would be provided with food and drink containing medicine so as to put their minds in order. They could then be led, and by being induced to conform by such means, gradually recover and return home one day, considered by all to be well. For those who would not ultimately recuperate, it would be even more appropriate to have compassion on them and allow them to live here in security for the rest of their lives."

Consequently, they selected a place to the west of the city and constructed buildings to house both male and female mental patients. Bearing in mind the unhealthy conditions under which men and women had been treated together in the city hospital, they constructed a separate building for the men [in 1859], while the women occupied the original building, and the combined institution was named the [Pennsylvania] Hospital for the Insane. The grounds encompass more than three hundred *mou* [about forty-five acres], with the buildings occupying about one-tenth of the area and the remainder devoted entirely to gardens and surrounded on all sides by trees. Entering the main gate, one sees trees, plants, and flowers winding all around, growing everywhere. A square pool is situated in the middle of the grounds, with pure refreshing water. Carriages [entering the grounds] travel about two hundred paces before arriving at the entrance to the buildings.

Inside the doors one finds a doctor's office, guest room, and cafeteria on the left, while to the right are a library, music room, and pharmacy. Further back, there are doors on both sides, and a corridor two hundred [English] feet long and twelve feet wide runs all along the inside. The doors of twenty-eight individual rooms face each other along it: Seventeen of them are the bedrooms of mental patients, twelve feet high, nine feet wide, and eleven feet deep; four are the living quarters of the attendants, and so on; the other seven function as a library, music room, a room for reading newspapers, and bathing and dining areas. The bedrooms are furnished with a bed, table, chair, and chamber pot, and there is a window in the rear with its panes protected on the inside by iron grillwork. Outside the window is a bright and tidy garden. There are also larger separate rooms, as well as doubles, which open in the center to become generous apartments, complete with a variety of cabinets, chairs, *kang* [Chinese heated beds], curtains, and screens for the wealthy and important patients. All together there are sixteen corridors and 560 rooms, all laid out in identical style.

The patients come to the asylum by carriage, its doors tightly secured, and are stopped on arrival at the gate. They are examined there by the doctors, who question them about the circumstances of their individual illnesses and record their findings. After the severity of their ailments has been ascertained, the patients are sent to the appropriate corridor and room for their individual problems. Initially, three months' room and board is collected. The wealthy pay more and the poor less—or not at all. On recovering, the patients may not be released until their families or neighbors furnish a guarantee to assist them. The asylum has three doctors, and one among them is selected to act as the director. The other staff and workmen number no less than sixty or seventy peo-

A New
Account
of a Trip
Around
the Globe

147

A New
Account
of a Trip
Around
the Globe

148

ple. The basement is given over to a large machine upon which they rely for grinding grain for bread, cooking meals, drawing water, washing clothes, ventilation, and warm air heating. The area in back of the asylum is wooded with a separate large gate through which one enters the women's asylum. This is identical to the men's in number and style of rooms and in its overall scheme. Aside from the doctors, all of its personnel are women. The two institutions jointly select an individual to superintend who conducts an inspection once every week. The total cost of purchasing the land and constructing the buildings, landscaping, and buying machinery came to about one million dollars, which was donated by wealthy and charitable patrons.[11] The annual operating expenses for both asylums come to about two hundred thousand dollars, the majority of it from wealthy contributors who have been treated for illness at the hospital. At the appointed date at the end of every year, the superintendent must report on the annual revenues and expenditures, the number of patients entering and leaving, their different illnesses, and the complete circumstances of those presently in the hospital. These reports are all collected into a book and a number of copies are printed and submitted to the national leadership and local officials and notables. Visitors coming to the hospital for a tour are also sent a copy to examine in order to prepare for their inspection of the institution. (In Western countries, every government office and business office must publish these facts for the public to see at a certain time at the end of every year.)

Li somewhat abruptly switches his narrative from the Hospital for the Insane to the nearby Almshouse complex.

The chief physician [of the Philadelphia Almshouse and Municipal Hospital], Dr. [Francis Fontaine] Maury, possesses extraordinary medical abilities. His skills are imbued with a humanity[12] that

11. McCabe put the cost at eight hundred thousand dollars. *Illustrated History*, 121.

12. Li here uses the all-important Confucian term *ren*, usually rendered as "humanity" or "humaneness." The previous line says, literally, ". . . excels all others in the attainments of the *Qihuang* [a legendary medical treatise]." Francis Fontaine Maury (1840–79) trained at Philadelphia's Jefferson Medical College, served as an Army surgeon during the Civil War, and for several years was renowned as editor of *The Photographic Review of Medicine and Surgery*. He was also the distant cousin of Matthew

Inaugural ceremonies at the Centennial, Memorial Hall, May 10, 1876. (Courtesy of Free Library of Philadelphia, Print and Picture Collection, Centennial Digital Collection no. c030356.)

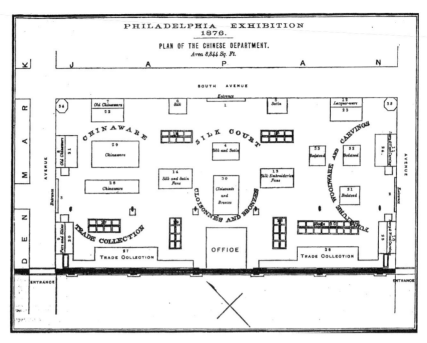

"Plan of the Chinese Department, Main Hall, Philadelphia Centennial Exhibition." (Catalog of the Chinese Imperial Maritime Customs at the United States International Exhibition, Philadelphia, 1876.)

Pailou, or ceremonial gateway, to the main entrance of the Chinese exhibit. The three large characters read, "The Country of the Great Qing." The Silk Court is immediately behind the gate, while hangings from the Japanese exhibit may be seen to the left rear. (Courtesy of the Free Library of Philadelphia, Print and Picture Collection, Centennial Digital Collection no. c020617.)

Carved bedstead, furniture, and screens at the Chinese Centennial exhibit
in the Main Building. Li reported that foreign observers were awestruck
at the intricacy and detail that marked the objects in the Chinese display,
proclaiming that their ingenuity "surpasses even that of the Westerners."
(Courtesy of Free Library of Philadelphia, Print and Picture Collection, Centennial
Digital Collection no. c021384.)

Japanese Centennial Exhibit, front entrance. As were most visitors, Li was
impressed by the orderliness, craftsmanship, and taste of the Japanese
exhibit, though he was less taken with their Western-influenced dress and
products. (Courtesy of Free Library of Philadelphia, Print and Picture Collection,
Centennial Digital Collection, no. c02247.)

709—CORSETS—ENGLAND

"Thomson's Patent Glove-Fitting Corsets." The display of women's foundation garments at the British exhibit in the Main Building had momentarily baffled Li until a solicitous staff member explained to him the function of various items. On realizing the details of their restriction and enhancement of women's bodies, he pronounced them as much a form of torture as footbinding in China.
(Courtesy of Free Library of Philadelphia, Print and Picture Collection, Centennial Digital Collection, no. c020709.)

Peruvian mummies and pottery (stereograph). The displays of Chile and Peru in the Main Building were nearby the Chinese section, and Li felt their objects to be of some archaeological interest. Unfortunately, the staff members on scene were unable to answer his questions about the methods involved in the mummification process. (Courtesy of Free Library of Philadelphia, Print and Picture Collection, Centennial Digital Collection, no. co62216.)

Exterior view of the Women's Pavilion. Li was much impressed by the unique architecture and innovative concepts embodied in the display of women's accomplishments at the exposition. This view is taken from the grounds of the American Government Building, with its 20-inch Rodman gun in the foreground. (Courtesy of Free Library of Philadelphia, Print and Picture Collection, Centennial Digital Collection, no. co11625.)

The Corliss engine, Machinery Hall. The largest and most powerful mover of its day, the 1,400-horsepower Corliss was the centerpiece of the Hall's impressive technological display. It powered nearly all the machines in the building, and its enormous size and futuristic lines made it the most recognized symbol of the exhibition. Li periodically watched transfixed as it sprang to life and operated smoothly and silently for several hours each day. (Courtesy of Free Library of Philadelphia, Print and Picture Collection, Centennial Digital Collection, no. co24020.)

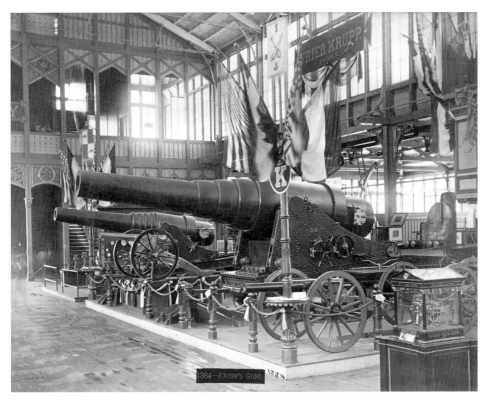

Krupp's "killing machines." Unlike the largely cultural display of books, paintings, maps, and musical instruments in the German exhibit in the Main Building, the 13.85- and 9-inch guns on display in Machinery Hall projected an air of menacing technical perfection. Like most other visitors, Li was taken aback by the size and capabilities of these weapons. Ironically, Krupp could not find a buyer for the larger gun and presented it as a gift to the Ottoman Sultan Abdul Hamid II (1842–1918) at the close of the Centennial. (Courtesy of Free Library of Philadelphia, Print and Picture Collection, Centennial Digital Collection, no. co21384.)

Frederic Bartholdi's "Liberty's" hand and torch. These first completed elements of the Statue of Liberty, billed as "Bartholdi's Electric Light," were erected at the Centennial to generate interest and funds for the project. Strangely, given its prominence and outlandish appearance, the structure escaped comment in Li's account, as did another exhibit made famous at the exposition—Alexander Graham Bell's telephone. (Courtesy of Free Library of Philadelphia, Print and Picture Collection, Centennial Digital Collection, no. co12025.)

"Headquarters of the Women's Centennial Executive Committee, 903 Walnut St. Mrs. E. D. Gillespie Receiving Reports from Subcommittees." (Centennial Exhibition, 1876 Philadelphia Scrapbook. Courtesy of Free Library of Philadelphia, Print and Picture Collection, Centennial Digital Collection, no. c180430.)

Interior of the Women's Pavilion. Li found his docents forthright, patient, and well informed and used the occasion of his visit to survey what he considered to be the sorry trend of women's education in China. (Courtesy of Free Library of Philadelphia, Print and Picture Collection, Centennial Digital Collection, no. c010747.)

Broadway and Twenty-third Street, looking north, ca. 1890. The large building in the foreground with the porticoed entrance is the Fifth Avenue Hotel, where Li stayed during his visit to New York City. (Collection of the New-York Historical Society.)

Centennial skyline from the Girard Avenue Bridge. Li's survey of notable Philadelphia sights included a description of this structure, considered by many to be the finest bridge of its type. The outlines of the towers on the Main Building and the dome of Memorial Hall may be seen on the hill across the Schuylkill River. (Courtesy of Free Library of Philadelphia, Print and Picture Collection, Centennial Digital Collection, no. c180020.)

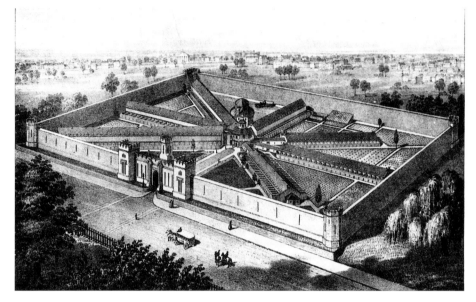

Eastern State Penitentiary. A bird's-eye view by Samuel Cowperthwaite, "convict no. 2954," April 1856. Unlike some observers, most notably Charles Dickens, Li found the silence and solitary confinement employed at the prison to be liberal and generous, a treatment "akin to a Buddhist monastery." (S. P. Duval Co., Courtesy of the Library Company of Philadelphia.)

"Panoramic View of New York City, Lower Manhattan from Brooklyn Bridge, 1876." Li was astonished at the sight of the main piers of the bridge under construction and likened them to mountains rising from the water. Third of five photographs by Joshua H. Beal. (Collection of the New-York Historical Society.)

MANDARIN YUNG WING.

"Mandarin Yung Wing," from *Harper's Weekly*, May 18, 1878. Li had found Yung an imposing man during his visit two years earlier and felt that China's fortunes overseas would be well served by such people. Though Yung and Chen Lanbin had been appointed assistant minister and minister to the United States, Spain, and Peru, respectively, Chen's participation in treaty negotiations with Spain concerning the ending of the coolie trade to Cuba delayed his arrival until the summer of 1878. Wood engraving, artist unknown; from sketches by Theodore R. Davis. (Connecticut Historical Society, Hartford.)

Yung Wing and his students, sometime in the late 1870s. From left to right, Woo Kee Tsao, Yang Chan Ling, Yung Wing, and Woo Yang Tsang. Woo Kee Tsao had arrived with the fourth group of students in 1875 and later became a naval officer; Yang, identified in the photograph as having come with the second group two years earlier, had in fact arrived with the third group in 1874; he later became a railroad official. Woo Yang Tsang, in the first group of 1872, subsequently had a career as a mining engineer. Though posed here uncharacteristically in full Chinese dress, when Li met the boys at the Centennial their outfits consisted of Chinese jackets worn over American-style shirts and trousers. Yung Wing himself avoided Chinese dress whenever he could, calling his ceremonial wear "grotesque habillements." For the careers of the students, see Thomas LaFargue, *China's First Hundred* (Pullman: Washington State University Press, 1941; reprint, 1987), 173–76. (Connecticut Historical Society, Hartford.)

THE COLLEGE.

"The College," Yung Wing's school, *Harper's Weekly*, May 18, 1878. Plans for
the larger and more elegant Chinese Education Mission building were already
approved and construction begun at 400 Collins Street when Li traveled to
Hartford in early September 1876. He seemed fully satisfied that the new
building designed by Yung would, in addition to providing improved facilities
for the boys, express more completely China's "national dignity." Wood
engraving, artist unknown; from sketches by Theodore R. Davis.
(Connecticut Historical Society, Hartford.)

Park Row, Printing House Square and Chatham Street, looking north, summer 1877 or 1878. From right to left are the buildings of the *New York Times,* the *Tribune* (with the clock tower), the *Sun,* and the *Staat-Zeitung.* Li toured the *Sun*'s complex and talked for several hours with publisher Moses Sperry Beach. (Collection of the New-York Historical Society.)

The Praya, Hong Kong harbor, 1873. Li felt Hong Kong's waterfront, with its godowns and residences climbing the adjacent hills, resembled the scales of a fish. The large building in the center of the picture is the complex of the opium firm of Dent and Company. (John Thomson, *Illustrations of China and Its People* [London: S. Low, Marston, Low, and Searle, 1874; reprint, New York: Dover, 1982], vol. 1, plate 6.)

proceeds from a profound generosity of spirit, and his colleagues cannot but praise his service. He accompanied me on my tour of the hospital. This hospital, he said, is the largest of its kind in the world. In Austria there is also a large institution in the capital, but it is not quite the equal of this one. The patients here ordinarily number more than four thousand, all of whom are poor, and all the medicine and provisions come entirely from public funds. The staff members are extremely attentive, and the bedding in the rooms is all spotlessly clean. Patients suffering from external ailments are in the majority, and many of those beginning the practice of medicine come to this hospital in order to see a variety of diseases.[13] The specified number of doctors is thirty, and they see the patients every day. Every three days, he [the chief physician] must pay a visit to examine and diagnose all of the most difficult cases, discussing the circumstances of each in turn, and allowing the group to benefit from his medical expertise. There was a case of bladder stones (Chinese people are not susceptible to this disease, though Westerners are very much so; the former French emperor Napoleon [III] died from it), and through an incision made below the kidney, they entered and extracted them with iron forceps. With the application of medicine, the incision was then closed to heal. There was also a man who had injured his thighbone, completely shattering it inside. They first placed a hand towel soaked in medicinal liquid on his face, and he gradually fell asleep, snoring thunderously. Using a scalpel to cut him open, they removed the shattered bone—which was very large—and then

A New
Account
of a Trip
Around
the Globe

149

Fontaine Maury, oceanographic pioneer, a founder of the U.S. Naval Observatory, and Confederate naval hero. "John Minor Maury," in *Appleton's Encyclopedia*, online version http://famousamericans.net/johnminormaur, pp. 5–6.

13. The Philadelphia Almshouse, or Blockley Hospital, as it was sometimes called, was located in the late nineteenth century in West Philadelphia near the Hospital for the Insane and the University of Pennsylvania, and was one of the oldest charity institutions in the country. It was administered by the Guardians of the Poor, who also ran the city's municipal clinics and handled the distribution of food, clothing, and shelter to the area's indigent. In 1865, a separate Municipal Hospital was opened for the treatment of contagious diseases, and in 1874, the House of Correction was opened with its own medical facilities for vagrants and light offenders. F. F. Maury was the chief surgeon of the Almshouse from 1865 to 1878, replacing the world famous Samuel D. Gross, the subject of the Thomas Eakins painting, *The Gross Clinic*. See Charles Lawrence, *History of the Philadelphia Almshouses and Hospitals* (Philadelphia: Charles Lawrence, 1905; Arno reprint, 1976), 280, 281, 295.

A New
Account
of a Trip
Around
the Globe

150

applied the medicine. With the procedure concluded, the patient regained consciousness painlessly.

Western medical studies constitute a most excellent curriculum, and also a most demanding one. From fear that inadequate skills might jeopardize the lives of patients, the students must first be examined on the structure of the body, the arteries and veins, internal organs, and so forth, and understand these thoroughly before they may go into practice. The physicians of the entire city, together with the notables and people of the region, publicly selected Dr. Maury's staff. The hospital's annual operating budget comes to six hundred thousand dollars, a great deal of which is supplied by the contributions of the wealthy and generous. Not only does Dr. Maury not take a medical fee, but he also donates money to the hospital, which is something especially rare. To this one can only sigh in admiration the phrase, "work together for humaneness and longevity" [*gong deng ren shou*], a sentiment the entire world cannot but share. If we are to succeed in applying it to our own country, then the many capable people who would administer such ventures and the wealthy and generous who would donate their funds must honestly and wholeheartedly show sympathy and consideration in designing and carrying out their plans. We must restrain those merely seeking fame from participating in order to have a proper selection of candidates, and as the injured, suffering, and dying among the people are sure to be helped, perhaps our gentle village doctors will not be completely without such men. Maybe then the world's great hope of uniting in cooperation for humaneness and longevity could truly be said to not be in vain.

The [U.S.] Mint is on Chestnut Street, and the building is quite large. On the twenty-first day of the seventh month [September 8], I accompanied my Western friend Mr. Knight to see the techniques involved in the coining of money. On arrival, a man delivered our names on a piece of paper to request a visit with the superintendent, Mr. [James] Pollack, who was out on business.[14]

14. James Pollack was director of the Mint from 1861 to 1866 and, after duty at the Treasury Department in the intervening years, became superintendent at Philadelphia in 1869. He served until 1879. While Li does not mention names, his docents at the mint may have included the assayer, William E. DuBois, the chief clerk, H. C. Hickock, or the coiner, Louden Snowden.

The man there knew of our coming and sent a member of the staff to lead us around and direct our attention to various things. Arriving at the first location, we saw vast quantities of gold and silver. There were perhaps thirty or forty pieces of gold about five [Chinese] inches long, two inches wide, and one inch thick [i.e., ingots], every one worth fifty-five hundred dollars. The silver pieces were eight inches long, three inches wide, and two inches thick, and there were about two hundred of these, each worth fifteen hundred dollars—the value of the bullion being subject to daily fluctuations. Placed nearby were scales of matchless precision, capable of weighing objects from the tiniest grains all the way up to several thousand ounces. It was said that the gold and silver here comes entirely from places in Nevada, California, and so forth, and one can plainly see that the mines of these two states are certainly flourishing.

Moving on, we entered a room used for smelting. There are iron furnaces arranged separately in two rows, and these are about five [Chinese] feet square. The melting vats are made of plaster and resemble soup cauldrons. The small ones are like cups and are used to take the molten metal from the vats and pour it into iron molds. The molds are eight [English] inches long, three inches wide, and seven-tenths of an inch thick, and their centers are made in the shape of a mortise. Every group of four molds is joined together and sheathed in an iron cage held together by screws. The silver is poured in and then [after cooling] the screws are loosened and the silver comes out of the mold as two ingots, seven inches long, eight-tenths of an inch wide, and three-tenths thick, and these are called "blank strips." Next we went to a room where copper was melted. In terms of their present relative value, the need for silver coins is most widespread and thus the production of gold and copper had been suspended and the workers were making only silver coins.

The blank strips are all returned to a room of machinery in which they are pressed into finished [planchet] strips. In the middle of these devices two steel shafts are mounted vertically, as thick as huge cups, alongside of which are large wheels. The blank strips are milled between the two shafts while the action of the wheels passes the finished strips through, which are now two to three [Chinese] feet long and the width and thickness of a coin. They

A New
Account
of a Trip
Around
the Globe

151

A New
Account
of a Trip
Around
the Globe

152

then enter a machine [the drawing table] that presses and smoothes them, making them straight and even, and perfectly regular in thickness and width. Small round pieces are then repeatedly cut from them called "coin blanks" at a rate of 160 a minute. Another machine run by a women worker places them edgewise into what appear to be small cylindrical rolls. The blanks all have a blue-black color to them and so are first placed on an iron screen and immersed in a chemical bath and washed until they shine. Then they go into a machine that stamps the blanks. This device is made of pure steel and is four [Chinese] feet high, round on top and square below. In the middle two steel dies have been set up directly opposite each other above and below. The designs of the imprints are carved on the dies, as both sides of the coins have artwork on them. There is a copper tube about four inches high in front of the dies, underneath which is a set of copper [actually steel] tongs ["feeders"]. A woman worker sits at the machine and places the piles of coin blanks into the tube, and by the action of the machine, each blank drops into the opening of the tongs, is placed between the dies, and simultaneously stamped from above and below. The coins emerge and accumulate in a space below the dies, and the machine can make 80 coins per minute. For the smaller denominations of coins, this type of method is even faster and can produce 120 coins per minute. The techniques employed in minting gold and copper coins are like this as well.

After the coins are finished, they are arranged on wooden [counting] boards and counted and boxed. Under the boards there is also a machine. Those [coins] of slightly inferior quality fall through holes under the boards to be remelted. The silver blank strips from which coin blanks have been cut, each one with round holes, are stored in cabinets. At the end of the day, they take the strips out and count the holes and therefore know the amount of the day's finished coinage, and the next day the strips are remelted. The floor of the smelting room is laid with iron strips, giving it a rough, grainy appearance, with every piece about a foot square and an inch thick through the middle. Shards of broken metal lost below are fished out and separately appraised. Every year these metal scraps yield about ten thousand ounces of silver. I had previously asked them whether this material was not as valuable as that which is melted in the furnace. They replied that the dust that sticks to it makes it of indifferent quality and requires a separate process to completely extract it, and this facility does not have the free time to do so. For myself, I had assumed that Western coins must have been made by melting gold and silver and pouring it into molds, just like the casting of copper cash in China. Now having seen this, I realized I had been grossly mistaken . . .

This is followed by a brief section on the chemical extraction of gold, silver, and copper residues.

A New
Account
of a Trip
Around
the Globe

153

Next to this [the chemical lab] on the second floor is an area that is circular in design and quite ingenious in construction [the dome and gallery in the center of the mint]. Here all the specimens of America's gold, silver, and copper coins of previous years are stored. Examples of the gold, silver, and copper coins of other countries, along with different styles of *yuan bao* [Chinese silver in weights of approximately fifty ounces], *tiao* [ingots], and *ding* [weights in the shape of ingots] are kept here as well. The coins of China, Japan, Vietnam, and Siam are all displayed, some of them cast as far back as two thousand years ago. There are also some excavated from as deep as 120 feet. Among these were many I had never before seen.[15]

As we were just about to leave, the superintendent returned, and we were again conducted to the guest room, where we sat and talked for a bit. He noted that this is America's most important coin depository and the second largest in the world. He went on to say,

The general use of silver coins among different nations, in addition to being a convenience for the people, is also beneficial to the country. The Western countries all mint their own, each with a distinctive style, but all having uniform weights and contents. Recently, Japan has also followed suit. Since Chinese merchants already like to use for-

15. Interestingly, McCabe reports, "Of late years, the mint has been largely engaged in coining money for China and Japan." *Illustrated History*, 62. If this was mentioned directly to Li, it was never recorded in his account. Nonetheless, the problems of the use of foreign coinage, uneven exchange rates, profiteering by shroffs, and counterfeiting are all discussed in the section following this one.

eign coins, why not mint your own instead of sitting by and watching other countries receive the benefits of China's economic power?

A New
Account
of a Trip
Around
the Globe

154

He then asked about Chinese methods of making *yuan bao* and casting copper cash, so I briefly explained these. On our way back, my Western friend [Knight] said,

> Regarding China's use of *yuan bao*, what purpose does it serve to have coins of uneven quality and different contents and weights, which allow markets and shops to raise and lower prices at will, thus causing considerable problems for the government? Without a way to regulate such profits and losses, how can China really follow the example of the wealthy nations and benefit her people? In this case, our Western methods might indeed be applicable to China, too.

Judging from what I have seen, it would appear that he is quite correct. Nevertheless, our country has a long history of using *yuan bao,* so we cannot just discontinue it. To remedy fraud and malpractice, staunch the flow of silver abroad, and return economic power to China, it would indeed be better to make our own silver coins, and to purchase the machines for it as well. Not only would this greatly reduce the labor involved, but it would also prevent the easy counterfeiting of coins among the people. Their size, weight, color, and silver content would then accord with those of other countries, while the design and engraving would, of course, be distinct. A suitable version would have the appropriate Manchu, Chinese, and English script in all its particulars, with the design taken from that of the dragon flag currently used in traveling abroad. China and foreign countries would then all be able to circulate them. Given that the illegal sale and casting of copper coins is rampant, rendering the investigation and prohibition of such cases extremely difficult, it might be just as well, in any case, to adopt these methods.

There is also a wax museum on Chestnut Street.[16] I had once

16. This appears to be a reference to the College of Physicians' Mütter Museum, which at the time was located on Locust Street, several blocks from Chestnut. The museum had been founded in 1849 as the Museum of Pathological Anatomy and was

remarked to [Maritime Customs] Commissioner [Alfred] Huber, "In China there are ancient bronze engravings depicting the arrangement of the arteries, veins, and organs of the human body, how food and drink are digested, and so forth. Did foreign countries ever have natural sciences like this?" He said they did, but only when the return ship [for the voyage to Europe] was about to sail was I able to visit this museum.

The building is of three stories, and tall and spacious. There are figures made of melted wax, men and women, old and young, declining and robust, infants, fetuses and afterbirth, all absolutely lifelike; their hair, skin, membranes, orifices, bones, *jingluo*,[17] pores, internal organs—the entire body, inside and out, is completely fashioned from melted wax. Assembled they become one body; separately removed they become a hundred parts, large and small, with nothing omitted. To which places are food and drink transferred and digested in order to expel disease and heal injuries? Which diseases are visible on the outside of the body? What forms and colors do various types of wounds assume as they extend inward from the surface? How does a wife become pregnant? After seven days, as the fetus begins to develop and gradually assume its complete form, what determines the ease or difficulty of the birth? Why does a pregnancy pass its due date, or not reach it at all? Not one of these particulars was unclear or lacking in detail. Furthermore, there was a statue of a doctor curing a disease: What was the cure? How was the cure received? Westerners also use doctors in cases of childbirth because of the difficulties involved in removing a stillbirth, the many complications related to delivery, and the possibility that, though the mother may not be saved, the child in her abdomen [*sic*] might still be alive. Hence there is a small detailed statue of a cesarean birth, also extremely lifelike. If one can concentrate on examining these thoroughly, one may perhaps attain 20 to 30 percent of the skills of a physician. No wonder the medical arts of the Westerners have advanced beyond those of China! Consequently, if one must suffer a broken arm, then its

A New
Account
of a Trip
Around
the Globe

155

hugely augmented by the donation in 1863 of the collection of Thomas Mütter, a professor of surgery at the city's Jefferson Medical College. In 1910, the museum moved to its present location at Twenty-second Street and Ludlow Avenue. "The College of Physicians of Philadelphia," unpublished museum guide ms.

17. In Chinese medicine, the main and collateral *qi* meridians running through the body, along which acupuncture points are located.

A New
Account
of a Trip
Around
the Globe

156

severity and duration, and thus the use of surgical instruments and medications, are sure to be completely correct. Those who "follow the wall to get away" ultimately end up outside the gate; how can one cross the five mountain ranges with a sail, or cross the seas with shoes? [That is, "How can we accomplish our goals with improper tools and methods?"]

Considering how the Westerners have designed this museum, it is also useful for those who are not medical specialists. If one is studying the natural sciences and yet woefully ignorant of one's own body, can we then say that this is a thorough understanding of those sciences? By making possible the examination of the human body, the essentials of recuperation, and the cure and prevention of disease, these displays will certainly help prevent the bungling of quacks. In benefiting the world, can this be called insignificant? Nearby there are also statues of the world's unusual and unique medical cases, such as conjoined twin brothers, their organs linked together; and twin sisters, their two bodies joined with an arm in the area of their stomach. There are others whose bodies differ from ordinary people, all of them extremely strange and difficult to describe. All of these things I have seen have been put on display just for the people, and I understand that there are those in the government who have further particulars on them, so these may also be consulted.

CHAPTER 12. THE AMERICAN CAPITAL OF WASHINGTON

In the American east there is a place named "Columbia," which is the capital district of America. It lies in southeastern Maryland and northeastern Virginia and occupies an area acquired jointly from both of these states, a most unique situation. Its area is calculated at 2,320 square li. The capital city is named "Washington" and is built toward the end of the western branch of the Chesapeake Bay on the eastern shore of the Potomac River, with a length and breadth of about 10 li, Philadelphia being about 450 li to the northeast. Originally, after Washington had founded the state with the English coalition [of the colonies], it was decided to make this the capital. The names of officials and people are accordingly used in naming cities from a desire to perpetuate their memory and so are not tabooed or barred from further use. (It is usually the practice among Westerners not to consider certain names as being forbidden.)[1] The buildings are neat and orderly, the scenery peaceful and elegant, and the weather, to describe it briefly, is like that of Jiangsu province. The streets and roads are wide and clean, mostly using oil mixed with earth in their construction, and very level and firm. There is relatively little traffic, the pedestrians are friendly and amiable, and the lack of noise and bustle is very different from Philadelphia. Because Philadelphia is a commercial center where people from all quarters mingle, its markets are prosperous and abundant and horses and carts push and squeeze along its streets. Here, however, mansions, government bureaus, private residences, gardens, and woods predominate. All the foodstuffs and items for everyday use found in the shops are brought in from Philadelphia and New York, and there are no factories or warehouses. Although there are boats and ships running on the river, the great merchants and powerful firms seldom come here. It is, however, connected by electric [telegraph] wires to the world's great cities and railroad lines from all the adjacent states pass through it.

In the center of the city stands a huge building, towering and remarkably lofty, which houses a library. The left side is for the Upper Deliberative *Yuan* of the *Libu*[2] [the Senate], and the right side is for the Lower Deliberative *Yuan* [the House of Representatives]. To the southeast are a navy yard, barracks, and to the extreme south facing the river is an arsenal [Fort Humphreys].[3] To the west are a museum [the Smithsonian] and the Department of Agriculture. South of the museum is a new machine proving ground. Farther south is the Postal Department. West of the Department of Agriculture facing the river is the president's mansion. The State Department and the Navy and War Departments are on its right, and the Treasury Department is on its left. Further

1. From ancient times it had been the practice among the Chinese to taboo the names and titles of the powerful, especially emperors and empresses. The characters in their personal names would be barred from use, often with homophonous ones substituted.

2. The Board of Civil Office or Ministry of Personnel under the Qing. Li is using this as a term for Congress as a whole.

3. From 1869 to 1881 Ft. Humphreys functioned as an arsenal and weapons development center. Federal Writers' Project, *Washington, City and Capital* (Washington, D.C.: GPO, 1937), 878.

A New
Account
of a Trip
Around
the Globe

158

west there is an observatory [the U.S. Naval Observatory] and also several schools and colleges for missionaries. Separate schools have been built especially for the education of black people (Africans who had been enslaved but are now full citizens).[4] In a deeply wooded area to the northwest, there are a number of large buildings for the recuperation of homeless wounded veterans [the United States Soldiers Home]. As for the remaining buildings, there are so many government departments and embassies of various countries that it is difficult to list them completely. According to the census for the ninth year of the Tongzhi emperor [1870][5] (by law this is done once every ten years), the entire population of the city is 109,200, including three Chinese, and with black people comprising about one-third. Further northwest is a city called "Georgetown." Farther south across the river there is also a city called "Alexandria," which has a college, a fort, and a charity, which serves the capital and the surrounding community.

On the twelfth day of the seventh month [August 30], I accompanied Imperial Maritime Customs Commissioner [J. L.] Hammond on a visit from Philadelphia to the capital city of Washington. We boarded the train at 12:30 and traveled along the western bank of the Delaware River. As we arrived in the vicinity of Wilmington, we turned to the southwest, leaving Pennsylvania and entering the state of Delaware. Traveling a bit more to the west, we entered the state of Maryland, crossing three large bridges, the longest of which spans a branch of the Chesapeake Bay about three li long in a place called Perryville. Further on we passed through five tunnels, the longest one in the area called Baltimore being about five li long. When passing through tunnels, the train's inside lights are turned on beforehand. On reaching the tunnel opening, it swiftly enters, and the sound of the air rushing by one's ears is like the sighing of ten thousand pines in the wind. The appearance of the tunnel opening is at first like that of a round door containing a full moon, very small and distant like a bowl. A bit further on and already one cannot see. Soon, however, one

4. Perhaps Li here refers to the original sectarian character of nearly all of Washington's institutions of higher education. The premier center of African-American higher education, Howard University, had been chartered in 1867.

5. The margin notes in the Hunan People's Press edition (256) incorrectly list the date of the census as 1872.

catches sight of a glimmer in the front of the train and then we are already through. Thinking back to my recent journey from San Francisco to Philadelphia, eight days by train and covering more than 10,000 li, I passed through a great many tunnels but had never before been able to see the actual situation with regard to the tunnel entrances. This time, however, my seat was in an opportune position in the rear of the train, and so I had this view, a chance situation not easy to come by. The area through which the train passed is heavily wooded and verdant, the shade reaching to the sky, with neat and orderly towns and villages. At 3:30 we reached the capital city, a travel distance of 449 *li*. We repaired to the Arlington Hotel,[6] which charges a daily rate of five dollars for room and board.

A New
Account
of a Trip
Around
the Globe

159

The Presidential [Executive] Mansion is built entirely of white stone,[7] and so is popularly known as the "White House" (translated as *baiwu*).[8] It is quite grand and extensive, with gardens and pavilions on all sides, shaded by trees, and with an abundance of flowers throughout the year. Outside the grounds is an iron fence. The main entrance faces south[9] and to the east and west are entrances like those of ancient Chinese government buildings; entering the east gate one approaches a *zhaobi* [a wall that screens the gate] and descends from one's carriage. Since the president was on summer holiday at a separate retreat and had not yet returned, we went to see the high official in charge of the mansion, who gave us a tour. Inside there are two large halls, capable of holding several hundred people. Hanging from the four walls are portraits of former presidents, and these rooms are used for receiving the different categories of subordinate officials. There are separate Red, Green, and Blue Rooms, for meeting the higher officials and foreign envoys of various countries. There is also an Oval Office and a ballroom, the furnishings of which are rather austere and frugal. The upstairs is used as an office for governmental

6. On H Street near Lafayette Square. The Arlington played host to presidents-elect from Grant to McKinley until its demolition in 1912. Federal Writers' Project, *Washington, City and Capital*, 653–55.

7. Actually sandstone and brick, painted white.

8. Zhang Deyi reported during his 1868 trip to the Executive Mansion that the term *White House* was also an American colloquialism for "outhouse." If this was true, Li seems not to have been similarly informed. See translation excerpts in Arkush and Lee, *Land without Ghosts*, 35.

9. Considered a propitious direction in Chinese architecture.

affairs, and one then comes to the residence, which is closed to all, so we were unable to enter it.

I went to pay a courtesy call on the secretary of state, [Hamilton] Fish (a post similar to that of a minister [*Shangshu*]).[10] I saw that the department's internal affairs are divided into six branches, each with a superintendent [assistant secretary]: An ambassadorial division; a consular division, which handles the posting of American diplomatic and consular personnel; a foreign affairs division, for the diplomatic personnel of other countries and consular officials posted to America involved in negotiations; an accounting division, in charge of receiving money and paying bills; a records division, in charge of the flow of official correspondence and record keeping; and a correspondence division, in charge of sending and receiving the records and telegrams of various countries. There is also a tower containing a library of twenty-five thousand volumes, all pertaining to international law, geography, history, and discussions of negotiations in collated volumes. Secretary Fish asked me: "How do these methods of managing public affairs compare with those of China?" I replied that they are for the most part the same. He went on to say that since the business of government is best kept to a minimum and that it is inadvisable for it to proliferate, the use of personnel should likewise be kept small and not be allowed to grow too large; thus, salaries should be generous and not inappropriately meager. Matters are therefore kept simple and easy to understand, the small number of personnel prevents any shifting of responsibility, and the generous salaries ensure that they will be focused and purposeful. These are sound principles indeed.

The Treasury Department is where all customs, tax revenues, and public funds are managed. There are four silver depositories, and the value of the gold and silver coins and government notes stored there is approximately $40 million. On one side is an area where notes are printed. A printing press utilizing steel plates engraved with the finest designs and script is used to print them. Every note must pass through many hands and several machines

A New
Account
of a Trip
Around
the Globe

160

10. A term first used in the *Shujing* (Classic of documents) for the Canons of Yao and Shun. It subsequently referred to high metropolitan officials and presidents of the Six Boards. By Qing times, it designated a high minister in charge of a specific region or function. See Charles O. Hucker, *A Dictionary of Official Titles in Imperial China* (Stanford: Stanford University Press, 1985), 411.

from the beginning of the process to the end, so as to avoid irregularities. The ten-cent and twenty-five cent notes are 2.5 [English] inches wide and 1.5 inches long; the one, two, five, ten, twenty, fifty, one hundred, two hundred, five hundred, and one thousand dollar bills are all five inches wide and two inches long. The paper is not very thick, but unusually strong and pliable, and visible in the sunlight are what seem like broken veins of ice [i.e., visible fibers] along with the Treasury Department's pictures and bank designs, and these [notes] are circulated freely throughout the country. The personnel employed there comprise about two thousand workers, of whom there are more women than men. There are also copper coins, of red copper, every one worth one- or two-tenths of a silver coin; the five-cent pieces are made of nickel and of excellent workmanship. There are five-cent, ten-cent, twenty-five-cent, and fifty-cent silver coins. The silver dollar coins are not numerous and slightly heavier, and thus not as convenient as the notes. The gold coins are valued at $2.50, $5.00, $10.00, and $20.00 in silver. The $20.00 gold pieces are as large as the silver half-dollars and as heavy as nine coins. In America these may be exchanged for $23.00 in notes; for customs duties, however, they are still worth $20.00. Those used in our Chinese treaty ports are worth no more than $18.00 or $19.00 [in exchange]. Because of this the people of other countries are rather critical of them as being inferior to the gold and silver currencies of England, France, and other countries, which are convertible to notes of equal value for public use. Previously, when I was in Japan, the various styles of their notes that I saw were much like these except that they mostly used Japanese and Chinese script, and they, too, were able to circulate freely. These countries do not issue notes primarily as a means of seeking profits, but do so instead as a reliable way to help regulate the circulation [of money]. If the legislation is properly arranged, why worry that it will not work? As for gold, silver, and copper coins, Japan also mints these itself, and the benefits accrued are not at all inconsiderable.

In the evening we went to the U.S. Soldiers Home. Mr. Hammond said of the American system: Fifteen cents per month is collected from the pay of common soldiers and noncommissioned officers. This money, with interest, is then used to support them in retirement. For those soldiers killed in action during wartime, the

A New
Account
of a Trip
Around
the Globe

161

A New
Account
of a Trip
Around
the Globe

162

money is used to support their families. Those who are wounded or disabled return to their families, while those who are without families live in this home, recuperating for the rest of their lives. Although the government does not pay a penny, this has become its largest philanthropic endeavor. At one time China, too, understood the advantages and drawbacks of this Western military system. But their arrangement of monthly pay deductions to cover the costs of those killed or wounded is especially advantageous, and it would be a simple matter for us copy it. This is because the number of soldiers who would collect the money is small, no more than one in ten in China. If a small amount were deducted from the other 90 percent, the large numbers would already be in place to sustain them. Moreover, the Westerners collect funds not only from soldiers but also from those in all categories of government service. Therefore, the interests of all, public and private, high and low, are well served. Just as substituting this [system] would help us economize, it would also prepare us for any contingency. This is certainly something about which we could happily agree.

In the center of the city is the Capitol building [*yicheng yuan:* "Congress Hall"], the exterior of which is of white stone blocks, while the inside is done completely in various types of marble and is incomparably beautiful. This [institution] has general authority over the nation's administrative bureaus and offices. The presidential mansion does not even approach it in size.

Rising from the center is a dome of 180 [English] feet, which contains a library [Library of Congress] of more than three hundred thousand volumes, old and new (I heard that there is also a dome in Boston that holds three hundred thousand books), and the officials of the country may take them out and read them, but must return them as per its [the library's] restrictions. The people are also allowed to come and read inside the library. I heard that twenty years ago, they had not exercised sufficient caution about fire in this dome and as a result many books were burned. Now, therefore, the roof members, pillars, and flooring all employ iron in their construction. Hanging in the dome are eight paintings, each about fifteen [Chinese] feet square. The events of Washington's war with the British during the early days of the nation are depicted, along with the stories of the forming of the coalition [of the colonies] and the founding of the state, and the brushwork truly "paints the water and paints the sound." Every picture is said to be worth $40,000 in foreign silver dollars. I also heard that there is a Frenchman, Meissonier, who is currently considered to be the premier painter.[11] He once painted a picture only five or six feet square of the former French emperor Napoleon in battle valued at $60,000, and a wealthy American [merchant][12] paid even more for it. Western paintings of such value indeed create a sensation.

The Senate is on the left side of the dome, and the House of Representatives is on the right. Every year from a group of all the *dufu* [lit.: governors and governors-general] convened by the vice president, a group of two hundred notables is elected to serve in the Senate [*sic*]; then a group of four hundred men of outstanding ability is elected by the people and they meet as the lower house, to discuss the governing of the country. Affairs of state like forming alliances, war, trade, plans for raising revenue, expenditures, proper procedures for elections, and so forth are all debated and then sent to the appropriate administrative branch (also in the Capitol); the president is then requested to implement them. The Congress meets in the hall for half of each year and then returns home for half a year. During their deliberations they are required to allow the newspapers to send reporters into the hall to record the proceedings and they supply them with seats, paper, pens, and ink. The governments of the different states are run by their governors, and the president does not consult them in advance.

Mr. Ge [unknown], an American official, explained to me: Each American state is like a country, and the union of the states forms the nation. The various states, therefore, have certain rights. All the officials below the governors are elected by the people for a term of four years. Originally, it was the practice for each state to elect a president separately. In forming alliances with other countries and other affairs, however, circumstances rendered it difficult to exert the authority to unite them as separate countries, and so one man from among the governors [*sic*][13] is publicly elected to hold this power, also for a four-year term. When his term is over,

A New
Account
of a Trip
Around
the Globe

163

11. Jean Louis Ernest Meissonier, 1815–91. A meticulous painter of military subjects, widely considered by contemporaries to have been the premier painter of the mid–nineteenth century.

12. Li omits the character *shang* for merchant, but it is inserted into the HPP edition; see p. 24a in S and p. 259 in HPP.

13. Li seems to be referring to the Electoral College system here.

A New
Account
of a Trip
Around
the Globe

164

if the people consider him worthy, he is elected to another four-year term. After leaving, he returns to the status of elder among the people (this precedent was begun by the nation's founder, Washington). While he is serving, should a situation arise in which the people no longer want him to continue, they do not actually have the power to make him step down. In addition, if the people of the country want to make a proposal for legislation or change a law, the president may hold it back [veto], and they can then do nothing about it.

The Post Office building is also constructed of white stone, four stories high, and has about five hundred rooms. It is organized with a postmaster-general and various department officials and is therefore also called the Department of the Mails. The number of superintendents is in the dozens, their subordinates are not less than a thousand, and women among them outnumber the men. There are post offices throughout all the states, cities, villages, and towns of the country, and within these areas they repeatedly select a number of strategic points among the offices of officials, and the gathering places of merchants and people, to set up mailboxes. The boxes are made of iron, about a [Chinese] foot high, and six inches wide and deep. They are tightly sealed, except for a small slit. Those who wish to mail a letter, regardless of whether they are officials or people, place it inside the box at their convenience, and every half [Chinese; one English] hour a postman comes from the post office and removes and sorts them; thus it [the post office] may be considered the control center for all the boxes. All letters posted weighing up to five *zhu* [about an ounce] sent to any city or town within the same state cost one cent for postage; outside the state, regardless of the distance, the postage is five cents. If the weight exceeds five *zhu,* then additional postage is required according to a system of fixed rates. The postage is then recorded in the office by means of a machine that prints a tiny stamp about seven-tenths of a [Chinese] inch square, and officials and people buy these and paste them on the front of their mail. After the post office receives the mail, it is registered there and the stamp is stamped [cancelled] to prevent fraud from reuse. The [cancellation] stamp bears the date and place-name so that in case the delivery is delayed, it can be reported to [the appropriate] office for investigation. As for mailing parcels of various sizes and weights, there is also a regularized system, and its fees, too, are quite reasonable. In order to comply with the customs on goods, one first pays the customs fee through the post office, which then registers it on behalf of [the customs service]. Because the post office and the customs service together serve the entire country, they work together to complement each other. For example, if among the letters are money orders or bank drafts, these must be verified on mailing and receive a separate permit in order to guarantee that there are no errors with them, and the fees for this are also arranged according to a fixed table. On the whole, the management of the mail is rigorous and precise and therefore easy to use.

A New
Account
of a Trip
Around
the Globe

165

I heard that Western countries formerly had systems similar to our Chinese courier stations for the special handling of official papers, but not for transporting the mail of the populace. In the initial year of the reign of the Qianlong emperor [1736], it was first proposed that the people are the foundation of the state, since the state cannot exist without the people.[14] This system, however, while convenient for the state, had not been convenient for the people. Thus, post offices were established throughout the different regions of all these countries and officials sent to manage them, with a high official to superintend. Regardless of whether it is official correspondence or [private] letters, it is all handled together and the people greatly praise its convenience. Now, this method of management has been in place for many years, and so has already produced considerable benefits. The income from postal fees is used to pay the expenses of transporting the mail, and in the calculations at year's end, the surplus is divided among the departments so that those with shortfalls need not worry about deficits. Actually, because the postal fees are cheap and the sending of mail swift and error-free, everyone is pleased to use it. Several years ago, the various countries decided that the overall management of postal services in all the nations of the globe should

14. Cf. *Mencius*, bk. IV, pt. 1, chap. 5, line 1 (p. 295): "Mencius said: 'Men are in the habit of speaking of the world, the state, and the family. As a matter of fact, the foundation/root of the world lies in the state, the foundation of the state lies in the family, and the foundation of the family lies in the individual.'" The significance of the date of 1736–37 is somewhat obscure in this context. It may refer to Benjamin Franklin's appointment as colonial postmaster in Philadelphia, during whose tenure numerous improvements were made in the speed, efficiency, and cost of mail delivery throughout the area.

A New
Account
of a Trip
Around
the Globe

166

employ a uniform system in order to speed delivery among them. Japan, in the Eastern Ocean, has also entered their ranks.[15]

In serving the main objects of government, postal courier stations have for countless generations been careful about profit and loss. Only in the West over the last century have the public and private postal systems actually been combined into one. This unified system would be desirable to adopt and put into practice in China as a means of enriching the country and accommodating the people. Those who still consider this to be impractical do not understand that it can in fact be done. The reason for this is that in the conduct of their own affairs they have habitually cut expenses but never personnel, and so their servants have, to some extent, remained dependent upon them. If expenses are then reduced, they fear that many of them will not have ample savings to support their families. My response is: Having postage fees among the people will help remedy this. A *yamen* runner with an official packet; a courier starting off on his way; how much must this cost? The cost of mailing a single private letter through a courier station, traveling only a bit over a hundred li, must be thirty or forty cents.[16] Isn't this altogether wasteful, in addition to being too expensive? The institution of a unified system could eliminate these ills, thereafter enriching the country and accommodating the people within. To consider this unworkable is, for this reason, simply inappropriate.

The [U.S. Naval] Observatory is in the west of the city.[17] Suspended on a huge mechanism in its center is a giant telescope, thirty-six feet long, with an objective aperture of twenty-six inches. It cost forty thousand dollars, and its lenses came to seven thousand dollars.[18] The ingenious [mounting] mechanism of the telescope allows it to be turned in any direction. Although its body is

15. The Universal Postal Union, established in 1874.

16. As noted in the introduction, Li's enthusiasm for the speed, efficiency, and profitability of the Western posts led to his playing an instrumental role in memorializing the Throne for their adoption. For the costs of using the government's *yizhan* and *pu* mounted and foot couriers, see Cheng, *Postal Communication*, 32. The rates for the [*min*] *xinju*, or private commercial carriers, generally varied from 10 to 400 *wen* (cash) according to distance; parcels would be charged at a rate of 60 *wen* per *jin*, or catty (1.33 pounds). Cheng, 41.

17. During Li's visit it was still located near E Street between Twenty-third and Twenty-fifth Streets.

18. The telescope at the Naval Observatory was a twenty-six-inch refractor built by Alvan Clark and Sons of Cambridgeport, Massachusetts, in 1873. When assembled, it was the largest refractor of its time. Post, *1876*, 93.

extremely heavy, its turning motion is extraordinarily smooth and easy. The roof of the building resembles a parasol on which a door opens to a width of perhaps three [Chinese] feet. The telescope's objective lens faces the door, which can also be rotated in any direction. Below this there are steps, and on them reclining chairs have been set up on which people sit in order to observe. The steps can also follow the rotation of the telescope and the observatory's roof. It is so ingenious that it is unbelievable!

In a separate building there is an instrument about six feet long for measuring the sun's position [a heliostat], used to determine the precise time. When the sun approaches noon, the instrument's end is pointed upward, with a man lying beneath to observe it. At exactly noon, through a telegraph mounted on the wall, reports are sent to various cities providing an exact time for clocks and time-pieces. Next to this there is a large case in which many types of timekeeping instruments are stored. Every foreign ship arriving in port must set its chronometers to the standard time until it sets sail for home. Inside there are a number of instruments, with those coming from England set to the English standard time, which, compared to America, is already two and a half [Chinese; five English] hours different. Exact noon in [eastern] America is England's early *you* period [5:00 P.M.]. If we compare [eastern] America and China, then the difference is exactly six Chinese [twelve English] hours. When it is day in America, it is night in China. Indeed, then, China's position is on the front of the earth, while that of America is on the back. Can there be any doubt that this proves the shape of the earth to be that of a globe?

The assorted other buildings serve as the living quarters for the astronomers and the library, and are nearly full of globes of the earth, sun, moon, and the five planets, but unfortunately we did not have the free time to examine them closely. Also, that particular evening happened to be overcast so, regrettably, we could not get a look at the stars and moon.

A New
Account
of a Trip
Around
the Globe

167

CHAPTER 13. THE AMERICAN CITY OF HARTFORD

Hartford is in the northeast corner of America and is the capital city of the state of Connecticut. On the twenty-fourth day of the

A New
Account
of a Trip
Around
the Globe

168

seventh month [September 11], I went on a visit there in the company of Mr. Knight.[1] The train left Philadelphia and after traveling perhaps one [Chinese] hour, passed through New [*sic*] Jersey City, where we left the train and boarded a ferry to cross the Hudson River to New York City. The distance from Philadelphia to here is calculated to be 297 li. After dinner we again boarded a train and covered 330 li, arriving in the city the following day at 1:30 A.M. The city is 10 li in length and breadth and overlooks the Connecticut River to the east. The climate is cold, more or less like that of China north of the Great Wall, with snow lingering into the beginning of the fourth month and appearing again in the ninth. The soil of the region, however, is quite good, the people have few illnesses, and the streets and roads are clean and well maintained. Commercial activity is not extensive, schools are numerous, and there are also a number of well-known factories. The inhabitants number about forty thousand and are simple and honest in their customs and dealings, with neither enormous wealth nor dire poverty. There are boys from our country studying here [the Chinese Education Mission], and an overseas headquarters has been set up for them.

The headquarters building is leased and stands three stories tall. Entering the door, there is a drawing room on the right, behind which are a translation office and dining room, while on the left are classrooms and the boys' dining room; upstairs are a business office and bedrooms. The uppermost[2] floor is used as a Confucian Hall, with a window facing north as a mark of veneration for the imperial palace.[3] This room is rather small and narrow, and inadequate for its purpose. On the twenty-fifth day [September 12] when we came to pay our respects to [newly appointed Assistant] Minister [to the United States, Spain, and Peru] Yung Wing, Ou Eliang, the director of the Education Mission, and Rong Zhixiang, the senior instructor, happened to have gone to Philadelphia to see the

---

1. The *Hartford Courant* of September 13, 1876, ran a brief item on Li's visit, including his proposed itinerary of the Education Mission, the Pratt and Whitney factory, the Colt works, and the Cheney Silk Manufacturing Company.

2. The Shanghai edition uses the characters *zai shang* for "uppermost," while the HPP edition shows them as *zui shang.*

3. Confucian temples typically consisted of a series of three courtyards arranged in a south to north direction.

exposition.[4] In addition to Minister Yung, therefore, the people we talked with were limited to the head translator, Kuang Qizhao,[5] and the teacher Liu Qichun. Minister Yung is held in high regard by Westerners, and it is fortunate that our country has entrusted the office to such a qualified man. From now on, we will not only be able to have complete confidence in those Chinese who have lived abroad, but matters bearing on Sino-foreign negotiations and trade relations will also grow smoother over the long term. This is because Minister Yung is thoroughly conversant with the politics and governmental decrees of Western countries and has a comprehensive understanding of their folkways and customs, national commercial interests, and any number of [other] topics. Having studied the literature of Western countries for decades, Minister Yung has been able to attain an extensive knowledge of these matters.

A New
Account
of a Trip
Around
the Globe

169

In the afternoon, Minister Yung accompanied us on a visit to Collins Street to tour the new headquarters building under construction. The craftsmen are in the process of beginning work, and the construction should be completed sometime next spring. It will be lofty and expansive, spacious and quite elegant. Four stories tall, with the main entrance facing south, the roof will have a cupola rising from it, and there will be wooden flagstaffs set up to fly the flags for the first and fifteenth of the lunar month. Minister Yung drafted the plans himself. The property is two hundred feet wide and three hundred feet deep and will be perhaps three times the size of the present building. Actually, were it not for this, not only would the current headquarters remain inadequate for its purpose, but it would continue to display an insufficient sense of Chinese propriety and decorum [*tiqong*] as well.

Currently there are only 113 students. They are placed in pairs with various prominent families along with their own children to aid in language practice. Every student's tuition, room, and board cost four hundred taels a year.

The mission headquarters has two Chinese teachers, and the

4. In its coverage of the visit of the Chinese students to Philadelphia, the *Hartford Courant* of August 22 noted that "in the first week in September the Chinese commissioners resident here will visit the Centennial."

5. Kuang Qizhao was the mission's chief translator from 1875 until its recall in 1881. Quite popular with the local press, he published *A Dictionary of English Phrases with Illustrative Sentences* in 1881. See McCunn, *Chinese American Portraits*, 21.

A New
Account
of a Trip
Around
the Globe

170

students come once every three months to review their Chinese. Twelve students come each time and stay for fourteen days. When the time is up, these twelve return to their families and another twelve come, each group taking its turn in the cycle. They awaken every day at 6:00 A.M. and retire at 10:00 P.M. They study books, write characters, hear lectures, and compose compositions all according to a set curriculum. All the students also write letters home twice a month at regular intervals. Clearly, attention is paid to even the smallest details.

Earlier, I had watched them as they traveled with some prominent Western families,[6] happily comparing notes among the group and in complete harmony with each other, so they are certainly successful in their social relationships. Both the Chinese and the Western children benefit from this. In addition, our Chinese students continue to combine such studies with immersion in Chinese works without becoming muddled or confused. Such methods are certainly laudable in enabling them to concentrate without fear of losing what they have gained. One day, when their studies have been completed, they will have both *ti* and *yong*, and will aid splendidly in carrying out our country's grand design. Then, the Sacred Dynasty's generosity in directing others to good will indeed not be neglected!

Minister Yung accompanied us to the Pratt and Whitney factory. Of all the various machines used for manufacturing weapons, most are fabricated in this plant. The building is huge with several hundred machines of various sizes, all having pulleys harnessed to leather belts extending to [iron shafts in] the building's rafters. The iron shafts are all powered by a large, centrally located engine capable of eighty horsepower and costing twenty-five hundred dollars in foreign money; every day it burns about twenty-five hundred catties of coal. The steam engine drives a great wheel, and all the hundreds of small wheels in the building then turn; the mechanics use these in running their machines as the occasion

6. Toward the end of August the students traveled to the Centennial in the care of the Bartletts and the Kelloggs, two families long associated with Yung Wing and the Education Mission. In addition, in 1875, Yung had married Mary Louise Kellogg in a ceremony performed by his closest friend, the Reverend Joseph Twichell. The couple had two sons, Morrison Brown Yung and Bartlett Golden Yung, before Mary Louise's death in 1886. For Twichell's account of the nuptials, see LaFargue, *China's First Hundred*, 42–43. A full account of the boys' visit to the Centennial, including a meeting with President Grant, is given in chapter 17.

demands. All the different machines in the Gatling Gun Factory were made here, and many of the European countries like Russia, Germany, Sweden, and so on also come to this factory to place orders. We heard that last year Germany placed an order calculated at $1.5 million in foreign money for machinery to manufacture guns. Germany is presently considered to be a powerful country with many factories, but still they come here to place orders. Obviously, then, this factory is superb.

The manager demonstrated a Gardner gun so that we might inspect the manufacture of the weapon. Under the barrel is a steel mount on which twin barrels are arranged side by side. In the breeches are positioned a square type of brass magazine, seven or eight [Chinese] inches high, containing the ammunition. In the back there is a small crank that when turned by hand allows the twin magazines to [load] and fire simultaneously and continuously, and it can fire several hundred rounds per minute. After a continuous firing of several thousand rounds there are no worries that the barrels, although very hot, might explode. Regarding the manufacture of the guns, the materials used start with properly selected, fine grade steel. The more expensive mechanisms are simple and few, rugged, and easy to repair. This gun has only two large moving parts in it, unlike other guns, which require a multitude of small components. There is a separate carriage for transport, and on the carriage is a limber chest that can hold six thousand rounds. It can also be mounted on an iron tripod and elevated, traversed, and rotated at will. The gun weighs 110 pounds, the stand, 70 pounds, and requires a crew of two. To transport it in mountainous areas only requires four men. All in all, the carriage, stand, and ammunition cost one thousand dollars in foreign money, and different countries have continually come to buy them. (Note: Previously, in "A Brief Account of the American Exhibition," I made mention of this weapon, though briefly.)

The Colt foreign arms factory is in the eastern part of the city on the banks of the Connecticut River. Mr. Knight accompanied us as we paid a call on the manager, Mr. Franklin[?]. Mr. Franklin said: Twenty-five years ago, there were no repeaters among foreign firearms. In the Western calendar's year of 1851, the American, Colt, first developed the model for them. Other countries copied their design, and as a result they are now used all over the world. This factory has therefore used his name to this day. He led us to a

A New
Account
of a Trip
Around
the Globe

171

A New
Account
of a Trip
Around
the Globe

172

place where there were old and new guns, no less than several
score to a hundred kinds produced throughout the ages, collected
and displayed to compare their advantages and disadvantages.
Then he led us to the factory building, a vast area of four stories.
On the bottom floor are various kinds of steam engines ranging
from two horsepower to as large as ten. They are shaped like barrels and unusually versatile and simple to run. The two-horse-
power model is only four or five feet long, costs four hundred dollars, and uses only a little more than a hundred catties of coal per
day. The rest are all used in manufacturing the small mechanisms
employed in the guns. On the second floor the manufacture of
gunstocks and pistol grips is carried out, while on the third floor
the various parts are assembled into finished guns. In addition,
there are a great many typewriters and sewing machines, as well as
Gatling rotary guns. This type of gun was invented by an American
named Gatling, who contracted this factory to manufacture it, and
so it is also called the Gatling Gun Factory. Mr. Franklin added:
This factory can produce any kind of machine regardless of type. If
someone invents a new device but lacks the capital to produce it,
he may bring the model to this factory to manufacture it for him. If
additional machines are required, these can then be sent out from
Pratt and Whitney. Because the Pratt and Whitney factory specializes in making all kinds of machinery, it occupies an essential place
in the manufacturing process. We then took in a demonstration of
a model of [Gatling] rotary gun, described earlier in "A Brief
Account of the American Exhibition." Following this, Mr.
Franklin presented me with a new model six-chamber revolver and
several books and diagrams. He said that the material in the books
on the workings of the factory is quite lucid and clear, and that it
was a shame that I could not understand all of the foreign words.
Shortly after one o'clock in the afternoon we returned to the Education Mission headquarters and ate our fill at a lunch of Chinese
fare.

To the northeast, about sixty li from Hartford in the vicinity of
the village of Manchester, there is a textile mill.[7] I went on a visit
there accompanied by the owner of the factory, Mr. Cheney, for-

7. The Cheney Brothers Silk Manufacturing Company in South Manchester, known
locally as Cheneyville.

mer Connecticut governor [Joseph] Hawley,[8] Minister Yung, and Mr. Knight. The factory grounds form a perfect square, a bit over three li per side [i.e., a square mile]. They are heavily wooded and boast a luxuriant lawn, forming an altogether excellent site. The factory has a number of large buildings, two of which are residences, and there are also houses for workers, a private school, and a chapel. There are more than fifteen hundred workers and more women than men. All of them are required to bring their families there to live, and all the sons and daughters of these people must attend a nearby school [the Cheney School] to study. This allows them to be free from worries about caring for their families, and they can then concentrate on their work. We first went to Mr. Cheney's residence. After lunch he guided us to his son's house to sit for a bit. His son had lived in Japan for several years as a purchaser of silk thread, and so both houses have a great many Chinese items on display.

At 3:30 we went to the factory, a building of several floors, with an estimated four to five hundred rooms. The front entrance has two iron rails extending for perhaps twenty li on which steam trains are run. The trains and tracks all belong to the owner and are used to move his goods to and from the main rail line. This kind of factory specializes in taking spoiled silk cocoons and, using machines to extract the thread, weaves cloth that binds this silk together with good silk thread, thus producing top-grade silk cloth. Entering the door of one large room, one sees cocoons and eggs piled high, nearly filling the room, spoiled in color and with a powerful stench. They said that these were all cheaply purchased and imported from Japan. Their technique consists of spreading the spoiled cocoons out on a machine. Here they are flattened by the action of a roller and then the threads are coiled onto an iron-toothed shaft. The waste spills down and accumulates in a space below. When used as fertilizer, it grows the most beautiful flowers. The jumbled thread on the shaft is taken down and at this point resembles wadding. It is brought to a second machine with finer iron teeth, rolled and combed as it passes and, somewhat whiter in color, is cut into short strips of perhaps eight [Chinese] inches and pressed between

A New
Account
of a Trip
Around
the Globe

173

8. Hawley was also president of the U.S. Centennial Commission from 1871 to 1876.

A New
Account
of a Trip
Around
the Globe

174

wooden boards. It moves on to a third machine with very fine iron teeth, is again combed as it passes, and is [now] spotlessly clean and white. Reaching the fourth machine, operated by two women, the short threads are pressed by flat horizontal boards, and passed onto a long board extending to a wooden wheel, the action of which presses them into one long strip. In the fifth and sixth machines, the long strip is drawn into fine strips, which are passed through the mouths of small copper tubes to enter into a thicker iron tube. On reaching the seventh, eighth, and ninth machines, it is alternately combed and brushed finer and finer, becoming ever more clean and bright, and absolutely indistinguishable from the silk thread of the best cocoons. It moves on to a tenth and eleventh machine, each of which has thirty wooden bobbins winding the thread on to them. As for the twelfth machine, it passes through this repeatedly, going from coarse to fine and from loose to tight. Passing to the thirteenth machine, the mechanism is separated into two levels. On the upper level are positioned two hundred spindles, while the lower space has one hundred empty ones; the threads from each two on the upper level are made to pass onto the lower level's wooden spindles and the two threads are thus joined together into one. It then goes on to a fourteenth machine that makes large loops from the thread wound around the wooden spindles. If it is to be woven into natural color silk, it is then put on the loom. That silk to which color must be added enters a vat to be dyed. Every day they can obtain five hundred pounds of clean silk thread. The ability to take terribly spoiled, rotten cocoons and successfully make excellent silk thread in such daily quantities is not merely the achievement of machines, but also of the men whose minds specialize in such ingenious ideas and are unwilling to allow the world to waste these materials. The famous silk-producing regions of our China must certainly have a great many spoiled cocoons, and if a determined individual were inclined to copy this process and pursue it, it would be unrivaled as the single greatest trade!

There is also a room used for dying, where red, purple, and all different colors are prepared. The vats are large and deep holding twenty *dan* [each *dan* is equivalent to 23.4 gallons]. Then we went to a room where shuttles flew back and forth with a great clatter, weaving the thread previously made from the spoiled cocoons into fine silk cloth. One machine can weave twenty-five to thirty yards of silk per day. The wages for every yard made cost five cents.

There are four hundred machines in all, every one costing $60 in foreign money. The cloth is stored in a separate room, nearly filling it, and they were just then in the process of inventorying, packaging, and shipping it to stores and shops for sale. There is one kind that is like Hangzhou corded silk, also similar in width, and every yard costs $2.50. I asked them why the price is so expensive, and they replied that the tariff on cocoons and silk is heavy, set at $60 in duty for every $100 in goods, which I found shocking. The machines in the two factories for unraveling cocoons and spinning and weaving are set up to run on one steam engine of five hundred horsepower, which requires ten tons of coal a day.

The School for Deaf-Mutes [the American School for the Deaf] has grounds covering a large area, with many buildings and rooms, and was built more than sixty years ago. It is sustained by a public endowment drawn entirely from the willing contributions of the wealthy, the interest on which gathers $25,000 per year. Its system: All of the people in the six northeastern American states who have hearing impairments and speech impediments who wish to come to the school for an education, whether male or female, must first obtain permission from their local authorities. Each year every person pays $175 for board, with the wealthy paying more and the poor paying nothing, and the curriculum takes seven years to complete. There are presently a total of 240 people in the academy. An instructor is engaged for every 10 to 12 people, and by using sign language to act out written words—a most remarkable instructional technique—they can enable mute people to speak and read books, fully compensating for their natural disabilities. Everyone sleeps and eats, studies and works, and pursues their daily activities entirely according to a prescribed schedule. Girls live in a separate building, and their teachers are also women. Every dorm room has more than ten beds, and everyone must have a partner to attend to due to concerns about fire hazards and the unexpected. Their bedding is clean and thick and soft, the dining room spacious, bright, and clean. The salaries for the headmaster, administrators, teachers, and staff are funded by the interest on the endowment.[9]

9. The American School for the Deaf was founded in 1817 by Thomas H. Gallaudet and Laurent Clerc and is the home of American Sign Language. It was the first school in the United States founded strictly for the education of deaf students, and its sign-based curriculum became the model for such institutions throughout the remainder of the century.

A New
Account
of a Trip
Around
the Globe

175

A New
Account
of a Trip
Around
the Globe

176

I heard about an academy for the blind in the state of Massachusetts that uses raised words [Braille] that a person's hands touch
and recognize, but unfortunately we were unable to visit it. Examining the history of the techniques employed in Western countries
for teaching the deaf and mute, these were developed 150 years ago
by a Frenchman. The deaf, mute, and blind of that era were considered disabled. Although they might have suffered physical
injury, however, their mental faculties remained intact. Properly
educated, they would be enabled to avoid impoverishment and
harsh treatment because of their disabilities; moreover, they might
even volunteer their own services as well—and what could be better than that?

At a livestock fair [the Connecticut State Fair] the cattle were
twice their usual size and weighed more than two thousand
pounds. This fair is held once every year for only ten days or so for
the special purpose of exchanging information on the best methods of livestock breeding. Because livestock are a basic necessity
for the people's livelihood, the results enable them to multiply
greatly and grow large and firm, and so this also constitutes an
important aspect of the people's prosperity. Indeed, this fair seems
just like something in the tradition of our ancient kings.

Minister Yung had also arranged for us to go to the city of New
Haven to inspect the university there [Yale, Yung's alma mater].
Later, though, he received word by telegram that the university
had not yet reopened from its summer break, so we ended up not
actually going. We thereupon boarded a train and discussed our
return [to Philadelphia]. There is a route of about 120 li that passes
through the city of New Haven and, after perhaps another 60 li,
reaches the vicinity of Bridgeport. All the train stops were for several minutes. At 3:30 P.M., we arrived at the Harlem River and
boarded a steamer. The ship has iron rails, and the train stops on
it and is then transported by the ship. The passengers all go to the
ship's cafeteria to eat or drink tea for a bit. The ferry is 236 feet
long. On the river, merchant ships come and go like shuttles, and
both shores are densely crowded with houses and buildings. To
the east is Brooklyn and to the west, New York City. At this time
the wind and waves had greatly increased, and there were a number of small, fast, lifesaving boats that regularly patrol the river. By
5:30 we had reached the pier in New Jersey. The rails on the shore

were connected to those on the ship, and the train again began its journey, returning to Philadelphia at 9:30.

Regarding the previous trip up to Hartford from Philadelphia, we passed through New [sic] Jersey City and crossed the Hudson River to New York and changed trains. On this trip we bypassed New York; it was unnecessary to change trains, and we traveled directly, with the fare also being quite economical.

CHAPTER 14. THE AMERICAN CITY OF NEW YORK

A New
Account
of a Trip
Around
the Globe

177

The state of New York lies in the northeast corner of America and is bordered on the south by the states of Pennsylvania and New Jersey, on the north by the English territory of Canada, and on the east by the three states of Connecticut, Massachusetts, and Vermont. On the west it faces the Great Lakes, and to the southeast, one corner fronts on the Atlantic Ocean. It is considered to be the richest of the thirty-nine states. Its principal city, located in the southeastern corner of the state facing the Hudson River, is named "New York" and is forty li long by thirteen li wide. The climate is rather cold, and the inhabitants number about one million. The buildings range in height from three stories to seven or eight and are most imposing. Pedestrians, vehicles, and horses crowd the streets and alleys and run unceasingly through the night. In the river a forest of masts and sails extends as far as the eye can see, while railroad tracks and telegraph wires run like arteries and veins linking everything together. Trains that of necessity run through the interior of the city move on long elevated trestles [i.e., the Elevated], or through tunnels under the streets. The mode of road construction is the same as in Philadelphia, and the different streets and alleyways have mailboxes set up everywhere for postal collection. As for the grand boulevards, one is Fifth Avenue, which is a place where the wealthy and prominent gather; another is Broadway, which has a number of famous stores.

The city's volume of commerce is considered by the Americans to be unsurpassed. If we are speaking of the entire globe, however, it must in all honesty be said that along with the English capital of London and the French capital of Paris, it should be seen as one of the three legs of a *ding* [an ancient ceremonial tripod vessel]. In

A New
Account
of a Trip
Around
the Globe

178

terms of the uniformity and opulence of the houses, however, the reputations of England and France are still unapproachable. Because of this city's optimal strategic location, merchants on land and sea flock here in great numbers from Chicago west to San Francisco, and across the Pacific to Japan and China; and to the east from the Hudson River over the Atlantic Ocean to Europe.

As for the administration of the city, there is the governor of the state (he is called *Gewener* in the Western language), and the mayor of New York City. Of the rest, such as the great and minor civil and military officials, the majority live here. There are a great many shipyards, factories, and military academies. In addition, there are several dozen very large hotels, and all the stores are quite luxurious. There are also abundant gardens for sightseers. On the south shore of the Hudson River is New Jersey, and to the east is Brooklyn, both thriving commercial regions as well. At a place on the northwest shore near the city are two reform schools, even larger than those in Philadelphia. There is also a place called "Poughkeepsie" complete with a prison, mental hospital, and convalescent home.[1]

In the middle of the river is a place named "Hell's Gate" [the confluence of the Harlem and East Rivers] that has many submerged reefs. Along the shore there is crushed rock piled up like mountains, and I discovered that they use gunpowder to blow up the reefs, and the rock is then continually removed from the water. The water flow is very rapid, and merchant ships entering port are unable to go from here directly down to the city, so it is necessary to first circle around to the south in order to enter. The river's shallows are dredged deeper by machine, and the mud is then utilized to fill in the nearby shore and expand construction of the port. A great bridge extending to Brooklyn is being built to straddle the river, with a height of two hundred feet. On both shores stone piers have already been raised, though the construction is not yet completed. Looking up to view them, they are like a pair of mountain peaks facing each other, and I have no idea how much it all costs. When it is finished, though, it will be an even more splendid sight.

From Philadelphia to New York City is 297 li and not quite two

1. Hudson River State Hospital, opened in 1871.

hours by train. Our lodgings were at the Fifth Avenue Hotel. The hotel's several hundred rooms were completely filled, and many of the single rooms had also been converted to double occupancy. It happened to be the time of the presidential election, and officials, gentry, merchants, and people of all the states were meeting in the city.[2] This evening, one of this city's wealthy and influential men, [Henry O.] Havemeyer,[3] came to see me and invited me to visit several places with him. On the following day, we went to the Havemeyer residence, a home of four stories, magnificent and opulent. I had become acquainted with Mr. Havemeyer's wife and family in Philadelphia.[4] These people, in entertaining guests, were overwhelming in their hospitality.

A New
Account
of a Trip
Around
the Globe

179

The New York City public school [we visited], an extremely large building, had already been in existence for seventy-two years.[5] In the auditorium were seated 957 students, all around ten years of age. There were five male teachers and twenty-five female teachers, and they begin every morning all gathered here. A woman teacher plays the piano and all the students sing songs together and learn various methods of calisthenics in order to make the blood circulate. They also employ lavish praise and allow them to breathe comfortably, and about half an hour goes by before they leave. As they withdraw they divide into groups of two and march in step like soldiers drilling, and one can even hear the sound of their shoes in time with the piano. Next, they divide into classes of fifty-six and everyone returns to their original rooms to study. I then saw a group of 570 girls come in, with a woman teacher playing the piano and singing as before. Finally, there was the youngest class, around 500 boys and girls, who were just being introduced to the routine. Their movements all conformed to the model without a sound.

Later on we went to a room with a class of the most advanced students, fourteen to twenty years old, who had been attending

2. New York governor Samuel J. Tilden had been nominated at the Democratic Convention in St. Louis that June. Democratic representatives were in the city during Li's stay (October 13 to 17) as the campaign was building toward its climax.

3. For a brief biographical sketch of Havemeyer, see introduction.

4. Havemeyer, along with General Hector Tyndale, had been one of the biggest purchasers of Chinese and Japanese objects at the Centennial. See introduction.

5. New York City began to fund public education at the end of the eighteenth century. The city's board of education had been founded in 1842, though compulsory schooling had not been mandated until 1874, shortly before Li's visit.

A New
Account
of a Trip
Around
the Globe

180

school anywhere from six to nine years. In a room upstairs there
was an advanced class of girls very similar in age. They said that
through the system of examinations and grades, one may be pro-
moted and enter an academy or college to study. Whether older or
younger, the time during which the students gather every day in
the auditorium, read, write compositions or characters, study art,
or take their ease and exercise, as well as when they rest and return
home, is all done according to an exacting schedule. Every Sunday
they have a day of rest. Every room is outfitted with maps, globes
of the earth, and models of the solar system. There is also a
wooden blackboard hanging in the room on which white chalk is
used to write out lessons. New York City has in all 107 schools that
follow this system, divided into upper, middle, and primary levels.
There are twenty-five hundred male and female instructors teaching over 110,000 students. Every year the expenses run to $4 mil-
lion, raised from the public funds of the community. There are two
universities, one for men and one for women, but they are rather
far away from the city, so we were not at leisure to go and visit
them.

I have heard that the schools and students favor the silent accumulation of knowledge [mo zhi] and are not inclined toward recitation.[6] This is because by taking knowledge in silently, the substance of a book may be fully comprehended by the mind. If this
process is treated only as a formality, those who do no more than
learn by rote will surely be unable to understand a single word.
Therefore, the silent accumulation of knowledge is considered to
be the most effective method. The purpose of the singing, leisure,
and stretching resembles that of Chinese music and dance.[7] To
summarize, the instructional methods are skillful and detailed,
while the texts and lessons are chosen to be simple but exacting.
There is therefore no need to employ the rod [xiachu], and there is
affection and harmony between teachers and students. In addition, by means of successive graded promotions, the students are
not allowed to pass over the prescribed steps by advancing through
luck or favor. This concentrates their physical and mental efforts

6. That is, as in China. See chapters 13 and 17.
7. Li seems to refer here to *qigong* exercises and perhaps the general Confucian belief
in the efficacy of correct forms of music in directing the development of *li,* or proper
decorum.

on study, with no empty or wasted years, and they can therefore develop into useful adults according to their abilities. At the same time, if there are those who are haughty or dissolute, they too will be compelled to suddenly change and conform to the rules. We also heard that by the age of eight Westerners have already been taught how to read and write by their mothers. Thus, on entering school outside [the home] they are easy to teach. Obviously, this is also one of the major benefits of women's education.[8]

A New
Account
of a Trip
Around
the Globe

181

The school administration building is organized around a superintendent, twenty assistant superintendents, and scores of principals who specialize in managing all the matters pertaining to the operation of the schools. In the rear of the building great quantities of books, paper, pens and ink, and stationery materials are stored, and all the schools draw their supplies from here as needed. The upstairs is used as an examination hall for educators. All of those who wish to become teachers are selected by means of these tests before they are permitted to teach students, and the tests consist entirely of essay questions. While I was there I saw four men and two women, for the moment lost in thought. Facing them were two examiners seated above, lofty and majestic, wearing very stern expressions. Since the teachers must pass the test, they exercise great care in taking it. With able teachers, the students can become educated and refined, and so the system of testing teachers is also regarded as a guiding principle of the schools.

In the evening I visited a police station. The precinct captain said that in New York City there are all together thirty-five police stations and twenty-three hundred policemen. This one is the Seventeenth Precinct and has ninety-two men. They are divided into two shifts of forty-four with an additional four lieutenants. As it happened, it was just midnight and the shifts were changing. The captain called the roll, and the group marched out in ranks just like in a military drill. In the morning, each man must report everything he has observed the night before, and these items are then recorded. I noticed several policemen bringing in people under

8. Here, as in a number of places throughout Li's account, he dwells on what he considers to be the deficiencies of traditional Chinese pedagogical techniques by heaping almost unqualified praise on Western methods. One might speculate that Li's experiences with the techniques of his own education were not entirely happy ones. As for additional comments on women's education, see chapter 10, "The Women's Pavilion."

A New
Account
of a Trip
Around
the Globe

182

arrest, some drunk and disorderly, others petty thieves and the like. The captain demanded their names and addresses, which were duly recorded in a separate book [from the policemen's incident register], and they were put into cells. There are separate cells for men and women, some holding just a few people and some holding a dozen or so. Their walls are all stone and the doors are made of iron bars.

This day they had already arrested sixty-eight people. Among them were seven or eight pretty young girls, beautifully dressed, together in a cell "weeping helplessly at their desperate situation."[9] I was quite surprised at this and when I asked about it discovered that they were nude stage performers who were subject to arrest because they too easily arouse lascivious intentions; the next morning they were to be sent to court. I heard that the following day they were all fined and released.

The courthouse has separate jails for men, women, and juveniles, perhaps five or six cells each for those who had been arrested the previous day and are about to be arraigned. The courtroom is fifty or sixty [Chinese] feet deep and broad, with a raised platform about three feet high similar to a *nuanke* [Chinese heating platform]. A desk is placed on it with three seated judges, each with paper and pen interrogating the participants and recording their answers. Off to the side is a table at which are seated three or four newspaper reporters. Before the bench stands a clerk who calls those to be examined. To the left is a chair for the plaintiff or a witness; the accused all stand to the left of the bench outside a short railing. On the left corner of the bench is a copy of a religious scripture [i.e., a Bible]. The accused is brought into the courtroom by a policeman and first takes the book and puts it to his lips, giving it a brief kiss, then replaces it as a gesture that he swears to tell the truth. Below the platform, twenty or thirty people, all of whom are lawyers and witnesses, are seated at long tables and benches. The courtroom can hold perhaps several hundred gentry and people who are allowed to watch and listen, and the judges are elected from among the gentry and people. There are dozens of cases every day, and after being arraigned some are released, some fined or

9. *Chu qiu dui qi;* "The captives from Chu wept with each other." An allusion from the *Zuo Zhuan* used to illustrate helpless fear in desperate circumstances.

released on bail, and some indicted and sent to a government court for further deliberation. Some whose questioning has not been concluded are sent back to their cells until it is resumed the next day. This system is identical to that used in the Shanghai Mixed Court.[10] I was told that New York has six such courts, each for specific districts according to strict regulations. In Western countries, regardless of whether the cases are serious or trivial, everyone is permitted to observe the proceedings, and news reporters are allowed to take notes on them so that everyone may stay informed. This being the case, how can there be any irregularities? Anyone wishing to attempt something improper would be unable to do so. Yet is it not rather meddlesome and intrusive to handle so many cases per day in each place? Is this really necessary in order to keep things peaceful and orderly? The Western countries would do well to ponder this.[11] As for this swearing on the book, that is simply meaningless.

A New
Account
of a Trip
Around
the Globe

183

The customs house is very large and imposing. We entered the door to a central room that can accommodate fifty or sixty people where business travelers make their declarations. Moving around to the left, there is also a large room for the cashier in front, with various offices to the rear. Upstairs are the offices of the customs inspectors and deputy inspectors. The customs inspectors were out on business at the moment, so we met with an assistant customs officer, Mr. Carr[?]. Inquiring about the tariff duties, I discovered that according to the customs regulations, they are extremely heavy on all foreign imports. For every one hundred dollars of an item's appraised value, the duty varies from ten to sixty dollars. Domestic products exported overseas or sent through this port to another [U.S.] port are entirely duty free. Also, foreign goods on which customs duties have already been paid are not subject to additional duties on being shipped to another port or to the inte-

10. Like the Imperial Maritime Customs, the Shanghai Mixed Court was a Sino-foreign institution that grew out of the dislocations of the Taiping Rebellion and the treaty port system. The court was set up in 1865 to try cases before both Chinese and Western magistrates on the basis of a ruling in British consular court that extraterritoriality did not exempt foreigners from Chinese law. See Wright, *Last Stand*, 258–59.

11. *Xiguo he shensi zhi;* literally, "Western countries, why not ponder it?" As much as he apparently admired the orderliness of Western cities, Li's obvious preference was for the informal controls of Chinese civic and village life based on family and clan, where a district magistrate might have responsibility for a half million people.

A New
Account
of a Trip
Around
the Globe

184

rior.[12] Their intention in this proceeds from a desire to tax foreign imports heavily in order to make their prices extremely high; this in turn makes their own people unwilling to buy many [foreign products], which enables them to concentrate instead on strengthening domestic manufactures, and thus stem the flow of gold and silver abroad For example, silks and woolens are taxed at a rate of 60 percent[13] because these are classes of goods that can be domestically produced. Also, items like tobacco and liquor, while not prohibited by law, are nonetheless considered harmful, so the tax on them is especially high as well. Books and printed materials, on the other hand, are imported duty free so that by availing themselves of the literatures of other countries, their own people's arts and letters will perhaps be improved. Recently, the tea exported by China and Japan has also been made duty free, because American soil is not suitable for tea cultivation and the tea merchants have for many years complained bitterly that the costs were excessively high; moreover, since clothing and foodstuffs are considered necessities, they had no choice but to make tea duty free as well. Their domestic products are exported duty free from a desire to use cheap domestic goods as a means for merchants taking them abroad to accumulate increasingly larger profits, since the volume of trade will necessarily grow larger day by day as a result. The logic of this is perfectly sound and practical. In concentrating on acquiring profits from other countries, Westerners must dredge the sources of profit in their home countries deeply and widely, and they do not lightly consent to releasing many of them. In this their approach is exacting and deeply resolute. *Ai!* This is most unsettling! Every year their import duties come to around $40 million, 1.5 percent of which is used to defray customs expenses. The customs inspectors are paid twelve thousand dollars a year; deputy inspectors, five thousand dollars; and officers, seven thousand dollars. All told there are around fifteen hundred personnel. The

12. This was a vitally important point for Li and his readers. In China, the fees charged for internal transit duties, or *likin (lijin)*, were increasingly seen by self-strengthening officials as hampering the empire's commerce. The practice began in July 1853 around Yangzhou as a way to raise money to fight the Taipings. It was continued, among other reasons, as a way to get around the low tariffs on imports dictated by the succession of "unequal treaties" with the foreign powers. In the event, versions of the tax survived the Qing dynasty and a series of successor governments until it was finally abolished in 1931.

13. Cf. Li's visit to the Cheney Brothers' mill in chapter 13.

inspection of warehouses is carried out separately in the port. As we left, Mr. Carr presented us with a volume on customs rules and regulations.

Mr. Havemeyer had mentioned firefighting equipment, so I went along with him to a fire station to inspect some of it. In the middle of the building sat a four-wheeled horse cart mounting a fifty-horsepower steam engine. This is used for drawing and spraying water and is pulled by two horses. Inside the engine, coal and kindling have been prepared in advance. The crew is made up of four men and the cost of the apparatus is forty-five hundred dollars. There is another cart loaded with rubber hoses for drawing water, also with four wheels, drawn by one horse, and with a crew of two, costing five hundred dollars. The power of the engine is enormous, and it is capable of shooting water to a height of three hundred feet. The underside of the nozzle is fitted with numerous pinholes, so that during the extreme heat of a fire the fireman can give it a turn and wet himself down with the water from the pinholes in order to stay cool.

Even more remarkable is an electrical device, next to which is mounted a bell, on the left-hand wall of the station house. Whenever a fire breaks out anywhere, the bell is automatically rung in response to the arrival of an electrical signal, and the tethers securing the horses stabled in the rear are automatically released. The horses, hearing the bell, quickly move forward and take up their positions before the various vehicles, and within five seconds the firemen can be prepared to leave. If it is evening, the great commotion of the horses moving across the floor awakens the firemen upstairs. Their coats, boots, and hats have already been carefully prepared before they go to sleep, and they can be dressed within five seconds. Thus, the time from when the alarm sounds to that of the carriage leaving the gate is calculated to be five seconds during the day and ten seconds at night. The wagons can travel at one li per minute; bells mounted on them are rung to clear the streets, as the firemen are not held legally responsible if pedestrians are injured or killed. There are only twelve firemen, divided into two shifts. Every day they are permitted to return home for an hour and a half by turns, and every month they allowed to sleep home twice; during the remaining time they are not allowed any leave. Every man receives a very generous monthly wage of one hundred

A New
Account
of a Trip
Around
the Globe

185

A New
Account
of a Trip
Around
the Globe

186

dollars because he must remain constantly on the alert. Their horses are selected for their size and strength and are trained until their routines become second nature. Next to the electrical device is a board displaying a list of all the streets and the various zones inside and outside the city. As methods of fire rescue, these are indeed the most effective and every large city should promptly adopt them.

The foundling hospital [New York City Foundling Asylum][14] has more than a hundred rooms, all of them quite spacious. Presently, there are about six hundred boys and girls from newborns to those seven or eight years of age, and sometimes as many as three thousand. Every floor has sixteen beds arranged in pairs facing each other, one of which sleeps two infants and the other a wet nurse. The screening curtains, bedclothes, shirts, and trousers are all spotlessly clean; likewise, the kitchens and washrooms. The superintendent and staff are all nuns of a religious order, like Chinese Daoist *po*, and it is said that they strictly observe their order's regulations. Boys and girls four to five years old are taught to recognize words and read, and also taught to make small toys like folded tricornered paper [a Chinese game] or clay figurines, and with these they begin to develop their thinking. There is also a hall that seats two to three hundred children, all six to eight years old. Women teachers instruct them in songs and join in with them in techniques of light stretching and breathing exercises. The boys and girls stand on each side. Another female teacher in their midst plays the piano with them, quickening the pace as all beat time and clap together. During the time before they come of age, their various abilities are assessed and jobs recommended for the future. The yearly cost is calculated at $261,000, half of which is from public funds and half from donations.

The community civic association [*shenmin gonghui*] is a place where the gentry and people go to devote themselves to reading newspapers and various kinds of books. Those entering the association pay yearly dues of five dollars, and there are currently more than eighty-five hundred members. The newspapers of various

14. The asylum (later hospital) had been founded by the Roman Catholic Sisters of Charity in 1869. The building Li visited was opened in 1873 on Sixty-eighth St. and was the product of a one-hundred-thousand-dollar grant from the state and matching funds from local donors. It had also expanded its services to care for unwed mothers and handle adoption placement.

countries and cities are all available there, and the library has a collection of 165,000 books. Those joining from the stores and shops pay five dollars per year if they are the proprietors and four dollars if they are employees. The various people responsible for the association's affairs are all elected, and they are not allowed to choose any one person too much. Regardless of the business or profession, civic associations are established in all the Western countries and employ conventions along these lines.

A New
Account
of a Trip
Around
the Globe

187

The editor-in-chief of the *Sun* newspaper, Mr. [Moses Sperry] Beach, came to meet us and said that there are over sixty large and small newspapers in New York City. This paper prints 140,000 copies every day and has six huge printing presses. Of the great newspapers, aside from the *Times* of London, the *Sun* is considered to be the largest. He went on to say: Newspapers cover everything from government affairs down to those of the neighborhood, omitting nothing. Indeed, in effectively providing access to official information for the upper classes, and increasing useful knowledge for the benefit of those below, they do a great deal of good. He then asked what the Chinese press was like. I replied: "Recently, it too has become quite popular."

"City Hall" may be translated as this city's *yamen,* and Mr. Havemeyer accompanied me to pay my respects to the mayor (similar to a prefect), Mr. [William H.] Wickham, and we had quite an agreeable conversation. In this office there are 140 administrators. Mr. Wickham led us to the first floor to view the paintings, all of which were portraits of the country's early notables and former mayors. Also on the first floor was a room of weapons, flags, banners, suits of armor, a magistrate's desk, and various writing implements and other objects from the time of the nation's founding. One of Mr. Havemeyer's esteemed relatives had formerly served as mayor and won the people's support for three successive terms, quite an unusual number of times. Unfortunately, he died last year and we could not meet him.[15]

Mr. Havemeyer then went along with us to the New York State governor's office [the Governor's Room in City Hall] to visit Gov-

15. Henry O. Havemeyer's cousin, William Frederick Havemeyer (b. 1804), served as mayor in 1845, 1848, and again, after a long interval, in 1872—not in three consecutive terms as reported by Li. Though he worked closely with Governor Samuel J. Tilden, his last term was marred by scandals growing out of city appointments, and he died in office in 1874. He was succeeded by William Wickham, elected in 1874. Johnson and Malone, *Dictionary of American Biography,* 4:404–5.

A New
Account
of a Trip
Around
the Globe

188

ernor Tilden, and we sat and talked for a considerable time. He was curious to know why, given China's preference for using the silver coins of other countries, it does not mint its own and gain the economic power this brings. We also talked about the minting of American coins [see chapter 11]. He presented us with two small, signed photographs, and I reciprocated with a small picture that he very happily urged me to autograph using Chinese script. The members of his family were also each introduced, and he led us in person to see different places of interest. The sitting room was very spacious and the library has a collection of ten thousand volumes. Mr. Havemeyer said that the governor is addicted to books and that his free time is spent with a book constantly in hand. Presently, two men are campaigning for the American presidency: one is [Rutherford B.] Hayes, and the other is this governor. Whether the winner will be Hayes or the governor is as yet undecided.[16]

The safety depository is a facility built to store gold and pearls, gems, license certificates, deeds, and the like. Regardless of whether they are officials or ordinary people, families who have valuable objects and are afraid of fire or loss can send them here to be stored for them. One can see iron strongboxes of all sizes requiring large amounts of rent. For example, a single box, seven inches square, rents for fifteen dollars a year; the largest of them costs three hundred dollars a year. The room is built of stone and is outfitted with thick iron plating above and below and on all four sides. The stands for the cases are also of iron, and there is not a scrap of wood throughout the room. Security guards circulate around the room to furnish protection for the wealthy. The various doors of the building are all locked, and entry cannot be had without several keys. Outside the room there is a time clock with the hands and the dots on the clock face each having small iron tubes. Every half a [Chinese; one English] hour, a guard must take a pencil and draw a circle inside the tube to record it. As the clock hands rotate, if there is a space without a mark then it is known that this man at some hour was not at his station and he is punished with appropriate severity. Also, there are electric wires running to concealed spaces on all the doors so that if there is an intruder, an elec-

16. The Sunday *New York Times* of October 15, 1876, carried the following small item in its "City and Suburban News" column: "Two Chinese Commissioners to the Centennial came to visit the City Hall yesterday, accompanied by Henry Havemeyer. They were shown the Governor's room and the various offices."

trical device is activated at once and a bell sounds. The purpose of all of these [precautions] is to safeguard completely against theft.

Mr. Havemeyer's sugar refinery is in New [sic] Jersey City,[17] and specializes in purchasing raw sugar from various countries, first inspecting it for quality and then putting it into a huge cauldron and boiling it. The cauldron can hold two thousand pounds of sugar. The sugar water is black in color and is combined with the ashes of cattle bones in order to clarify it. It is then piped to large vats, where a small portion of ox blood is mixed with it to make the impurities rise to the top, while the purified material gradually thickens. From there it enters a round boiler turned by steam power where it gradually becomes clean and white and is finished as top-grade sugar. The yellow colored liquid in it is piped into another boiler, which rotates it again into second-grade white sugar. The sugar water still remaining is piped into a boiler on a lower floor, where it is made into yellow sugar. The residual liquid, which cannot be boiled down further, is then made into syrup. Every day they process three hundred thousand pounds of raw sugar, the vast majority of which is made into sugar and syrup, while the rest consists of waste and impurities. They have five or six machines, which every day burn forty tons of coal. The price of the land and construction of the building are figured at $140,000, with $160,000 for the machines, and the workers number more than 130. The cost of the raw sugar is nine cents a pound, while the selling price for the finished product is fifteen cents a pound. The import duties are two and one half cents a pound on [raw sugar], and the exports are duty free. The ox bones and ashes come to three cents a pound. Every day, the value of the sugar sold comes to $50,000–$60,000.

There is a large department store on Broadway, established by the American, [A. T.] Stewart. The building is of white stone, five stories tall and shaped like a cube, with perhaps more than three hundred rooms.[18] There is every sort of flowered carpet, men's and

A New
Account
of a Trip
Around
the Globe

189

17. Li may be in error here. The Havemeyers had both a Lower Manhattan and a Brooklyn refinery. Johnson and Malone, *Dictionary of American Biography*, 4:404–5.

18. While Alexander T. Stewart (1803–76) had earlier opened a women's department store called the Marble Palace on Broadway, Li appears to be describing instead his famous Cast Iron Palace. Opened in 1862, its innovative, Italianate iron exterior was painted white, and its five floors occupied an entire city block between Broadway and Fourth Avenue, making it the world's largest retail establishment. By the time of Li's visit, Stewart's anchored a Broadway retail district known locally as Ladies' Mile.

A New
Account
of a Trip
Around
the Globe

190

women's clothing and hats, and all manner of items for one's dress. In the basement is an engine of six hundred horsepower that runs all the working machinery. The store requires about fifteen hundred people to run it, and every day they sell goods worth about $70,000 to $100,000.

The theater's main stage is very wide with perhaps a thousand gaslights and more than two hundred actors and actresses, who performed a play that was set in Turkey. Wearing makeup, wigs, and gaily colored clothes embroidered with gold, they thrust and parried with swords and spears. In front of the stage there was an orchestra of sixty or seventy musicians. At the close of every act, the stage curtain fell and was then raised momentarily for the next act. There were dramatic and acrobatic acts, music and weeping, demons with a hundred different expressions, and seventy or eighty beautiful women, their clothes of filmy silk, joining hands and dancing. All of this was unimaginably strange and magical. There were one or two thousand people in the audience and Mr. Havemeyer's box for one performance cost twenty-five dollars in foreign money. The next night we went to another theater that was even better.[19]

19. Either of two productions advertised during the week of Li's stay in New York might correspond roughly to his description. Booth's Theatre was running a ballet version of Lord Byron's play *Sardanapalus*, set in the ancient Near East, and Niblo's Garden mounted a production called *Baba*, billed as "the grandest spectacle ever produced."

BOOK III
Notes on Sightseeing

CHAPTER 15. THE ENGLISH CAPITAL
OF LONDON

London is the capital city of England and the great metropolis of the West. Now that I have crossed the Atlantic Ocean from the east coast of America to visit this city, seen its dense population and the richness of its markets and shops; its houses and buildings as tall as mountain peaks, and its streets and roads criss-crossing in dense profusion, its special reputation is indeed well deserved. In comparison to America, however, it presents an altogether different scene. Because America is a newly founded country, there is on the whole nothing there that has not been recently constructed. Here, things have more of a feel of antiquity, like an old aristocratic family whose vigor is yet undiminished. The city is in the southeast of the English homeland (the English state is composed of three islands,[1] one called "England," another called "Scotland," and a third called "Ireland"), south of Middlesex *fu* [prefecture] and north of Surrey, spanning these two prefectures. From the mouth of the Thames River it is about 160 li. The river winds in from the west, flowing through the city and then east out to sea. In ancient times there was a wall, the site of which now stands in the middle of the modern city. While the ancient ruins are mostly gone, those remaining in the city center are said to have survived from antiq-

---

1. Li here repeats a mistake made by Xu Jiyu and other earlier commentators. See *Yinghuan jilue*, 45b.

A New
Account
of a Trip
Around
the Globe

192

uity. Actually the whole is referred to as a city [*cheng*] and is not divided into inner and outer sections [i.e., as are Chinese cities]. Modern buildings and houses are packed into a space calculated to be 22 li long and 3o li wide with additional buildings and homes extending all around for another 7o li or more. There are more than four million residents, and there is no country whose gentlemen and merchants are not represented among them. In the twelfth year of the reign of the Tongzhi emperor [1874], it was calculated that there were already more than 520,000 buildings and every year since approximately 2,000–3,000 more have been built. The streets within the center of the city are narrow, but along the perimeter they are broad, completely level, and spotlessly clean, without dirt or odors. It has been determined that the combined length of all thoroughfares is 21,780 li. The street lamps total more than 360,000 and every night use gas in the amount of 10 million *qiaobi* [cubic feet] (every *qiaobi* is a square *chi* [foot]).[2] Electric wires extend everywhere, perhaps 2,000 of them, and the railway tracks are like spider webs, their length and number running through the city unknown.

Protecting the city are five thousand soldiers, wearing red coats and blue pants, or a black uniform. Their hats are made from black bear fur and are as tall as a *dou* measure.[3] Every palace, government office, barracks, and factory office has guards stationed to protect it, and at the end of the day they are not the least bit fatigued. There are eight thousand policemen equipped with special short sticks, wearing black [*sic*] uniforms with leather belts and hats made of black felt, keeping watch on every street and alley in different areas, diligently maintaining order. The pedestrians come and go quietly amid the incessant traffic of people and vehicles. As for the climate, in winter the thermometer registers about 18 or 19 degrees [Fahrenheit]; during the hottest period of the summer it only rises to 8o degrees. In the spring, summer, and fall it is mild; in winter, foggy and colder. The eleventh month [in 1876, mid-December to mid-January] is particularly so, sometimes to the point where people cannot see each other if they are more than a few feet apart. Because the residents are so numerous and all the buildings use furnaces for heating, the coal smoke and fog blend

2. Literally, "rectangle" or "square foot"; the implication is "square square foot."
3. A *dou* is a measure of volume equal to approximately 2.34 gallons.

together, acquiring a yellowish tinge. Even newly constructed buildings no more than a few years old are already blackened from it. Just as the *wei* hour turns to *shen* [around 3:00 P.M.] the lamps are already burning in all the homes. During this time, the Parliament adjourns, the monarch goes to stay at an auxiliary palace[4] on the Isle of Wight, and everywhere the nobles, gentry, and wealthy businessmen generally retreat to their country houses and villages. The horse-drawn vehicles are calculated at several hundred thousand per day, trotting and galloping everywhere, and continuing throughout the night without letup. The streets are mostly paved with small cobblestones, and the wheels hitting the stones make a noise like thunder, causing the buildings to shake. Those riding in the carriages cannot hear themselves speak, and in the evening it is especially disturbing to one's sound sleep.[5]

Four of the monarch's palaces are in this city: One is Buckingham; another, [St.] James; a third is Whitehall, and finally there is Kensington. The crown prince's residence is Marlborough House, and all of these are in the city's West End. Set amid the most beautiful gardens and parks are three separate auxiliary palaces: one, in the city of Windsor to the south of the capital, called Windsor Castle; one on the Isle of Wight in the sea to the south of the country, called Osborne; and one in Scotland, called Balmoral. Except for the palaces on the Isle of Wight and in Scotland, I have visited them all. Every one is grand, magnificent, lofty, and towering, and their battlements are done with particular skill, though Windsor has been singled out as the best in this regard.

In the center of the city is St. Paul's Cathedral, whose central dome is the highest point in the capital. To the west is the lord mayor's office (the lord mayor is like a *fu yin* [metropolitan prefect]). Facing the river on the southwest is the Parliament. West of the Parliament is the ancient Westminster Cathedral. In the city's southeast are many shipyards. There are also a number of colleges and academies, 1,540 private schools among the people, and about one thousand churches. The rest, like the Foreign Office, India Office, various ministries and departments, barracks, and factories

4. *Xinggong,* literally "mobile," or "traveling palace." During the Qing it referred chiefly to the Imperial Court's summer retreat in Jehol. See Hucker, *Dictionary of Official Titles,* 245. Li uses the term for the royal residences outside of London.

5. Li revisits this point in greater depth in chapter 25.

A New
Account
of a Trip
Around
the Globe

194

are mostly of fine stonework and incomparably solid and sturdy. The great library [British Museum]'s collections contain seven hundred thousand volumes. The *yuanlin* [parks] (in the English language, *pa*) number more than a dozen, with abundant flowers and trees, and both officials and people can stroll about and take their ease in them. Hyde Park is the city's largest, and there is an unusually pretty pavilion erected on its grounds, inside of which the current monarch has had placed a marble and gilded statue of her late prince consort. The residences of the gentry and the largest stores are in the west of the city, while the workers and poorer people tend to live in the eastern section. In the city center, called "The City," the banks are clustered. Famous people, ancient and modern, are honored in bronze and stone statues and commemorative monuments, most of which are set up at various large intersections and are too numerous for one to count. There are a number of brothels as well, whose guests are greeted with smiles of welcome, some even soliciting their customers right out on the major streets.

In America, many of the streets have iron rails laid in them for running streetcars, in order to transport passengers conveniently. This city, however, has underground tunnels through which trains are run. Different districts have ticket offices set up, and whenever passengers want to go to one section or another they purchase the appropriate ticket, go down forty or fifty stone steps to the underground train station, board the train and ride. Next to the station there are also stalls and small shops for the convenience of the passengers, and these constitute a blurred, half-lit, totally different world. The reason for this is that there is limited space for the vast numbers of people, and all of the nation's traffic—the pedestrians on the streets, horses, and wagons—had been unable to move freely about. They therefore created the underground so as to facilitate the people's travel.

My residence in the city was at number 2 Spanish Place.[6] The lodgings were on the third floor, splendidly arranged, and the weekly rent for the suite of three rooms came to two "pounds" (every "pound" is a gold coin equivalent to five silver dollars), ten "shillings" (every "shilling" is roughly equivalent to twenty-five for-

6. *Xiban'nian jie.* It is just off Manchester Square, which seems to accord with Li's observation that the trip from Euston Station was about a mile. See chapter 30.

eign cents). Food for two [Li and his interpreter, Chen Chiyuan], coal, a female housekeeper (Western law prohibits the purchase of women for use as servants, but many hire poor women as household staff), and wages for the cook came to about sixty dollars a week. The food here is cheaper than in America, and the carriages even more so, with the cost amounting to less than a dollar for a ride of more than ten li, unlike in America, where it cost two to three dollars.

A New
Account
of a Trip
Around
the Globe

195

The Imperial Maritime Customs official James Duncan Campbell is the man who has been sent by our country to handle our affairs in London.[7] I went to pay him my respects and met his assistant, Mr. Bullock, and also former Zhejiang [Ningbo] customs commissioner [F. W.] White, who was home on leave, and Mr. Jones, an engineer in the customs service. During the four years Mr. White was in Ningbo, we had got on quite well, and coming across him today in this remote corner of the world was indeed a happy occasion.[8]

The Houses of Parliament are to the west overlooking the banks of the river Thames. Thirty-five years ago the court authorized officials to select the beautiful stone with which to renovate the building, which covers an area of forty-eight *mou,* and cost more than £2 million. The building has more than a thousand rooms and over a hundred different stairways. Hot air registers are employed throughout the building during the winter with their estimated length coming to more than fifty li, while the yearly cost for gas lighting comes to thirty-five hundred pounds. On the southwest corner of the Parliament building a tall tower has been

7. James Duncan Campbell (1833–1907). Li transliterates his name as *Jin Deng'gan* ("Jim Duncan"). His actual title was non-resident secretary of the Inspectorate General of the Imperial Maritime Customs. Campbell served at this post from its inception in 1874 until his death, and much of his correspondence with Robert Hart has been published in Chen and Han, *Archives;* and Fairbank, Bruner, and Matheson, *The I.G. in Peking.* See introduction.

8. F. W. White was on leave in London from 1874 to 1876. In the last line of this passage Li is referencing his meeting with White as analogous to one of the four proverbial "happy moments in life." The identity of the man Li calls *Yibuluo* is strictly guesswork. I have identified him as Thomas Lowndes Bullock, former British consul at Tianjin. He was known to be in London during the time and worked with Guo Songtao's party shortly afterward. Though he was not, by any means, Campbell's assistant in the formal sense, he was perceived to be so later by several in the retinue of the newly arrived Chinese embassy. See chapter 30, note 4. Other possibilities include H. O. Brown, IMC interpreter and commissioner at Dakao, Taiwan, on leave in London in 1876; and M. J. O'Brien, an English instructor at the Tongwen Guan, also on leave in London in 1876.

A New
Account
of a Trip
Around
the Globe

196

erected for the storage of archival materials from different years. There is also a 320-foot clock tower on which a great bell has been mounted [Big Ben], which is rung automatically, and [the clock] is able to run for eight days [without attention]. The bell weighs thirteen tons and the diameter of the clock face is twenty-two feet, while the hourly chiming of the clock can be heard for dozens of li.

The inside is divided into upper and lower houses. The Upper House [House of Lords] is ninety-seven feet deep and forty-five feet wide, and is where the high officials and aristocracy deliberate. In front is a raised platform, two feet high, like a screened alcove, in the middle of which sits an elegantly decorated, gilded throne for the monarch. Next to it is a comparatively smaller one with a slightly lower seat, where the crown prince sits. Mr. Campbell, who accompanied us on our visit, said the crown prince is called the Prince of Wales. "Prince" translates as *Qin Wang;* "Wales" is the name of a territory of twelve prefectures to the west of the capital. This is actually a title traditionally conferred on the heir apparent throughout the history of England, though he does not really reside in the territory of Wales. The present crown prince is currently studying at Christ Church College [Oxford]. On completion of his studies he will undergo examinations in different subjects of study, and will then be sent to nearby countries in order to obtain an extensive knowledge of world affairs, following which he will be prepared to rule. The quality of his wisdom will thus be improved while his education is being furthered by travel. His benevolence, virtue, and ability will therefore be extended, something for which the entire country cannot be but gratified. Below the platform two large tables are placed on which the edicts and proclamations are prepared for discussion in order to become law. Flanking both sides are a number of chairs on which the members sit. Whenever the monarch is present in the Parliament, it is considered a set rule that after an hour and a half, he or she must return to the palace.

The Lower House [Commons] is sixty-five feet deep and forty-five feet broad, and is where the men of learning and ability among the common people hold public debates. In the middle is a chair on which the Speaker sits and a number of chairs and tables are also set up on four different levels, seating perhaps several hundred people. There is a gallery, bright and spacious, where the people are allowed to attend the debates. Reporters from all the newspapers are also present in the gallery calmly listening and taking notes. Aside from these areas are a Great Seal Room, Guards Room [a reference to the Parliamentary Police], and the [Royal] Robing Room. There is also a long corridor [the Royal Gallery] hung throughout with paintings of the victories and heroic deeds of former monarchs painted by famous artists. Examining the procedures of the Parliament, one finds that they are identical to those of other Western countries. They thus join together all classes in order that the affairs of the country may be run without interruption. As a rule, one can frequently visit the Parliament when the great political issues are being aired, and even as venerated an object as the monarch's throne is open to inspection by the people without restriction.

A New
Account
of a Trip
Around
the Globe

197

The [General] Telegraph Office is four stories high and opposite the [General] Post Office, and under the administration of the head official of the posts. Mr. White and Mr. Bullock accompanied me as I went to inspect the electrical instruments installed on the second floor. There are wooden cabinets about forty feet long, six feet high, and a bit over a foot deep, all divided into two thousand and several hundred cubicles. Every space is like a small box, and every one has an iron wire. These are connected to the major cities in all different countries of the globe, all of which can send messages. There are over a thousand and several hundred telegraphic instruments of all sizes employing about seven hundred operators, of whom there are more women than men, each one operating two or three devices. To send a message from one office to another, a code is substituted for the letters and keyed into the instrument, which transmits the telegram as it is entered. No sooner is the transmission completed than it is received at the other station. As for messages from other stations, as soon as they detect the motion of the electrical instruments, the operators instantly decode the letters and write them out, then send the messages on to another room.

The method by which these are sent is quite astonishing: The envelope containing the message is placed inside a rubber sleeve. The sleeve is three or four inches long and two inches in diameter. Next to all the instruments are mounted air [pneumatic] tubes. Facing the tubes are indicators like clock dials. The rubber sleeve

A New
Account
of a Trip
Around
the Globe

198

is placed inside the pneumatic tube and sent off by means of suction from an air pump. The personnel in the other room hear a bell ring on the indicator and know that the rubber sleeve is on its way; seeing the indicator needle pointing to the left, they know it has arrived. Following this, the letter is put in another envelope and sent to its respective destination through the postal system. You could not begin to fathom the ingenuity of the full variety and extent of the regulations. I heard that the power of the suction in the pneumatic tubes is such that, with the twisting and turning calculated, every three minutes a message can go five li. The idea for setting up these pneumatic tubes came about because the building is so large that the telegraphic area, the registration office where the messages are drafted, and the areas where they are posted could not all be consolidated into one room. Without these tubes to send messages all around, the whole operation would require staff to do it. Not only would using so many people be enormously expensive, but it would also interfere with the operation of things and cause mistakes.

In the basement three machines have been installed, all of them of fifty horsepower, just to create the suction for the tubes. Every day, incoming and outgoing messages number about forty thousand. Every year, the salaries of office personnel come to about six hundred thousand dollars in gold; as for the expenses of other items, I do not completely know how much they come to.

In the central office, to the right of the building is a room for receiving letters of remittance [the Receiver and Accountant General's office]. Each piece of mail carrying money is brought in here and inspected and counted in accordance with the remittance. Mr. Bullock said that the English post office, telegraph office, and remittance office work together and bring in large surpluses. This is indeed of the utmost profit to the country and convenience to the people.

The London customs is in a huge building in the city's East End facing the Thames. It is organized with four chief inspectors who stay at the customs in order to superintend. The man in charge is named Gowen [unknown], and we had a friendly initial discussion centered mostly on the topic of administration. He said that last year import duties (under English law, exports of domestic products are also duty free [as in the United States]) came to £10,114,992 and, presently, every day total about £32,000 with the figures on Saturdays and Sundays rising to more than £40,000. Only eleven customs officers handle the fees, while the Bank of England receives the customs revenues twice a day, every day. Those conducting official business are divided into inner and outer branches, the inner branch comprising about seven hundred people, and the outer branch about sixteen hundred. Accordingly, they select [only] five out of the several hundred who apply and pay all of their salaries and expenses.

The highest duties are on tobacco, liquor, and tea. For cigars (*lu song* [Luzon] *yan;* the English call them *sigai*), every pound in weight carries a duty of five shillings. Tobacco leaves are assessed at 5 percent; and every "gallon" (equivalent to about five Chinese *jin*) of liquor is taxed at ten shillings. Fine liquors are taxed as much as sixteen shillings per gallon. For tea, the duty is six pence (every "pence" is a copper coin equal to two foreign [U.S.] pennies) per pound of weight. Silk and cotton are duty free.

Every year they confiscate about £5,000 worth of goods. There is a contraband warehouse nearby, the stocks of which were at the moment rather small. The smuggling techniques are quite remarkable, and the methods of seizing smugglers are in turn most exacting. One man was found to have cigars concealed inside loaves of bread, while another was discovered with them when the soles of his shoes were searched.

We next went to the first floor, where they inspect tea. All tea sent from China must be inspected to determine what kind of filler is mixed in with it. If the examination discloses that it contains a great deal of material unsuitable for consumption, then it is destroyed; if the foreign matter is minimal, they will permit the tea to be reshipped to other countries for sale. This inspection is not to determine the duty on the tea, but only to ascertain whether or not it can be used, so as to prevent the people of the country from getting sick from it. We then went to a room where they inspect liquor, for which they employ experts in the examination of imported wines. They must determine the percentage of alcohol among the different kinds of wine, and if the inspection shows the alcohol content to be higher than the specified amount, the duty must then be increased. Nearby, merchant ships are gathered at anchor, and there are numerous warehouses built by the mer-

A New
Account
of a Trip
Around
the Globe

199

chants themselves [i.e., as distinct from government warehouses], holding 150,000 chests of Chinese tea.

The *Times* newspaper is respected as authoritative in every capital. It is the most accurate at reporting the current events of different nations, and its opinions are masterly and extremely precise. From the monarch to the masses, nearly everyone deems it a pleasure to be among the first to read it. The building is four stories tall, red brick and white stone, imposing and grand in aspect.

In the basement, adjoining spaces have been constructed as composition rooms, where the matrices—the method of which utilizes a machine to arrange the words—and the character boards are prepared on thick paper. These enter a machine to press them, and the words are then embossed in a convex manner on the paper. The paper will be placed onto a mold and melted tin poured into it to complete the matrix, which corresponds to the convex pattern of the words, outlining each one clearly. The original character boards and thick paper are now all useless, but the cast matrix is installed in the press for printing. No other technique can approach this for speed.

We then came to a large hall, which functions as the pressroom. Here there were six huge machines. A long sheet of paper is passed into the end of a machine, the matrices having been previously inked with black ink felt (the felt is soaked in black ink). The paper is first wound around an iron shaft having large blades. As the machine revolves, the sound is like thunder. It emerges at the end of the machine and is simultaneously printed and cut. Once cut, the sheets are piled onto a wooden bench and every [Chinese] half hour, the six machines together print more than seventy thousand sheets. The finished newspapers are very long and wide, and, since they want to fold them into smaller and narrower sizes, there are also machines to do this without the need of human labor. The machines are like tall cabinets and utilize the power of the main engine for their action. As the newspapers rest on the cabinet, the motion of the machine repeatedly folds them very quickly. Every time they reach one hundred copies, the machine briefly stops and the papers are taken down. The machine then resumes folding, and does several thousand copies in no time. It is truly astonishing. Every machine costs fifteen thousand dollars. The main engine is

A New
Account
of a Trip
Around
the Globe

200

rated at 250 horsepower and can put out several hundred thousand sheets per day.

In the city there are more than ten large newspapers and an unknown number of smaller ones. There are also many so-called evening papers, Sunday papers, and monthly papers. In fact, the number of all the papers published daily is unknown. This is true of the capital as well as of other cities. Moreover, it is true of other countries as well as of England. In forming an estimate of these throughout the entire globe, one could not guess the number of papers per day. In addition, more and more papers appear daily, since those who remain uninformed potentially stand to be ruined. In my humble opinion, I note that Westerners have established newspapers from a desire to thoroughly understand the world's affairs. People must comprehend world affairs in order to be capable of participating in them. Thus, the founding of these newspapers can indeed be said to be quite advantageous and their benefits considerable.

The [South] Kensington Museum [presently the Victoria and Albert Museum] has every kind of article of dress and adornment used in different countries. There are cat's eye gems as large as pigeon's eggs. The regalia and weapons of ancient and modern rulers are set out in a dozen cabinets, with treasures and antiques in dozens more. There is a bronze bell cast for the "Perceptive Being" Buddhist temple during the reign of the Dao Guang emperor [1821–51]; gold and jade bracelets, hairpins, and so forth, cloisonné, and lacquerware, all of which was obtained from China. There are also very ancient bronze Buddhist statues and a variety of porcelain and bronze objects on loan from Japan. There are jars and vases perhaps three feet in height, objects that are three thousand years old found buried in Egypt. In the center large banners hang depicting the great towers of different countries. The highest among them is the dome of a cathedral in the Italian city of Rome [St. Peter's] at 550 feet. The Chang Gan Pagoda of Jiangning, since destroyed, is also listed here at 210 feet tall. A hundred years ago, the men of England, France, and other countries mostly wore wigs of plaited hair falling to their shoulders and very long coats, closely resembling Chinese styles.

The building housing the British Museum (the English refer to

A New
Account
of a Trip
Around
the Globe

201

A New
Account
of a Trip
Around
the Globe

202

their own country as *Bailitishe*, the name under which the union of
the islands of England, Scotland [*sic*], and Ireland is generally
known) is constructed of white stone, grand and colossal in scale,
the whole costing $5 million. Inside there are more than ten gal-
leries of antiquities from the past three thousand years unearthed
in Egypt, the Holy Land, Greece, and other countries. There are a
number of statues of ancient idols, their clothing and adornments
strange and eerie, said to be four thousand years old. There are
also statues of ancient Greek warriors and goddesses riding horses
made of stone from the front of a temple, fourteen feet tall, all fashioned from a single piece of stone and exquisitely carved [the Elgin
Marbles frieze from the Parthenon]. There are several ancient sar-
cophagi, some of stone, some of bronze. On the lids of the coffins
are sculpted images of the deceased in repose. The stone, a pur-
plish black color [diorite], is very unusual; tapping it makes a ringing sound, and the coffins are made of entire pieces of stone. The
bronze coffins are cast, not made of bronze plates compressed
together. There are perhaps a dozen wooden idols, some with
human torsos and horses' legs, others with horses' heads and
men's bodies, all completely different. The ancient ink slabs were
somewhat like those of China. The ancient Greek bronze mirrors,
dozens of large and small ones, have writing on the back closely
resembling tadpoles,[9] and also some resembling the form of birds
and beasts [hieroglyphs]. I had suspected that these objects might
have been native to China, but they were in fact obtained from the
Greeks. The [cuneiform] script of the papyrus books of the country
of Babylon (now part of Turkey) resembles the *zhongding wen*
inscriptions on ancient Chinese *ding* tripods, and there is also a
room that contains more than a dozen corpses [mummies] over
three thousand years old, all sleeping in their coffins.

My Western friends tell me that the dead of ancient Egypt were
treated after sundown to lessen the heat. After being painted with
fragrant oil and wrapped tightly using a great many cloth strips—
with a picture included depicting the deceased—and wrapped in
another two to three hundred yards of cloth, they were placed into

9. A possible reference to the so-called tadpole or wiggly worm script said to be on
the Tablets of Yu, legendary founder of the Xia dynasty (ca. 2205–1818 B.C.E.?). In several
places in his account, Li is anxious to show perceived connections between early Chinese states and those of the West in remote antiquity.

their coffins and interred, not spoiling for ages. Now, however, we do not hear of this [practice] anymore. These have all come from Egypt, and their outer wrappings are already gone, so they are preserved only by the inner bindings. Dozens of cabinets are set up nearby, with all kinds of cattle, sheep, cats, dogs, fish, and birds, also wrapped using the ancient methods as funerary objects. The styles of the boats, weapons, and tools are identical to those of China.

A New
Account
of a Trip
Around
the Globe

203

I also saw antique swords with jeweled hilts bearing ancient seals of two characters, though they were too rusty and corroded to make out. In addition there is a crown, the style of which is like a gourd, nine [Chinese] inches tall, with a seal cut of six characters on it. In the center there is a yellow satin wrapping for holding the hair. The headgear is as heavy as eighty-two [silver] ounce coins and eight cash, and made of 50 percent gold. All of these came from our China.

In the center of the museum is a library holding volumes of the ancient and modern works of many countries, seven hundred thousand of them, including about ten thousand Chinese books. Next to it is a circular room, 150 feet wide, seating three to four hundred people. The literati of the country and those of other countries traveling for study who receive a permit are allowed to enter to read. The building's construction is of iron and stone, with no wood, as a precaution against fire. There are also two large rooms, one with various kinds of animal skins and one for bird skins and feathers, with their internal organs stuffed with other materials and sewn up as if they were living, selected as completely as possible from all the world's countries for display. There was a bird as small as a peacock, splendidly colored like our Chinese pheasant, which the Westerners call a "dodo." It was said that they had still existed six hundred years ago but are now extinct. I asked how they knew that there were no more, and they replied that they had "studied their bones, and at present there are no others like them; therefore we know they are extinct." Pursuing this further I said:

> Reading our classics, Westerners are always saying that they
> do not believe in the existence of the dragons, phoenixes,
> and unicorns [*qilin;* three of the so-called four intelligent

creatures] in the sages' stories. My reply has been that regardless of whether later generations have been misled by the sages' stories, or whether these creatures actually existed in antiquity and are currently extinct, it is impossible to say for certain that they never existed at all. Westerners as a rule do not make light of this. Now seeing this "dodo" bird, and after your saying that it existed in the past and is now extinct, how do we know that the dragon, phoenix, and unicorn did not exist in the past and have not now become extinct? How can we know this was true of the "dodo" but not the phoenix?

A New
Account
of a Trip
Around
the Globe

204

One of the staff, who held the rank of "Professor" (the initial rank held by prominent scholars), and who had been in China as an assistant consul was deeply impressed by this argument.

Among the holdings of the Kensington and British Museums, antiquities are in the majority. This is because knowledge of the past can lead to an understanding of the present, and so teaching about the past can serve to enhance this understanding. Thus, for the English people attending these museums, only those pursuing research in the reading rooms must obtain permits to enter and everyone else may stroll about the exhibits within the walls and on the grounds, entering to observe and study as they please. The majority of the staff are learned men, drawing on not just the detailed reports of travelers, but even more upon focused, extensive research, and from this breadth of knowledge and experience, they become ever more skilled and resourceful. They are therefore not conceited or wasteful, because they also genuinely desire to use their wide knowledge and experience, wisdom, and skill to substantially benefit the people.

Westminster Abbey is to the west of the Parliament. The church is in the shape of the character *shi* [i.e., a cross], 120 feet high, built of white stone with finely detailed carvings. Over the course of more than a thousand years, however, the stone has become increasingly worn and blackened. Below the church are the mausoleums of ancient monarchs, princes, and the famous; inside the church there are stone carvings like coffins with their likenesses on the outside, underneath of which they are interred. It is taken care of by religious adherents and visitors pay a fee of fifteen cents on entering.

St. Paul's Cathedral is in the center of the city and also built of white stone blocks, soaring and magnificent, and easily capable of holding several thousand people. Inside there is a stone statue of the admiral Nelson [Nelson's Casket], who won a victory against the French sixty [*sic*] years ago, and his captured flags. During that time there were two great commanders, one named Wellington and the other, Nelson. A bronze equestrian statue of Wellington has been erected at a major intersection [Hyde Park Corner], while the statue of Nelson is here. All of this is done in order to honor such men.[10] In the center of the cathedral rises a dome like an inverted cup, to a height of 404 feet. All in all there are 540 steps to the very top, the highest point in the capital. Climbing it, one can see at a glance the entire city at one's feet. On all sides for seventy li, houses, mountains, and rivers command one's attention.[11]

The Crystal Palace (*Kuiseer* translates as "crystal," while *pailiesi* is a *gong* [palace]) is twenty-three li distant to the south of the city. This area is called Sydenham and the site is high on a hill. The building is very tall and spacious, bright and clean. There are towers north and south in which water is stored so that it is available when required. The stairs are in the form of a spiral in order to climb to the top. This building and towers are all made of iron beams and columns, with glass panes in the roof and walls, translucent and brilliant inside and out, employing not a scrap of wood; hence the becoming name of "Crystal Palace." There is a particularly elegant pool and waterside pavilion with abundant greenery and grasses of all kinds, and many rare birds and animals. Even more unusual are the marine creatures, all of which are in dozens of large tanks similar to cabinets fitted with glass and filled with seawater, about five or six feet high and wide, and organized according to species. At the top and bottom of the tanks are mounted two pipes, which circulate water and keep them full but never to overflowing. Sand and rocks, seaweed and plants have

10. Li apparently missed Wellington's Casket, which is also in St. Paul's, as well as confusing the chronology of Trafalgar and Waterloo.

11. The official height of the Ball and Lantern atop the cathedral dome is 355 feet, while there are 530 steps to the top.

A New
Account
of a Trip
Around
the Globe

206

also been taken from the sea. The visitors can see the creatures swimming about from the outside, with even the smallest details entirely visible. Houses in the styles of different nations have also been built along with bronze and stone statues from different countries in ancient and contemporary apparel, with utensils and native products organized and classified, and there were also statues of the aboriginal inhabitants of all the continents. In the center of a pond is an arrangement of pipes for a fountain, greatly refreshing for people's moods. Visitors are all charged twenty-five cents. On the Westerners' Saturday it is sixty cents. There is a theater stage and a music stage, and plays and songs are performed. The restaurants, taverns, and food and drink are all quite elegant. The Crystal Palace had formerly been erected in Hyde Park (translated previously) where it had stood twenty [sic] years ago. I heard that it had been conceived by the wealthy of England on the one hand to expand the peoples' knowledge and experience, and on the other to realize unlimited profits.[12]

The zoological garden [London Zoo] ("zoology" translates as "the classification of living things," *jiadeng* as "garden") is in the city's northwest corner [i.e., in Regent's Park]. It was built fifty years ago by the natural scientists of England who specialized in animal research. The display area grew larger year by year and is now the most extensive in the world. There are calculated to be five hundred species of animals, a thousand species of birds, a hundred kinds of turtles, dozens of varieties of monkeys, and fishes and insects beyond calculation. Of these, the most difficult to obtain were two giant seahorses sent as gifts by the khedive of Egypt. Every visitor pays twenty-five cents. On the Western Sunday it is closed and the time is given over to research.

The [London] Mechanics Institute: Under the English system, all scholars who specialize in a branch of mechanics, after passing a succession of exams, may be hired by manufacturing concerns and shipyards who then draw upon their collective expertise.

12. See introduction. The Crystal Palace was closed in Hyde Park in 1852 and, after extensive Parliamentary debate about its future, was purchased by a group of investors called the Crystal Palace Company that summer. The structure was reconstructed on a hill in Sydenham with assorted alterations—such as the water towers mentioned by Li—and reopened in June 1854. A fire in 1866 took out its north transept, but the Palace remained a popular attraction until consumed by a spectacular conflagration in 1936. Gibbs-Smith, *The Great Exhibition*, 39.

Thus, those who are skilled in seeking to improve machinery have donated money to create this institute. Here they pool their talents, discussing older types [of machines], researching new techniques, and constantly improving and refining them. In striving to conquer nature while reducing human labor they leave no stone unturned and no area unexplored in pursuit of that which is beneficial. Every year's discussions are compiled into special books of four or five volumes and there is an auditorium that can seat over a hundred people in which the discussions are held. In addition, there is a reading room with about ten thousand books on machines in the languages of different countries. Mr. White is a member, so I accompanied him for a visit.

A New
Account
of a Trip
Around
the Globe

207

On the Westerners' Sunday, government offices are closed, the schools suspend classes, and stores and shops shut down for business, as do most of the famous sites. The religious go to church to recite Scripture while the nonreligious amuse themselves in the countryside or drink and enjoy themselves at home. Each Sunday follows the regular cycle of the daily constellations *fang, xu, ang,* and *xin.* The months thus have four or five days somewhat like the Chinese intercalary holidays.[13]

As we stopped for a drink, Mr. Campbell raised a point about the national debt: Various countries borrow money from England— since practically no country can do without it—and England also raises money by borrowing from wealthy merchants, some of whom have capital worth as much as £100 million.[14] The smaller the amount borrowed, the higher the interest charged on it. It is said that on the whole, the differences among the concerned parties tend to connect those who have with those who lack, while the power of interest and principal also serve to even out such discrepancies. But how can the pursuit of profit among all parties be reconciled with the need to avoid putting the country at risk? For this reason, interest rates are dependent on the amounts borrowed

13. Each day in the twenty-eight-day Chinese lunar month is associated with a particular constellation. *Fang, xu, ang,* and *xin* mark the four seven-day intervals that Li associates with Western weeks. The difference between the solar and lunar years requires the addition of an intercalary month to the Chinese calendar every three years. The Western 1876 was such an intercalary year.

14. The British national debt was figured at £776,670,544 in 1876. Cited in Frodsham, *First Chinese Embassy,* 131 n. 2. The figure itself is from *Whitaker's Almanack* (London, 1877), 116.

A New
Account
of a Trip
Around
the Globe

208

and must therefore be studied to determine whether or not they are appropriate.

Windsor Palace (the following four places are not in London and have thus been added afterwards) is in the city of Windsor. The English call it Windsor Castle ("Castle" may be translated as "fortress"; since this palace has towers all around and its form is like that of a fort, to this day people refer to it as the ruins of a fortress), and it is seventy-three li southwest of London and serves as one of the monarch's three auxiliary palaces. Mr. White, who came along with us, said that all of England's palaces allow people to enter and get an impression of the inside at specific times. This palace's regulations specify that every year from April 1 in the Western calendar to the end of October, every day from 11:00 to 4:00, and in the remaining months, from 11:00 to 3:00, the public be allowed to come inside. During the specified times on every Western Monday, Tuesday, Thursday, and Friday, one must first go to a permit office and receive a pass, while on Wednesday and Saturday a pass is not required.

We boarded a train from London and rode for a little more than half an hour before arriving there, and saw woods and trees by the thousands stretching as far as the eye could see. Within these [woods] was a stone building like a strong walled city appearing to reach toward the clouds. Flagstaffs were mounted on the tops of the buildings, though no flags were flying, indicating that the monarch was not present. (The monarch's presence in the palace is signaled by a hanging flag.) Getting off the train, we walked half a li to the palace gate, where we climbed over a hundred stone steps [the Hundred Steps] before we came to the lowest level. Anyone may come to this point; in the center is a great gate requiring a permit for one to pass through. Mr. White presented his pass to the soldier at the gate and we entered the office of a high official in charge of the palace and sat for a bit, following which he sent a man to guide us on our visit. We first came to a room on the west, very large, high, and magnificent. The door is made of pure bronze and the decorative figures and animals are quite exquisite. All around the room they have employed all manner of carved stone inscriptions, and the walls are covered with inlaid, multicolored stone carved with historical figures, marvelous to behold, to which no detail could be added; truly extraordinary work. The windows are fashioned of large pieces of stained glass with images of the present monarch's prince consort, his clothes resplendent, depicting scenes from his life. In the chamber toward the front is a stone pedestal on which a statue of this monarch's former prince consort reposes [the Albert Memorial Chapel]. Below this chamber, twenty-four monarchs are now interred.

After observing this, we exited and proceeded east, entering a heavy gate and climbing more than ten steps, and moved through a long corridor, at the end of which is a great hall for banqueting the royalty of other countries. In a hall beside it the ambassadors of other countries, high officials, and the host country's great officers and women are commanded to present themselves to the monarch, and this is arranged wonderfully. There are porcelain vases three to four feet high, all of which are ancient Chinese antiques. The four walls are hung with banners, most with colorful tapestries of people, landscapes and trees, and are even more vivid than paintings [St. George's Hall]. There is also another place called Waterloo Chamber for use as a banquet hall. Outside of this there is a great room about three hundred feet long and sixty feet wide. A raised platform is set up there with a large seat on it. In the center of the room is a long table that can seat two hundred. This is for entertaining the royalty and officials of other countries, as well as the wealthy and aristocrats of this country. High up on the walls one finds weapons of ancient times, armor, shields, and so on used as decoration. There are also maps of different countries and flags hanging on the walls to please the eye. We entered another large, resplendent room called the "Dance Palace" [Ballroom] (*danshi* may be translated as *tiaowu*). Continuing, there are the sleeping chambers; turning to the south, there is a library to the front, with an office for governmental affairs and a music room. Every year the monarch stays in the palace sometimes for one month, sometimes for two or three, keeping to no fixed schedule. Outside there are gardens, woods for shade, and abundant flowers and plants. There are over a hundred deer and a great deal of wildlife. In the exact center is a road from the palace gate directly to a place on a hill to the south with a stone equestrian statue, estimated at ten li [the Long Walk],[15] flanked by tall, planted pines and ancient cypresses,

15. The statue, of George III, is actually of copper on a stone base.

so green and luxuriant that as the carriage went through them the dust of the world was completely wiped away. Regrettably, the day was already growing short, so we only went 30 or 40 percent of the way before turning back.

The city of Oxford is 208 li northwest of London and is host to a great university. I went to pay my respects to *Daode* [Doctor] Mr. [James] Legge (in England, a "doctor" is similar to a Chinese *jinshi*[16] degree holder). Mr. Legge has spent many years in China and is extremely well read. Formerly, he had translated the *Daxue, Zhongyong, Lun yu, Mengzi, Zuozhuan,* and *Shijing* into English and is presently serving as this university's civil official-lecturer [*wenguan jiaoshi*] on Chinese literature. After lunch, Mr. Legge gave us a tour of different places and we saw that there were not so many streets and lanes in the city, and that the shops and stores there only sold groceries and necessities for the convenience of the university community nearby. The university has total of twenty-one colleges, six lecture halls, an examination hall,[17] and a library. The library holds four hundred thousand volumes and there are ancient books on parchment and writings in very elegant script, thousands of examples in their original state. The building itself is the most ancient one, having stood for a thousand years, and its stonework has largely become blackened. The largest college is called Christ Church College, and the present crown prince is currently studying there. The students number twenty-five hundred among the twenty-one colleges and they all must finish at the top of their primary schools, from which they enter the university on graduation, staying from the age of seventeen to twenty-one. Each student's fees for room and board come to about $1,000 per year. The university's annual expenses run about $2.5 million, and from ancient times this has been drawn from an endowment. The curriculum is divided into astronomy, geography, natural science, composition, mathematics, chemistry, medicine, military science, and politics. Students enter the particular field in which they wish to study and specialize in it. There is a "tutor," translated as *yuan-*

A New
Account
of a Trip
Around
the Globe

210

16. The highest, or metropolitan, degree in the old imperial examination system. Legge (1815–97) had become Oxford's professor of Chinese history in 1876. See introduction.

17. Li here uses the term *gongyuan*, which denotes the halls where provincial-level Chinese official examinations were given.

shi, to direct their day-to-day studies. At different times there are lectures by *pufeisi* [professors], translated as "official-teacher" and similar to *juren* degree holders.

Students enrolled in the university must take three levels of exams. The first level is taken on entering a college and tests them in comprehensive fashion. There is no set time limit in the specialized curricula, and after passing another test to monitor their progress they may enter their specialization. There is then a test to graduate, which ascertains their quality within their specialized area. Following this, they are ranked and become tutors. Notable ones can become professors, and there are some who acquire the honorary title of professor immediately upon graduation. A person who wins renown as the author of a book on a particular subject or theory may also become a "doctor." Those who are doctors can also become professors. The three exams are not arranged according to particular grades or classes, and the graduates may listen in as well as those students waiting for the appointed time of their own impending tests. Most students entering are from noteworthy families, and there are few poor ones, since the yearly fee of $1,000 for room and board is unaffordable to them. There are, however, also those who are poor but ambitious to study, and relatives or friends are willing to help with the fees. Considering the organization of the colleges, the advantages of their specialization of study, and the systematic order of the curriculum, problems with the tests are few. The reason for this is that all of the university's students have been promoted from primary school, and coming here they must excel among each other for years in order to succeed, and the people therefore cannot skip the normal steps in their desire for a speedy and fraudulent outcome. Unfortunately, in the course of years of study at a thousand dollars per year, the poorer students must unavoidably be disappointed for lack of opportunity, or else rely on philanthropy, if their abilities are not to be squandered.

In the colleges the instructors wear long black gowns like Chinese *doufeng,* and over this, another black, red-bordered cape. There are also black hats with flat, four-sided tops and black tassels in the center. The students' caps are the same and the clothes are similar, only the gowns are half-length, like a Chinese person's *beida* jacket. When not in class, they wear ordinary clothes (for

A New
Account
of a Trip
Around
the Globe

212

example, at one of the colleges a white shirt and blue trousers are worn; at another, blue shirt and white trousers. All of the outfits of the twenty-one colleges are distinctive), and go out to compete in rowing races, in order to take exercise and improve the circulation. Their everyday clothes worn on the street are appropriately refined, and, if they are returning from a boat race, the students tend to be rather jaunty.

England's three greatest university sites are one in Scotland [sic] called Cambridge; one in the Irish capital, called Dublin; and this one.

On the banks of the Thames 264 li to the east of London is a place called Woolwich, where the English manufacture military ordnance. The area covers 780 *mou* [124.8 acres] and is surrounded by earthen ramparts of four li in circumference. The complex is very spacious and wide with dozens of buildings, including a foundry for bronze and iron, a forge and hammer shop, cannon factory, small arms factory, ammunition plants for guns and small arms, a gun carriage shop, rifle stock shop, rocket works, and torpedo factory. There is also a large building for storing older types of military hardware. Twenty steam engines have been installed for powering the assorted machines. There are twelve furnaces for smelting iron, each one about twenty feet square, and the molten iron flows like a river channel. There are twenty iron [steam] hammers hanging from high beams, the larger ones forty tons in weight. Each blow from one of these carries the power of a thousand tons. It requires only one man to pull a lever on the machine in order to make the hammer drop, with the force of the blow controlled by the operator. There are ten thousand workers, and sometimes as many as fifteen thousand. All day long the furnace fires light the heavens and the sound of the hammers shakes the earth unceasingly. Should the necessity arise, regardless of the cost or the nature of the affair, they are in a position to cope with it immediately without anxiety.

There are fifty machines for manufacturing small arms ammunition, and each one can make sixty thousand bullets per day. The cannon factory presently makes four types of large guns, up to a weight of eighty-one tons. The technique consists of using a large piece of steel to make the barrel of the gun, and then taking strips of iron four inches square, putting them into the furnace to heat them, winding them around the body of the gun, and hammering them on [a so-called built-up gun]. They repeat this process three times and the three straps around the gun barrel become bonded to it like one. The gun can then be fired without worry of it being destroyed or split. The shells are four feet, two inches long and weigh seventeen hundred pounds; the head is pointed and base square [*sic*][18] and the actual powder charge weighs twenty-one pounds. The gun's chamber receives 370 pounds of powder and the shell has a range of twenty-three li. The projectile can penetrate an iron slab two feet, five inches thick set up at five hundred yards. We heard that several months ago, Italy had a gun built weighing a hundred tons, very nimble and easy to operate, which has already been transported back to their country and set into a fort, and this is said to be the biggest cannon in the world. I also heard that England now plans to build four guns weighing up to two hundred tons, and will begin fabricating them sometime next year.

A New
Account
of a Trip
Around
the Globe

213

The torpedo plant makes dozens of types of large and small marine mines and torpedoes. One model is elliptical with a pointed head and tail. On the tail are mounted four brass sheets like the fins of a fish, with an electric wire running from a small reel to the point on the torpedo's head. Placed in the water, it runs forward while an operator controls its range and direction. When the tip of the head makes contact with an enemy vessel, an electrical current flows [in the weapon] and it blows the ship up. The body of the torpedo is made of thin sheet iron, and it is actually armed with 180 pounds of gun cotton, the power of which is more than five times that of [black] powder. The largest one is twenty feet long, and we saw one here of fourteen feet costing $1,750. This type of system was designed during the fourth year of the Tongzhi emperor [1866–67] by an Englishman named Whitehead. It is called the *feishi duopiduo* [fish torpedo], translated as "fish explosive" because its shape resembles that of a fish.

Afterwards, we boarded a small train to a parade ground inside the complex to see a firing of a Gatling rotary gun. They then demonstrated the gun cotton. Gun cotton consists of two types, dry and wet. The dry kind can only be set off by burning, while the

18. All versions use the character *fang*, literally "square," here, an apparent mistake.

A New
Account
of a Trip
Around
the Globe

214

wet variety is detonated by electricity. They first took a piece of the wet cotton about three inches square and an inch thick, and only a couple of ounces in weight, and tested it in a fire, where it remained for perhaps several minutes without exploding. Then they set it on a large rock a hundred paces away and detonated it with a metal wire connected to an electrical current, where it made a tremendous noise and pulverized the rock. Inquiring about this, I discovered that the rock was about three hundred *jin* [approximately four hundred pounds]. The price of the cotton is very cheap. In an unused area in the factory there are assorted sizes of older model guns and ammunition displayed. Several years before, these had been brand-new types; now they have become obsolete and are piled up like so many hills. Presently, they will be melted down and remanufactured into new models. The arsenal's director is a general. The civil and military officials at the upper levels number forty and of the various specialists staying at the arsenal and the minor officials, the number is unknown.

"Portsmouth" is the name of place three hundred li southwest of London on a river outlet to the sea, and is England's naval shipyard. Eight hundred *mou* [128 acres] in area, it is protected by batteries all around, and ten thousand men are stationed there. When I visited this place, the officials in charge of the yard sent a man to guide me around. We first went to the ironclad *Thunderer*.[19] The ship's hull is wooden and about one foot, eight inches thick, with one foot and two inches of iron plate, displacing 4,650 tons, and with engines that deliver a thousand horsepower. The ship's stern has twin screws, which can turn right or left [i.e., to move forward or in reverse]. On both bow and stern are round-style turrets, also made of fine iron, which can be rotated in any direction. The front turret mounts two guns, each weighing thirty-eight tons. The stern also has two guns, each weighing thirty-five tons; the shells weigh eight hundred pounds. The mechanism for elevating and lowering the guns in the front is operated by steam, while that in the rear is operated by hand, both moving quickly and easily. Below decks there are two small iron tracks for a cart to haul ammunition. Every

19. H.M.S. *Thunderer*, built in 1872, was the sister ship of the pathbreaking H.M.S. *Devastation*, and among the first of a new class of twin-turreted ironclads constructed without sails.

[Chinese half hour; English] hour the ship can travel more than sixty li [eighteen to nineteen knots], and the construction costs were $2.5 million. We also went to a ship named *Shah,* built for the shah of Persia, who had visited the shipyard and is named for him because Persia calls its monarch the "shah." The style of the ship is wooden in construction, 6,040 tons, and it is the largest modern wooden warship. Inside are mounted twenty-six guns, all twelve tons, with 280-pound shells. The crew numbers 673 and it can make sixty-five li in half a Chinese hour [nineteen to twenty knots].

We went next to a pair of exploration steamers, one named *Alert,* and the other named *Discovery,* which had recently returned from an expedition to the Arctic Ocean. Both ships are only 450 tons. Previously, when this country had sent these two ships out, the crews reported that the ships were small and the way dangerous, and they were afraid that they could not return the way they had come. They did not realize that though small, the ships' hulls were extremely strong compared with those of other vessels and completely able to go straight ahead and withstand the rigors beyond 10 degrees north latitude in the area called the Arctic Ocean and return intact. Because of this, the people throughout the country could not but gasp in awe at the voyages and the tremendous capacities of their equipment. The captain is named [George S.] Nares, elderly and dignified, and it was said that he had been rewarded for meritorious service.[20]

There are sixteen levels for constructing ships, built of white stone, and connected to a waterway allowing the ships to enter the water through an iron sluice gate [i.e., a dry dock] to a wide and broad area. The workers are extremely skilled, and there are also a dozen large buildings for masts, sails, rigging, paint, and various factories for types of machinery. Unfortunately, this day was very rainy, and because we would have had to go through the mud and our clothes would have got soaked and smeared, we were not able to look around.

20. Sir George Strong Nares led an arctic expedition that reached 83 20' 26" N. in the summer of 1875. His expedition caused a sensation in England, as did his account, *Narrative of a Voyage to the Polar Sea during 1875–76,* 2 vols. (London: Her Majesty's Stationery Office, 1877). Kuo Songtao also met Nares and was fascinated by the hardships encountered in arctic exploration. See Frodsham, *First Chinese Embassy,* 19, 20, 60, 62.

A New
Account
of a Trip
Around
the Globe

215

A New
Account
of a Trip
Around
the Globe

216

Paris is the capital city of France. (In England, America, and other countries, places with dense populations are generally referred to as *cheng* [lit. "walled city"], though they do not actually have any walls. In France, however, there actually are some with walls.) The city sits astride the Seine River in the northwest corner of the country. About thirty *li* in length and forty in breadth, it is surrounded by stone walls lacking crenellations and having forty gates. A ring of eighteen formidable forts has [also] been constructed along defensible positions outside the city.[1]

There are twenty districts [arrondissements] within the city limits, each organized around a supervising official and under the jurisdiction of a prefect. All the gates require tolls in order to pass through. The Seine enters the city from the southeast and its shape is like a bow flowing toward the southwest and out, deep and broad, clear, and navigable by steamer. The population comes to about 2 million. The boulevards and streets are magnificent, wide and clean, both sides being planted with trees and greenery to provide shade. The shops are arranged like the cells of a honeycomb, orderly and pleasing to the eye. The buildings are six or seven stories, with the doorways on each level protected by ornamental iron grilles painted a golden color, extraordinarily pretty in a way that neither England nor America comes close to approaching. Day and night the carriage traffic never stops. The inhabitants enjoy entertaining visitors, and their clothes are stylish and colorful. Most of the foreigners who come here do so for vacation or amusement and cannot help but envy the Parisians, even to the point of enjoying themselves so much that they all but forget about returning home. In short, if we are to compare England's capital of London with Paris, we can say that London is the world's commercial and financial center, while Paris is the West's most scenic city. Four years ago during the military occupation [following the Franco-Prussian War and Paris Commune] many homes were destroyed, but now it is already the very picture of peace and tran-

---

1. The Enceinte, a system of barriers and parapets twenty-one miles in circumference, built during the early 1840s. See K. Baedeker, *Paris and Its Environs* (London: Dulau and Co., 1878), 166–67.

quility, and the country's wealth and prosperity are everywhere evident. There are a great number of palaces and halls, government offices, dwellings, and factories, as well as very many gardens here, and it is a pity that we could only visit for four or five days. In addition, it was mostly rainy so we were unable to tour very extensively. The French did not speak English very clearly, either, so the account of this city is comparatively short. Within it, I am afraid mistakes have been inevitable as well.

The Tuileries are in the center of the city and within them is the old palace of the former emperor Napoleon [I] [the Palais des Tuileries]. The halls and chambers are very tall and wide with stone carvings of exquisite workmanship. Four years ago, during the disorders and the looting of the halls, only the galleries survived. The French claim that in the past it was magnificent and inspiring, and that there was truly nothing wonderful that it lacked, nor any exquisite object not displayed; and that it had a deeply beautiful dreamlike quality to it. The restoration has only now just begun, and when its reconstruction is fully under way, they intend to make it even better than before.

The Louvre museum was in earlier days the Louvre Royal Palace, and it has now been transformed into a huge museum. Stored inside are invaluable portrait collections of ancient and modern notables, some of them appraised at tens of thousands of dollars. I saw a great number of learned gentlemen armed with colored pencils and paper sketching them every day. There are many stone statues as well. There are ancient monarchs and aristocrats along with royal officials in many styles of clothing and weapons, jewelry and raiment over the course of three or four thousand years in stone and bronze—as well as some Chinese objects—all available for unrestricted public inspection.

To the west is a huge glass building [the Palais du Champs de Mars] similar to the English Crystal Palace built several years ago [1867] for the Paris Exposition. Now it houses a great many tapestries of every color thread featuring the famous fictional characters of different countries; like paintings, only even more exquisite.

The former French ruler Napoleon I's tomb was built as a cathedral, the church's spire and dome shaped like an inverted bell, gilded, and making a magnificent appearance. When he died while in custody of the English during the first year of the reign of the

A New
Account
of a Trip
Around
the Globe

217

A New
Account
of a Trip
Around
the Globe

218

Dao Guang emperor [1821], they returned his remains, and he is interred here along with his two brothers. He is called "the First" because the monarchies in Western countries have numbered titles, in the same way as Qin Shi Huang [the First Emperor of the Qin, 221–209 B.C.E.] is called *Shi* [the First], so that the next ones are called "the Second," and "the Third," and so on. On the left of the church is a large building for the recuperation of wounded soldiers [Les Invalides]. There are several old soldiers there who served with Napoleon and can still reminisce about those times. The dome is of iron, 134 feet high, its interior constructed of stone and the exterior encased in iron, and in the middle is a spiral staircase leading upward. At the very top is a statue of Napoleon I cast from his own guns that were used against his enemies during those years.

A district dedicated to commemorating Napoleon's military successes is marked by the 152-foot Arc de Triomphe in the northwest corner of the city. Inside there is a stairway to the very top, and one can see the features of the entire city from it. Erected as a memorial to Napoleon's victories, it cost $1.86 million and is constructed of white stone and very large. Its four walls have stone carvings depicting people and battle scenes of the era.

The city's two largest Catholic cathedrals are called the Pantheon[2] and Notre Dame. Both are large in size and magnificent, with numerous tall towers and spires. In the middle [of Notre Dame] is a large nave dedicated to a woman holding a child, considered to be the mother of Jesus and her son. On the right and left are six chapels, each having a statue of one of Jesus' twelve disciples. The faithful pray to them as they wish. They also light candles, which are white.[3] Kneeling to worship, the people have cushions arranged before them and some prostrate themselves, bowing and folding their hands, and murmuring unintelligible words very much like the movements of Buddhist monks. In the case of Protestant churches, the interior space is open and empty [of statues and ornamentation] and the preacher lectures in the center with nothing but the rows of pews for the listeners near him. All in

2. The Pantheon, built toward the end of the eighteenth century, was made a national shrine during the Revolution. In Li's time its crypts housed the remains of Voltaire and Rousseau. It had also been the site of the first demonstration of the Foucault Pendulum in March 1851.

3. For Li's comments on the significance of white for Westerners, see chapter 5.

all, this is essentially correct, though I was only able to go to these two [cathedrals].

The zoo[4] is like England's zoological garden and is north of the Arc de Triomphe. There are unusual animals, flora and fauna, fish, plants, everything. I do not know the names of 70 to 80 percent of them, like the pure white peacocks, the all-blue chickens, the all-red waterfowl, or the trees with white bark that seem whitewashed, all of which I had never seen before. There is no bamboo among the various European countries and so there are only a dozen or so kinds of green bamboo shoots here, which were said to have been brought from South America. Having crossed several tens of thousands of li just to meet with "these gentlemen,"[5] they are most adamant about sending people every day to report on their well-being. I also saw some flowering crabapple of a type like that found in China, but with even fatter fruit and surprisingly fragrant; it must have been transplanted from Changzhou![6]

The Opera House covers an area of twelve thousand square feet and is constructed of the world's most beautiful stone. It took twenty years to complete and cost $7 million. The stage can hold seven hundred people and the building has several levels with a seating capacity of ten thousand. Inside and out are exquisite carvings, all the floors and furnishings are richly arranged, and it truly is a most magnificent building. As for the story performed, it was quite unusual and the special skills of the players greatly surpassed my expectations. Though I had feared that what was offered would not resemble proper singing, it proved instead to be very much so, and it is said that their skills are unsurpassed by the performers of other countries.

The Circus [Cirque d'Hiver] has an indoor ring, and the floor is smooth, covered with sand and earth, and more than a hundred feet across. There were the most beautiful girls there, perhaps fifteen or sixteen years old, clothed in sharkskin tights and galloping around on horseback. Standing on horseback while riding around the ring more than ten times, they smiled brightly as if

4. The Jardins des Plantes, with the Gallery of Zoology and Botanic Garden.

5. *Ci jun* (these gentlemen), a euphemism for bamboo. This appears to be part of the collection of forty-five hundred species of tropical plants brought back from the Americas by Alexander Humboldt in 1805. See Baedeker, *Paris and Its Environs*, 244.

6. Li here inverts the more standard construction of *feide* for "must." Changzhou is near Nanjing; hence it is for Li a local tree.

A New
Account
of a Trip
Around
the Globe

220

seeking to be casually reckless. The spectators applauded and howled. They also had twelve elephants that had been trained to dance, the elephants lifting their feet to the tempo of the music. As they held their trunks and turned in a circle, the elephant driver had them strike a pose with their trunks in a spiral; or putting his head into their mouths, he made them hold it without the slightest injury to himself. They say that the elephant's body though huge is not inelegant, but I had no idea they could actually dance. Among the *Man* peoples,[7] elephants are used in battle formations. A nimble creature indeed!

We saw a wagon fitted with an iron grille, seven or eight feet high, and more than twenty feet long and six or seven feet wide, with seven lions inside. They had two elephants pull the cart out and a man entered and used an iron rod to smack the lions and stir them up. They fought for quite a while, but since this was not sufficient, they fired a gun to make a loud noise. They roared furiously with a sound like a bronze *zheng* [an ancient instrument]— ferociously, as if they were about to pounce—and the spectators shuddered with fear. Just as they were becoming anxious, the man suddenly emerged from the cage through the barred door. Although the men are quite skillful, they are still no match for a lion, and I understand that some have been mauled by them.

CHAPTER 17. THE VISIT OF THE CHINESE EDUCATION MISSION STUDENTS TO THE CENTENNIAL

On the third day of the seventh month of the second year in the reign of the Guangxu emperor [August 21, 1876], the 113 students from our country currently studying in America accompanied their teacher, Liu Qijun, Chief Translator Kuang Qizhao, and their six male and female instructors from Hartford to Philadelphia to see the Centennial Exposition. Their leader was the American, D. E. Bartlett, who acted as Education Mission director, and the party

7. *Man* is a generic term for the non-Han, southern peoples considered by northerners to be aboriginal or semicivilized.

stayed at the Atlas Hotel outside the exhibition.[1] Every day they entered the exposition at 9:00 A.M. and returned to the hotel at 5:00 in the afternoon, taking lunch in the restaurants at the fairgrounds for the sake of convenience.

Both the hotel and the restaurant [the American Restaurant, near Agricultural Hall] received them quite cordially, with the yellow dragon flag flying atop the buildings and musicians playing as they passed in and out, all of it done with considerable pomp and appropriate courtesy. The newspapers from various quarters, having publicized the visit for some time, repeatedly offered their opinions over the last few days on the ways in which it will be immensely helpful to China.[2] The students are clever and learn well, are mannerly and affectionate toward one another, and quite capable of making appropriate conversation when meeting people. Those enrolled in the school for little more than a year are also proficient in the Western language. As a further means of increasing their knowledge and experience, this brief visit to the exposition should prove very helpful indeed.

The fourth [August 22]. It appears that for the most part, the students talk and move about freely and fearlessly among the many thousands here as they tour the exhibition halls. Their clothes are like those of Westerners, though with a short scholar's gown worn over them in order to remain close to the Chinese style of dress. Meeting me, they were very friendly, and spoke excitedly in the manner of those who have lived overseas. The younger students were accompanied by their women teachers, and were able to respond when the teacher pointed things out for them to see. The

A New
Account
of a Trip
Around
the Globe

221

1. Aside from Bartlett and the others mentioned, the students were accompanied by William Kellogg, Yung Wing's brother-in-law; L. N. Carleson, a professor at the State Normal School in New Britain, Connecticut; and Connecticut Board of Education secretary B. G. Northrop. See the *Hartford Courant,* August 22, 1876.

2. In addition to the Philadelphia newspapers, the *Hartford Courant,* as noted in the introduction, provided frequent coverage of the Education Mission and what amounted to daily reports of the boys' activities at the Centennial. The August 26, 1876, *Courant* contained the following item:

> The Chinese boys have received much attention and admiration at Philadelphia, both at their hotel and within the Centennial grounds and buildings. They dined at the Grand American Restaurant Tuesday and Wednesday. Out of compliment to them and their attendants, the Chinese national flag was hung upon the flagstaff in the rear of the restaurant building. As the boys passed out of the dining saloon they surrounded the flag and cheered it lustily.

bond of affection between them in this regard is not unlike that of mothers and children.

The fifth [August 23]. I met Mr. Liu and Mr. Kuang, together with Education Mission director Bartlett, at the Agricultural Hall. All the students were gathered together as well, and before long we went to lunch, during the course of which I singled out one of the older boys and asked him whether this exposition was, in fact, worthwhile. He replied:

> Collecting the objects of the world and allowing people to examine them enhances knowledge and understanding. New machines and ingenious ideas can be copied and utilized. Furthermore, it is enormously helpful in enabling friendly contacts among various countries. Before my classmates and I started on our journey, the teachers urged us to take notes as we pleased on what we would observe. When we return to school, we will all write essays discussing these things in English and then translate them into Chinese.

I asked him about his favorite things and he replied, "Foreign printing techniques and Chinese ivory carvings." Doesn't he miss home, though? "There's no use being homesick. But if we attack the books, then when we do return home it will be for a lifetime." How about the food and drink, and your daily routine? "The food and drink seem very pure and clean, and our daily activities move according to a set schedule. We must also exercise periodically for our qi[3] and circulation, and this is a particularly good way of helping to prevent disease." What are your hosts like? "Those who take care of us treat us like members of their families. They become deeply concerned if I come down with so much as a case of sniffles, but since Hartford's climate is healthful, we have few illnesses." Why do you wear Western clothes? "We don't change our clothes sometimes when it is inconvenient, so we follow the local customs with two exceptions: We do not cut our queues, and we do not go

A New
Account
of a Trip
Around
the Globe

222

3. Chinese cosmology and medicine both hold that the universe is permeated by qi, "life force" or "material force." In the human body, qi flows through meridians, or channels, and its unhindered circulation is believed to be enhanced by prescribed exercises—like $qigong$—as well as treatments involving acupuncture and moxibustion. Here, the reference is to general health (see also chapter 14); for qi as gravitational force, see chapter 26, note 5.

to church."[4] His words were absolutely plain, forthright, and reasonable, and I felt quite fond of him. Exactly how much of this is a product of Western studies, however, is impossible to say.

I have heard that in developing one's character, the techniques used in Western countries do not emphasize empty formalities, but concentrate instead on practical results. In this curriculum, things are simple yet strict, the instructional methods clear and earnest, and between teacher and student there is a feeling of family harmony. Better still, they build up a quiet comprehension of the material and do not stress chanting and recitation, thereby avoiding the perils of rote learning.[5] They are calm and cheerful, and do not stand on ceremony, thus anxiety and depression do not lead to illness. Though they are sightseeing, they must also write about their experiences. Hence, this is not casual viewing, but an effective way of encouraging study and carefully assessing their knowledge. Also, they [the teachers] do not resort to bribing them to behave, nor do they punish them in anger, things which harm both the clever and the slow, and keep both from progressing. Of all these students, who among them will not be successfully molded into "good pottery" [lit.] to serve you?

But it is said that China does not value Western learning, and now these students have been sent tens of thousands of li to study. Is this not like "flying from lofty trees into dark valleys?"[6] Whether this is true or not, I cannot really say. Those students who travel for study find that their learning is enhanced. As far as extending the Way [*dao*] and the Virtue [*de*] of our sages, as well as the "three

A New
Account
of a Trip
Around
the Globe

223

4. The boys lived with their American host families and attended primary and high schools in Hartford and in the area around Springfield, Massachusetts. Their long, braided queues were a mandatory emblem of loyalty to the Qing dynasty and could not be cut. In order to minimize their exotic quality and reduce the schoolboy teasing to which they were periodically subjected, the students resorted to a number of stratagems to conceal their braids. Some tucked them into high collars; others wound them into a coil on top of their heads and covered them with a hat. Fears among Chinese officials of attempts to convert the boys to Christianity—emanating in large part from Yung Wing's assertive Congregationalism—resulted in regulations barring the boys from attending church. Though only a few ultimately converted, the issue remained a contentious one until the Education Mission's recall in 1881.

5. Literally, "eating without digesting." See also Li's comments on rote learning in chapter 14.

6. This is a reference to a passage from Mencius in which he says, "You turn away from your master and become [another's] disciple. Your conduct is different indeed from the philosopher Zeng. I have heard of birds leaving dark valleys to fly to lofty trees, but I have not heard of their descending from lofty trees to enter into dark valleys." *Mencius*, bk. III, pt. 1, chap. 4, lines 14–15 (p. 255).

A New
Account
of a Trip
Around
the Globe

224

bonds and five principles," the students have taken these firmly to heart and are quite comfortable with them, and do not commit the slightest errors from studying Western subjects. Moreover, learning from others to correct one's faults cannot really be confined to one's own lands. Thus, in furthering the ambitious plans of today, having an unsuitable disregard for Western affairs is certainly not to learn. The Way and Virtue, the bonds and principles, constitute the *ti,* or essentials; the techniques of the West are *yong* [practical application]. We must have both *ti* and *yong* so that in the future we will have a nation whose abilities are utilized and whose knowledge cannot but exceed that of the present.[7]

The sixth [August 24]. I ordered Chinese food at the restaurant with Kuang and Liu, and together with the chaperones and boys there were more than 140 people. At 3:30 in the afternoon they were to meet the American president and the officials in charge of the Centennial. Just before coming to Philadelphia, the president was very pleased to hear of the arrival of the students and directed the exhibition officials to schedule a visit.[8] At the proper time, the president stood up in the middle of the hall, Customs Inspector [J. L.] Hammond came forward with me together with the leaders of the Japanese delegation, and we clasped hands on meeting each other. Mr. Bartlett led the boys inside, and they shook hands and said a few words face to face with the president. At 5:00, we returned to the auditorium, directed the boys to sit, and several of the exposition's leaders and teachers, as well as a Japanese official [Fujimoro Tanaka, vice minister of education] took turns passing through the hall, speaking movingly on the meaning of close relations between our two countries, and also encouraging the boys to study diligently. The boys applauded together and stamped their feet, praising them in unison. On dispersing, all raised their hands

7. The passage above previously appeared in Desnoyers, "One Enlightened and Progressive Civilization," 143. *Dao* and *de* are key Chinese philosophical concepts: *Dao,* often translated as "the Way," refers to the operative principle of the cosmos; *de,* or "virtue," might here be described as the way in which the *dao* manifests itself in human affairs. The "bonds" and "principles" are the individual relationships and attributes one observes and strives for in seeking to follow the *dao* in Confucianism. *Ti* and y*ong,* or "essence" and "application," are part of a family of "root and branch," or *benmo,* dualities popular in Neo-Confucian epistemology. Here, they refer to the increasingly popular formulation of China's self-strengthening advocates, "Chinese studies for the essence *(ti),* and Western studies for practical application *(yong)."*

8. For brief accounts of the affair, see the August 25, 1876, *Philadelphia Inquirer* and the August 29, 1876, *Hartford Courant.*

to speak individually, and I found myself feeling quite attached to them. However, early tomorrow morning they must return to Hartford.

CHAPTER 18. A COMPLETE ACCOUNT OF THE ACTUAL CONDITION OF THE CHINESE IN AMERICA

A New
Account
of a Trip
Around
the Globe

225

The ancients repeatedly journeyed from their native lands, despite the fact that travel anywhere throughout the neighboring regions was not easily undertaken. If such is the case, that the men of old had dealings everywhere, could it then be said that the ancients misled others? Though we know little about what occupied them, they still merit our appreciation. How could the one in ten who fought with awls and swords and knives, or gambled and threw away their lives overseas, be mentioned in the same breath with them? And yet, such people are certainly entitled to our sympathy as well.[1]

Because gold was produced in the region, Chinese people came to refer to the city of San Francisco in the American state of California as *Jin Shan* [*Gum Sam* in Cantonese; Gold Mountain]. Later, Australia in the South Pacific also became a site of gold production and was called *Jin Shan* as well; these were then differentiated as "New" and "Old." The one called Old Gold Mountain is a large city on America's west coast. It is estimated that the Chinese population in America, men and women combined, comes to approximately 160,000, of whom about 40,000 live in San Francisco. Around 100,000 live in other cities in California, and the rest are dispersed among various places in the hinterlands. In San Francisco six large *huiguan*[2] have been established among the Cantonese: the San Yi ["Three Counties," for the three counties of]

1. Li is here addressing the lingering prejudice among his readers toward the emigrants as traitors, opportunists, and malcontents, considered deficient in virtue for wanting to leave their homeland, and deserving of whatever hardships they encountered abroad.

2. *Huiguan* are organizations set up overseas along regional or clan lines to assist the freshly arrived in settling into their new environment. In America they would help in clearing the emigrant's paperwork with local authorities, act as surety if necessary, broker passage money, and in Li's time, acted as unofficial consulates. The different *huiguan* to which Li refers were known in San Francisco as the Six Companies. As ten-

A New
Account
of a Trip
Around
the Globe

226

(Nanhai, Xingyu, Xunde, with Sanshui, Qingyuan, and Huasi attached to them), with 11,000 people; the Yang He *huiguan* (Xiangshan, Dongwan, Zengcheng, with Boluo attached), with about 12,000 members; Gang Zhou (Xinhui, with Heshan and Sihui attached), about 15,000 members; Ning Yang (Xinning, excluding people surnamed *Yu*), about 75,000; He He (for the people from Xinning surnamed *Yu* and [all] those from Kaiping and Enping), approximately 35,000; and Ren He (Xin'an, Guishan, and Jiayinzhou), about 4,000. Those who do not join one of the *huiguan*, including people from other provinces [i.e., other than Guangdong], Christians, actors, and actresses total about 2,000. There are about 6,000 women and girls, with those among the wives and families of respectable people numbering only about 10 to 20 percent, the remainder being prostitutes. These are the statistics from the end of the summer of the year *bingzi* [1876].

It should be noted that the state of California had formerly belonged to Mexico and its southern regions had been used by the Mexicans for pastureland and ranches, while the north remained entirely in the hands of the native aborigines. Later, for a variety of reasons, it became American territory. During the autumn of the twenty-eighth year of the Daoguang emperor [1848] reports began to surface that gold had been discovered in the region. These were initially discounted, but when subsequent investigations showed them to be true, the people of various countries scrambled there like a flock of ducks, spending every day digging for it. At the time there were Chinese crewmen aboard foreign ships who, catching a glimpse of the huge fortunes to be had, jumped ship and made their piles. On returning home they spread word of the situation and the employment opportunities abroad, inducing friends and relatives to sail for America, and were treated no differently than the Europeans. Such was the beginning of Chinese emigration to America.

By the first years of the reign of the Xianfeng emperor [1851–1852], those leaving grew more numerous by the day and the first three *huiguan* — San Yi, Yang He, and Si Yi ([including the

sions grew between the Chinese and other ethnic groups in the city and region—particularly, the Chinese believed, due to the activities of the Irish—the Companies were regularly accused in the press and by California politicians of fostering "coolie slavery" and trafficking in prostitutes, among other crimes.

four counties of] Xinhui, Xinning, Enping, and Kaiping) were founded. By the third year [1853], the Xinning division of Si Yi had split off and become Ning Yang, while Yang He's Xinan division had become Ren He. During the first year of the Tongzhi emperor [1861], the people of the Yu clan in the Xinning *huiguan* had once more joined with the Enping and Kaiping divisions of Si Yi and formed He He. The name Si Yi was then changed to Gang Zhou, thus forming the current six *huiguan.* All of them choose directors to oversee their affairs. In addition to having *chufan* and *lishumu,* these titles change each year, with those who are capable holding office for several years.

Their bylaws stipulate that, as a rule, Chinese entering port are to be met by representatives sent by the different *huiguan* who lead them to the [appropriate] organization, where they are registered at no charge. Instead [of paying immediately], they wait until they have enough to return to China, and when they report back to the *huiguan,* the personnel there check to see that their debts have been cleared and, only after booking passage for the returnees, do they settle the *huiguan* dues, which vary from five to ten foreign dollars. No dues are charged for the elderly, poor, or sick who want to return to China; moreover, in such cases their passage fees are donated in addition to their booking arrangements being made for them. I understand that the wishes of those unwilling to join the *huiguan* are respected, but such cases are very few. The dues collected are used for rent, and wages and food for workers. If there is any surplus beyond the requirements of sustaining the group, it is used for philanthropy. If bickering arises among people from their home villages over some trivial matter, the *huiguan* can step in to compel mediation and enable a peaceful outcome. What the Six Companies take care of therefore consists of this relative handful of things, and since they have no official status and their funds are minimal, they are actually not completely able to carry even these out. Hence, all the rest must be done entirely by the local officials who have jurisdiction over them.

Of the different kinds of workers, the figures from the first year of the reign of the Tongzhi emperor [1861] put their numbers at no more than sixty thousand. Twenty percent of them were cigar rollers, earning wages of two to three dollars a day. The statistics for the other trades were somewhat similar, though their wages

A New
Account
of a Trip
Around
the Globe

228

were generally a bit less. The remaining 60 percent specialized in mining. At the time, the claims of miners among the different countries were separated by distinct borders, and all were self-supporting. Later, due to the decline of gold mining, they all reverted to laboring and pursuing trades. They made cigars, fashioned boots, shoes, textiles, and work clothes; twisted rope, laid railroad tracks, did farm labor, and raised cattle and sheep. The Chinese worked well at all of these occupations for low wages and were frugal in their daily needs, and so the trades and crafts of foreign workers were all being taken over by them. Moreover, the numbers of those entering the Ning Yang and He He *huiguan* increased daily, while the cost of labor dropped accordingly (wages had already declined to only sixty or seventy cents to a dollar per day), and because of this the foreign workers grew to hate them more and more each day, creating a difficult situation for both sides.

The most cruel and cunning among the foreigners are the so-called Irish (men from the English territory of Ireland), who spend the greater part of their day's wages on drink and delight in stirring up trouble. They succeeded in founding an organization whose express purpose was to interfere with Chinese laborers,[3] and the Chinese therefore protested the support of this organization by the political parties. A number of incidents of bullying, humiliation, and beating have come about because of this. There is a law in America that allows foreign nationals to become naturalized citizens after living in the country for six years. Irish who had already been naturalized have become officials in California and also form a majority in the different political parties. Among our Chinese, however, because of the differences in their natural disposition, clothes, and food, and despite the fact that they have lived in America for many years, there are none who have become naturalized. This, too, is something the Americans deeply regret.[4]

Because all of America was once inhabited entirely by the red-skinned aborigines, those who achieved its independence relied

3. This appears to be a reference to the so-called People's Protective Alliance, a coalition of a number of "anti-coolie" and "anti-Mongolian" organizations. Following extensive rioting the following summer, during which the Pacific Mail docks would be set ablaze, the San Francisco anti-Chinese movement would be increasingly centered on the famous "sandlot" agitator Dennis Kearney and his Workingmen's Party. For a brief survey of the literature, see introduction, notes 2 and 41.

4. Li seems to have not been informed about the recent efforts to ensure that Chinese would be denied citizenship. Yung Wing, to cite a prominent example, had been natu-

completely upon masses of people emigrating from other countries, and together they built the premier state of the Western Hemisphere. The Chinese who came at first also intended to become naturalized, not to make money and return to China.[5] Now, those coming to the ports every year number about eight thousand, and those returning to China, approximately five thousand, with these numbers increasing each year. Also, the Americans do not legally prohibit immigration, so although there may be obstructions, such difficulties cannot, in the end, hold it back. Thus, all manner of humiliation, fear, and intimidation is practiced with the aim of spreading word back to China that those coming by ship should think twice about doing so. The upright people of America, however, have never been unwilling either to scold or register their support, unlike the majority of politicians, who tend to avoid making enemies. This spring the Six Companies were falsely accused of buying [contract] laborers, taking fat profits for themselves, setting up private government offices, and so forth, and a petition was sent to the American capital to demand the prohibition of Chinese immigration. Have they not indeed, then, dealt properly to some degree with this all along?

A New
Account
of a Trip
Around
the Globe

229

Among those Chinese who are merchants, only four or five out of a hundred specialize in handling Chinese goods and selling them to the other Chinese residents. Formerly, the merchants' profits were fairly high, but recently the steamers have been coming two or three times a month, and the various goods have thus become difficult to hoard against any mounting scarcity. In fact, those seeking them can obtain them even more easily than in China. Such things as the traffic in prostitutes, which cannot help

ralized during his student days in the 1850s; his successors in the 1870s were to be less fortunate. In 1870, Congress had changed the criteria for citizenship to include "aliens of African nativity, and to persons of African descent." Subsequent interpretations during the decade left unclear the status of the Chinese and others who did not fit into either this category or that of "free white persons." Several attempts made by Chinese in San Francisco, including that of the San Yi *huiguan* director Hong Chung, to file for naturalization were struck down by the courts throughout the decade. See Charles J. McClain, *In Search of Equality: The Chinese Struggle against Discrimination in Nineteenth-Century America* (Berkeley and Los Angeles: University of California Press, 1994), 70–72.

5. Li here touches upon what would later come to be known—and bitterly contested—as the "sojourner thesis." In addition to the books listed in this chapter and the introduction that address this and related issues, see also Chen Yong, *Chinese San Francisco, 1850–1943: A Transpacific Community* (Stanford: Stanford University Press, 2000) for a critique of the sojourner idea; and Josephine Khu, *Cultural Curiosity* (Berkeley and Los Angeles: University of California Press, 2001) for useful case studies in the creation of identity among overseas Chinese.

but injure the country's dignity, I hear all come by way of Macau and Hong Kong. The *huiguan* have always sought strict prohibitions on this but by law cannot prohibit women from entering the country. As a rule, approximately 70 to 80 percent of the homicide cases in San Francisco result from prostitution.

A New
Account
of a Trip
Around
the Globe

230

I stayed for six days while passing through this region. A certain country's official[6] I visited told me:

> The Chinese here number more than one hundred thousand and are subjected to bullying by foreigners more and more every day; their situation is dire. How can your honorable country continue to give no thought to providing officials to protect them? For example, the workers and merchants of some countries living here number only two thousand people, yet they have set up a consulate. Some countries have only five or six hundred and have a consul. By sending a consul here, your honorable country would on the one hand protect the national dignity and on the other, protect the people's interests. The office's expenses and consular salaries could be raised immediately from local funds and would be easy to arrange. Who, in studying this, would not make it an urgent priority? I too am a foreigner, and I say bluntly that we honestly cannot sit by and watch the Chinese be humiliated so. Do you not agree?

I replied:

> I don't presume to speak on national affairs. In considering this matter, however, our two ministers, Chen [Lanbin] and Rong [Yung Wing] have undertaken this important national responsibility, and in connection with this precarious situation will certainly formulate a plan to resolve it advantageously. As for setting up a consulate here, that is no doubt not far off.[7]

---

6. Li mentioned meeting with the Japanese vice-consul, Takagi Saburo. This may have been part of their conversation. See chapter 28.

7. In fact, Chen Lanbin, having taken his Cuba Commission findings back to China in 1874, was delayed from taking up his post in Washington until the summer of 1878. Inthe interim, Yung Wing acted as de facto minister from the Education Mission in

In addition, there is an American official, a quite fair-minded and very energetic man [Colonel Frederick Bee, 1826–92]. Out of his great affection for our Chinese people he has persevered admirably in championing them in this, and our good people are increasingly indebted to him for his outstanding work.

I recently heard that an official has already been selected for the post of consul in America. Seeing our Chinese, he will obtain an understanding of their dire circumstances. Peaceful Sino-foreign relations will then be maintained, labor affairs will be eased, the national dignity will be upheld, and friendship will then be strengthened and the people pleased. Moreover, the entry and exit of the Chinese will not take place under the circumstances of the past as outlined in this essay. Under the responsibility of a consul, this will certainly not be so serious a matter.

A New
Account
of a Trip
Around
the Globe

231

CHAPTER 19. A BRIEF ACCOUNT OF
THE SUEZ CANAL

The Suez Canal was formerly a stretch of desert occupying an area bordering the continents of Asia and Africa under the jurisdiction of the Turkish Governor-general of Egypt. In the north it fronted on the Mediterranean Sea and in the south on the Red Sea, forming an overland route of 238 li, which, at the time, was uninhabited. Those arriving at the end of the Mediterranean from the west by ship had to take a train from the port of Alexandria (the largest port in the southern Mediterranean and controlled by Egypt) and

Hartford but was severely hampered by his lack of official credentials. Nevertheless, he kept up a steady drumfire of correspondence to the State Department protesting the deteriorating situation of the Chinese in the American West. One of the new ministers' first acts after their official installation was to set up a consulate in San Francisco with Chen Shutang as consul-general and Colonel Frederick Bee as vice-consul in the fall of 1878. Key English-language correspondence on the period may be found in Seward to Fish, February 29, 1876, in Jules Davids, *American Diplomatic and Public Papers: The United States and China*, vol. 13, *Chinese Immigration* (Wilmington, Del.: Scholarly Resources, 1979), 228–29, 232; Seward to Fish, June 29, 1876, U.S. Department of State, National Archives Microfilm, "Diplomatic Dispatches, China: Minister's Dispatches," M92, Roll 42, number 95; and Prince Kung [Gong] to Seward, M92, Roll 42, number 95, enclosure 1. For the appointments of Chen Shutong and Colonel Bee, see Chen [Lanbin] to Evarts, November 8, 1878, U.S. Department of State, National Archives Microfilm, "Notes from Foreign Legations, China," M98, Roll 1. Li Gui's reference to an appointment that had already been made may have come from Li Hongzhang, who mentioned that Chen Shutong had already been added to the projected personnel for the legation in the fall of 1876. See Li to Chen Lanbin, in *Li wenzhong gong: Pengliao hangao* (The works of Li Hongzhang: Correspondence with friends and colleagues), 16:39a.

travel overland to the vicinity of the northern Red Sea port of Suez, then board another ship to continue east, unable to go directly by water.[1] The *Yinghuan zhilue* records that the *Haiguo Wenjian Lu*[2] even says: "How regrettable that one cannot take a sword and slice it off," in reference to this.

In the sixth year of the reign of the Xianfeng emperor [1856], the Frenchman [Ferdinand] de Lesseps developed a proposal to cut a channel that would allow merchant ships to sail directly from the Mediterranean to the Red Sea, and negotiated with the Egyptian khedive Ismail [Pasha, 1830–95]. The Egyptian governor [initially] disregarded it,[3] remaining obstinate in the face of M. de Lesseps's amicability. Consequently M. de Lesseps returned to France to raise the capital, with every share selling for five hundred francs (every franc is equal to twenty cents in foreign silver).[4] One concern was the temperature in the region, so they first constructed devices to supply water. Their method was to run iron pipes underground and join them to sources of water from other places; they also prepared supplies for the workmen. These initial essentials obtained, the work then took another eight years. They utilized sixty to seventy enormous dredging machines to dig it out and regularly employed twenty to thirty thousand men each day. They were repeatedly troubled by shifting sands clogging the channel, so they obtained yellow mud from other locales and, along with clamshells, used it to fill in and press into the banks [to stabilize them]. In the tenth month of the seventh year of Tongzhi

1. Travelers went via the Alexandria-Cairo and Desert Railways, built by railroad pioneer Robert Stephenson in the mid-1850s.

2. *A Record of News in the Maritime Countries,* Chen Lunjiong, 1730.

3. Li's chronology appears compressed here. Lesseps's initial negotiations in 1856 with Mehemet Said, Ismail's predecessor, went sufficiently well to get the project under way—with Said being a major shareholder—though it lacked an official *firman* from Constantinople. Ismail's accession to the governor-generalship of Egypt in 1863 and the complex tensions between his impulses toward modernization and his fears of European dominance on completion of the canal tended to keep his relationship with de Lesseps in somewhat of a parlous state throughout the decade. D. A. Farnie, *East and West of Suez: The Suez Canal in History* (Oxford: Oxford University Press, 1969), 56–93, passim. There also appears to be a mistake in all versions of the text in which the character *wei,* "the right" has been substituted for *wéi,* "to disregard or oppose."

4. Lesseps's Universal Canal Company was incorporated in France in 1859 as a "foreign" enterprise. Shareholders were required to pay 40 percent of their share costs within the first year of the company's existence; this was later reduced to 20 percent. Ibid., 53.

[November–December 1869][5] its completion was announced. After eleven years, and at the huge cost of a billion taels,[6] the finished canal was 287 li long, 192 feet wide, and 26 feet deep. The French emperor gave de Lesseps high honors and ennobled him.

Ships passing through the canal pay a fee of ten francs for every ton of cargo according to the size of their hulls, and every passenger also pays ten francs. It is inadvisable for ships in the canal to speed or veer from side to side, or start and stop erratically, and so they all proceed according to the canal company's regulations, and everyone gladly accepts their directions.[7]

Initially, when the French began this great project, there had been numerous other proposals from all over the world. Some might have succeeded; others seemed more dubious. England, however, simply decided that the project could not possibly succeed because the land was a vast desert and while the earth and rock were easy to work, it would be necessary to continually open the channel. They had therefore already dismissed M. de Lesseps's plan out of hand when it reached them. England is generally the leader in initiating the great affairs of the West and unwilling to lag behind. In this instance, however, their lack of participation stood to lose them their rights to a way from east to west, which for the English would have been unwise. In the first year of the reign of the Guangxu emperor [1875], the English crown prince passed through the canal while traveling east on a visit to India. The Egyptian governor, anxious to keep close relations with England, offered four hundred shares to the prince as a mark of respect. The prince repaid in gold, and the English were naturally pleased to obtain an ownership in the canal.[8]

Examining the success of de Lesseps in this great enterprise, he was possessed of a firmness of purpose and determination, and

A New
Account
of a Trip
Around
the Globe

233

5. The inauguration ceremonies took place from November 16 to 20, 1869. Of the cultural effects springing from the opening of the canal, the most famous is perhaps Verdi's *Aida*, composed the following year. Ibid., 84, 87.

6. The actual costs came to £18,144,000 or $90,720,000, the equivalent of about 64,080,000 *liang*/taels.

7. The Canal Company's *Navigation Regulations*, issued prior to the opening ceremonies in August 1869.

8. Li, of course, omits the crucial information that British Prime Minister Disraeli purchased the remainder of the bankrupt khedive's shares for four million pounds in November 1875.

A New
Account
of a Trip
Around
the Globe

234

was thus unafraid of difficulty or danger; having deep understanding and foresight, his firmness and determination could therefore be strengthened. If one merely has the necessary desire to succeed but is in fact incapable of doing so, then what can be accomplished? Therefore, [both] deep knowledge and foresight were actually de Lesseps's great talents. The country's rulers were able to entrust him with special responsibilities as an official for a specific time without hindering him in the least, and he got on well with the ruler's ministers, a quality that is not accidental. But was the judgment of the English that the project could not succeed the product of a thorough understanding derived from meticulous examination? Or was it "an inadequate glimpse of a cartload of firewood"? I say it was indeed a mistake and thus like the old proverb that says: "Even the wise are not immune from error."

Now I also hear that the Westerners intend to dig a canal across the isthmus called Panama connecting the Western Hemisphere's two continents (Westerners use this word *jing* [neck], as they say it is like a person's neck) to allow ships to pass directly between the eastern and western oceans. This land's width is only a bit more than a hundred li. It is not even half as wide as the Isthmus of Suez, but the land is all hard rock and difficult to excavate. Moreover, in discussing the conditions of the water in the two oceans there are many who say they are not suitable.

CHAPTER 20. A SHORT ESSAY ON CHINESE AND FOREIGN MERCHANTS ABROAD

Once, during the course of a conversation with Westerners on the proper ways of governing the people, one of them said: "Those who lead,[1] nurture. Those who nurture allow all to pursue their livelihoods." In discussing Chinese and foreign merchants who travel to different countries, he went on to say,

This, too, is simply allowing them to pursue their livelihoods. Therefore, our Western countries have employed

---

1. Significantly, Li uses the character *mu*, "shepherd," here to denote officials or leaders. Mencius at one point uses similar terminology to denote a country's leadership, referring to them as "shepherds of people" *(ren mu). Mencius,* bk. I, pt. 1, chap. 6, line 6 (p. 137).

modest, competent, high officials to act as resident ministers in China so that under their leadership, the friendly relations between our two countries will ensure that all classes of Chinese and foreigners may live in harmony and safety without incident. Thus, magistrates have been installed to handle routine cases, with consuls to handle commercial affairs. Ancillary matters are decided and discussed by attachés and counselors, who assist in their implementation, while translators interpret the spoken and written languages. Concern for the possibility of the unexpected requires that provisions be made for protection, so water forces are organized. Anxious to prevent fighting and pilfering, funds are appropriated for investigation and arrests, and thus a police force is set up. In arranging for the salaries of all civil and military officials, as well as for barracks, warships, ordnance and munitions, and a million other annual necessities, no effort can be spared. All of this is done from a desire that merchants living in China may all pursue their livelihoods in the same manner as they do in their native countries—even though we Westerners living in China number no more than a few thousand people. The Chinese living abroad, however, number more than a million, yet without Chinese officials to protect and nurture them, how are they to avoid being humiliated?

A New
Account
of a Trip
Around
the Globe

235

I replied:

I have heard this before and, moreover, I can point to any number of instances of it. The Chinese in San Francisco are not tolerated by the Irish party [see chapters 18 and 28] and are most certainly in a precarious position. Chinese in Singapore have been maimed or killed by the locals, while those suffering the hardships of Cuba and Peru are uncountable. Such barbarities I cannot even bear to describe. Even the Chinese in Japan are at the moment not completely accepted by the local governments there. As for all the Chinese in other places like Australia, Malacca, Java, and Penang, while we have not heard of any additional incidents, it is nevertheless feared that they might not be able to remain in complete safety. Since the aim of our Imperial

A New
Account
of a Trip
Around
the Globe

236

Court, however, has been to care for the people tenderly, without in fact departing from the sage kings of the ancients, how could they begrudge such a small expense as this? Though at first they were especially reluctant to allow Chinese to go abroad, things have now taken their present turn.[2] The recently appointed ministers and consuls who are to reside in various countries will go through fire and water to protect them and allow all to be completely safe and happy in their livelihoods. From the further necessity of carefully arranging matters on a secure and orderly basis, they may live permanently abroad without anxiety, trusting in the assistance of the caring benevolence of the imperial intention.

The Westerner happily replied, "With this, I wish the Chinese living abroad my most profound good wishes." Accordingly, I have written this short essay on Chinese and foreign merchants abroad.

CHAPTER 21. GETTING ALONG IN WESTERN COUNTRIES: AN INTRODUCTION TO THE ESSENTIALS

Passing through ten or more countries and covering eighty thousand li on this present trip around the globe, the people with whom I have come into contact have mostly been English, French, and American. On the whole, these people have been earnest and perceptive,[1] lively and straightforward, calm and tranquil, modest, and clean, and not constrained by outmoded views; as for the

---

2. Since the period of turmoil accompanying the dynastic change that brought them to power in the seventeenth century, the Qing viewed Chinese who went abroad for any length of time as *han jian,* or "Chinese traitors." Despite the immigration treaties of the later half of the nineteenth century, Qing statutes still carried the death penalty for emigrants, though enforcement was, by this time, essentially nonexistent. As noted previously, issues revolving around the treatment of emigrants as well as their potential as sources of revenue and technological expertise for the regime were a primary reason for the posting of Chinese diplomats overseas. Nonetheless, one can detect throughout Li's account a palpable sense of tension as he strives to defend the propriety and loyalty of the emigrants from the lingering animus of his Chinese audience, while attempting to answer as honestly as possible questions from his bewildered Western friends as to why his government doesn't do more to protect its overseas subjects. Additional examples of this tension may be found throughout chapter 18.

1. The exact usage Li is after for the term *min* is difficult to pin down. Definitions I have listed here, including "perceptive," "quick-witted," and "clever" (as in Li's preface) may be found in the *Analects,* 1:14, and in the *Xiaojing* (Classic of filial piety), 1a.

exceptions, they may be discounted. Having seen the situation in these places, though admittedly with little time spent in any of them, I have come to realize that while the main threads of it are complex and rather tangled, the heart of the matter lies in their earnestness and perception. Only earnestness gives rise to forthrightness and good humor, with no trifling or prevarication, or indecisiveness or doubt about where one is going. Forthrightness and good humor indeed follow from earnestness, and those who possess it also tend to stay calm. Such tranquility is present not only during times of leisure, but even more so when things get difficult. Why is this the case? Examining their parliaments, monarchs, ministers, gentlemen, and all classes of the people en masse, I am not sure that I can express it in only a few words. Although they may argue, they do so quite calmly. Ordinary situations do not bring about harsh words or looks, or shouting and abuse; not even servants are subjected to this. At close quarters in buildings and dwellings, one does not hear families making noise at the end of the day. Their understanding of things and their unwillingness to cling to stale opinions comes from long experience and practice, broad learning, and especially from reading useful books. There are also many Chinese books there and those who can read them are neither pedantic nor undisciplined and they do not bother with trivial or superfluous works. Thus, after reading useful books, and examining ancient and modern, Chinese and foreign works, how could they not be far-sighted and free of outdated opinions?

Westerners must bathe daily and wash their clothes after a day or two, their food and drink must be pure, and they do not wipe tears or mucus into it or cough on it. Their houses are without a speck of dust and their persons without the slightest bit of dirt. Admittedly, this is perhaps true of the people I have come to know intimately, but I am not aware of having met any exceptions to this—who would no doubt have excited ridicule and disgust—so in the essentials they are most refined. Everyone who travels among them must be circumspect and not excite their mockery or disdain on account of their refinement, which might further cause one to be taken lightly. This cannot be disregarded and must be taken seriously. During such times, we cannot but trust their words and follow their lead; then, regardless of the importance of

A New
Account
of a Trip
Around
the Globe

237

A New
Account
of a Trip
Around
the Globe

238

the affair, any problems will invariably be smoothed over. Of those Chinese traveling there, shouldn't we not only worry about allowing them to see the important things, but also about seeing those things that are trivial? However superficial in its essentials, those who have been getting along in Western countries for a long time do not consider this explanation off the mark.

CHAPTER 22. A FEW WORDS ON RUNNING WATER

All people place considerable emphasis on keeping their houses, clothing, food, and drink clean, and this is especially true of Westerners. Westerners are even more particular about water, and if it is sandy, turbid, or dirty, they believe that this causes disease. Therefore, they do not drink all the river water, well water, or rainwater that is collected. Rather, their method of obtaining water in metropolitan areas is to first carefully investigate the sources in the surrounding regions. Regardless of the distance involved these must be as pure as possible. It is then conveyed underground through iron pipes winding high and low, bending around, and drawn up into a reservoir. The reservoir must be located in a high place, otherwise dirt can easily collect in it. From the reservoir the water is distributed all around to every residence. The houses all have additional iron pipes to bring the water in and thus depend entirely on mechanical devices to supply it. They examine the number of people concentrated [in the service area], for the size of the devices must accord with the size of the population; otherwise, it will either oversupply or undersupply them, neither of which would be suitable. This being the case, one can draw water without having it run out, and it can then be used widely for drinking, rinsing [the mouth], washing, and irrigation. With the unlimited use of water, the poor may be relieved from want, and it can truly be said that the advantages of this excellent idea are universal.

China's water comes from lakes, rivers, streams, and wells, and as such is [ultimately] rainwater. There are devices for water storage, but no methods of distribution and, from time immemorial, the people have had no control over whether there would be an abundance or lack of it. If there is too much, it overflows; too little, and it cannot be supplied, nor is it pure and clear. Some even go so far as to allow muddy water to settle and then drink it, as they seek to avoid illness and see this as a way to drive away pestilence! For this reason, Westerners living in China often go to the mountains to get spring water to bring back for drinking. Time and again, they have sought to transfer their techniques [of water supply] for application in China, but their influence has so far been somewhat unsuccessful in securing it. Water is a natural substance the nature of which is to flow downward.[1] There have been hollowed-out bamboo tubes linked together to draw running water from high places where our country's mountain dwellers have permanent supplies. However, there has never been a system of distribution down from these higher areas winding all around and run underground, so can we really say that this is running water? Even so, the water does run to some degree, so I mention it here by way of example in the interest of fairness.

A New
Account
of a Trip
Around
the Globe

239

CHAPTER 23. A FEW WORDS ON HOTELS

Hotels are neither ancient nor modern, nor Chinese or foreign, but something common to everyone. Throughout the world there are no places that people do not visit, and so there are no places without hotels. Once, simply because the country had no lodgings, Duke Xiang knew that Marquis Chen must be worthy of great blame. Although Marquis Chen was not censured merely for this,[1] its importance as an aspect of good government has been univer-

1. As famously expressed by Mencius in likening it to the disposition of human nature to seek the good. *Mencius*, bk. VI, pt. 1, chap. 2, line 2 (pp. 395–96).

1. In the entries for the reign of Duke Xiang (named Wu) of Lu (ca. 573–542 B.C.E.) in both the *Chunqiu* and its extended commentaries in the *Zuo Zhuan*, the duplicity and despotism of the rulers of Chen, a small state to the west of Lu, are routinely cited. Perhaps the best summary is offered in a *Zuo Zhuan* commentary for the thirtieth year of Duke Xiang, shortly before he died:

> Ch'in [Chen] is a doomed State with which we should have nothing to do. (Its government) is collecting rice and millet, and repairing the walls of its capital and suburbs, relying on these two things, without doing anything for the comfort of the people. The ruler is too weak to stand to anything; his brothers and cousins are extravagant; his eldest son is mean; the great officers are proud; the government is in the hands of many families: in this condition and so near to the great State (of Ts'oo [Chu]), can it avoid perishing? It will perish within ten years.

Zuo Zhuan commentary on *Chunqiu*, "Duke Xiang," Thirtieth Year, line 5, "The King's son Jia fled to Jin." Translation in James Legge, *The Chinese Classics*, vol. 5, part 2 (London: Trubner and Company, 1872), 551, 553 (for Chinese originals); 555, 557 for English translations.

A New
Account
of a Trip
Around
the Globe

240

sally recognized. In discussing hotels, however, whether in ancient times or modern, inside China or in foreign lands, the countries of the West must really be considered to set the ultimate standard. Why? Without going into other reasons, I say that we may simply generalize from this: In their travels, the rulers of neighboring countries trust to hotels for their nightly lodgings and, consequently, everything entailed therein. Needless to say, the buildings are huge, elegantly appointed, and the food and drink of the finest quality. There are stores and shops within them for obtaining necessities on the spot, and they even provide books. In addition, though, complete arrangements for telegrams and posts may be had inside the hotels. Steamships, trains, and all manner of horse-drawn vehicles may be engaged, as well as interpreters, servants, laborers, and so forth. This promptness and convenience we found over and over, and because this is not entirely covered in "A Diary of a Journey to the East," I am writing something about it here. In addition, their ability to suit the tastes and preferences of various nationalities and to meet their needs appropriately allows one to forget that one is a traveler at the far corners of the earth. Does this represent nothing more than servicing the weary, albeit on a grand scale? Moreover, the regulations are orderly, and each hotel accommodates hundreds or thousands of people with everything impeccably run, so what about these additional skills of theirs? It is just this that enables travelers to gather throughout the world and in so doing improve relations in all countries. Governments therefore actually depend on them for this and do not see the hotels as merely hosts.

CHAPTER 24. SOME COMMENTS ON WESTERNERS ENTERTAINING GUESTS

The *Zuo Zhuan* says: "The visitors came as if returning home," and this should be the motto of a host in entertaining guests, as it suggests that there is nothing that will not be provided for them. It goes on to say, "He instructed them in what they did not know and provided them with what they did not have," which goes further than merely [treating them] like they were returning home. Westerners, however, in entertaining guests have progressed even beyond this.[1] During this trip around the globe, I have covered a distance of over eighty thousand li, and my hosts have truly been too numerous to mention individually. They have nonetheless been very gracious and completely considerate in every way, in each case diligently and conscientiously treating us like family. The manner in which Westerners entertain guests like this is something that, unless one has personally experienced it, would in itself be scarcely believable.

Generally speaking, we Chinese traveling abroad are for the most part seeing and hearing things we have never experienced before. Thus, we must receive guidance from others on all sides about a variety of things. The information they impart must therefore be expressed candidly in clear and distinct language, concealing nothing, as their sole concern is that their guests have every detail in its entirety. As for room and board, one need only to seek it as appropriate, and it can indeed be obtained. This is all the more so in speaking of the great hotels. Who knows how many strangers, having never had the pleasure of meeting before, searching out every sight and sound, must have arranged introductions and exchanged words of good luck? They thereby enable the travelers' residence to be even more delightful, like a [pleasant] surprise. Although activity and rest must each be examined in detail, regardless of sickness, hunger, and fatigue, are they being nothing more than solicitous in suppressing talk and laughter, and remaining amiable and dignified? All the families I visited accompanied me on my sightseeing. This, again, appears to surpass what the ancients had to say about host and guest being indistinguishable.

It might be asked: "Were all the places through which you traveled like this?" I would have to say they were. The one that was surpassing in this regard, however, was America, and I hear that the

A New
Account
of a Trip
Around
the Globe

241

1. Etiquette, protocol, and diplomacy are consistent themes in the *Zuo Zhuan*, a history of the tumultuous period between 722 and 468 B.C.E. The reference employed by Li comes from the "31st Year of Duke Xiang (542 B.C.E.)," and is part of a speech by Zi Chan expounding on the virtuous example set by Duke Wen of Jin in caring for guests. As translated by Burton Watson it reads, "The duke did not detain his visitors longer than necessary, yet none of their affairs was neglected. . . . He taught them things they did not know, and took pity on their needs. Thus the guests felt as though they were at home." *The Tso Chuan: Selections from China's Oldest Narrative History* (New York: Columbia University Press, 1989), 158.

A New
Account
of a Trip
Around
the Globe

242

Americans also say this about the Germans. Presently, I have a sufficient understanding of Westerners to get along with them. In what I see as an unbiased observation, however, the essential thing in guessing their intentions to some degree lies with the host. These countries in their affairs desire [to strengthen] earnest friendship, broaden understanding, and cultivate talent and so cannot presume to look at this factor with indifference. Hence, their feting of guests is most admirable and beneficial, completely proper and appropriate to their national honor, and their desire to assist and counsel is endlessly celebrated. In former times, when cities were not on friendly terms, those with great reputations could bring them together, and the *Zuo Zhuan* accords with this as well concerning relations with neighboring countries. The present path has in fact advanced even further with the times, and can therefore be said to be a means of proclaiming Sino-foreign understanding.

CHAPTER 25. SOME THOUGHTS ON CARRIAGE NOISE

To detest noise and enjoy quiet is, though perhaps rarely attainable, a fixed principle both during the day's work and the evening's rest. This is true of both Chinese and foreigners, and there has never been the least difference in this regard. When things go against one's wishes, however, the situation becomes intolerable in a different environment, precisely because one may then lack anything with which to objectively compare it.

On this present tour of the globe, passing through many countries, I stayed for some time in the American city of Philadelphia. I stayed in England and France for no more than a few days. Usually, in traveling about within these places, regardless of cost or distance, I went by steamer over water and by train over land. The carriages running on the streets did not have a pair of wheels [as with many carts in China], but instead had four, and the rumbling of their running all day and night was incessant. It is said that Du Fanzhuan's [the poet Du Mu, 803–52] "Sudden Thunder" was directly inspired by the fear of the noise of the royal chariots by the people of Qin; but it was not one-tenth of the noise on Western streets. All Fanzhuan's thunderclaps in every direction cannot remotely compare to the noise made by Western vehicles. The residents themselves actually find it somewhat taxing. I once stayed four stories up in a hotel, a building that could be said to be very tall and unusually solid. With the noise of these carriages shaking it I was surely not alone in being unable to sleep, and with the bed and building shuddering continuously, how could one call this an evening's rest? Even if one perhaps likes clamor and dislikes quiet, it was unbearable.

Nonetheless, Westerners particularly hate noise, so how is one to account for this apparent difference in results I observed among them? I say it is this so-called phenomenon of things going against one's wishes and finding them intolerable in a different environment! Yet Westerners living in China, although the vehicles have only a single set of wheels, hate the noise of them, so again, what is the reason for this? Is it because they have nothing with which to objectively compare it?

BOOK IV
Diary of a Journey to the East

CHAPTER 26. A FEW WORDS ABOUT THE MAP OF THE GLOBE

The earth is shaped like a globe and orbits around the sun, while the sun remains fixed as the earth moves. Although there are a great many Chinese who understand this in principle, perhaps eight or nine out of ten do not believe it. Formerly, I, too, was inclined to doubt it, though now, having traveled abroad by imperial edict and circled the globe, I have come to accept it. Traveling east from Shanghai, passing through Japan, and crossing the Great Eastern Ocean [the Pacific], I reached San Francisco in the western part of America, a distance calculated to be 22,149 li. The crewmen regularly measured the sun's position in degrees on the hour, and every day at sunrise we routinely gained seventeen minutes or so. Thus when it is exactly noon in Shanghai, the time in San Francisco is already *xu* [8:00 P.M.]. Boarding the train in San Francisco and traveling east for 10,785 li, the sunrise was still advancing when we arrived at the city of Philadelphia in the eastern part of America; at noon in San Francisco it is *shencheng* [3:00 P.M.] in Philadelphia and slightly less than six [Chinese] hours ahead of Shanghai.[1] Then, crossing the Great Western Ocean [the Atlantic] from Philadelphia, another 11,748 li east to the English capital of London, the sunrise is increasingly later each day [in relation to Shanghai]. At noon in

1. Philadelphia is actually eleven hours ahead in absolute terms, but because of the international date line, somewhat over twelve hours behind.

A New
Account
of a Trip
Around
the Globe

246

Philadelphia, England is beginning *zhen* [7:00 A.M.].² Again, travel-ing east from England, from the port of Marseilles through the Suez Canal, passing through the Red Sea and Indian Ocean to Hong Kong and back to Shanghai, the distance is reckoned to be 36,739 li. Continuing to calculate the sun's position, in England it is just at the beginning of the *mao* hour [5:00 A.M.] while in Shanghai it is already exactly noon; compared with Philadelphia, the difference is slightly less than six Chinese hours [twelve English hours]. Thus, from Shanghai to Philadelphia constitutes a hemisphere, with China having day while America's east is having night; and from Philadelphia back to Shanghai is also a hemisphere, with America's east having night while in China it is still day.

If the shape of the earth were perhaps a square,³ and it remained stationary while the sun was in motion, how could one travel east from Shanghai and ultimately return to Shanghai, a distance total-ing 82,351 li over land and sea, without ever taking a half-step to the west? Because the shape of the earth is like a globe, there is essentially no separation into "east" and "west." Thus, the time of the sunrise varies in locations everywhere around the globe throughout the year. China's length and breadth are more than ten thousand li, and still there are variations. If calculated like those in America on the opposite side of the world,⁴ then the differences will vary even more widely [than in America].

If we can say that the shape of the earth is like a globe, then why do the earth's myriad objects not fall off of it? I say it is because they are held by *qi*.⁵ Since the earth moves along with everything attached to it, how could things fall off?

As for the Eastern and Western Hemispheres, these derive from

2. This appears to have been a misprint on Li's part: The situation is exactly the reverse of what he describes. That is, 7:00 A.M. in Philadelphia would be noon in Lon-don. Noon in Philadelphia would be 5:00 P.M. in London, as Li has it in chapter 12.

3. Traditional Chinese cosmology posits the earth as square and heaven as round. This is depicted in a wide variety of media from the design of coins—round with a square hole in the center—to the shape of buildings, with the distinctively round Tem-ple of Heaven in Beijing as perhaps the most dramatic surviving example.

4. Lit.: "Separated like front and back."

5. The concept of *qi* permeates Chinese thought in any number of areas: meta-physics, science, medicine, and aesthetics, to list just a few. For Li, educated within a continuum of officially favored Neo-Confucian epistemology extending at least as far back as Zhu Xi (1130–1200), the best approximation of his use of *qi* here might be, vari-ously, "energy," "force," "vital force," or "material force." For a good general overview of the subject in relation to the development of Neoconfucianism, see William T. DeBary, ed., *Sources of Chinese Tradition*, vol. 1 (New York: Columbia University Press, 1960), 455–514, passim.

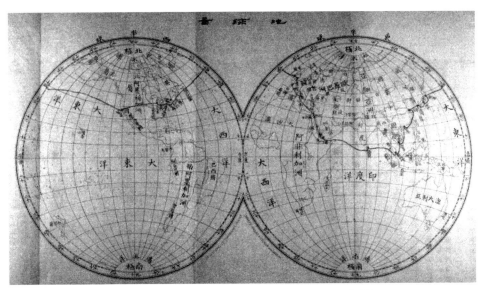

A Map of the Globe. Li's route through the Eastern and Western Hemispheres is depicted by the line on the twin maps (done in red on the original). (From *Huan you diqiu xin lu*, Shanghai, 1877–78; courtesy of University of Pittsburgh.)

the inability of the Westerners to depict them as connected [i.e., as a complete globe on a flat map], so they are drawn separately. Because things are also arranged according to divisions of latitude, there are northern and southern hemispheres as well.

The common people also persist in saying that the winds from the south are warm while those from the north are cold, a sentiment that is practically universal. Actually, however, it is untrue. Because the sun stays at the equator, the winds coming from the equatorial regions are warm while those from the polar regions are cold. Since China is north of the equator, the southern winds are warm and the northerly winds are cold; countries south of the equator experience the southern winds as cold while those from the north are warm. The important thing is that the winds from the sunnier areas will be warm and those from the opposite regions will be cold, regardless of whether they are to the south or north. This principle may be seen as evidence that the sun remains fixed while the earth moves, and is thus the cause of it.

A carefully drawn map of the globe precedes the diary of my eastern journey. All of the routes I followed are distinguished on the map by red lines, with the cities through which I passed marked by red circles. Readers will therefore come to realize that the shape of the earth is that of a globe, and will have absolutely no doubt that the sun remains fixed while the earth moves.

CHAPTER 27. FROM SHANGHAI
TO YOKOHAMA

A New
Account
of a Trip
Around
the Globe

248

On the twentieth day of the fourth month of the second year in the reign of the Guangxu emperor [May 13, 1876], I booked passage on the Mitsubishi Co. of Japan's American steamer *Nevada* (the joint-stock trading companies of foreign merchants are called *gongsi* [corporations]; the China Merchants' Steam Navigation Company[1] also follows this system), buying tickets for first-class cabins on two voyages, one from Shanghai to Yokohama, and the other from Yokohama to San Francisco. Despite the fact that all the passengers have had their fees reduced by half, the cost still came to about $150 in foreign silver (all those going to the American Centennial Exposition on official business—government officials, workers, merchants, and those participating in the fair—have had their fares reduced by half according to a commercial shipping protocol signed between our country and the Americans). Tonight at 9:00 P.M. we boarded ship. Accompanying me was my interpreter, a Cantonese, Mr. Chen Chiyuan.

At 6:00 A.M. on the twenty-first, we set sail from the *Pu* [Shanghai]. The ship is a paddlewheel steamer with two large masts, two funnels, and a displacement of twenty-five hundred tons (every "ton" is equivalent to 1,660 *jin*). The ship is open and wide, with separate cabins above and below decks. Chiyuan and I are in first-

---

1. The China Merchants' Steam Navigation Company was founded in January 1873, under the aegis of Li Hongzhang and other Chinese self-strengtheners as a pioneering *guandu shangban* (officially sponsored, merchant-run) enterprise. Its efforts were directed largely at winning back the carrying trade on China's inland waters from foreign firms. Under its director, Sheng Xuanhuai (1844–1916), and financed in part by Hu Guangyong, it achieved a considerable degree of success in the 1870s. A standard work remains Albert Feuerwerker, *China's Early Industrialization: Sheng Hsuan-huai and Mandarin Enterprise* (Cambridge: Harvard University Press, 1958; reprint, New York: Atheneum, 1970); see also Chi-kong Lai, "The Qing State and Merchant Enterprise: The China Merchants' Company, 1872–1902," in *To Achieve Security and Wealth: The Qing Imperial State and the Economy, 1644–1911*, ed. Jane Kate Leonard (Ithaca: Cornell University Press, 1992). The *Nevada* was built in 1865 and began its service with the Pacific Mail line in 1874. The following year, Mitsubishi bought the Pacific Mail routes between Shanghai and Nagasaki and Yokohama and acquired the *Nevada*. Toward the end of its service, the ship's name was changed to *Sakio Maru*.

class berth number 25. The cabin is over seven [Chinese] feet square, and has two beds with clean and tidy quilts and pillows, and thick, soft mattresses (the passengers do not carry their own bedding, as these are provided on board ship). On the wall hangs a large mirror and a glass lamp (ship's regulations state that at about 11:00 P.M. the lights must be put out), and a washbasin, towels and soap, and assorted other items are provided, overlooking nothing. The bed covers and window curtains are all clean, white, and pleasant. Fore and aft on the deck are separate elegant rooms reserved for the first-class passengers. One is used as a study, while the other is for smoking and passing the time (ship's regulations prohibit smoking in the cabins and dining room), and the rooms are nicely appointed for sitting or dozing as appropriate. On the deck below there is a room amidships used as a dining hall, with six long tables, each of which seats about a dozen or so passengers. Flower vases are placed on them and their sweet fragrance is pleasant and strong.

Breakfast is served at eight-thirty in the morning; lunch at twelve-thirty; and dinner at six-thirty. Not only are all styles of foreign food prepared, but our Chinese *zhoufang* [rice gruel] as well. Shortly before every meal a gong is sounded, and it is rung again as everyone gathers in the dining room and the meal begins. During mealtimes, every table is provided with a bill of fare, and each guest chooses his or her own dishes, but drinks and liquor must be purchased separately from the ship's mess. About half the stewards are Japanese and the rest Cantonese, diligent and attentive, and come immediately on hearing us call. I was feeling a bit seasick and did not go to the dining room to eat and drink, taking only small meals — a few vegetables, tea, soup, and fruit — which they brought as I wished. During this trip, I have given away most of the prepared food items I had brought along that I thought I would need, since I have no use for them and have come to regard them as a nuisance.

There are all together eleven different nationalities represented on this trip. Among those I have got on well with are an American, [Francis P.] Knight,[2] a merchant who is also serving as consul at Niuzhuang, whom I chanced to meet on his way to the exposition

A New
Account
of a Trip
Around
the Globe

249

2. For information on Knight and his role as Li's docent in the United States, see introduction, Li Gui's author's preface, and chaps. 3–13. Knight's official business was to serve as one of the Chinese Centennial commissioners on site in Philadelphia.

on business; a Japanese named Shinagawa Tadomichi who had served in Japan's Shanghai consulate and was now returning home; two or three English students traveling for study; and also a Cantonese merchant named Wu, who is going to America.

A New
Account
of a Trip
Around
the Globe

250

The twenty-second. At 9:00 P.M. the ship arrived at the Japanese port of *Zhangqidao*, which the Japanese call "Nagasaki," also using the two characters *zhangqi* because their written language is read the same as China's, but with a different pronunciation. The distance from Shanghai to here I judge to be only nineteen and a half [Chinese] hours [thirty-nine English hours], and 1,797 li.

The twenty-third. At 9:00 A.M., I paid eight small foreign cash and boarded a launch to go ashore to what my Cantonese friend called the *Hesheng* general store. In the boat were the store's partners, who carried two small bags, which the customs inspectors took away from them. The thrust of the conversation was that they must wait until they declare the bags, after which they will be returned. By law, even the duty-free goods in the luggage must be declared.

Presently, the boat approached the opposite shore. The shop managers, named Liang Yanzhuan and Zhou Zhaoting, said that our Chinese in the Nagasaki area are workers and merchants, with those from Guangdong numbering about three hundred, plus another three to four hundred Fujianese, and over a hundred people from Chejiang. They have organized a Guangdong *huiguan*[3] and a Fujian *huiguan* (to which the Chejiang people are attached), and find it easier to make a living here, though it was implied that they disliked the laws of Japan.

At eleven o'clock, Mr. Liang led us on a tour of *Wanshou shan* [*Manjuzenji*].[4] We took *jinrickshas* (in Shanghai, the so-called Japanese carriage), and the price was very cheap. We passed through all manner of large and small streets and alleys, all clean and smooth and level. The people's shops and stores are on ground level, and there are few buildings of more than one story. The styles of the government offices are like China's, and there are

3. For more on the organization and functions of *huiguan*, see chapter 18.
4. *Wanshou shan si, Manjuzenji* in Japanese, was a famous Zen temple and school during the Song period in China visited by the Rinzai Zen master Enni Ben'en (1201–80). As noted by Heinrich Dumoulin, the temple on Mount Jing in Chejiang "became one of the mainstays of the bridge across which Zen traveled to Japan." Enni himself established a number of monasteries in Kyushu. *Zen Buddhism: A History*, vol. 2, *Japan* (New York: Macmillan, 1990), 25.

also occasionally temples in Western styles, all of which have been built in recent years. All the streets have police on them just as in Shanghai, except that they are all Japanese wearing Western uniforms. The policing of the foreign treaty ports is also done entirely by the Japanese themselves.[5] Coming to the foot of the mountain after half an hour, we saw a ceremonial gate on which was carved the four characters "*Shengfu* Zen Temple" [*Sofukuji*].[6] We entered the gate and began to climb up fifty or sixty stone steps to another gateway with the three large characters *Wanshou Shan*.[7] Again, after fifty or sixty steps we came to a large hall, soaring and majestic, piercing the clouds, with a great horizontal sign reading "The Buddha Hall,"[8] and a statue of the Buddha—just like those in China. Nearby was a hall for *Guandi* [the Chinese god of war], large and spacious, built by Chinese merchants. Several Japanese monks came to visit it [the Buddha Hall], bowing in reverence. We climbed another thirty or forty steps winding up to the Zen Hall. We then removed our shoes outside the door and went in and sat down on the floor and talked. All around, the mountains lay low beneath us. The most ancient trees were a thousand years old and still luxuriously verdant. Some old monks entered bringing incense and refreshments, which were entirely agreeable, and before leaving I made a contribution of a gold coin for an offering of incense.

At 1:00 P.M. we went to a restaurant for a meal, also leaving off our shoes and sitting on the floor. Serving the meal and pouring the wine were young women and girls who permitted themselves to be teased and flirted with shamelessly, as it is customary to employ them this way.

At 3:30 we went to the customs, a Western-style building,

A New
Account
of a Trip
Around
the Globe

251

5. Unlike in China, where the treaty ports were policed by the imperial powers, often with troops from other parts of their empires. The British, for example, famously employed Sikh police in Shanghai.

6. Sofukuji is one of four Zen temples in Nagasaki built by the Chinese merchant community in the seventeenth century and has been designated as a national treasure by the Japanese government. The first character Li records, however, *sheng*, or *sho* in Japanese, appears to be in error. There is a famous temple in nearby Fukuoka called Shofukuji, reputed to be the site of the introduction of both Zen and tea to Japan in the thirteenth century; it not only does not fit the description in Li's account but also would have been impossible to reach in half an hour by ricksha.

7. "Longevity Hill"; perhaps the most famous *Wanshou Shan* is the one anchoring one end of the *Yihe Yuan*, or Summer Palace in Beijing.

8. Literally, "Hall of Great Treasures," a euphemism for the Buddha.

though it employed Chinese and foreign script to display the two characters for "Customs." We heard that every month they only collect slightly less than twenty thousand dollars in gold on large amounts of tea, lacquerware, porcelain, and tobacco. It is run by more than thirty men, with the upstairs given over to the business offices of the customs personnel and the lower story used as the cashier's office, but without a separate bank set up there. The room for examining the goods is to the right of the customs house, and very spacious. Western merchants write their declarations in Western languages, while Chinese merchants do so in Chinese, but all the receipts are issued in Japanese. It opens every day at 9:00 A.M. At noon they break, and after lunch they open again at 1:00. At 5:00 they close for the day. Although the customs house here was set up because of the Western trade, there are no Westerners employed. We heard that this spring, they began to employ one or two Westerners to assist in managing it, but only as first-level clerks.9

After returning to the store, Mr. Zhou told me that there are four government offices in the Nagasaki area: A division of the customs where only foreign duties are handled; a separate division farther away from here devoted exclusively to collecting dues from Japanese merchants; an office for foreign affairs, specializing in matters pertaining to foreign countries; and a court for handling the people's litigation. The affairs of Nagasaki's local government had become confused [due to the treaty port system and the changes wrought by the imperial government], and so five years ago it was reorganized. There is now one Nagasaki district for purposes of handling revenue, and there are specially devised household taxes and capitation taxes. The people pay a tax on every household each month of two and a half *tianbao* [*tempo*] copper coins (every coin being equivalent to about eight *kuanyong* [*kan'ei*] cash),10 and each

9. In marked contrast to the international composition of the IMC, with the highest spots going to Hart's trusted picks.

10. The transition from the late Edo to the early Meiji period in Japan was accompanied by a bewildering array of currencies, the values of which fluctuated considerably. In 1871, the government revamped the system along European-American lines by adopting the gold standard, and issuing gold and silver yen, with smaller decimal-based denominations of sen and rin. Despite efforts to reabsorb the existing Tokugawa coinages, these were still honored in 1876, though their values had sunk. The *tempo*, a large elliptical coin dating from the 1830s with the standard square hole of Chinese and pre-Meiji Japanese currency, was theoretically worth one hundred *kan'ei* type *mon*, or

A New
Account
of a Trip
Around
the Globe

252

man and woman must pay eight *tianbao* coins each month, with those sixteen years of age or less being exempt. All resident Chinese merchants, male and female, must annually pay two yuan [yen][11] in Japanese silver coins (they recently copied Western methods and mint these themselves); the employees of [Chinese] merchants pay a yearly tax of one-half yuan; those sixteen or younger pay half of this. Westerners residing in Japan do not have to pay. As for Chinese involved in litigation, this has been given entirely over to Japanese magistrates to adjudicate, unlike the practice in the Western concessions [in China] under consular officials. Likewise, Chinese living in the Western concessions [in Japan] are also exempt from the household tax. As for the school buildings, post office, telegraph office, mines, and steamship companies, all of these are run according to Western methods with [Japanese] officers in charge of them. They have paid particular attention to telegraphs and posts, with the result that the quality of these is almost comparable to that of Western countries.

There are also practices that are unsightly and offensive. The boatmen, carters, and ricksha pullers of the land generally leave their lower bodies naked in plying their trades, and wear only a white strip of cloth a mere two [Chinese] inches wide, which runs down from the navel and is wrapped through the buttocks. Words are inadequate to describe it. I hear that no trousers are worn among the gentlemen and merchants either, but that they wrap themselves instead in folds of cloth. The women and children do so as well. A high degree of cleanliness is part of their character and they must bathe every day. Yet dozens of people, men and women, all bathe together in bathhouses as a matter of course. The alleyways on the side streets also have tubs set up for men and women to take turns using. Fearing that they will be made a laughingstock by people from afar, the government has now ordered the practice discontinued. Their efforts so far, however, have been to no avail since this has been a long-standing custom and they must necessarily proceed slowly.

At 7:00 P.M. we returned to the boat and at midnight we cast off.

cash. Li here notes that they are now worth only eight *mon;* at one point they were worth only five. Bank of Japan, *A History of Japanese Currency,* http://www.imes.boj.or.jp/cm/english_htmls/history_17.htm (accessed 5/17/02).

11. The initial use of silver yen was confined largely to the foreign trade in treaty ports like Nagasaki. Ibid.

A New
Account
of a Trip
Around
the Globe

254

A few moments before, a gun had been fired on the ship to signal the passengers ashore to return, lest they miss setting sail.

The twenty-fourth. The ship sailed along the inner waters [Inland Sea]. Very calm. On both shores were scenic mountains and rocks, very beautiful and thickly crowded with forests and trees. The sea was azure all around the bay as it narrowed to no more than one li. Leaning on the rail and gazing into the distance, the shining mist descended onto the very foreheads of the people, as if in a painting come to life.

The twenty-fifth. At noon we arrived at *Shenhu*, which in Japanese is called "Kobe," and also "Yoke." The distance from Nagasaki to here is also determined to be nineteen and a half [Chinese] hours, covering 1,531 li. At noon, we all went ashore, and together with my shipmates I strolled to the Cantonese merchants' place [named] "Yu Xingtai" to sip tea and chat. A member of the company's staff, Mr. Mai, entertained us attentively. That evening it rained and we did not return to the ship, sleeping instead at Mr. Mai's establishment. Mr. Mai told us that Kobe and Osaka are divided into two separate areas, all together numbering about sixty thousand people, and the Chinese number about seven or eight hundred, all told. They have also founded a *huiguan* here, which is the same in extent as that of Nagasaki. The commercial situation and various aspects of the concession are comparatively better than in Nagasaki.

The twenty-sixth. At twelve-thirty we went to visit another Mt. Ji.[12] A winding path circles around it, and we passed through a dozen or so teahouses (it is necessary to have teahouses set up every half li along the path circling the mountain so that travelers can rest), before climbing to the very top. The mountain has a waterfall a dozen or so *chang* [about 140'] high, cascading down just like a crystal curtain. Japanese who are sick generally come here to pray and bathe, and it is regarded as the most scenic place in Japan.

At two-thirty, I took the train to *Daban*, which the Japanese call "Osaka," a trip of an [English] hour, about 120 li distant, for the higher ticket price of a dollar for foreign guests. The Osaka region is also a commercial port and densely populated because of its con-

12. A reference to a famous mountain in China's Henan province.

centration of business. The government offices are in the Western style, very tall and broad, and the streets are all clean and spacious. The river is clear and limpid, and there are calculated to be some eight hundred odd bridges spanning it, most of which are as long as twenty to thirty *chang* [a bit over two to three hundred English feet]. Among the Chinese merchants here is a Cantonese, Mr. Mai Xuchu, and we accompanied him for a tour of the gardens, which hold more than fifteen hundred kinds of trees and plants, the majority of which I do not know the names of.

The twenty-seventh. At ten o'clock I again accompanied him [Mr. Mai] for a visit to a government science museum, which also follows the systems and arrangements of the West in order to broaden the people's knowledge and experience. Everyone must pay fifty cents to buy a wooden token before entering the museum. Inside, the goods and machines of many countries are on display, along with different types of fossils—petrified wood, bones, and skeletons—all of which are the result of a long-term transformation. There are also the regalia of successive emperors and empresses, weapons, household utensils, male and female skeletons, and fetuses and embryos of birds, beasts, insects, fish skin and bones, and Chinese Bronze Age inscriptions on tablets, as well as paintings and calligraphy. For example, I saw the Song Emperor Hui Zong's [r. 1101–26] "Gerfalcon," calligraphy by Zhu Wengong,[13] Song and Yuan editions of block-printed books, and assorted treasures from all periods.

After the tour, I took the train back to Kobe. I heard that they [the Japanese] also mint three types of coins, gold, silver, and copper, copying the techniques of the Westerners, but unfortunately I did not have the free time to go and see it. This evening, a Japanese official, Mr. Shinasugi, invited us for a drink and treated us to a sumptuous dinner of delicacies. At midnight, we returned to the ship. No sooner had my head touched the pillow than I suddenly heard the sound of surging water and the twin paddle wheels began to turn.

The twenty-eighth. The running is still calm. As dawn was breaking early this morning I leaned on a railing to catch the sunrise. As it began, innumerable golden rays streaked out into the sky. In a

13. The Neo-Confucian thinker Zhu Xi.

flash they had already turned a reddish violet, the sun so dazzling as it emerged above the surging waves that I could not gaze directly at it. Gradually it rose higher and grew smaller and paler amid the embrace of the clouds; a wondrous sight indeed! After breakfast, the waves suddenly got rougher, and I lay down on one of the ship's long rattan chairs. I could barely manage a reply to my Western friends who stopped by to chat, and my head and eyes grew very dizzy as I realized I was on the verge of throwing up.

The twenty-ninth. At 9:00 A.M. we arrived at *Hongbin*, which the Japanese call "Yokohama." From Kobe it is a trip of fifteen and a half [Chinese] hours, and a distance of 1,341 li; all told, a distance of 4,669 li from Shanghai. We saw a steamer twice the size of our *Nevada* riding at anchor in the harbor flying the American flag. I asked about it and discovered that this was the ship to the United States, named "City of Peking," which had arrived here from Hong Kong a few hours before. At 1:00 P.M. we disembarked but had to wait until the morning of the second day, fifth month [May 24] before boarding for America. In order for our luggage to be properly taken care of, we again took a small boat ashore to the *Dong-tong Tai* Cantonese shop and engaged them to go to the *Wan Chang* [Pacific Mail Steamship] Company (the "City of Peking" belongs to the American company called *Wan Chang*) to exchange our tickets.

This evening a company manager named Liang Peilin invited us for a drink. Mr. Liang said that Yokohama's merchants and people number about forty thousand, with a Chinese population of about sixteen hundred, and the commercial environment is better than Nagasaki and Kobe, though not 30 to 40 percent of that of Shanghai. The foreign business houses number several dozen of families, more or less, and there are goods piled up like mountains. They mostly import foreign commodities and export brass, cloisonné, lacquerware, tea, and antiques. There are, however, no merchants who traffic principally in opium, like the firm of Sassoon in China, a great English trader who specializes in it. This is because the Japanese strictly forbid the smoking of it and users are severely punished, so their nationals do not dare violate the prohibition. Although the punishments are strict and impartial, one can also see that the law accords with the people's wishes. What a pity that we Chinese do not know when we will be able to extinguish this

A New
Account
of a Trip
Around
the Globe

256

poisonous flame! He went on to say that Chinese *huiguan* have also been organized here, and they have selected six directors and eight officers. Minor matters among the Chinese are handled by the *huiguan,* and if there is litigation, they can then refer it to Japanese officials. The duties and household taxes of the people here are all identical to those in Nagasaki. The officials in the region are the governor of Yokohama, a customs director, a magistrate, and the prefect of Kanagawa prefecture. Various countries have set up permanent consulates here. There is also a railroad directly to the Japanese capital, about a hundred li long, and the trains running on it are priced the same as those from Kobe to Osaka.

A New
Account
of a Trip
Around
the Globe

257

The fifth month, first day [May 23]. The weather is not good, nor do I feel well. At Mr. Liang's I wrote some letters home and recounted the events of the trip thus far. At 5:00 P.M. I boarded the train for a trip to *Dongjing,* the capital of Japan, also called "Tokyo." The many villages and houses en route were very neat and tidy, and the road smooth and even. Five forts closely modeled on Western versions have been constructed on the bay, Westerners having been employed to design and build them. The most striking feature of the area is the Tokyo city gate. At six o'clock the train stopped and we hired carriages to enter the city (the cost of the train is one and half yuan per half [Chinese] hour). There are five gates, and from the northeast corner of the city we circled around and back to the railroad tracks, reboarding the train at seven-thirty.

In another few minutes, it was already dusk and we could not look around. But we were able to see the city walls, which are all built of stone and incomparably solid. The river is deep and wide and clean. The roads are open and broad and washed constantly; passing along them there is not even a hair or piece of dirt. The palaces, government buildings, barracks, and regulations for soldiers partially follow those of the West, and the officers, soldiers, and police are all in Western dress. We heard that the emperor and empress have decreed this even for the wives of officials. At eight-thirty we returned to the Dongtai Company store, had dinner, and then boarded the ship.

In speaking of the unification of the Japanese state, my humble view is that as of the beginning of the reign of [our] Xianfeng emperor [1851–61], it was still ruled by the government of the shogun, while the emperor's position was strictly in name only, and the power of the country lay dormant. In recent years they have come to greatly esteem Western learning, have adopted beneficial Western methods, and largely pursued a determined course of reform. As a result of their ability to strengthen the roots and weaken the trunk,[14] they [the reformers] have come to dominate Japan, and since then the shogun has not controlled the government. Unfortunately, they have perhaps changed their calendar and forms of dress somewhat unthinkingly.

A New
Account
of a Trip
Around
the Globe

258

CHAPTER 28. FROM YOKOHAMA
TO SAN FRANCISCO

On the second day of the fifth month [May 24] at 4:00 A.M. we set out across the Great Eastern Ocean. The ship is named "City of Peking" and I understand that it is the largest [of its kind]. The hull is made completely of iron, 420 feet long and 46 feet in the beam, with a displacement of 5,500 tons, and has four large masts and two funnels.[1] There are thirty-four first-class cabins, and each one is seven feet square and sleeps two passengers. The second-class accommodations are ahead of the masts and called the "common berth" [steerage] and can hold a thousand people. On this voyage there are thirty-five foreigners and 3 Chinese in first class, while 109 Chinese and eighteen foreigners occupy the common berth.

I had heard that whenever there are Chinese laborers traveling from Hong Kong to America, there are, as a rule, not less than a thousand in the common berth. This spring, however, it is rumored that the Irish in San Francisco (who have already become naturalized Americans and whom the Chinese say have formed a political party) have vowed to cause trouble because the Chinese

14. *Ben* and *gan:* Formulations for fundamental and ancillary matters. Sometimes used in the context of self-strengthening formulas as equivalents for *ti* and *yong.* Here the reference is to restructuring the government around the emperor as the "root" while reducing or eliminating the power of his minister, the "trunk" or shogun. For a similar reference in the context of Han dynasty interest in *Zuo Zhuan*–inspired statecraft, see Nylan, *The Five "Confucian Classics,"* 45.

1. The *City of Peking* and its sister ship, *City of Tokio* (later to carry Chen Lanbin to the United States), were built in 1873 and 1874 respectively at the new John Roach and Sons shipyard in Chester, Pennsylvania, next to Philadelphia. They were both iron-hulled screw steamers and at the time the largest ships in the Pacific. The *City of Peking*'s registered dimensions were 419 by 47.3 feet, and it was officially rated at 5,079 tons. It was capable of sustained speeds on the Pacific run of over twelve knots. William A. Fairburn, *Merchant Sail,* vol. 2 (Center Lovell, Maine: n.p., n.d.), 1398–99.

compete with them for work, and so presently there are very few here on board. The foreigners here are all English, French, American, Swiss, Spanish, or Peruvian. Aside from the Americans, the rest are all returning home from business and purposely taking an easterly route across America in order to take in the Centennial in Philadelphia.

I went with Chiyuan to stateroom number 24, which is beautifully appointed, and far surpasses the one on the last ship. The doors and windows are paneled with beautiful wood and the carving and engraving work is extremely well done. The food and drink here may be brought up at one's convenience, with attendants to bring it around just like in the homes of the rich. The ship's captain is named Maury and had served as an American naval officer. He is turning sixty and is mature and dignified; his four chief officers are also skilled in their tasks. In addition, there are a secretary, doctor, and purser to manage things and a chef, butcher, night watch officers, and stewards; thirty-one people in all. Aside from these, they employ thirty-eight Chinese as stokers, thirty-eight as deckhands, one as a chief petty officer, twenty as stewards, and nine as cooks.

The third [May 25]. The running is calm. After meals, the passengers mostly gather in the ship's saloon to chat and enjoy themselves. This evening the sea and sky were all of one color, with traces of a crescent moon.

The fourth [May 26]; around noon. A hard northwest wind is blowing. For several days now the ship has been tossed around quite a bit, and it has been very difficult for me to get up. I have been unable to eat and drink as well.[2]

The ninth [May 31]. The wind has shifted to the southwest and the ship is a bit steadier. The Westerners are talking in groups of three to five in the dining room, library, and smoking room, or taking short walks together on deck. I, too, have gradually begun to do this. After dinner the captain noted that today is Wednesday and that tomorrow it will still be Wednesday. This is because we have gained seventeen minutes a day in our daily measurements of the sun's position at sunrise since setting sail from China, and when we reach San Francisco after a period of approximately twenty-

2. It is difficult to reconcile these consecutive, yet apparently contradictory, entries. Perhaps the calm in the previous day's entry was momentary.

A New
Account
of a Trip
Around
the Globe

260

eight days,[3] it will have gained over four [Chinese; eight English] hours. Noon in Shanghai is thus 8:00 P.M. in San Francisco. But because we will not have traveled a full day in advance of China's time, an arbitrary day must be inserted between China and America [the International Date Line].[4] Observing the time on the clock seemed to bear his words out. (The clock [ship's chronometer], after being set to Shanghai time, is never stopped.)

The eleventh [June 3]. During lunch, I sat with five missionaries who are also on board returning home, and all are able to speak Chinese. One had lived in China for twenty or thirty years and said that in doing missionary work in the interior, those who convert and those who do not are continually in a state of tension. When incidents arise, they prove equally implacable, and this appears to be premeditated and cleverly planned on both sides. I replied: "What you say certainly seems to ring true. But in my humble opinion it would be far better to not be so clever in converting them." There were also two men coming from Siam [Thailand] who said that in the regions nearby trusting the missionaries had proven difficult as well. In addition, there was an elderly man, aged seventy, his hair and beard like silver threads, who had lived in the area around Yunnan for several years and greatly enjoyed his dealings with the Chinese. His view was that the missionaries had not had much of an impact.

The fifteenth [June 7]. The sky was very beautiful with absolutely no wind or clouds. I strolled about the deck this evening, the moon round like a mirror, completely content in my thoughts. Looking around my cabin, I thought of all those having families in the West, how their wives and children would eventually be talking and laughing with them throughout the day, overjoyed, Heaven

3. Captain Maury is referring to the entire voyage from Hong Kong, not the final leg from Yokohama. The average run from Hong Kong to San Francisco was twenty-six days; from Yokohama, not quite seventeen days. Fairburn, *Merchant Sail,* 1399.

4. The phenomenon of "losing" a day was well known to long-distance navigators for hundreds of years, though no international standards governing where the change should be considered to occur were agreed upon until the nineteenth century. Agreements in 1845 and 1867 placed an imaginary line in the Pacific in various places to accommodate among others Spain (the so-called Philippine Adjustment) and the United States (the Alaskan Adjustment). At a later conference in Washington in 1884, the major maritime powers agreed in principle upon the 180-degree meridian as the line, with adjustments to place assorted island groups to the east or west of it as politically appropriate. The *City of Peking* crossed the line approximately where it would be reckoned today.

granting their households undiminished happiness. Without the ease to the traveler afforded by the steamship, how could all this be accomplished? Yet for the solitary voyager, it only increases his sense of loneliness.

The sixteenth [June 7]. I went to visit the Chinese passengers in the common berth. Here, too, everyone has a bunk, all of which are stacked on several levels. Some were sitting, others were lying down or standing around, and still others were in groups of three to five gambling. Some were playing instruments and singing, while others were smoking opium behind cloth curtains. All were Cantonese. I asked how many of them were going to America as laborers. They replied that no more than eighty were. I then asked them what exactly it was that they were after. They replied: "It's a little easier to make a living there." But why then are their numbers so reduced on this trip, I asked. They said that in telegrams to Hong Kong it had been reported that the Chinese in America had been the victims of hostility and resentment on the part of the Irish political party [see chapter 18], and because of the unpredictable prospects for the future, they did not dare to go. I asked why, having received such bad news, there are still men willing to go. All of them said that they had been driven by famine and had no choice.[5] I asked them how much the fare was for everyone. Their answer was that the passage from Hong Kong to San Francisco was fifty dollars. I felt enormous pity for them.

The twentieth [June 11]. I rose at dawn. The deckhands pointed to mountains all to the east and said: "Look! Land! That's the Golden Gate ahead of us. We'll pass through it to enter the bay, and put in shortly at San Francisco." I asked why it is called the Golden Gate. They answered, "The name Golden Gate is taken from the impression made by the mountains on both sides of the entrance to the bay of a gate facing west. They are bare of any vegetation and so take on a golden color in the afternoon sun."

The fog was very thick after entering the bay, but I did catch a glimpse of some buildings. There were numerous merchant vessels of all sizes in the harbor, and there were seals swimming in the water about them as if they were totally unafraid of people.

At 10:00 A.M., the ship fired two shots announcing its arrival in

5. Southern China had been subjected to widespread flooding in 1876, resulting in famine in a number of places.

A New
Account
of a Trip
Around
the Globe

262

San Francisco. From Yokohama to here is calculated to be 17,480 li, and the ship's passage took eighteen days and nights and three [Chinese] hours. The Chinese call this body of water the Great Eastern Ocean. During these eighteen days we saw not a speck of land, nor another ship, and this is the largest of the world's oceans, covering about one-third of the globe. Mr. Knight calls it the "Pacific," translated as *Taiping Yang*, because it does not have strong winds or big waves. But when the northwest winds rose, how could it really have been called "pacific" in the minds of the passengers?

We saw two small boats coming with oars flying, which I took to be a customs patrol. On inquiry, they turned out to be connected with the hotels and were coming out in search of business. There is one called the Palace Hotel, a name I had previously encountered in China, and the best hotel in America. After talking it over with Mr. Knight, he explained to the staff that this is the hotel where we would be staying. A small paddle steamer was also sailing by and came alongside our ship as it rode at anchor. I learned that this was the [Pacific Mail] company's launch, which had come to arrange for the passengers' luggage to be taken aboard, so I directed Chiyuan to have our bags put aboard the smaller craft.

At 11:00 A.M. we landed. There was a man there to pick up our luggage, and he directed us to identify our bags so that they could be arranged for customs inspection. As two or three customs agents opened the pieces one by one for inspection, we were unable to hide our impatience. The foreign men and women, however, were completely indifferent, not stubborn or stiff-necked the way they would have been in China. Looking over my bags, they saw the foreign words on my passport and so did not inspect them, but marked them instead with white chalk and moved on. The hotel staff then loaded the luggage onto wagons while we hired a waiting carriage and, with Mr. Chen and Mr. Knight, started off for the hotel.

1:30 P.M. Throughout the ride to the hotel, the streets along the way were large and grand, and the houses and buildings towering and lofty—more so than in Shanghai. The one called the "Palace" may be translated as *gongfu*, with the word "Hotel" rendered as *geyu*. The building is as immense as I had heard. It is nine stories and 120 feet high with over 1,100 rooms. There are 755 guest rooms, all of which are numbered using gold-painted metal plates on the doors. Inside [the rooms] there are also lavatories, toilets, and baths. All told, they employ a staff of 325, and in the evening there are 10,050 gas lamps.

Every guest's room, board, and daily necessities cost a total of five dollars. The bed, table and chairs, curtains and carpets are all very beautiful. There are three dining rooms with a total capacity of two thousand, and the food and drink are fine and pure; liquor, however, must be purchased separately and is not included in the five-dollar-per-day charge. If one orders the waiter to bring food to the room, this is figured separately from the five-dollar daily fee, as are tea and snacks, with the attendant's tips given according to the cost [of the service]. These practices are the general rule in hotels. Even more amazing is a spiral staircase that runs to the very top of the building. Constantly having to climb it, though, is quite exhausting, and so on selected routes [between floors] there is a machine from which hangs a small, well-constructed room, more than ten by ten [Chinese] feet, with a capacity of a dozen or so people. A man is there exclusively to operate it, and guests wanting to go up or down are hoisted or lowered by the device as they wish, regardless of the floor on which they find themselves.[6]

On the walls of all the rooms there is a button for a bell. If one wishes to call a bellhop, one pushes it and the device signals them at the bellhop's desk that so and so on such and such a floor and room requests an attendant, and he comes immediately to the correct room. Arriving outside the proper door, he does not dare to just barge in without announcing himself, but instead knocks lightly on the door or calls out before entering. The bathtub has two copper pipes from which water flows into the tub, one hot and one cold, adjusted according to one's wishes and with as much or as little as one wants. Washing one's face [in the sink] is like this, too, and the toilet also uses copper pipes to draw water whenever it is flushed. As for the use of such copper supply pipes in Western countries, I have heard Westerners say that regardless of size, all

6. Other Chinese visitors were taken with the Palace's amenities as well. Chen Lan-bin, on arriving at the hotel two years later, received the press in his suite, having first taken the elevator, which, one of the reporters observed, he "gravely entered." Because Chen did so with a confidence born of experience, his retinue decided to chance the appliance as well. See the *San Francisco Call*, July 27, 1878.

A New
Account
of a Trip
Around
the Globe

264

the residences are generally outfitted this way. They have also told me that this is the biggest hotel in the West.

The twenty-first [June 12]. I went to pay my respects to the former American minister in Beijing, Mr. [Frederick Ferdinand] Low and the Japanese consular official, Mr. Takagi Saburo.7 These gentlemen had heard that there were people coming over from China, and so were most anxious to meet with us. I heard that the population [of San Francisco] did not exceed two hundred thousand and that the Chinese accounted for 20 percent of this. The city and region are thriving, the port is open and wide, and there are also numerous merchant ships.

The twenty-second [June 13]. I visited the directors of the Chinese Six Companies [*huiguan;* see chapter 18] and also went to a carpet factory to inspect the machines.

The twenty-third [June 14]. The *huiguan* invited me to a banquet, but feeling a little indisposed, I did not attend.

The twenty-fourth [June 15]. I bought train tickets from San Francisco to Philadelphia, a distance of more than ten thousand li, at a cost of $136. The train has sleeping compartments, so there is an additional charge of $3 per night. This evening I wrote and mailed some letters home.

CHAPTER 29. FROM SAN FRANCISCO TO PHILADELPHIA

[Fifth month,] twenty-fifth day [June 16]. At 6:00 A.M., along with Mr. Knight and Mr. Chen, I hired a carriage from the hotel. The distance to the train station was about three li, and we had already sent our luggage ahead to be weighed. The railroad regulations stipulate that every passenger may carry up to 250 pounds of lug-

---

7. Born in Maine, Frederick Ferdinand Low (1828–94) had been a Forty-Niner, businessman, and banker in California before serving in Congress from 1862 to 1863. He was later elected governor of California (1863–67) and, most significantly for Li, sent as U.S. minister to China from 1869 to 1874, during which he gained experience in dealing with the consequences to both countries of the free emigration provision of the Sino-American Burlingame Treaty (1868). Johnson and Malone, *Dictionary of American Biography,* 6:445–46. Takagi Saburo was Japanese vice-consul from 1874 until the end of 1876, when Yanagiya Kentaro became the first Japanese national to hold the rank of consul in San Francisco. Takagi also appears to have attended the Centennial, as his calling card, along with General Saigo's, is contained in a scrapbook for the exposition held by the Free Library of Philadelphia.

gage (every "pound" being equivalent to twelve Chinese *liang* [ounces]) with fifteen cents charged for each additional pound over the limit. After all the bags had been laid out on a brass scale equipped with an indicator to give their weight, they were separated and organized according to type and had nameplates fastened to them; later, on arrival in Philadelphia the nameplates will be removed. Small personal items and bamboo baskets of necessities must be carried on the train unchecked.

After taking the train station's steamboat [across the bay] for about three-quarters of an [English] hour, we landed in Oakland.[1] The boat landing is out in the bay and connects with the train station by means of a long bridge. Both sides [of the bridge] mount stout wooden poles, from which five or six electric wires are strung (the wires are made of iron[2] and use electricity to transmit messages; one by one, all the Western countries have put them up) parallel to the railroad along the entire route. The method of construction of the rail bed is this: First, the grade is leveled, following which wooden ties of six or seven [Chinese] feet in length and three or four [Chinese] inches thick are laid horizontally across the bed. The space between the wooden ties is a bit more than a foot. On both ends of the ties iron rails configured like tenons are spiked, each more than ten feet long and one to two inches wide and thick, and these mate with the mortise shape of the train's wheels to fit the rail like a mortise and tenon joint. The train then runs on them swiftly and smoothly.

At 8:00 A.M. we boarded the train and started east. The train consists first of an engine that uses fire to boil water, and the steam produced enters different pipes and tubes through which it is transferred to the wheels for propulsion; the next car [the tender] holds the fuel; the next, freight; the next, livestock and horses; the next, luggage; the next carries the mail, as well as the conductors, porters, and staff; and following these are the passenger cars without sleeping quarters—inside of which the seating space is rather

A New
Account
of a Trip
Around
the Globe

265

1. Li's estimate seems on the mark: The Central Pacific Railroad timetable gives the estimated passage time as forty-one minutes. See Dale Morgan, ed., *Rand McNally's Pioneer Atlas of the American West* (Chicago: Rand McNally, 1956), 21. Notes below on distances and population are taken from the "Central and Union Pacific Railroads and Chicago and Northwestern Railway Time Card" shown there.

2. Copper wires did not come into general use until the following decade.

A New
Account
of a Trip
Around
the Globe

266

cramped. The next cars are for passengers who will be sleeping
(Westerners call this class of car a "sleeping car"), and all those
boarding these cars are in first class. The sitting area is more broad
and open and gorgeously painted. Every car is like a separate
dwelling seventy [English] feet long and nine feet wide. Both sides
are laid out with ten rows of small bench seats along a central aisle
for moving about. [Sets of] two bench seats face each other and
seat two with a bed hanging overhead. At night the attendants take
the beds down and make them horizontal, each one sleeping a single person. The lower two benches can also become a bed to sleep
one. All of them have wooden partitions, curtains, and a mattress,
which is thick and comfortable. Each passenger's personal belongings are stored under the bench. Every car can seat twenty people
during the day and provide a bed for each one at night. Both sides
have twenty large glass windows that can be opened or shut as
each person wishes, inside of which are curtains and shades
against wind and sun. Sitting and sleeping, standing up or sitting
down, eating and drinking, and looking around can all be done as
one pleases. In the rear of the car is a small room having only two
beds. Passengers with family members who are nauseous or dis-
ruptive ride there at the cost of an additional ten dollars. In the
front of the car there is a sink, a smoking area (smoking is not permitted inside the car, so smokers come here), a toilet, and an ice-
box. There is a separate water supply system piped in so that the
passengers may conveniently have a drink, and hand towels, soap,
and clothes brushes are all readily available. In the evening the
lamps are brilliantly lit until the start of the following day. The
attendants are mostly black men (from the continent of Africa, but
now naturalized American citizens), and very attentive. When
changing trains they receive a tip of half a dollar. The cars following these range in number from eight or nine to as many as forty or
fifty, and because of this we see a great many goods and passengers
on them. Just before the wheels are set in motion (every car has
four wheels on both right and left sides) the engine's whistle is
blown and its bell is rung twice. At first it moves along rather
slowly, but after several dozen paces it speeds along like lightning
with hills, woods, houses, villages on both sides as fleeting as birds
in flight. Outside the windows the sound of the wind merges with
the friction of the wheels, rolling onward like spring thunder.

Every day there are three stops at regular intervals along the route, each from a quarter to a half hour. The passengers get off the train and go to small restaurants along the wayside in which all the dishes range from seventy-five cents to a dollar. Just a bit of refreshment costs fifty cents, and the stopover is so hurried that one's hunger cannot be assuaged.[3] There are also those passengers, primarily women, who carry along their own food or who send the black men to purchase some. The men disdain to do so, preferring instead to get off the train to get some exercise for their health and well-being. When the train starts up again, its bell is rung and its whistle blown to signal the passengers to return. In addition to these, the train also makes anywhere from a few to a dozen or so daily stops at regular intervals for the convenience of the short-run passengers getting on and off. Just as the wheels of the train come to a stop, there are children everywhere, coming to the cars to sell newspapers, magazines, and postcards of scenery along the way, as well as milk, coffee and tea, and different kinds of fruit and melons all for the convenience of the passengers.

A New
Account
of a Trip
Around
the Globe

267

7:30 P.M. We stopped in the vicinity of Dutch Flat (the aforementioned are all in the state of California). The region's hills are completely barren, but gold production is high and there are quite a few miners. San Francisco is 680 li distant. As the train pulled out, there was a great river [the Humboldt] running, it seemed, unbounded along the northwest corner of the area. Occasionally, along the side of the rail line one would find villages and houses, flowers blooming, forests and woodlands, and grain and millet, all of which were quite plentiful. After half a day, however, there was nothing but dull hills, the ground completely rust colored and without a drop of water. In the car the breeze was very hot and dry and the heat was withering.

The twenty-sixth [June 17]. At noontime we began to see water in an area called Palisade (translated as "grassland" [*caodi*] in the state of Nevada), 1,200 li from Dutch Flat.[4]

The twenty-seventh [June 18]. At 7:15 A.M. we passed by Salt Lake

---

3. The transcontinental trains did not yet carry dining cars. Moreover, at a time when a daily wage of a dollar was considered respectable pay, the implication is clear that the prices inflicted on this captive clientele were grossly inflated. On the whole, Li was not terribly enthusiastic about American food. See chapter 30.

4. Li's translation of the name Palisade is obviously mistaken here. He may have been thinking of an earlier stop at Rye Patch, which certainly comes closer to his rendering of "grassland." This is confirmed by the fact that the rail line intersects the Humboldt River at Palisade, which is 367 miles, or slightly less than 1,200 li, from Dutch Flat.

A New
Account
of a Trip
Around
the Globe

268

City. The people in the car all wanted to visit it but, unfortunately, there is no stop so they could not.[5] I asked what was so attractive about this place and what it was they wanted to visit. According to what they said, there is a lake here high in the mountains estimated to be 264 li long and 165 li wide, and its waters are extremely rich in salt. Simmering the water in four tubs will yield one tub of salt, and so it is called Salt Lake, similar in this regard to China's salt wells. Next to the lake is a city of about twenty to thirty thousand people, many of whom come from England and Switzerland and by nature enjoy recreation and entertaining. While their religion is similar to that of Protestant Christianity, their practice of polygamy (one husband and several wives) is opposed to Christian doctrine. Their leader[6] himself has more than twenty wives. Traditionally, they had lived in the eastern part of America but in time, because this practice departed from the accepted Christian canon and they could not be induced to give it up, their countrymen could tolerate them no longer. As a result, they migrated here thirty years ago. The Americans refer to them disparagingly as "Mormons" (the meaning of the two words *mao* and *mu* is unknown to me) and to their religion as "Mormonism," and they have been exiled here for some time because of this. I should point out that the American government actually exercises considerable tolerance in merely ostracizing those who are opposed to orthodox beliefs and cannot be persuaded to change. This is unlike the manner in which religions are treated in other countries where, although [different] beliefs may spring from the same source, fire and sword are still used to force compliance with approved doctrines.

At 9:30 A.M. we arrived in Ogden, a town of four thousand (in the state of Utah), 1,016 li from Palisade. Here we changed trains and stopped for more than a half [Chinese] hour.[7] At 1:30 P.M. we

5. The isolation of the Mormons is pointedly suggested here by the fact that the main line ran through Ogden without a regularly scheduled stop in Salt Lake City. Li, however, is not quite correct that passengers could not go there altogether. The Central Pacific and Union Pacific brochures advertised excursion trains to the city and lake from Ogden. Passengers stopping off would then have their reservations honored on the next transcontinental train.

6. Li uses the term *doumu*, often rendered as "chieftain" or "headman," the implication of which is that the group in question is a bit uncivilized or disreputable.

7. At the Ogden depot they changed from a Central Pacific to a Union Pacific train. A time change was also mandated at this point on the schedule from San Francisco time to Laramie, Wyoming, time.

passed through a mountain tunnel of 2 li, extremely dark and gloomy. Electric wires on both sides continue to run right through the mountain peaks.

At 3:00 p.m. we arrived in the area of Evanston [Wyoming] and saw three or four Chinese men dressed in short Chinese-style jackets wearing foreign hats and shoes. Asking about this, I learned that there are three or four hundred [Chinese] people specializing in railroad work and receiving monthly wages of forty dollars who have already been here for seven or eight years.[8] We talked intimately, like family. The restaurant's walls were all decorated with picturesque scenes of Chinese subjects and landscapes, and they also had Cantonese slippers and socks for sale along with other assorted items. Seeing all these things from home made me long to be there.

After reboarding the train, we had only gone a few li when we saw another majestic series of mountain peaks devoid of vegetation. The snowpack had not yet melted and everywhere around was covered by more than a foot of it. Wherever the train's rail bed must go through deep snow, wooden roofs have been built over it [i.e., "snow sheds"] like deep, dark alleyways along four or five li of track. The trains then pass through the alleyway, allowing the snow to remain on the roof. Where there are mountains that are not terribly high, the train runs through them; if they are extremely high and there is no alternate route or separate road, tunnels are bored through them. If water is encountered, trestles are erected, even up to lengths of several li. Problems such as these are considered more or less routine. Large wells must also be provided every several li along the train's route, next to which are wooden outbuildings and windmills. The train requires a great deal of water and the windmills serve to supply it. Therefore, even if the area is an arid wilderness, there are no worries about running short.

The twenty-eighth [June 19]. In this mountain wilderness I saw a herd of wild cattle, brown in color, with black beards and heads of hair like hedgehog bristle galloping swiftly by [i.e., American bison, or buffalo]. The wild sheep, also very numerous, are as large as donkeys.

At 1:30 p.m. we arrived in Sherman. This is considered the high-

8. Since the railroad tables give Evanston's population as fifteen hundred, this was a substantial segment of the community.

A New
Account
of a Trip
Around
the Globe

270

est region in America, the mountain peaks 8,242 feet above sea
level.9 Westerners measure the height of mountains from the surface of the sea since the water is perfectly level, and as a result the
heights may be calculated correctly. On the day we began our journey, the heat was scorching—unusually so. Since then, as the terrain has become higher, it has decreased to the point that here one
needs clothes of heavy cotton. I heard that farther east of the
mountains it gradually warms up again. From Ogden, this place is
figured to be 1,465 li.

At 3:00 P.M. we arrived at a town named Cheyenne (in the state
of Wyoming). A man who said he was a newspaper reporter came
out to ask my name and where I was going and coming from.

At 7:30 P.M. we passed through the area of Sidney [Nebraska],
and the train stopped for half a [Chinese] hour. I saw small wild
dogs only the size of rats [prairie dogs] that are native to these
mountains; the local people raise them in birdcages. I also saw
types of men whose hair was draped over their shoulders, with reddish skin and features much like those of Chinese, dressed in short
blue coats and red trousers. The women wore long cloaks of
flowered cloth or red coats. They carried their children on their
backs, with those as young as a few months wrapped tightly with
string and standing up in rattan baskets. The baskets were long
and finely made, and their children, despite their crying, were
bound up in them and carried on their backs. Their speech was
twittering and they scurried about barefooted in a wild manner.
Some of them bounded up onto the train, squatting, laughing, and
sporting with the passengers, the conductor being helpless to prevent it. Seeing that the train was about to depart, they got off quite
boisterously. I asked about them and found out that these red-
skinned aborigines live scattered throughout the mountains and
number all told more than 90,000 to 100,000.10 The foreigners disparagingly refer to them as "Indians." The Americans consider

9. Li refers to Sherman's status as the highest elevation reached by the railroad as it
crosses the Continental Divide in the Medicine Bow Range of Wyoming. See Morgan,
Rand McNally's Pioneer Atlas, 35.

10. Bureau of Indian Affairs figures for 1876 estimate the entire Native American population in the United States to be 291,161. The issue of whether that population was
growing or shrinking was hotly contested through the remainder of the century. For
one stridently argued view, see J. Worden Pope, "The North American Indian—The
Disappearance of the Race a Popular Fallacy," *The Arena* 16 (November 1896): 945–59.
BIA figures for various years in the late nineteenth century are given on p. 947.

them to be the landlords here and do not permit the Indians to be bullied or humiliated, serving them with appropriate solicitude. Every year officials record their names and distribute blankets and sets of clothes [to them]. Their nature is such that they do not fear death, and they are skilled in the use of arrows, and in fishing and hunting to support themselves. In the past they had regularly battled government soldiers, and so troops have been sent to garrison these places in order to guard and pacify them.[11]

There was a soldier holding two unrefined gold nuggets, one black in color and the other yellow. Both weighed two to three ounces, and he wanted to sell them for fifty dollars.

The twenty-ninth [June 20]. At midday they changed our baggage tags in order to prevent error or mishap. At three-thirty we arrived in Omaha (in the state of Nebraska). From Sherman to here it is 1,984 li. The town is fairly large, with a population of thirty-five thousand. The train stopped here briefly and then began to move again. Farther on we crossed a long iron bridge, 2,750 [English] feet long and 50 feet wide, underneath of which were twenty iron columns supporting it at a height of twenty feet, two feet around and weighing eight tons apiece. The route across the bridge has a number of double ridges between which are laid wooden ties and stone on which the train tracks run back and forth. Tall poles rise from it on which more than twenty electric wires are strung. On both sides are scattered buildings and houses, clusters of thick woods, and scenic surrounding countryside. About a hundred paces after crossing the bridge was a railroad yard and a large building where we were to change trains. All the passengers got off the train and boarded another. The luggage on the first train was taken by the porters and unloaded with no fear of losing it; small articles were carried on, or one could request the black men to load them for a half-dollar tip. At four-thirty we resumed our journey with the makeup of the train as before.[12]

The thirtieth [June 21]. At 7:30 A.M. we reached Loudon [Iowa], 1,033 li from Omaha. The way is lush with flowers, trees, and grain,

A New
Account
of a Trip
Around
the Globe

271

---

11. Ironically, less than a week after this encounter came the climactic episode of the Plains Wars, the battle at Little Bighorn on June 25. As noted in the introduction, if Li was aware of this, it is not reflected anywhere in his account.

12. At the Omaha Union Pacific Depot Transfer Yard the passengers changed to a Chicago and Northwestern Railway train.

A New
Account
of a Trip
Around
the Globe

272

and the weather and climate are entirely agreeable. From here on east, it slowly becomes increasingly delightful—not a repeat of the previous days' mix of wind and hills, winding around mountain peaks, being surrounded by desert, and other sorts of frightening things. With me in the car were the members of five families, mostly Europeans and very nicely dressed, the manners of the women being quite refined. They delightedly asked about things Chinese, so we began to chat for a bit. Some things amazed them and struck them as heavenly; others shocked them as bizarre; and some simply caused them to nod their heads in agreement. Then from a small case they took out a translation book to consult, and asked me to write out some Chinese characters and read them aloud. By day's end, we had talked without a break, honestly and directly. Before retiring we shook hands and said good-bye.

At 9:30 P.M. we crossed the Mississippi River at a place named Clinton (in the state of Iowa). The train crossed an iron bridge, also very big and broad, from which were suspended more than thirty electric wires. This is considered to be the world's longest river and the steamer traffic is unremitting (these are all American merchant vessels; by American law the merchant ships of other nations are only allowed in the seaports and may not enter the inland waterways).[13] Mr. Knight said: America's most prosperous regions are all in the east. From this river directly west to the port of San Francisco is a distance of approximately seven thousand li. In the past, white men (Westerners refer to the native aborigines as "red men," Africans as "black men," and themselves as "white men") seldom came to this area, and all the inhabitants of the region were aborigines. Deserts, dense forests and thick grasses, wild cattle [buffalo], bear, and deer were all plentiful. With the coming of the railroad the area has been opened up to white settlement, and, gradually, villages and towns have been founded. San Francisco, for example, is now regarded as the chief port on the western sea. Ogden, Omaha, and so on have also grown into cities where thirty years before there had been only wasteland.

13. Since the actual lengths of the Nile, Amazon, and Yangzi Rivers were not yet calculated accurately, Li can be forgiven for taking his hosts' claim at face value. His note on the U.S. regulations limiting foreign vessels on interior waters and its implications for China's efforts to recapture its own carrying trade would certainly have been noted by his readers. See chapter 27, note 1, for the efforts of the China Merchants' Steam Navigation Company in this regard.

One can readily see that having railroads and trains has been of no small benefit to the country. Moreover, in each village established, churches and schools are built at public expense and thus lend themselves to guiding the people toward cultivation and refinement. In the practice of good government, nothing is more beneficial than this.[14] In the end, however, the land is vast, but its fertile and barren regions are distributed unevenly. The good lands may still be cultivated, while the poorer areas will for the most part remain wasteland. Nonetheless, the gold and silver mines are highly profitable, and one may suppose that in another ten or twenty years the land will be criss-crossed by railroads in every direction.

A New
Account
of a Trip
Around
the Globe

273

At 1:30 P.M. I accompanied Mr. Knight to the front of the train to have a look at the locomotive. Its construction is that of a large, straight, iron cylinder lying horizontally on a carriage, about twelve [Chinese] feet long, ten feet in circumference, and twelve feet in circumference in the rear. The front of the cylinder's body is outfitted with a smokestack, two or three feet high, with a large funnel and a narrow trunk, while in the rear hangs a brass bell. Farther back is mounted the steam dome. On both sides are copper pipes as thick as cups, through which the steam passes from the bottom of the carriage out to connect to the wheels, causing them to move. At the rear of the cylinder rises a small cabin about five feet square, like the pilothouse on a steamship, for the two men who operate the engine. One handles the various devices for the water and fire [the engineer], while the other shovels coal [the fireman]. Inside the cabin are mounted a clock, temperature and steam pressure gauges, and the engine's speed and motion indicator. The upper half of the inside of the boiler is used for water storage, while the fire [box] is below. As the fire begins to boil the water, the steam flows into the two pipes on the right and left and various smaller pipes. They then check the pressure on the steam

14. As Li interprets Knight's account of the opening of the west, he does so using terms from which his readers will draw strong correspondences to long-standing Confucian themes used to define the progress of "civilization." The rubric within which all of these are couched is the idea of government as an active moral agent. More specifically, Li, glossing Knight, relates the narrative in roughly the same hierarchical order as did Confucius: as the population grows numerous, it should be enriched; having been enriched, it should be educated. In the end, one will have a government in which "those near are happy and those far off are attracted." *Analects*, 13:9, 16. See also chap. 6, note 2.

A New
Account
of a Trip
Around
the Globe

274

gauge to see if it is sufficient to make the engine run. If there is enough steam but the train has not yet begun to move, or if the train must be stopped while running, they can release steam from all of these pipes. On the roof of the cabin run two belts; pulling on the left one rings the bell, while the right one goes to the steam whistle. There is also an iron device like a saw-toothed carpenter's square that, when pushed forward, makes the needle on the speed indicator point straight up while the train is moving and, when pulled back, causes the needle to lie horizontally, showing that the train is stopped. Movement and speed are thus entirely controlled by the engineer. Attached to the front of the engine is an iron device whose sides are like a plow with two blades that are progressively smaller on the sides and shaped like a tongue, only a few inches above the rail [i.e., the cowcatcher]. If there are rocks, etc., blocking the train's passage, this clears the way, whisking them off to either side.

The engine produces four hundred horsepower and can ordinarily travel about 260 li per [Chinese] hour [approximately forty-three miles per hour], with a maximum speed of 400 li [sixty-six miles per hour], and burns four tons of coal per day. There are still more pipes run to smaller mechanisms, more than a dozen devices of various kinds, but it is difficult to include them all. Within the space of a minute all this machinery can move like a clap of thunder and one cannot understand a word heard face to face.

I also witnessed an extraordinarily rapid method of carrying the mail: Without stopping, the train picks it up with a device like an arm. They said that there are special postmasters who wait along the line for the train do this at prearranged places.

At three-fifteen we arrived in Chicago (in the state of Illinois) 587 li from Loudon. The buildings and houses are very neat and uniform, and the city is flourishing and prosperous, with a population of 350,000. It is perhaps ten times larger than Shanghai,[15] and the

---

15. It is difficult to account for a mistake of this magnitude, which occurs in all versions of the text. Though figures are only irregularly available, Shanghai's population appears to have been roughly comparable to that of Chicago in 1876, certainly not 10 percent of it. Li may be referring to his impression of the city's area, but this, too, seems to be a considerable stretch. B. R. Mitchell, *International Historical Statistics—Asia, Africa, and Oceania, 1750–1993* (London: Macmillan, 1998), 42, for example, gives Shanghai's population as 149,000 in 1865 with no other data available until 1895, when the numbers reach 423,000.

train tracks extend in all directions. Here we left the train and had a two- or three-hour [Chinese hours] stopover. I went with Mr. Knight for a short stay at the Hotel Sherman to have a bath and relax.

At 5:00 P.M. we hired a carriage and visited several famous places, then continued on to the Waterworks to see the machinery there. According to what was said, all the water used throughout the city comes from the action of these machines, which draw water from springs and sources in other areas into a reservoir. Separate pipes then run underground from the reservoir back and forth to the homes of all the residents. This arrangement of machines and pipes therefore conveniences everyone.[16] While in use, the revolution of the machinery ceaselessly moves all of the water from one place to another. The engine house faces the street, and there is a tall tower of more than one hundred feet on which stands a giant iron tank. They said that this also serves as water storage. There is a spiral stair on the tower of 232 steps. Climbing the tower and looking about, one floats in the air, as if standing in the clouds. Mr. Knight said that being extremely particular about obtaining potable water is something all Western countries have in common. If there are sources of spring water nearby, then these are used; if not, it is piped accordingly from other places, no matter how far. This is because the inhabitants suffer if food and water are not clean and pure and can even become sick from it.

After dinner, we went to a theater to see a play, the plot of which centered on a village fool and was absolutely true to life. The theater was identical to Chinese ones, with a large seating area, beautiful appointments, and an abundance of lighting. The stage was high and wide. Unfortunately, I did not understand the words and could only get a general sense of the plot. At ten o'clock we were back on the train, and, shortly thereafter, it pulled out.

I heard that four years ago Chicago had suffered a devastating fire. Within a year, however, the buildings and houses that had been burned had all been rebuilt. The extent of the buildings is already calculated to be about sixty-six li. Now the restored city is even bigger and taller than the old one, and its wealth and large population are widely evident. The Chinese inhabitants here num-

A New
Account
of a Trip
Around
the Globe

275

16. This visit to Chicago's tower and Waterworks provides the basis for Li's essay on "Running Water" in chapter 22.

A New
Account
of a Trip
Around
the Globe

276

ber about two hundred, and the cigar makers among them earn about twenty dollars a week in wages.

Intercalary fifth month, first day [June 22]. I saw forests along the way, thickly wooded without a break, the largest trees having trunks more than several tens of arm-spans around and sur-rounded by smaller ones — a lumber-producing area of America. A fellow passenger in the car who had once been to China said to me:

> Broad expanses of woods help to moderate the climate, improve people's minds, and also allow those suffering from minor ailments to have some relief from them. In the wake of the ravages of your honorable country's soldiers [during the Taiping Rebellion], your forests were largely cut down. If your officials and merchants were to widely urge their replanting, this too would appear to be something indis-pensable.

From this I inferred that our country had once ordered that the people be urged to plant trees, but that it had simply never been fully carried out.

At 7:00 P.M. we came to the city of Pittsburgh, 1,544 li from Chicago. In the city there are a great many iron mills for the mak-ing of machines, and the inhabitants' dwellings are also high and spacious. There are over a hundred Chinese, all of whom are employed in making knives. In the area east of Chicago and west of Pittsburgh are the two states of Indiana and Ohio. After changing trains here,[17] at 8:30 we resumed our journey.

The second [June 23]. In the morning I heard a companion say: "Since last night when the train started east to Philadelphia, we have been traveling entirely within the state of Pennsylvania." The scenery is very pretty, plants and trees abundant and flourishing, with flowers and scenic places. When the train was about 20 li from Philadelphia, the conductor came around and collected our tickets. At 9:30 A.M. we arrived in Philadelphia. From Pittsburgh to here is 1,240 li.

Getting off the train, I accompanied Mr. Chen and Mr. Knight for a brief stay at the Globe Hotel, which is directly across from the exposition, while the hotel staff, holding our special brass luggage

17. To a Pennsylvania Railroad train.

tags, set about retrieving our bags.[18] At the time, I looked at the clock and, comparing it with the time in San Francisco, found that it was perhaps another two [Chinese; four English] hours faster; midnight in China is noon in the American east. From San Francisco to here is 10,715 li. It is ten states away and having been on the train for seven days—and having changed trains four times—everyone was exhausted. In all, the meals and snacks were not terribly satisfying, the drinks were of ice water or tea with milk, I was dirty and greasy, and it had all become simply unbearable. Beyond this, the thunderous racket of the train's machinery has affected my hearing. What an arduous trip! Yet, traveling more than ten thousand li these seven days and nights, I can also say that it was extremely convenient and, if not for the train, how could it have been accomplished?[19]

A New
Account
of a Trip
Around
the Globe

277

From Shanghai to Philadelphia, land and sea, is reckoned to be 32,864 li. On the third day [June 24], we moved from the Globe Hotel to the house of a German named Liebig[20] in a part of the city on Girard Avenue. Our rooms are on the third floor, very spacious and grand, and expenses for room and board come to one hundred dollars per month.

The fifth to the sixth month, twenty-first [June 26 to August 10]. I visited the Centennial Exhibition and other places of interest. Again, I was not quite acclimated and so was sick for several days. See diary entries, "A Brief Account of the American Exposition," and "Notes on Sightseeing."

Sixth month, twenty-second [August 11]. To Chestnut Street to a place even larger than the Liebig house, though for about the same price.

Twenty-third to the seventh month, eleventh [August 12 to 29]. To the exposition, see journal entry under "A Brief Account."

18. The Globe, at Elm Street and Belmont Avenue, was both directly across the street from the exposition and adjacent to the Pennsylvania Railroad Depot built especially for the fair. At five dollars per day, it was one of Philadelphia's most expensive hotels as well as one of its largest, with a thousand rooms and a capacity of four thousand. See McCabe, *Illustrated History*, 257.

19. Note Li's parallelism in weighing the pros and cons of steamships (at the end of the preceding chapter) and railroads.

20. The identity of this person is somewhat problematic. While *Gopsill's Philadelphia City Directory for 1876*, comp. Isaac Costa (Philadelphia: James Gopsill Publisher, 1876) contains some possible candidates for this transliteration living on Girard Avenue, the most likely one is a George Liebig, whose address was on adjacent Columbia Avenue. Since renamed Leidy Street, Columbia ran from Girard to Belmont and was within easy walking distance of the train station and exposition.

A New
Account
of a Trip
Around
the Globe

278

Twelfth [August 3o]. Visited Washington [D.C.]; stayed at the Arlington Hotel at five dollars a day.

Fifteenth [September 2]. Returned to Philadelphia due to illness; see journal entry under "Notes on Sightseeing."

Twenty-fourth [September 11]. Went to Hartford, staying at Allyn House at $4.5o per day.

Twenty-ninth [September 16]. To Philadelphia; see journal under "Notes on Sightseeing."

Eighth month, first [September 18]. Returned to Liebig house, again took in the exposition during the following days; in journal under "A Short Account."

Twenty-fifth [October 13]. To New York City, where I stayed at the Fifth Avenue Hotel for $5.oo a day.

Ninth month, first [October 17]. Returned to Philadelphia; see "Notes on Sightseeing" in the journal.

CHAPTER 30. FROM PHILADELPHIA
TO LONDON

Ninth month, ninth day [October 25]. There is a steamer set to leave Philadelphia tomorrow for the English city of Liverpool, and, accordingly, I have purchased a first-class ticket. For two passengers it came to £3o, or $15o.

I spent the morning packing, and in the afternoon said my good-byes. Right after dinner we hired a couple of carriages for our luggage and ourselves, and at seven-forty-five set off from the Liebig house to a wharf on the Delaware River several li to the east to board the ship. After arranging for our baggage, Chiyuan and I went over to stateroom number 2. Just then, Mr. Hart, Mr. Hammond, and Mr. Huber appeared, the three Maritime Customs commissioners having made a date to see us off, and we clasped hands with great emotion. They prevailed upon the captain to take especially good care of us, for which I was extremely grateful.

The ship is named *Lord Clive* and is 4oo long, 4o feet in the beam, and displaces 3,4oo tons.[1] The engines are extraordinarily sturdy

---

1. The *Lord Clive* was built in Liverpool by R. & J. Evans in 1871 and chartered to the Philadelphia-based American Line in 1875. Rated at 3,386 tons, the ship was 381 feet long and 40 feet in the beam. See N. R. P. Bonsor, *North Atlantic Seaway* (Cambridge: Patrick Stephens, 1977), 2:8o3. Also posted to "Ships List," http://www.fortunecity.com /littleitaly/amalfi/13/shipl.htm, p. 26.

and generate 550 horsepower. Inside and out the ship is also very clean and attractive. Right now there are only four passengers in the first-class cabins, all of whom paid fifteen pounds; the second-class passengers, numbering eighty or more, all paid six pounds, with those twelve years old or younger paying half price. Every day there are three meals, with two sets of refreshments in the morning and evening, and the cooking is all quite palatable.

A New
Account
of a Trip
Around
the Globe

279

The tenth [October 26]. We cast off at 7:00 A.M., and at 11:00 the ship stopped while we awaited the tide. At 2:00 P.M. we were under way again. Still apprehensive that the water was too shallow for the ship, they stopped once more at 3:30. Just after dinner we heard a sound like a sharp clap of thunder from the ship's stern. Anxiously, I went up on deck to investigate and discovered that it was only a sailing ship coming into the wind whose crew had been a bit careless. It had dashed its bowsprit against our iron taffrail and was now suddenly unable to break loose. The shouts of the men boomed, and after a short time we were back under way. Fortunately, the damage was not extensive, though we had quite a scare. The captain made some inquiries and found out the name of the vessel, and the next time [he is in port] he will put in a claim for the repairs.

The eleventh [October 27]. We got under way at 7:30 A.M., and at 11:00 cleared the mouth of the Delaware River and sailed northeast.

The twelfth to the fourteenth [October 28–30]. The wind and waves have been very heavy. I am feeling rather dizzy, though with tea and rice things are still bearable, if not terribly pleasant.

The fifteenth [October 31]. At 12:30 P.M. we passed by the island of Newfoundland. The island belongs to England and lies in the ocean off the northeast corner of America, and there is a lighthouse on it. There are many fishing boats near the island and the English have sent warships to protect them.[2] This evening on deck we saw such dense fog and spray that sea and sky melded into one. A bright moon set the fog off, suffusing it with a pale yellow glow.

The sixteenth to the twentieth [November 1 to 5]. As the ship sails east the wind and waves have become heavier. I have slept once in five

2. Newfoundland remained a possession of Great Britain following a vote in 1869 not to join the new confederation that formed the Dominion of Canada two years before. Following periodic tensions arising from contested fishing rights, the United States gained legal access to the fisheries of the Grand Banks by the Treaty of Washington in 1871.

A New
Account
of a Trip
Around
the Globe

280

days, taken no food or drink, and have continually vomited white foam, my strength remaining at a very low ebb. My ears hear only the all-powerful wind and waves while sea and ship struggle for mastery. Suddenly, the dining room utensils are flung to the deck with a sound like shattering jade; in an instant the luggage comes crashing down a dozen feet from a storage shelf. A shipmate who came to my bunk to look after me said that sometimes the wind and waves are even worse than this; so if for no other reason, there is really nothing to worry about since these conditions are normal. I told him, "How can I be worried about dying when, to be honest, I can scarcely stand this tossing around?" My friend then had the steward bring me some milk, and after drinking it I felt a bit better. Not a moment later I threw up again.

The twenty-first [November 6]. The wind has gradually lessened and the waves have died down a bit. We are already far out in the middle of the ocean and are gradually nearing the eastern shore.

The twenty-second [November 7]. I am now able to take a short walk on deck, and my stomach is somewhat restored. From here the ship sails in a southeasterly direction. The captain said that this is called the Atlantic Ocean, what [we] refer to as the Great Western Ocean, and its winds and waves are famous for being dangerous. Every fifth, sixth, and seventh month it becomes a little calmer, and ships can sail at top speed, making 1,200 li per day. During the remaining nine months, even with no wind, the waves are still heavy. When the wind and waves are high, a ship can only make a little more than 100 li per day. On foreign ships they do not fear wind and waves, but are quite concerned about reefs and rocks. This ocean has no reefs, so the crew's duties do not require much in the way of keeping watch for them. At 7:30 P.M. the ship passed within the vicinity of Fastnet [Rock], about 12 li from shore, and a light could be dimly seen flashing on and off. The ship's mast also has a light on in response to it. Asking about this, I learned that this point is only about 228 li from Queenstown[3] (on the southeast of the English island of Ireland) and has a beacon on it. When the lights on a ship's mast are sighted, they can tell by the particular colors that it is such and such a company's ship, and can then tele-graph the news to Queenstown. By doing so they [at Queenstown]

3. Presently, Cobh.

can then prepare to take on passengers from other places and load and unload the mail. At the same time, Queenstown can telegraph Liverpool, informing them of the ship's approach, and Liverpool in turn can send the news back to Philadelphia. Before the ship has even landed, the Liverpool and Philadelphia papers will have already published the news of our approach so that friends and relatives of the passengers may rest a bit easier.

The twenty-third [November 8]. At 2:00 A.M. we landed at Queenstown. The ship only stopped for an hour and was then under way again. Today I wrote some letters. At 9:30 P.M. a pilot came on board.

The twenty-fourth [November 9]. At 4:00 A.M. we reached Liverpool. From Philadelphia to the mouth of the Delaware is 388 li. From the mouth of the river across the Atlantic to Queenstown is 10,731 li. From Queenstown to the mouth of the river Mersey is 874 li; entering the mouth of the river, it is then 19 li to Liverpool; all told, it is 12,012 li, the steamer having sailed for fourteen days (an ordinary passage is eleven days, the fastest ones only nine and a half; the high winds and waves on this trip made it extremely slow). By the captain's calculations, every day the sunrise was advanced by about two *ke,* and over the course of ten days gained about two and a half *shi* [five English hours]. Philadelphia's noon is 7:00 A.M. in England [*sic*].[4] I ordered the stewards to take out the luggage and tipped them a pound for their service on the voyage. At the same time I asked permission for the local deputy Imperial Maritime Customs commissioner [James] Twinem[5] to come on board to

A New
Account
of a Trip
Around
the Globe

281

4. Li's interpretation of this seems a bit garbled. The captain's calculations, based on a ten-day trip, do indeed put the time advance to the correct five hours, or two and one-half Chinese *shi.* Li, however, seems to have again reversed the Philadelphia and London times: 7:00 A.M. in Philadelphia is 12:00 noon in London.

5. The exact identification of this man has proved troublesome to past commentators. Li gives the transliteration of his name as *Tu ma lun,* which the Hunan People's Press version's index has identified as "Twinem" (357). This seems a likely guess since Twinem did indeed hold the post of deputy commissioner and was on leave in London in 1876–77. Soon after Li's visit he was enlisted as an interpreter for Guo Songtao's Chinese Embassy. Later, while customs commissioner at Qiongzhou, he was lost at sea in 1886. See Fairbank, Bruner, and Matheson, *The I.G. in Peking,* letters 121, 144, 157, 166, 180, 181, 357, and 359. Frodsham, on the other hand, identifies him as Thomas Lowndes Bullock, who had been a British consul at Tianjin, not a member of the Maritime Customs (*First Chinese Embassy,* 78). Zhang Deyi, however, does mistakenly identify him as the Tianjin customs commissioner (Frodsham, *First Chinese Embassy,* 151–52). I have identified Bullock as the man Li refers to as *Yibulou,* though this, too, is admittedly a guess. See chapter 15.

meet me, as he had received a telegram from IMC commissioner [James] Hart in Philadelphia asking him to come and look after me.

After breakfast, we got into a small steamer along with Mr. Twinem and went about five li to Princes Dock, where we disembarked. The length of the wharf is about two li, with a customs house specially set up to examine transient passengers. The baggage room is very large and spacious, with five gates. The passengers' baggage is arranged inside the appropriate gate, which is bordered by a wooden railing. The passengers are transferred here in boats run by the customs service, whose officers wear caps trimmed in red and bearing numbers. On their right arms are fastened round bronze name tags. As the luggage from the various ships comes up, one or two uniformed customs inspectors holding lists with foreign writing on them ask the passengers whether or not they are carrying *sigai* (*sigai* are cigars, the so-called *lusong yen* ["Luzon smokes"] of the Chinese). The passengers open their own luggage and prepare it for inspection. My belongings carried nothing requiring a declaration and were packed so tightly and bundled up and tied so securely that once opened they could not be repacked. I therefore told them I carried no cigars, nor did I have anything to declare. I also said that because of this, and because I had to catch a train to London, I was afraid that opening the bags would delay us and cause us to miss our departure. The inspection was therefore waived and our luggage received a seal and was passed. Mr. Twinem found a couple of carriages and engaged them at a cost of three silver shillings apiece.

After traveling about three li we arrived at the railway station and bought two tickets for the express train, costing one pound, nine shillings. With our luggage arranged, the time was just 9:00 A.M. and we still had more than half an hour [considerably more than an English hour] before the train departed, so Mr. Twinem and I talked for a bit. From what he told me, the river on which the steamers enter port is called the Mersey, on the left of which is the city of Liverpool, while on the right is the region of Cheshire. There were ships anchored on the left shore holding their sterns in an unbroken line for twenty li,[6] with those coming and going to various countries in the Western Hemisphere and Ireland consti-

6. A fair estimate; Kirkaldy gives the length of the Liverpool docks as six and a half miles. *British Shipping*, 517.

A New
Account
of a Trip
Around
the Globe

282

tuting the majority in port, and those sailing east numbering no more than 10 or 20 percent. The city of Liverpool is about twenty li in length and breadth and is in the southwest of the county of Lancashire. Its population is about six hundred thousand, and it is considered to be England's second busiest region. Just then, Mr. Twinem received an opportune telegram from the IMC commissioner [non-resident secretary to the Inspectorate General] in London, Mr. James Duncan Campbell, inquiring as to how many days my group and I would be in the capital and if perhaps he could secure lodging for us. I answered "seven days," and a telegram was dispatched in reply. (The railroad stations in Western countries all have telegraph offices, posts, bookshops, refreshment stands, and taverns for the convenience of passengers.)

At eleven o'clock we boarded the train and headed southeast, our way lined with trees whose leaves were turning a golden yellow, farms and fields in good order, and everything quite peaceful and well laid out. The village women and children played in the woods or tended their livestock. The dwellings, while rather small, were all neat and clean, most having plants and flowers planted outside their doors and windows. At intervals from ten li or so to twenty or thirty li it is necessary have stations, and the train stops for perhaps several minutes for passengers to get on and off. By two o'clock we reached Rugby, 452 li from Liverpool, where there is a town that also has a private academy. From this point on throughout the journey, there were many fine school buildings, the population grew ever more dense, and orchards stretched as far as the eye could see. The tracks are constructed in parallel rows, perhaps more than ten sets of tracks, and the trains come and go like a flowing stream. Trains carrying coal from the mines to various places are also ceaselessly on the rails.

At 4:00 P.M. we arrived in the capital of London, a total of 736 li. The train was even faster than those in America. The arrangement of the train is this: Every car is divided into three compartments with doors on both sides—slightly different from those in America. In appearance and style they are a bit inferior to those in America, as is their height and size, but the seating area is wider. The name of the place where the train stopped is Euston, in the northwest corner of the city. An Englishman surnamed Hugh [?] (sent by IMC commissioner Campbell) arrived here to guide us.

A New
Account
of a Trip
Around
the Globe

283

A New
Account
of a Trip
Around
the Globe

284

We thereupon secured our luggage in a horse cart and after traveling perhaps 3 li, came to a hotel on the city's Spanish Place. The building was high and spacious, beautifully built and furnished, and had been prepared after Mr. Campbell received our telegram. At six o'clock Mr. Campbell came and talked with us for perhaps half an hour. That evening, all the street lamps were lit and there was music and singing. Asking around, I learned that it was the birthday of the English crown prince, and everybody was celebrating.

The twenty-fifth to the tenth month, ninth day [November 10 to 24]. I remained in London; the weather was similar to that in the northern part of America, so I wore a heavy fur coat. This is recorded in "Notes on Sightseeing."

CHAPTER 31. FROM LONDON
TO MARSEILLES

The tenth [November 25]. In the morning I bought railroad tickets [with the channel crossing included] from London to the French port of Marseilles, the first-class fare being seven gold pounds, five shillings a person, the equivalent of $36.25 in foreign silver.

The eleventh [November 26]. At 7:45 A.M. the train started off. At 9:25 we reached a place called Folkestone, with a neighboring town by the same name near the railroad line. The conductor came to inspect the tickets, tore off a copy, and returned the rest. At 9:40 I estimated we had gone 297 li and arrived at the port of Dover, where we boarded a ship. I tipped the porters who transferred our luggage and the ship's sailors a half-dollar. Dover is an English seaport directly opposite northern France, and the channel between them is only eighty li wide. When the weather is clear, both sides are visible to each other. The inhabitants number about twenty thousand. There is a fort, very solid looking, built about six hundred years ago to ward off the French. Along the coast a lookout tower and lighthouse have been erected, and there is a customs house, a school, and a barracks. Outside the port, the water is shallow and ships with a capacity of up to 100–150 tons can enter, though larger ones risk running aground.

At eleven-thirty we reached the French port of Calais. The wharf is built of wood and extends out into the sea for about three li. Disembarking, we boarded a train and traveled two to three li before arriving at the station inside the city. The conductor handled the transfer of our luggage, and at twelve-thirty we again boarded a train and headed southwest. On one side of the city of Calais's shore there is a wall and battlements with well-planned and positioned forts also built six hundred years ago. Outside the port are crowds of fishing boats. When the tide goes out, it is all sand for many li, but when it is in it comes right up to the city; hence, large ships are unable to enter. The lighthouse is very tall and employs the newest technology, its light being able to rotate. The population is about twenty thousand. Once every year, their fishing fleet plies the North Sea for eels, and the catch is quite large and profitable. At one-fifteen, when the train had traveled eighty-nine li, we passed through the city of Boulogne [-sur-Mer]. Boulogne relies on its geographical situation southwest of Calais. The population numbers about forty to fifty thousand, and there is a small river running through its interior. From the English Channel steamers entering the port of Calais have a fairly short voyage, but the railroad does not go directly to the French capital, necessitating a diversion to the southwest to enter the line at Boulogne. Generally, the majority of the ships arriving in France from England go through the port of Calais to enter the country; the majority of those leaving France for England, however, depart from Boulogne. Presently, the merchants traveling back and forth are inconvenienced because the ports on the coasts of both England and France cannot accommodate large ships. I heard that the governments of the two countries have agreed to draw up plans for an undersea tunnel and construct a railroad to run through it, which will start here when and if it is completed.

We stopped briefly here, then continued on to the southeast for another 550 li, and at 6:00 P.M. we arrived in the capital city of Paris. There was a Frenchman expectantly awaiting our arrival at the station—another person whom Mr. Campbell had prevailed upon to look out for us. Customs inspection was waived, a carriage hired (the carriages as cheap as those in England), and we rode 3 or 4 li to the Hotel du Jardins [des Tuileries] in the city center.[1] Along the smooth and even streets, the city was bustling the entire

A New
Account
of a Trip
Around
the Globe

285

---

1. See Baedeker, *Paris and Its Environs*, 6.

A New
Account
of a Trip
Around
the Globe

286

way, its gaslights like a multitude of stars, the pedestrians jostling each other in the crowds, carriage traffic coming and going unceasingly; even the New Year's Eves of other places are not as magnificent as this.

The hotel, in which we are staying on the third floor, has two bedrooms and a parlor. The tables and chairs are very new and elegant, and the curtains, drapes, and carpets are all bright and beautiful; every day the rooms cost twenty-one francs (every franc is equivalent to twenty cents, and five small cash equal one). Meals are figured separately. Chiyuan is only conversant in English, and since not many of the French understand it and we wanted to do some minor sightseeing, we were totally unsuccessful in finding someone to accompany us. Having no alternative, I hired an interpreter, a Frenchman who understood a bit of English whom I recruited from the hotel's business office. In French this is called a *commission*, translated as a "guide," and his work and meals every day cost ten francs. The food from the hotel kitchen is absolutely wonderful and everything is delicious. In England, they still have not achieved this level of refined preparation, and in America, even less so. I can believe that the French who have lived in America say in conversation that while they did not starve there, they most certainly did not crave the fare either. From London to Paris by land and sea it is 981 li.

The twelfth to the fifteenth [November 27 to 30]. Stayed in Paris. Weather a little bit warm and so I changed into cotton clothes. See journal under "Notes on Sightseeing."

The sixteenth [December 1]. At 12:15 P.M. I went to the home of IMC commissioner [Alfred] Huber (who had recently returned to France from the exposition in Philadelphia) for lunch. At five o'clock, we repaired to the train station's office to dispose of our luggage, and then to a restaurant for dinner, after which I went beforehand to arrange for first-class train seats (this class of car is called a *coupé*), for which one pays an additional eleven francs. At seven-thirty the train started southeast. Most of the women and children in the car were dressed in men's clothing for convenience while traveling.

The seventeenth [December 2]. At 5:00 A.M. we arrived in Lyon, 1,053 li from Paris. Asking about it, I learned that this is the second largest city in France, with a population of about four hundred thousand, and the *Du Cha Yuan* resides here as well.[2] (France has two *Du Cha Yuan*, one in this city and one in Paris.) There are two large rivers, one called the Saône, and one named the Rhône, which flow from the northeast; their streams are divided until after they reach the city, where they then join and run to Marseilles and the Mediterranean Sea. The water and land routes generate a great amount of commerce. The spinning and weaving of cloth here is very skillfully done, and the dye work is particularly bright and lovely. Perhaps sixty thousand people are employed in the textile trade. There is a large college, as well as public schools, churches, gardens, and parks. There are walls constructed all around along with seventeen forts with thirty thousand soldiers. The train stopped here for several minutes, and passengers stepped off for some refreshments.

A New
Account
of a Trip
Around
the Globe

287

Resuming our way south for 716 li, at noon we reached the seaport of Marseilles. I stayed at the Grande Hotel, also a great, splendid building. After lunch we secured carriages to tour the southwest seawall, and the scenery was very clear, pleasant, and uplifting to the mind and heart.

I learned that the population of Marseilles is about three hundred thousand and the passengers passing through are innumerable. There is a new and an old seaport. The old port had proved too small, and over twenty years gradually expanded northward and became the new port. It is quite spacious and able to accommodate two thousand ships, making it the principal port on the Mediterranean (the "Sea at the Center of the Earth"). Formerly, the old port had forts facing each other. After developing the new port, these were no longer used and now, on several small islands outside the port, they have built forts from which they are fully able to defend the harbor. There are mountains to the southwest, and from one of the peaks rises a church steeple and roofs with gilded bronze statues of a goddess holding a child. The church is 130 feet tall, the statue is 20 feet high, and from sea level to the head of the goddess is 450 feet, and the work was extremely expensive. In the city there are many sugar mills, and the locals manu-

2. In China, the Board of Censors. A possible reference to the Conseil d'Etat; another possibility is to the dismissal of Lyon's municipal government, its division into arrondissements like Paris, and its rule by a prefect in the turbulent wake of the founding of the Third Republic.

A New
Account
of a Trip
Around
the Globe

288

facture soap and excellent candles. There is also a mint and a college. One hundred li beyond to the southeast there are two cities: One is called La Ciotat, and the other, La Seyne. These two places are not far from each other and there are manufacturing concerns and shipyards there. All told, the overland route from Paris to Marseilles is 1,769 li.

The eighteenth [December 3]. At 7:30 A.M. we left the hotel and took a carriage to ride 2 or 3 li to the new port and boarded ship. The ship's name is the *Ava* and it is a screw steamer, 131 feet [*sic*] long and 42 feet wide, with a depth of hold of 22 feet and displacing 3,500 tons.[3] The ship is a French *paquebot,* and the cabins are divided into four classes: first class has thirty-five cabins and sleeps seventy people, with everyone paying ninety-five pounds in silver (every gold pound coin is equal to about five dollars in foreign silver) from Marseilles to Shanghai; second class has ten cabins sleeping thirty-nine people, and everyone pays seventy-one pounds; third-class and fourth-class accommodations are common berth in the front of the ship; third class costs forty-three pounds and fourth class, twenty-eight pounds. The crew comprises 172 men in all from the captain on down to the sailors and deckhands. There are 50 black men, 23 Chinese, and the rest are French. The cabins are spacious and arranged magnificently, and the cuisine skillful and delicious; the ships of other countries cannot even come close to it. Every day there are three meals, and in morning and evening there are refreshments. In the second-class cabins they do not offer a midday meal; otherwise everything is the same as first class (the liquor on the ships of other countries must be purchased separately, but on French-registered ships red wine is served at all three meals). All those on board in first class were educated people, with half of the group composed of French military officers and missionaries.

The passengers are for the most part English, French, and Dutch. The English were going to India, the French to Saigon (a port in Vietnam now under French control), and the Dutch to Java

3. The *Ava* was one of a series of five *paquebots* commissioned by the Messageries Maritimes specifically for regular runs to British, French, and Dutch colonial outposts and treaty ports in East Asia. Li's description of the ship's size is off because he has given its length in meters and its beam in feet. *L'Ava*'s true length was 117 meters, or approximately 380 feet. It was rated at 3,307 tons burden and 4,420 tons in displacement.

(the island of *Kaluoba* in the *Nanyang*, presently a dependency of Holland). In fact, officials and merchants are constantly coming and going among the possessions of these three countries. The rest of the passengers are Germans, Americans, Japanese, and Indians. There is a German surnamed Li who, a few months before, had accompanied several of our country's officers to study military affairs and governmental methods in Germany and is now returning to China to report back on his mission.[4] The three Japanese were all children of high officials and had gone to Germany to study law and medicine; one has completed his studies and is returning, while the other two are being transferred home due to some slight illness. I heard that this country [Japan] still has more than eighty outstanding boys studying in Germany, as well as many others in England, France, and America acquiring [various] professions. Today at 10:00 A.M. the ship started east. In a short time, however, a boiler broke down, so we paused briefly for repairs. At 6:00 P.M. we resumed.

A New
Account
of a Trip
Around
the Globe

289

CHAPTER 32. FROM MARSEILLES BACK TO SHANGHAI

[Tenth month,] nineteenth day [December 4]. The wind and water surge while the ship swerves and sways, and the passengers are unable to stand up much. A Westerner once told me that the wind and waves on the Mediterranean are sometimes even worse than those on the outside oceans because there is land all around, which harbors changeable winds. Now indeed I see it.[1]

The twentieth [December 5]. At 3:30 P.M. we came to the Italian city of Naples, 1,702 li from Marseilles. The city rests partially on mountains facing the sea, has grand buildings, lofty towers and spires, and a population of 450,000. It has the prince's [the future Humbert I] auxiliary palace, great cathedrals, and also many extensive gardens and wooded areas. Along the shore, there are forts

4. Li Gui refers to a German drill instructor in Li Hongzhang's Anhwei Army named Lehmayer, who had taken seven Chinese officers for advanced training in Germany earlier in the year. Richard J. Smith, "Li Hung-chang's Use," 133. Lehmayer's arrival is also mentioned, along with that of Li, Chen, and the Maritime Customs officer Viguier, in the shipping news column of the *North China Herald* for January 18, 1877.

1. Guo Songtao received similar information during his Mediterranean passage. See Frodsham, *First Chinese Embassy,* 60.

A New
Account
of a Trip
Around
the Globe

290

strongly positioned on the hills and numerous lighthouses. It was founded over two thousand years ago and is considered to be the largest seaport in Italy. To the southeast there are two volcanoes, and the one called Vesuvius is usually smoking. The produce of the area includes fine fruits, the sea yields coral, and the climate is pleasant. Westerners are inclined to call it a famous scenic spot, though many of the mountains are full of bandits and traitors who have escaped arrest by going deep into the hills. The ship stopped here for two and a half [Chinese] hours, receiving and delivering mail, and, after unloading some cargo, we departed at 7:30 P.M., the ship now turning south.

The twenty-first [December 6]. At 7:00 A.M. the ship departed Sicilian waters.[2] To the south is the island of Sicily, the mountains on both shores very rugged and the earth a yellowish color, few trees and woods, but producing grapes and fine quality mulberry leaves [for silkworms; see chapter 3]. To the northeast there is a port called Messina, with a population of about eighty thousand. The mountains yield sulfur, and more than half of the ships entering and leaving these waters are carrying it, since Sicily also has a number of volcanoes. Before the Suez Canal was opened, the packet boats all stopped here; now they have moved on to Naples. As the ship travels southeast, the weather has gradually warmed and I have changed into light clothes.

The twenty-third [December 8]. At 6:00 P.M. we reached Port Said, the far point on the Mediterranean and the northern terminus of the Suez Canal. At one time this had all been uninhabited desert; since the opening of the canal, however, a city has been gradually established. The area is controlled by Egypt and most of the ten thousand inhabitants are Muslims. Those who are not are Europeans from different countries, and there are a number of gambling establishments. The canal has a 180-foot lighthouse and is 4,180 li from Naples. We anchored here because movement in the canal is restricted and the ship is not permitted to pass through it at night. In addition, we must take on a pilot. The passengers have mostly gone ashore to sightsee for a bit.

The twenty-fourth [December 9]. At sunrise we untied from our

2. Literally, *haigang*, "harbor"; or "port." Since Li specifies that the *paquebots* no longer put in at Messina or other Sicilian ports, he perhaps means the adjacent sheltered waters of the Straits.

mooring and entered the canal. The ship's passage is very slow as it is feared that too much speed will cause the screws to create a surge in the water, which will damage the canal way. At 5:00 P.M. we came to the canal's midpoint, Lake Timsah, and the ship stopped after traveling only 132 li. On the lake's western shore is Ismailia City. The city was named for the khedive of Egypt after its construction had begun. The inhabitants number about fifty thousand, and the Frenchman de Lesseps (the designer of the canal) constructed a separate villa here for him. It is on a rise several li from the lake and is the Egyptian khedive's traveling residence.

The twenty-fifth [December 10]. At 6:00 A.M. we began moving again, reaching a lake [Great Bitter Lake]. This lake was connected long ago to the Red Sea, but over time shifting sands filled it in and the lake water evaporated into salt flats, which piled up like hills. After the canal was opened, the lake's water suddenly rose and the salt was dissolved. We also heard that in the past it could go for a decade here without raining. Now, since the canal water flows through the area, it rains perhaps once in three or four years, even once every one or two years, while for days on end the desert is stiflingly hot and the scorch of the heat is in the air.

At 2:00 P.M. we cleared the southern canal entrance and came to Suez, a distance from Lake Timsah of 155 li. This place is said to have once been prosperous, with goods and passengers coming and going from east and west landing here to be transhipped. After the canal opened, it gradually became deserted. There are around fourteen thousand inhabitants, with Muslims, French, and Italians in the majority.

The ship stopped for one or two [Chinese] hours and resumed at five-thirty. Moving south, we entered the Red Sea. The climate is extremely hot and the passengers have all changed into summer clothes. The dining room is using fans, and we have been unable to sleep in the cabins at night. Previously, when the passengers came on board at Marseilles, they rented long rattan chairs to set up on the ship's deck, and now they lie down on these in search of coolness in order to sleep. Every night as the evening wanes they begin to return to sleep. Actually, because the sea's configuration is long and narrow, and both sides are mountainous with a southerly wind blowing from the equator, it is hot all the time. From morning to evening, half the sky is made up of red, rosy

A New
Account
of a Trip
Around
the Globe

291

clouds, which are reflected off the sea like myriad branches of coral, and so because of this phenomenon, the Westerners call it the Red Sea.

The twenty-sixth to the twenty-ninth [December 11 to 14]. We have been cruising through the Red Sea. The water has not been terribly rough, and every day I have been able to do fine [brush] work. Seagulls fly after the ship, relying on the passengers for food, and there have also been a great many flying fish.

The thirtieth [December 15]. This afternoon the southern wind was very strong. The ship was rocky, and it was midnight before it began to calm down. I have been hot for days on end, drinking a good deal of ice water every day and bewildered by this nagging thirst.

Eleventh month, first day [December 16]. At 12:30 p.m. we reached Aden. This is an English territory, with Suez 4,970 li to the north. Sometimes small African children, their skin a deep black color, come here beating drums. Their boats are carved from trees and only a few feet long, and they are fearless in the face of the wind and waves. Those on board the ship fling silver coins into the sea and the children compete to see who can dive in first and retrieve them, which greatly pleases the passengers.

At one-thirty, I accompanied a Frenchman named Viguier ashore (also rather important in our country's customs, now returning to China from leave), to sit for a bit at the ship's agent's office. We then took a carriage to sightsee. There is a mountain path winding around rather ugly crags with bizarre rocks, the hills being utterly devoid of vegetation. To the east there is a neck (Westerners say it looks like a person's neck, so that is what it is called) and at low tide one can cross over into Arabia. In some strategic passes overlooking the sea, the English have carefully and thoroughly constructed impregnable forts. The mountain passes are like gates and can be defended by a single man. Also, a road has been cut in the front of the mountains for transport, and there are dozens of outposts quartering perhaps two thousand soldiers who, along with a governor and a general, constitute the garrison. Because these mountains serve as both a coaling station for ocean-going vessels and a gateway to the Red Sea for ships to and from India, it is of vital importance to England.

The populace numbers about twenty-five thousand here. Muslims and Africans are in the majority, all of them servicing this

A New
Account
of a Trip
Around
the Globe

292

stream of traffic. These people are simple, natural, and peaceable, living their lives without ever coming to blows. The place is very hot, sometimes raining once a year, sometimes going two or three years with no precipitation, and there is a lack of fresh water. The English devised a plan to dig reservoirs as collection basins in different mountain areas around the bay in order to provide water everywhere. Westerners say these look like forts, and indeed they do. Their construction is unique, a bit like supernatural works completed by demons. When it rains, the mountain water is collected for drinking and for use in food, and also for watering flowers and plants (all the potted plants have been brought over from India). Alternatively, by means of the ships' engines they are able to utilize the twin forces of fire and water to change seawater into freshwater and to make ice [through distillation and compression refrigeration] (the food served on the steamers of Western countries sailing the seas requires freshwater and also employs this method), and also many places have water wells dug. Those living here have full-length, open-seam sheepskin pouches, five or six of which are placed on the back of a donkey; or a camel is used to carry a large keg; or the black people, men and women, carry sheepskin pouches around their waists or on their backs, all endlessly coming and going with fresh water.

After the ship was completely loaded with coal we got under way at 8:00 P.M. We sailed east for a little while, peacefully and calmly for several days. But the weather is still hot, and in the evenings I have not been able to sleep. Every day hundreds and thousands of large fish about ten feet in length have gathered, arranged in ranks and leaping through the waves. I do not know what they are called, so perhaps they are also called "flying fish."

The seventh and eighth [December 22 and 23]. Continuing southeast. Approaching Ceylon [Sri Lanka] on a southerly course.

The ninth [December 24]. At 7:00 P.M. we arrived at the island of Ceylon. It was evening, so we were unable to enter port and had to anchor outside the harbor. This is a large island in the middle of the sea to the south of India and is presently ruled by England.

The tenth [December 25]. At 6:00 A.M. we entered the harbor, and after about half a [Chinese] hour the ship anchored. This place is called Galle and is Ceylon's most southern port, 8,113 li from Aden. Passengers bound for India's capital city of Calcutta (where En-

A New
Account
of a Trip
Around
the Globe

294

gland's governor-general resides) from England change ship here.
To the left of the entrance to the port is a white stone lighthouse,
as tall as the clouds. On the two shores lush greenery reaches to
the sky, extremely tasteful, with groves of coconut palms everywhere.

After breakfast we took a small boat [a catamaran] to go ashore,
for which each person paid a shilling. The boat's construction is
quite unusual. It is carved from a tree more than twenty feet in
length, no wider than a foot, and twice as deep. The passengers sit
side by side, and the bow and stern each have a paddler. To the left
of the bow and stern are thin cross-members, perhaps five or six
feet long, the ends of which reach almost to water level. Then
another long piece of wood is fastened to them, facing parallel to
the hull like a high and low boat [i.e., an outrigger]. Asking about
this arrangement, I learned that without it they could not avoid
capsizing when the wind and waves are high.

A warship had stopped in port along with several merchant
ships, full of flags of all colors fluttering in the wind. On the Western calendar today is December 25, the date of the birth of Jesus.
First, I went on a short visit to the English hotel [the New Oriental]
and prevailed on the hotel manager to find us a carriage for hire to
see *Wuwole* [Wackwelle Hill?] (which may be translated as "deep
forest") and *Xiniemenjiateng* (translated as "Cinnamon Garden").
We entered an ancient Buddhist temple to view a statue of Sakya-
muni.[3] The statue is venerated by adherents of Chinese and local
schools of Buddhism alike. The foreign monks [*fanjia*] have shaved
heads and wear yellow robes like [Chinese] *jiasha*, and visitors also
greet them with the clasped hands of Buddhist worship. For a
donation of a small silver coin I was given a look at several pages of
Buddhist scripture written on leaves. Later I returned to the ship
along the shore road and by then it was already five o'clock.

Regarding this city of Galle, it has crenellated walls like those in
China. Inside the walls are English and Indian soldiers on garrison
duty. The seaport's forts are constructed in a circuit of around
three li, guarded by a large force. Commerce, however, is not
extensive and the population is not quite ten thousand. The soil is
rich and the climate warm. There are [a long list of fruit and pro-

---

3. This may be the Valukarama Temple, which Guo Songtao and his group had visited a few days earlier. Like Li, Guo was shown ancient Buddhist sutras written on palm
leaves. See Frodsham, *First Chinese Embassy*, 26–27.

duce] . . . betel nuts and pineapples, which are most excellent. There are wildflowers everywhere, most of which I don't know the names of. The forests have many elephants, and the hills yield precious stones. The local people come to sell ivory, and the articles made of tortoise shell are skillfully done. The jade finger rings sold, however, are only fakes. Morning and evening the climate is like that of China at noon in late spring or even more like midsummer.[4]

The eleventh [December 26]. At 10:30 A.M. we boarded ship and started east. Day after day there have been headwinds, and it has been slow going.

The fifteenth [December 30]. Early this morning the ship headed on a southeasterly course. There are mountains on both sides, by turns distant and close by, now hidden, now appearing without a break. When I asked about them I found that the land on the left side was Malacca, and that on the right was Sumatra. In the straits from northwest to southeast it varies from three to four hundred li wide to as narrow as thirty to forty. Entering the mouth of the straits, there is an island on the left called Penang, colloquially known as "Newport," which is also under control of the British. On the right is a territory called Aceh, under the Dutch, the interior of which is mostly high mountain peaks and very scenic landscapes. We heard that among the transient populations of Penang and Aceh there are prosperous Chinese.

The sixteenth [December 31]. In the evening I saw two lighthouses along the left shore. One of them is seven or eight hundred li distant from Singapore; the other perhaps five hundred li.

The seventeenth [January 1, 1877]. At 9:15 A.M. I saw the left shore, which is all mountains, stretching in an unbroken chain for over a hundred li, like a series of [painted] screens. On the right were a dozen small hills floating on the sea, as luxuriant as jade lotus. There are many tigers in these hills, and they are able to swim back

A New
Account
of a Trip
Around
the Globe

295

---

4. Galle had been a major entrepôt on the Indian Ocean for at least two thousand years and was widely considered by Westerners in Li's time to have been the biblical city of Tarshish. The Portuguese in the sixteenth century and the Dutch in the seventeenth had given way to the English in the eighteenth as the city's overlords. Within a few years, Galle's commerce was largely removed to the renovated port at Colombo. Much as in Li's time, the stout walls of the Dutch fort surrounding the old city remain a popular tourist attraction today. For nineteenth- and early-twentieth-century descriptions, see Ernst Haeckel, *A Visit to Ceylon*, trans. Clara Bell (Berlin: n.p., 1883), chap. 9, "Point de Galle"; and Henry W. Cave, *The Book of Ceylon* (London: Cassell and Co., 1908), 158–66.

A New
Account
of a Trip
Around
the Globe

296

and forth on this stretch of ocean. At 12:30 P.M. we arrived in Singapore. Singapore is the southernmost port of Malacca [i.e., the Straits Settlements] and is now under English rule. After entering the port for about a half hour, our ship's bow pulled into its wharf slip and anchored. From Ceylon to here is fifty-seven hundred li. Southeast of the wharf is the English city with churches and towering spires.

At one-thirty we went ashore and hired a carriage at fifty cents an hour [English] in foreign money. I first went to see the stores and shops, temples, *huiguan,* theaters, restaurants, and brothels of the Chinese quarter all on display, and I heard that there are eighty to ninety thousand Chinese, 70 percent of whom are Fujianese, and 30 percent Cantonese. Some here have married local women and raised families for several generations without returning to China.

The local men are black and are fond of chewing betel nut, so their teeth are very red. They wear head coverings of flowered cloth and skirts but no trousers. The women are also black, and coil their hair up on their foreheads and stick a flower or coin in it. They wear brass rings in their right nostrils and both ears sport hoops in five or six holes, fully inlaid with copper designs, the wealthy sometimes using gold or silver; on their wrists and ankles they wear bracelets. Around their waists they have short shirts and also wear skirts without trousers. They rush about barefoot like the men, laughing and playing along the way. We heard that this class of people makes very good servants, and so Western families like to hire them in this capacity.

Since this was the Western New Year, the local people arranged a festival in an open area with a hundred games involving ball playing and dancing to music, and the spectators numbered up to tens of thousands. At five-thirty we went to the "Funan House" restaurant for a dinner featuring Chinese and local fare, which was not terribly good. At eight o'clock we returned to the ship.

The inhabitants here total more than 300,000, the overwhelming majority of whom are Chinese and native people.[5] The region pro-

5. The population figures vary considerably. Li's estimate seems excessively high and is probably meant to include the Straits Settlements as a whole. Guo gives Singapore's population as 200,000, which Frodsham feels is too high, citing 1871 census figures and 1877 Colonial Office estimates. His compromise figure, drawn from 1881, is given as 139,208, which includes 86,766 Chinese. *First Chinese Embassy,* 18 n. 3.

duces pepper and sugarcane, the climate is very hot, and every day it clouds over and rains for about half the time. It is in the extreme south, only 304 li from the equator, so the sun shines directly overhead and it remains summer throughout the year. It is mostly forest, and because of this there is no foul air and the inhabitants suffer little in the way of sickness. The English have built forts along the strategic passes and garrisoned them with troops. There is a customs house set up, and in discussing this, it may be said that the customs are rather light. The transient Chinese living within the borders of the colony do not pay any additional taxes except a monthly assessment for the police. But the Chinese are incompatible with the locals, and it takes only an angry stare to prompt an immediate reprisal, with the result that Chinese are often killed or maimed by them. Fortunately, the English officials are still able to investigate and make arrests, as such activity is prohibited.

A New
Account
of a Trip
Around
the Globe

297

The eighteenth [January 2]. A ship carrying goods from Java has not yet arrived, and so we are delayed another day. Because of this I returned to shore to see several of the gardens. There is a *Huang Pu* [Whampoa] (which sounds close to "wangpu") *Jiateng* (the translation of which is "garden") built by a Cantonese named Hu Xuanze for his family, with abundant, luxurious flowers and trees, and exotic birds and animals. Hu is a Cantonese from Huang Pu [Whampoa] and a longtime resident of Singapore who became a naturalized British subject. His trade is the largest among the ports of the Nanyang, and he presently serves as the Russian consul here. Westerners often call him "Whampoa" not realizing that his name is actually Hu. The English rely on his experience and have a great deal of respect for him. In cases where Chinese offenders are tried before an official, the hearing will not be conducted unless he is present.[6]

The nineteenth [January 3]. At 10:30 a.m. we cast off and left port, the ship pushing north. For several days the northeast wind [monsoon] was strong, and because of this the ship took a day longer than expected and the waves were unbearable. From Naples the journey east to Singapore was some twenty thousand li, and took

6. Ho Ah Kay, or Hu Qiongxian, styled Hu Xuanze (1816–80), was the most prominent Chinese merchant in Singapore and, as Li intimated, had also won considerable respect from the Western community. He had been appointed a justice of the peace in 1870 and unofficial member of the Straits Settlement Legislative Council in 1867. Guo was sufficiently impressed with him to named him Chinese consul to Singapore in 1877. Ibid., 81 n. 1.

almost a month. The ship's engines are running smoothly, though, and every day I have been able to do some passable writing. The sailors say that from Singapore to the northeast we will see constant headwinds strengthening by the day.

A New
Account
of a Trip
Around
the Globe

298

The twenty-first [January 5]. At 9:15 A.M. we saw several dozen mountains rising from the sea off to the west and were told that they are the Poulo Condore Islands [now called Con Son], three hundred to four hundred li distant from the harbor in Vietnam and now under French rule. Here amid the inhabitants the French have erected a barracks in the mountains and a prison to which criminals from Saigon are transferred. The mountains produce excellent birds' nests [for soup]. At 8:00 P.M. we reached the seaport in Vietnam and the ship stopped.

The twenty-second [January 6]. At 3:00 A.M. we entered port. Moving up the [Lang Cang] river both shores were lush with trees and plants, jadelike and dripping with beauty. A broad space of 2 to 3 li narrowed to no more than two hundred feet. This passage north I calculated to be 182 li, and at 4:30 we arrived in Saigon. From Singapore to here is 2,421 li. The wharf on the river's western shore rode up and down on the waves like a floating bridge.

I found that Saigon was Vietnam's southernmost port, within the borders of Jiading [prefecture]. The country's fashions, writing, and other things resemble those of China somewhat, and from the Han dynasty on they had been under our tutelage. In the first year of the reign of Xian Feng [1851], however, an incident involving the killing of Catholic missionaries and merchant seamen prompted the French to move troops in and occupy it completely. When this proved unsuccessful, they negotiated a peace and arranged for three provinces to be ceded to them. Saigon is in the middle of the three and situated in the most advantageous place. The French have set up a governor and also a commander of sea and land forces, together with four thousand troops who are billeted here in the city. As a precaution against any problems in the mountains, they have also built forts to defend them, covetously eying England's position in India and desiring to put France into a comparable situation. Is Vietnam not in danger from this?[7]

7. French domination of Southeast Asia is usually considered to have been accomplished in three stages. The first two are, roughly speaking, outlined above by Li. During the period from 1858 to 1867 the French, having long since championed the activi-

Three or four li southwest of Saigon lies the Chinese city called Cholon. Here there are numerous stores and shops, and two *huiguan* have also been established. Chinese merchants are involved in the rice trade and export a great deal of it. We heard that Saigon and Cholon have a population from Fujian and Guangdong of about twenty thousand. Scattered among the other French-controlled ports are still another fifty-five thousand. The streets, roads, houses, and buildings are just like those in China. The Fujianese merchant Huang Facheng invited us to lunch. Huang is a Zhangzhou native and also a naturalized British subject who has lived in the area a long time.

Afterward, we went along the riverside where the foreign ships rode at anchor in the bay and saw some twenty or thirty foreign houses. The French governor's mansion is quite grand and lofty and in back of it there are public gardens. There are many hotels in this place called "Saigon" [i.e., as opposed to the Chinese city, Cholon]. After sightseeing, we returned to the ship.

The climate here is more or less like that of Singapore, with lovely scenery and birds singing joyously. A hundred flowers and fruits grow continuously throughout the year, truly a delightful place. The French view the increasing numbers of Chinese coming here day by day as an avenue to financial benefit, and have developed new regulations specifically aimed at taking advantage of them. All the Chinese residents here are subject to import taxes, export taxes, a capitation tax, dwelling tax, land tax, and a sign tax; six in all. When first coming into port, they must apply to the *huiguan* and register with its directors, who submit their names to the French for permits. Everyone has to pay a customs tax of $2.50, of which $2.00 is returned to the French officials and fifty cents goes as a fee to the *huiguan*. The landing permits are good for a year and then must be surrendered at the appropriate time. Everyone, rich or poor, pays the capitation tax of $5.00, with females

A New
Account
of a Trip
Around
the Globe

299

ties of their missionaries and merchants in the area, absorbed the three prefectures mentioned by Li and reorganized them as Cochin China. Persistently seeking to extend their influence northward, they sent an expedition to Hanoi in 1873, only to have it repulsed by the Vietnamese and the Black Flags—mostly Chinese irregulars, many of whom had fought in the Taiping Rebellion. During the following decade, the French invaded again and, as a result of the Sino-French conflict of 1884–85, were ceded the remainder of the territory that constituted French Indo-China. Joel David Steinberg, ed., *In Search of Southeast Asia: A Modern History*, rev. ed. (Honolulu: University of Hawaii Press, 1987), 187–88.

A New
Account
of a Trip
Around
the Globe

300

below the age of sixteen exempted; after that they are subject to the entire amount. The land tax is based on the condition of the land in the area, which is divided into first, second, and third classes. In the uppermost class, every French *zhangfang*—square footage equal to a Chinese measure of 2.7 *chi* [i.e., a square meter] is assessed at 3.7 cents. The second-class land is half of this; and the third-class land, half of the second-class assessment. The dwelling tax is assessed at a yearly rate of $6.00 for every $100 of value. The sign tax is figured according to the size of the business, and is divided into five grades: first grade has a yearly tax of $200; second, $120; third, $80; fourth, $40; and fifth, $20. The shop owners' personal taxes are also adjusted accordingly: If the sign tax is a first-grade one, the owner is charged $60; second, $20; third grade is lower still, on down to $5.00. In the future, exports will be taxed at the same regulatory rates as imports—all goods at $2.50. Those paying import and personal taxes must have licenses and must carry them on their persons and be prepared to show them to the police for inspection. Customs are separately assessed, and decisions as to taxable items are made quite rigorously. Alas! There is no place in the entire world so annoyed by this kind of tyrannical treatment! Compared to the English regulations in Singapore, they are truly as far apart as heaven and earth. In observing England and France therefore, we should study them even more minutely on this.

The twenty-third [January 7]. At 5:00 A.M. we boarded ship, and at 9:00 we left port heading northeast with a headwind, the ship being quite rocky.

The twenty-fourth and twenty-fifth [January 8 and 9]. Even more so.

The twenty-seventh [January 11]. At 11:00 A.M. we arrived in Hong Kong, 3,477 li from Saigon. Entering port, Hong Kong Island [Victoria] was on the right, while on the left was the Kowloon district. On the sea, the merchant ships are many, their masts standing up like rows of chopsticks, and cannot be taken in all at once. In addition to the crowding of the city, the buildings are all of three or four stories, with their backs to the mountains and facing the sea, row upon row of houses, like the scales of a fish. When evening arrives, lamps illuminate everything brilliantly from the shore up to the many-storied buildings with countless thousands of lights— a magnificent spectacle.

The twenty-eighth [January 12]. I took a bamboo sedan chair to see the public gardens. The area is not very large, but nonetheless quiet and secluded for enjoyment. At eleven o'clock I met with Mr. Wang Tao [Ziquan] from Wuzhong [see introduction] and talked for half the day. He is extensively conversant with Chinese and foreign ways and policies. Although we sat and talked, he constantly wanted to get up and move about. How sad to meet by chance someone living in this strange and distant land whose talents remain unknown to the world! I heard that there are about 130,000 Chinese in this place and about four thousand foreigners.[8] The area is thriving, though somewhat less so than Shanghai, and the environment is not the same either. This is because Shanghai is on flat land while this area is surrounded by mountains. Guangdong's opening to the sea is about 264 li to the southwest of here, and steamers and boats come and go every day. The climate is still pleasant, with people wearing double-layer clothing and carrying paper fans. In morning and evening it is a bit cooler and the people change into cotton clothes.

A New
Account
of a Trip
Around
the Globe

301

The twenty-ninth [January 13]. At noon we got back on board.

Twelfth month, first day [January 14]. At 7:15 A.M. we passed Chaozhou [near Shantou]; at 7:30 P.M., we passed Amoy.

The second [January 15]. At midnight we passed Fuzhou.

The third [January 16]. At 10:00 A.M. we passed Wenzhou.

The fourth [January 17]. At 3:30 A.M. we passed Ningbo, and at 3:30 P.M. we landed in Shanghai. On this leg of the journey there were also headwinds, and the climate was cold all day. The passengers were all in the dining room around the stove having a drink and not going up on deck to move around. Since docking at Shanghai the new moon wind has become fiercely cold, and I have put on heavy clothes. From here to Hong Kong is 3,139 li. From the port of Marseilles in France by ship to Shanghai took forty-six days in all, 33,989 li (including the 287 li of the Suez Canal. Since this was originally a land route, it is still measured as land distance [i.e., not in nautical miles]). The ship's captain pointed to the clock and said to me: "In Shanghai it is 5:00 P.M.; in London, it is just 10:00 A.M.!"

The End

8. As with Singapore, population estimates vary, at least in part because of the flow of transients. Guo also gives Hong Kong's population as 130,000; Frodsham, citing the *Times* of London, December 13, 1876, puts the figure at 121,985. *First Chinese Embassy*, 7 n. 3.

Bibliography

WORKS BY LI GUI

Huan you diqiu xin lu. 4 juan. Shanghai, printed with illustrations by Ernest Grelier. Prefaces dated 1877, 1878.

Huan you diqiu xin lu. Reprint with introduction by Zhong Shuhe, in *Zouwen shijie congshu.* Changsha: Hunan People's Press, 1985. 191–353.

Jinling bing huilue. 4 juan. Ningbo. Prefaces dated 1887, 1888.

Sitong ji. 2 juan. N.p., 1880.

Tongshang biao. 4 juan. Haichang guan, 1895.

Yapian shi lue. 2 juan. Beiping: Beiping tuxuguan, 1931.

OTHER CHINESE WORKS

Chen Lanbin. *Shi mei jilue.* In *Xiaofang hu zhai youdi congqiao,* comp. Wang Xiji. Shanghai: n.p., 1892.

Chen Lunjiong. *Haiguo Wenjian lu.* N.p., 1730.

Chouban yiwu shimo. Tongzhi. N.p., 1880.

Guo Songtao. *Yangzhi shuwu yiji. 12 juan.* 1892. In *Xiaofang hu zhai youdi congqiao,* comp. Wang Xiji. Shanghai: n.p., 1892.

Li Hongzhang. *Li Wenzhong gong quanji.* Ed. Wu Rulun. 165 *juan.* Nanjing: n.p., 1905–8.

Liu Xihong. *Yingyao riji.* N.p. In *Xiaofang hu zhai youdi congqiao,* comp. Wang Xiji. Shanghai: n.p., 1892.

Xu Jiyu. *Yinghuan ji lue. 10 juan.* N.p. 1848, 1850.

Wang Xiji, comp. *Xiaofang hu zhai youdi congqiao.* Shanghai: n.p., 1892.

Wang Yenxi and Wang Shumin, eds. *Huangchao Dao Xian Tong Guang zouyi* (Memorials of the Dao Guang, Xian Fews, Tongzhi, and Guang Xu periods). Shanghai: n.p., 1902.

Zeng Guofan. *Zeng Wenzhong gong quanji.* 10 ce. Shanghai: n.p., 1888.

Zhang Deyi. *Ou mei huanyou ji.* Beijing, 1872.

Zhi Gang. *Chu shi taixi ji.* In *Xiaofang hu zhai youdi congqiao,* comp. Wang Xiji. Shanghai: n.p., 1892.

Zhongmei guanxi shiliao. Taipei: Institute of Modern History, Academia Sinica, 1968.

Zhong Shuhe, ed. *Zouwen shijie congshu.* Changsha: Hunan People's Press, 1985.

Zongli Yamen. *Ge guo saihui gong hui.* Institute of Modern History, Academia Sinica. Zongli Yamen Files on International Exhibitions.

WORKS IN OTHER LANGUAGES

Manuscripts and Unpublished Materials

Philadelphia Museum of Art. "Calling Cards of Centennial Attendees: Japan." From Philadelphia Free Library scrapbook, "1876 Japanese Meishi."

Government Documents

U.S. Department of State. "Diplomatic Documents, China." National Archives Microfilm, M92, Roll 42.

———. "Notes from Foreign Legations, China." National Archives Microfilm, M98, Roll 1.

Newspapers

New York Times, October 1876.

North China Herald and Consular Gazette, February 1876–December 1878.

Philadelphia Inquirer, June 1876–October 1876.

Philadelphia Public Ledger, June 1876–July 1876.

Hartford Courant, August 1876–September 1876.

San Francisco Call, July 1878.

General Works

Adas, Michael. *Machines as the Measure of Men.* Ithaca: Cornell University Press, 1989.

Arkush, R. David, and Leo O. Lee. *Land without Ghosts.* Berkeley and Los Angeles: University of California Press, 1989.

Auerbach, Jeffrey. *The Great Exhibition of 1851: A Nation on Display.* New Haven: Yale University Press, 1999.

Baedeker, Karl. *Paris and Its Environs.* London: Dulau and Co., 1878.

Bearse, Ray. *Centerfire American Rifle Cartridges, 1892–1963.* London: Thomas Yoseloff, 1966.

Bonsor, N. R. P. *North Atlantic Seaway.* Cambridge: Patrick Stephens, 1977.

Campbell, Robert Ronald. *James Duncan Campbell, a Memoir by His Son.* Harvard East Asia Monograph Series no. 38. Cambridge: Harvard University Press, 1970.

Carlyle, Thomas. "Signs of the Times." In *Critical and Miscellaneous Essays.* New York, 1896.

Carr, Caleb. *The Devil Soldier.* New York: Random House, 1992.

Carrier, James G., ed. *Occidentalism: Images of the West.* Oxford: Clarendon Press, 1995.

———. "Occidentalism: The World Turned Upside Down." *American Ethnologist* 19, no. 2 (1992): 195–212.

Cave, Henry W. *The Book of Ceylon.* London: Cassell, 1908.

Chen Chang-fang. "Barbarian Paradise: Chinese Views of the United States, 1784–1911." Ph.D. diss., Indiana University, 1985.

Cheng Ying-wan. *Postal Communication in China and Its Modernization, 1860–1896.* Cambridge: Harvard University Press, 1970.

Chen Lanbin, A. Huber, and A. MacPherson. *The Cuba Commission Report.* Shanghai: Imperial Maritime Customs, 1876. Reprint, Johns Hopkins University Press, 1993.

Chen Xiafei and Han Rongfang, eds. *Archives of China's Imperial Maritime Customs Confidential Correspondence between Robert Hart and James Duncan Campbell, 1874–1907.* Vol. 1. Beijing: Foreign Languages Press, 1990.

Chen Xiaomei. *Occidentalism.* Lanham, Md.: Rowman and Littlefield, 2002.

Chen Yong. *Chinese San Francisco, 1850–1943: A Transpacific Community.* Stanford: Stanford University Press, 2000.

Chiang Yee. *Chinese Calligraphy: An Introduction to Its Aesthetic and Technique.* Cambridge: Harvard University Press, 1973.

Chu, Samuel C., and Kwang-Ching Liu, eds. *Li Hung-chang and China's Early Modernization.* Armonk, N.Y.: M. E. Sharpe, 1994.

Cohen, Paul A. *Between Tradition and Modernity: Wang T'ao and Reform in Late Imperial China.* Cambridge: Harvard University Press, 1974.

———. *Discovering History in China.* New York: Columbia University Press, 1984.

College of Physicians. "The College of Physicians of Philadelphia." Descriptive manuscript.

Coronil, Fernando. "Beyond Occidentalism: Toward Nonimperial Geohistorical Categories." *Cultural Anthropology* 11, no. 1 (1996): 51–87.

Davids, Jules. *American Diplomatic and Public Papers: The United States and China.* Vol. 13, *Chinese Immigration.* Wilmington, Del.: Scholarly Resources, 1979.

DeBary, William T., ed. *Sources of Chinese Tradition.* Vol. 1. New York: Columbia University Press, 1960.

Desnoyers, Charles A. "Self-Strengthening in the New World: A Chinese Envoy's Travels in America." *Pacific Historical Review* 60 (1991): 195–219.

———. "The Thin Edge of the Wedge: The Chinese Educational Mission and Diplomatic Representation in the Americas, 1872–1875." *Pacific Historical Review* 61 (1992): 241–63.

———. "Toward 'One Enlightened and Progressive Civilization': Discourses of Expansion and Nineteenth-Century Chinese Missions Abroad." *Journal of World History* 8, no. 1 (1997): 135–56.

Dickens, Charles. *American Notes for General Circulation.* Reprint, Avon, Conn.: Limited Editions, 1975.

Drake, Fred. *China Charts the World.* Cambridge: Harvard University Press, 1975.

Dumoulin, Heinrich. *Zen Buddhism: A History.* Vol. 2, *Japan.* New York: Macmillan, 1990.

Dutton, Michael R. *Policing and Punishment in China: From Patriarchy to "the People."* Cambridge: Cambridge University Press, 1992.

Earl, Joseph. *Splendors of Meiji: Treasures of Imperial Japan.* St. Petersburg, Fla.: Broughton International, 1999.

Ebrey, Patricia. *The Inner Quarters: Marriage and the Lives of Chinese Women in the Sung Period.* Berkeley and Los Angeles: University of California Press, 1993.

Eskildsen, Robert. "Of Civilization and Savages: The Mimetic Imperialism of Japan's 1874 Expedition to Taiwan." *American Historical Review* 107, no. 2 (April 2002): 388–418.

Fairbank, John K. *Trade and Diplomacy on the China Coast.* Stanford: Stanford University Press, 1969.

Fairbank, John K., Katherine Frost Bruner, and Elizabeth MacLeod Matheson, eds. *The I.G. in Peking: Letters of Robert Hart, Chinese Maritime Customs, 1868–1907.* Vol. 1. Cambridge: Harvard University Press, 1975.

Fairbank, John K., and Su-yu Teng. *China's Response to the West.* Cambridge: Harvard University Press, 1954.

Fairburn, William A. *Merchant Sail.* Vol. 2. Center Lovell, Maine: n.p., n.d.

Farnie, D. A. *East and West of Suez: The Suez Canal in History.* Oxford: Oxford University Press, 1969.

Federal Writers' Project. *Washington, City and Capital.* Washington, D.C.: Government Printing Office, 1937.

Feuerwerker, Albert. *China's Early Industrialization.* Cambridge: Harvard University Press, 1958. Reprint, New York: Atheneum, 1970.

Finkel, Kenneth. "Philadelphia in the 1820's: A New Civic Consciousness." In *Eastern State Penitentiary: Crucible of Good Intentions,* ed. Norman Johnston. Philadelphia: Philadelphia Art Museum, 1994.

Frodsham, J. D. *The First Chinese Embassy to the West.* Oxford: Clarendon Press, 1974.

Garcia-Lahiguera, Daniel William. "The Diaries of Li Gui." M.A. thesis, University of California, Berkeley, 1993.

Gibbs-Smith, C. H. *The Great Exhibition of 1851.* London: Her Majesty's Stationery Office, 1950.

Gillespie, Elizabeth D. *A Book of Remembrance.* Philadelphia: n.p., 1901.

Giquel, Prosper. *A Journal of the Chinese Civil War, 1864.* Ed. Steven Leibo. Honolulu: University of Hawaii Press, 1985.

Gopsill's Philadelphia City Directory for 1876. Comp. Isaac Costa. Philadelphia: James Gopsill Publisher, 1876.

Gramont, Sanche de. *The French.* New York: Putnam, 1969.

Gunder Frank, Andre. *Re-Orient: Global Economy in the Asian Age.* Berkeley and Los Angeles: University of California Press, 1998.

Haeckel, Ernst. *A Visit to Ceylon.* Trans. Clara Bell. Berlin, 1883.

Hamberg, Theodore. *The Visions of Hung-siu-tschuen, and the Origin of the Kwang-si Insurrection.* Hong Kong, 1854.

Hariss, Joseph. "The Divine Sarah." *Smithsonian* 32, no. 5 (2001): 68–76.

Hevia, James. *Cherishing Men from Afar.* Durham, N.C.: Duke University Press, 1995.

Hostetler, Laura. *Qing Colonial Enterprise.* Chicago: University of Chicago Press, 2001.

Howland, Douglas. *Borders of Chinese Civilization.* Durham, N.C.: Duke University Press, 1996.

Hsu, Immanuel C. Y. *China's Entrance into the Family of Nations: The Diplomatic Phase, 1858–1880.* Cambridge: Harvard University Press, 1960.

Hucker, Charles O. *Dictionary of Official Titles in Imperial China.* Stanford: Stanford University Press, 1985.

Hummel, Arthur, ed. *Eminent Chinese of the Ch'ing Period.* 2 vols. Washington, D.C.: Government Printing Office, 1943–44.

Hung, William, "The Closure of the Educational Mission in America." *Harvard Journal of Asiatic Studies* 18 (1955): 51–73.

Imperial Maritime Customs. *Catalog of the Chinese Exhibition.* Shanghai: Imperial Maritime Customs Press, 1876.

Institute of Modern History, Academia Sinica. *Proceedings of the Conference on the Self-Strengthening Movement in Late Ch'ing China, 1861–1894.* 2 vols. Taipei: Academia Sinica, 1988.

Irick, Robert W. *Ch'ing Policy toward the Coolie Trade, 1847–1878.* Taipei: Chinese Materials Center, 1982.

James, Henry. *Hawthorne.* N.p., 1879.

Johnson, Allen, and Dumas Malone. *Dictionary of American Biography.* New York: Scribner's Sons, 1931.

Johnston, Norman, Kenneth Finkel, and Jeffrey Cohen. *Eastern State Penitentiary: Crucible of Good Intentions.* Philadelphia: Philadelphia Museum of Art, 1994.

Johnstone, Simon. *Diary of a Chinese Diplomat.* Beijing: Chinese Literature Press, 1992.

Khu, Josephine. *Cultural Curiosity.* Berkeley and Los Angeles: University of California Press, 2001.

Kirkaldy, A. W. *British Shipping: Its History, Organisation, and Importance.* London: Kegan Paul, 1914.

Kuhn, Philip. *Rebellion and Its Enemies in Late Imperial China.* Cambridge: Harvard University Press, 1970.

LaFargue, Thomas. *China's First Hundred.* Pullman: University Press of Washington State, 1942.

Lai Chi-kong. "The Qing State and Merchant Enterprise: The China Merchants' Company, 1872–1902." In *To Achieve Security and Wealth: The Qing Imperial State and the Economy, 1644–1911,* ed. Jane Kate Leonard and John R. Watt. Ithaca: Cornell University Press, 1992.

Lawrence, Charles. *A History of Philadelphia Almshouses and Hospitals.* Philadelphia: Charles Lawrence, 1905. Reprint, New York: Arno, 1976.

Legge, James, ed. and trans. *Confucius: Confucian Analects, the Great Learning, and the Doctrine of the Mean.* Oxford: Clarendon Press, 1893. Reprint, New York: Dover, 1971.

———. *The Hsiao King.* In *The Sacred Books of the East,* vol. 3. Oxford: Clarendon Press, 1879.

———. *The Works of Mencius.* Oxford: Clarendon Press, 1895. Reprint, New York: Dover, 1970.

Leonard, Jane Kate. *Wei Yuan and China's Rediscovery of the Maritime World.* Cambridge: Harvard University Press, 1984.

Leonard, Jane Kate, and John R. Watt, eds. *To Achieve Security and Wealth: The Qing Imperial State and the Economy, 1644–1911.* Ithaca: Cornell University Press, 1992.

Levenson, Joseph R. *Confucian China and Its Modern Fate.* 3 vols. Berkeley and Los Angeles: University of California Press, 1958, 1964, 1965.

———. "'History' and 'Value': The Tensions of Intellectual Choice in Modern China." In *Studies in Chinese Thought,* ed. Arthur Wright. Chicago: University of Chicago Press, 1953, 1967.

Lewis, Berkeley R. *Small Arms Ammunition at the International Exposition Philadelphia, 1876.* Washington, D.C.: Smithsonian Institution Press, 1972.

Leys, Simon. *The Burning Forest.* New York: Holt, Rinehart and Winston, 1985.

Lieberman, Victor, ed. *Beyond Binary Histories.* Ann Arbor: University of Michigan Press, 1999.

Maass, John. "The Centennial Success Story." In *1876, a Centennial Exhibition.* Ed. Robert C. Post. Washington, D.C.: Smithsonian Institution Press, 1976.

———. *The Glorious Enterprise.* Watkins Glen, N.Y.: American Life Foundation, 1973.

Mackerras, Colin, and Robert Chan. *Modern China: A Chronology from 1842 to the Present.* San Francisco: W. H. Freeman, 1982.

McCabe, James D. *An Illustrated History of the Centennial Exhibition.* Philadelphia: National Publishing, 1876.

McClain, Charles J. *In Search of Equality: The Chinese Struggle against Discrimination in Nineteenth-Century America.* Berkeley and Los Angeles: University of California Press, 1994.

McCunn, Ruthann Lum. *Chinese American Portraits.* San Francisco: Chronicle Press, 1988.

Meadows, Thomas Taylor. *The Chinese and Their Rebellions.* London: Smith, Elder and Company, 1856.

Metzger, Thomas. *Escape from Predicament.* New York: Columbia University Press, 1977.

Michael, Franz, and Chang Chung-li. *The Taiping Rebellion: History and Documents.* 3 vols. Seattle: University of Washington Press, 1966, 1971.

Miller, Stuart C. *The Unwelcome Immigrant: The American Image of the Chinese, 1785–1882.* Berkeley and Los Angeles: University of California Press, 1969.

Mitchell, B. R. *International Historical Statistics—Asia, Africa, and Oceania, 1750–1993.* London: Macmillan, 1998.

Miyazaki, Ichisada. *China's Examination Hell.* New Haven: Yale University Press, 1981.

Miyoshi, Masao. *As We Saw Them: The First Japanese Embassy to the United States.* Tokyo: Kodansha, 1994.

Morgan, Dale, ed. *Rand McNally's Pioneer Atlas of the American West.* Chicago: Rand McNally, 1956.

Mungello, D. E. *The Great Encounter: China and the West, 1500–1800.* Lanham, Md.: Rowman and Littlefield, 1999.

Nares, George Strong. *Narrative of a Voyage to the Polar Sea during 1875–1876.* London: Her Majesty's Stationery Office, 1877.

Nicolai, Richard R. *Centennial Philadelphia.* Bryn Mawr: Bryn Mawr Press, 1976.

Nylan, Michael. *The Five "Confucian" Classics.* New Haven: Yale University Press, 2001.

Paul, James Laughery. *Pennsylvania Soldiers' Orphans Schools.* Harrisburg: Lane S. Hart, 1877.

Perry, Elizabeth J. *Rebels and Revolutionaries in North China.* Stanford: Stanford University Press, 1980.

Pitman, Jennifer. "China's Presence at the Centennial." M.A. thesis, Bard College, 1999.

Pomeranz, Kenneth. *The Great Divergence: Europe, China, and the Making of the Modern World Economy.* Princeton: Princeton University Press, 2000.

Pope, J. Worden. "The North American Indian—The Disappearance of the Race a Popular Fallacy." *The Arena* 16 (November 1896): 945–59.

Porter, Jonathan. *Tseng Kuo-fan's Private Bureaucracy.* Berkeley and Los Angeles: University of California Press, 1972.

Post, Robert C., ed. *1876, a Centennial Exhibition.* Washington, D.C.: Smithsonian Institution, 1976.

Quesnay, François. *Le Despotisme de la Chine.* N.p., 1767.

Raphals, Lisa. *Sharing the Light: Representations of Women and Virtue in Early China.* Albany: State University of New York Press, 1998.

Realeaux, Franz. *Brief aus Philadelphia.* Braunschweig: Friederich Vieweg und Sohn, 1877.

"Review Essays: Orientalism Twenty Years On." *American Historical Review* 105, no. 4 (2000): 1205–49.

"Review Symposium on Orientalism." *Journal of Asian Studies* 39, no. 3 (1980): 481–517.

Said, Edward. *Orientalism.* New York: Pantheon, 1979.

Saussy, Haun. *Great Walls of Discourse and Other Adventures in Cultural China.* Cambridge: Harvard University Press, 2001.

Saxton, Alexander. *The Indispensable Enemy: Labor and the Anti-Chinese Movement in California.* Berkeley and Los Angeles: University of California Press, 1971.

Schein, Louisa. "Gender and Internal Orientalism in China." *Modern China* 23, no. 1 (1997): 69–98.

Shih, Vincent C. Y. *The Taiping Ideology: Its Sources, Interpretations, and Influences.* Seattle: University of Washington Press, 1967.

Smith, Richard J. "Li Hung-chang's Use of Foreign Military Talent: The Formative Period, 1862–1874." In *Li Hung-chang and China's Early Modernization,* ed. Samuel Chu and Kwang-ching Liu. Armonk, N.Y.: M. E. Sharpe, 1994.

———. *Mercenaries and Mandarins: The Ever-Victorious Army in Nineteenth Century China.* Millwood, N.Y.: KTO Press, 1978.

Spector, Stanley. *Li Hung-chang and the Huai Army: A Study in Nineteenth Century Regionalism.* Seattle: University of Washington Press, 1964.

Spence, Jonathan D. *God's Chinese Son.* New York: Norton, 1996.

Stanley, John. *Late Ch'ing Finance: Hu Kuang-yung as an Innovator.* Harvard East Asia Monograph Series no. 12. Cambridge: Harvard University Press, 1966.

Steinberg, Joel David, ed. *In Search of Southeast Asia: A Modern History.* Rev. ed. Honolulu: University of Hawaii Press, 1987.

Strassberg, Richard. *Inscribed Landscapes: Writings from Imperial China.* Berkeley and Los Angeles: University of California Press, 1994.

Sun Qianli and Jiang Kui. *Two Chinese Treatises on Calligraphy.* Trans. Chang Ch'ung-ho and Hans H. Frankel. New Haven: Yale University Press, 1995.

Teng Su-yu. *Historiography of the Taiping Rebellion.* Cambridge: Harvard University Press, 1962.

Tocqueville, Alexis de. *Democracy in America.* New York: Penguin, 1984.

Tonnesson, Stein. "Orientalism, Occidentalism, and Knowing about Others." *Nordic Newsletter of Asian Studies,* April 1994, 1–9.

Tsai, Shih-shan Henry. *China and the Overseas Chinese in the United States, 1868–1911.* Fayetteville: University of Arkansas Press, 1985.

Tu Wei-ming. *Way, Learning, and Politics: Essays on the Confucian Intellectual.* Albany: State University of New York Press, 1993.

Wagner, Rudolf. *Reenacting the Heavenly Vision: The Role of Religion in the Taiping Rebellion.* Berkeley and Los Angeles: University of California Press, 1982.

Wakeman, Frederic, Jr. *The Great Enterprise.* Vol. 1. Berkeley and Los Angeles: University of California Press, 1985.

———. *Strangers at the Gate: Social Disorder in South China, 1839–1861.* Berkeley and Los Angeles: University of California Press, 1966.

Waley-Cohen, Joanna. *The Sextants of Beijing.* New York: Norton, 1999.

Watson, Burton, trans. *The Tso Chuan: Selections from China's Oldest Narrative History.* New York: Columbia University Press, 1989.

Weigley, Russell F., ed. *Philadelphia: A Three-Hundred-Year History.* New York: Norton, 1982.

Wilde, Oscar. *A Woman of No Importance.* 1893.

Wollstonecraft, Mary. *A Vindication of the Rights of Woman.* Reprint, Mineola, N.Y.: Dover, 1996.

Wong, Kevin Scott. "The Transformation of Culture: Three Chinese Views of America." *American Quarterly* 48, no. 2 (1996): 217–25.

Worthy, Edmund. "Yung Wing in America." *Pacific Historical Review* 34 (1965): 265–87.

Wright, Mary C. *The Last Stand of Chinese Conservatism.* New York: Atheneum, 1966.

Wu T'ing-fang. *America through the Spectacles of an Oriental Diplomat.* New York: Stokes, 1914.

Xiong Yuezhi. "Difficulties in Comprehension and Differences in Expression: Interpreting American Democracy in the Late Qing." Trans. William Rowe. *Late Imperial China* 23, no. 1 (June 2002): 1–27.

Yen Ching-hwang. *Coolies and Mandarins.* Singapore: Singapore University Press, 1985.

Yung Wing. *My Life in China and America.* New York: Henry Holt, 1909.

Index